LEISURE IN AMERICA:

LEISURE IN AMERICA: a social inquiry

a social inquiry

MAX KAPLAN

Director, The Arts Center
School of Fine and Applied Arts
Boston University

JOHN WILEY & SONS, INC.
NEW YORK · LONDON

Preface

Two major problems confront life in the United States today: how can we insure survival as persons and as a nation and what will the conditions of this survival be?

Of these issues, the second is by far the more important. Survival itself is easy to arrange by the mere act of capitulation.

Why should we survive? A host of words, phrases, clichés, banners, and ideologies flood the mind: liberty, individualism, dignity of man, the American creed, democracy. . . .

Yet each of these ends—survival and the conditions of survival—provides us with a dual set of problems, one perennial, the other uniquely contemporary. Survival has challenged man since his cave days: survival in the face of animals, enemies, disease, and natural calamities. Here, the new dimension is total warfare or the possibility that atomic and hydrogen wars will wipe us out at a faster rate than we can reproduce ourselves.

The problem of man's goals and his meanings in life has been with him as long as he has been able to objectify himself, and probably all of the major philosophical issues implicit in the problem were well formulated by Socrates and Aristotle. Here, the new dimension stems from industrialization, and implicit in this are the ramifications of urbanization, mass education, mass culture, new transportation, and communication phenomena.

Obviously, the two new dimensions are closely interrelated. Just as atomic power is useful for great destruction as well as for industrial energy, it is part of the new attitudes of man toward himself and the world. These are attitudes, on the one hand, of futility, uprootedness, malaise, conformity, quest for certainty, alienation, and other-directedness; on the other hand, of new adventure, creative possibilities for

v

the broad masses, social-class fluidity, enlarged educational opportunities, comfort, longer life, and better health.

The topic of leisure emerges in the middle of these varying interpretations and significant issues, for it deals essentially with the nature of the Good Life. Assuming our current social projections and no major wars, our economic levels will go up and our free time will expand. Attention will be turned to such aspects of the problem as adult education, retirement, and old age. More books will be written to demonstrate that we are "status seekers"; the press will pay even more attention to consumption and expenditure patterns and will herald a new day for the middle class. We will, as a nation, be scolded, cajoled, and criticized.

What is needed now is a more sober, dispassionate analysis. What, indeed, is leisure? What factual trends in its use are observable? What are the factors in American life that affect these trends? Can a classification be developed that will go beyond the mere listing of activities and into the dynamics of meanings and functions? How is leisure activity patterned or structured in groupings and in time? How is it chosen and modified?

This book seeks to explore such issues. Neither its tone nor its conclusions are startling. Its ultimate temper, if one is needed, is a greater respect for the masses than is currently shown by the younger crop of social scientists, who (in my own view) have unwittingly been defending the values of a departed aristocracy and a feudal way of life. I also confess to a personal interpretation that some of my colleagues, although displaying increased virtuosity in quantitative methods, have little sense of history; if one looks back a thousand years, never has the Common Man been so free of dogma and conformity, and if we limit ourselves to American history alone never has he displayed more thought or more concern for human values, creative activity, or high quality of nonwork performance.

Given these personal leanings, this book is intended to suggest the wide scope of interrelationships between leisure and other facets of life. Policy formation may be touched upon here and there for professions concerned with leisure. Theorists in the social sciences may find clues and topics to further research and understanding in leisure as a phenomenon of culture. If the reader finds himself profiting in a personal way from these pages, the book will have pleasantly exceeded its intentions.

A deep sense of inadequacy overwhelms a writer on that happy and heavy day when he finally deposits a manuscript in the mail to the publisher. Among these inadequacies is the knowledge that even in his own mind he has failed to acknowledge the many by whose insight he has been nourished. In my own experience, surely, there was Florian Znaniecki, closest of friends and giant among sociologists, who passed away while this work of his student and colleague was in process; my other esteemed colleagues, William J. Albig, E. T. Hiller, Richard Dewey, Donald Taft, Benjamin Timmons, Robert Bierstedt, Ralph Englund, Oscar Lewis, all of whom served as sounding boards and as consciences in scholarship; Professor Charles Brightbill, across the campus in Urbana, Illinois, a leading authority in recreation; Professor Alfred Clarke, sociologist of Ohio State University, whose valuable suggestions were influential in the reworking of portions of the book; my many students at the Universities of Colorado, Illinois, and Boston; Claire Coppola, one of those rare secretaries who can read while she types; and Betty, one wife who too often found herself without the companionship of a leisureless husband busily working in a corner, scribbling about how to attain the Good Life through leisure.

Boston, Massachusetts   MAX KAPLAN
July 1960

Contents

Processes of Leisure

Evaluation and Implication of Leisure

Data, Methods, and Issues
of Leisure

An age of leisure I

We are in an age of leisure. When we have as much time during the day away from work as we have in work, what has happened? How did this come about? How widespread is this freedom? Is it really new, or have there been hidden hours of leisure in past days? What significance does the current trend have for the family, for social stratification, for the economy? What does it mean to the emotional lives and minds of people?

Is the leisure of today only a result of social factors, or does it in turn cause new ways of life? What does atomic power and automation mean for the future? Who spends leisure time with whom? How much money is spent for leisure activity? What is the meaning or the function of such spending? Why is activity A preferred in town X but not in town Y? Does the United States differ in this whole picture from other countries and cultures?

Speaking of the homogeneous nature of our culture, the historian Arthur Schlesinger, Jr., asks of the new age, "Will it be an epoch when the American people, seeking mass distraction and mass surcease through mass media, will continue to grow more and more indistinguishable from one another? Or will it be an epoch when people will use leisure creatively to develop their own infinitely diverse individualities?" [1]

Every facet of American life is included in the phrase that we are in an age of leisure. Our work week is shorter. Our family life has changed in character. Our "rootlessness" has taken new directions. Our familiar sources of control, such as the church or elders of the community, are no longer in dominance. We move about from state to state. A whole new world of visual images reaches us in the mass media. We find a large segment of older people among us. We travel to all corners of the country and abroad. Our clothing habits have caused

3

upheavals to that industry. Our houses are being planned differently. The search for a different style of life has led to the "exurbanite." A revolution in the price of books has affected the directions of our literacy. Increased material comforts have come to ever larger segments of our people. Retirement comes earlier. Old ideas about social class are modified. Labor union contracts are more concerned with time as an increment.

How deeply does all this affect our fundamental views of life, our purposes and goals, and our sense of direction as persons, as families, and as a nation? Has the age of leisure, at least to this point, modified the values that have been identified with those of a business and industrial society? Can the "acquisitive society" produce as one of its by-products those developments that, in turn, subvert or convert the values of the technical civilization?

These questions are more than academically intriguing; they touch upon many professional interests and applied fields; indeed, upon the resolution of such questions rests in part the welfare of all Americans as we move deeper into the "Nucleo-Hydro-Technico-Sputnico Age."

Leisure and the ends of life

On September 15–16, 1959, Chairman Khrushchev called upon President Eisenhower; they met later for serious conversations at Camp David. Perhaps the most significant aspect of this remarkable visit was overlooked by the world's press: *the Russian visitors returned home!* Why did not Khrushchev turn over the keys of the Kremlin to his host? Why did not Eisenhower volunteer to vacate the White House permanently to the Russians? In either case, survival might have easily been assured. The preposterous thought calls dramatic attention to an unspoken major assumption: it is more than survival that the world wants; it is a way of life, a content, a style, a self-defined outlook as to the good and bad, the important and superficial, the Path of Light and the Path of Darkness. Leisure and its use is one of the keys to the ends of survival.

Leisure as element in the diagnosis of culture

Leisure—however we shall later characterize it—deals with hours and ways of behavior in which we are freest to be ourselves. Thus what we do, whether on the noblest of levels and aspirations or the lowest of tastes, is a clue or indication of *what* we are, *who* we are, *where* we want to go. The morality of our entertainment—quiz shows on television or illegal gambling on school sports—cannot be separated from the morality of our whole life. In our leisure we stand exposed. Through our leisure we provide the elements for diagnosing our culture to the observer, and through the facts of leisure we may see how deeply we are in an age of leisure.

What is the factual extent of America's free time? Several approaches provide answers: expenditures, types of participation, tax income from free-time activities, case studies of persons and families, facilities provided by communities, the study of voluntary organizations, and so on. Such materials are distributed throughout the book.

There are wide discrepancies in the accounts or estimates given of our total expenditures for leisure. For example, according to a United Press summary, "Fun-loving Americans spend a whopping 35 billion dollars a year to entertain themselves—almost the exact amount they poured into the federal treasury last year (1955) in income taxes." [2] But *Business Week* has placed the figure for entertainment at 281.1 billion dollars.[3] Meyer and Brightbill estimate the total spent for leisure purposes as 20 to 40 billion dollars,[4] and United Nations publications arrived at the figure of 30 billion dollars a year, or about 15 per cent of the total income of the United States.[5]

The matter of definitions immediately enters into such estimates. For instance, it is not easy to determine how much travel money to put under "leisure" or "pleasure," how much under "business" or "necessity." In spite of such problems, the general facts are impressive: goods and services connected with leisure involved 11 billion dollars in 1950; over 580 million dollars in salaries went to workers directly serving the free-time needs of others; over 331 million dollars went into the Federal treasury in 1952 as taxes and revenues from admissions to some form of entertainment; 70 million dollars went to states in that year from hunting and fishing licenses; about 50 per cent of all families in the United States now have TV sets, and many have two or more; in 1952 an average of 50 million tickets were bought for the movies every week; the United States Department of Commerce reports that 836 million dollars were spent in 1952 on flowers, seeds, and potted plants (in comparison, all higher education got little more than 930 million dollars). Another 200 million dollars were spent for garden tools. In 1953 about 40 million dollars were invested in over 400 new drive-in theaters.[6]

Life finds a "national aquamania" developing: the pleasure-boat business, with a gross of over 2 billion dollars, has more than tripled since 1951; 8 million recreational boats are now in use, including 5.5 million outboards.[7]

Flat figures such as these, although impressive, mean more when the trend in spending is observed for a period of years. Table 1, from the *Business Week* report for the years 1929 to 1952, relates spending to types of activities.

TABLE 1

How We Spend Our Leisure Money: 1929–1952

As a Percentage of All Recreational Expenditures

	1929	1939	1952	In Millions of Dollars 1952
Spectator amusements	21.1	23.8	13.5	1,577
Movies	16.6	19.1	9.7	1,134
Theater, opera	2.1	0.9	0.7	87
Pro baseball	0.4	0.7	0.4	49
Pro football	0.1	0.1	0.1	10
Pro hockey	0.1	0.1	0.1	6
Horse, dog races	0.1	0.3	0.4	42
College football	0.5	1.1	0.9	105
Other nonprofit and amateur	1.2	1.5	1.2	144
Participation amusements	4.8	5.3	3.8	448
Billiards, bowling	1.3	2.0	1.1	129
Dancing, swimming, etc.	0.7	0.8	0.8	92
Amusement parks (devices)	0.4	0.4	0.3	36
Golf	2.1	1.8	1.4	169
Other	0.3	0.3	0.2	22
Individual recreation	63.9	59.4	72.2	8,466
Books, maps	7.1	6.4	5.4	638
Magazines, newspapers, etc.	12.4	16.1	12.5	1,468
Nondurable toys	7.8	8.3	11.0	1,284
Sporting goods	4.2	5.6	6.7	790
Boats, airplanes	0.6	0.6	0.7	79
Radio, TV, records, musical instruments	23.4	12.2	19.8	2,324
Photo developing, studios	1.7	2.3	3.8	442
Flowers, seeds	5.1	5.5	7.1	836
Other	1.7	2.4	5.2	605
Gambling Coin machines, Pari-mutuel net receipts	0.4	2.9	3.6	419
Other	9.8	8.6	6.9	806
Total	100.0	100.0	100.0	11,716

Of the ten activities in Table 1 in which we find increased spending since 1939, five have to do with the out-of-doors. These new patterns derive from enlarged technology, such as photo developing, from get-rich-quick ideas, such as gambling, and from travel, gardening, and fads for children.

Table 2 shows an increase of 2.2 per cent in total proportion of money spent on recreation in the United States from 1909 to 1950.[8]

TABLE 2

National Expenditure for Recreation in the United States: 1909–1950

Year	Total in Millions of Dollars	Percentage of Total
1909	1,081	3.6
1919	2,517	4.0
1929	4,327	5.5
1933	2,199	4.7
1937	3,374	5.0
1941	4,225	5.1
1945	6,314	5.1
1949	10,269	5.7
1950	11,290	5.8

TABLE 3

National Expenditure for Various Consumption Items—United States: 1909–1950

Item	Percentage of Expenditure 1909	Percentage of Expenditure 1950	Difference
Food	34.4	33.8	−0.6
Clothing	14.3	11.8	−2.6
Personal care	0.9	1.2	+0.3
Housing	19.1	10.3	−8.8
Household operation	14.1	13.7	−1.4
Medical, death expenses	3.2	4.9	+1.7
Personal business	1.1	4.4	+3.3
Transportation	5.2	11.7	+6.5
Private education and research	0.6	0.9	+0.3
Religious and welfare activities	2.9	0.9	−2.0
Foreign travel and remittance	0.4	1.0	+0.6

Except for the depression years, the proportion of expenditures for recreation went up regularly. These figures indicate a growth in absolute numbers of about 1000 per cent in 40 years. It is interesting to note how other items of expenditure went up or down in the same period.

As we might expect, the rise in expenditures for recreation of over 2 per cent has been accompanied by increases in such items as travel, medical care, and other personal expenses and by declines in amounts spent on clothing and housing.

Another method of obtaining data about leisure is by asking people what they prefer to do in their free time. Public opinion pollsters have done some of this work. A comparative summary of preferences, based on studies reported by Henry Cantril for the United States, Canada, Norway, and Hungary,[9] is presented here. These polls were fairly similar in their sampling techniques. The dates of each, and the question asked, were as follows:

1. United States, January 1938. Question: Which of these recreations do you enjoy the most?
2. United States, August 16, 1938. Question: What is your favorite way of spending an evening?
3. Canada, December 26, 1946. Question: Which of these do you like to do most in your spare time?
4. Norway, December 20, 1946. Question: How do you spend your spare time?
5. Hungary, June 1946. Question: What distractions have you? (Asked in Budapest and suburbs.)

The first three of the foregoing opinion surveys ask a more quantitative question than the one put to Norwegians and Hungarians. This should suggest caution in taking these comparisons too literally. They do not always compare the same kinds of items. Further, conversations about leisure with foreign students have impressed the author with various connotations of the word: in many cases, the term "leisure" meant little; conversely, the American would find it difficult to know what is meant by the question put to the Hungarians, "What distractions have you?" Third, what people *say* they prefer to do is not necessarily what they actually do.

A Gallup poll in 1959, however, did ask the question, "Which of the activities listed on the card have you, yourself, participated in during the last 12 months?" [10] The results are shown in terms of the percentage of persons who participated at least once, as well as the total.

TABLE 4

Comparison of Four Polls on Leisure Preferences
Source. Cantril: *Public Opinion*, 1935–1946

	Fortune Survey-Roper (Evening) United States 1(^{a})	American Institute of Public Opinion (Total) United States 2	Canada 3	Norway 4(^{b})	Hungary 5(^{c})
Radio	18.8%	9%	23%	3%	7.8%
Movies—legitimate theater	2.1	17	13	4	18.4
Reading—magazines, books	20.9	21	26	42	13.7
Newspapers	7.1				
Hunting—fishing	11.	1	4		
Watching sports	10.4	2	6	10	8.1(^{d})
Playing outdoor games	6.6	2	7		
Visiting friends		4	20	1	
Company—coffee house					2.1
Cards—indoor games	5.3	9	11	3	2.7
Parties—dancing		12	7		4.5
Car driving		4	6	1 (bike, boat)	
With family		7		1	3.2
Music listening— singing—playing		3		7	6.5
Drinking		1			
Walking		1		8	
Sewing—knitting		1		18	2.8
Dating		1			
Resting—sleeping				6	3.0
Gardening				3	1.8
Study				3	
Christian interests				1	
Playing with children				1	

^{a} These figures are averages of results for men and women.

^{b} These figures are averages of results for men and women.

^{c} In the original report both men and women were divided into groups of "under 40" and "over 40." The figures given here are averages for both sexes and age groups.

^{d} No distinction was made between watching and participating in sports.

TABLE 5

Gallup Poll, 1959—Recreational Participation

Percentage Participating Once or More		Total Number of Participants
33	Swimming	33,000,000
32	Fishing	32,000,000
32	Dancing	32,000,000
18	Bowling	18,000,000
16	Hunting	16,000,000
11	Baseball or softball	11,000,000
8	Golf	8,000,000
7	Badminton	7,000,000
6	Ice skating	6,000,000
6	Pool or billiards	6,000,000
5	Horseback riding	5,000,000
4	Roller skating	4,000,000
4	Tennis	4,000,000
4	Volleyball	4,000,000
3	Skiing	3,000,000
36	None of these	36,000,000

An additional study was made of spectatorship, with the following report:

TABLE 6

Gallup Poll 1959—Recreational Spectatorship

Percentage Attending One or More Games		Total Number of Adults
28	Baseball	28,000,000
23	Football	23,000,000
18	Basketball	18,000,000
9	Horse racing	9,000,000
9	Stock-car racing	9,000,000
6	Wrestling	6,000,000
4	Boxing	4,000,000
4	Ice hockey	4,000,000
2	Track and field	2,000,000
2	Dog racing	2,000,000
2	Tennis	2,000,000
1	Soccer	1,000,000
50	None of these sports	50,000,000
158	per cent *	

* Multiple answers were frequent.

Yet the most serious limitation of all of these studies, and of the polling technique in particular, is that a list of topics or activities was read or presented to the person. Whenever a straight choice is at issue, such as between political candidates, specific items are legitimately listed in interviews. Since a principal issue in leisure studies is precisely this—what do people perceive to be leisure time or activity—it is a dubious technique to limit the subject's thinking by presenting a ready-made list. This is not to say that this type of study is worthless. It can, however, be misleading. The field is at present not tilled sufficiently by scholars to permit of easy approaches; "yes" and "no" answers or checks of the pencil ignore too many fine points as well as the basic issues.[11] Polls can be most useful when they inquire into such matters as ownership of leisure items (television sets, swimming pools, musical instruments, etc.), activities carried on in a previous short period, or expenditures for activities. These and similar items are specific and worth knowing.

These facts, as we have already seen, raise serious questions about accuracy and validity of methods. Yet even if they are all accepted at face value they raise serious questions as to our values or ends as a culture "beyond survival." Do they provide incontestable evidence that all or most Americans are *conformists* or *status seekers* or *uprooted* or *alienated* or *other-directed*, as some articulate observers are claiming?

Perhaps these facts leave much unsaid. For instance, at a Congressional hearing in June 1954 [12] a report was heard that there are in this country about 1000 symphony orchestras, most of which (600) are community groups with a sprinkling of professional players among the amateurs, altogether involving about 30,000 persons. Turning to the nonprofessional community theater, a report by ANTA (American National Theatre and Academy) notes 1437 groups in 1952.[13] Theater activity involves persons other than actors, of course. On a conservative assumption that the average community theater provides some activity for 50 persons per year, more than 70,000 find some leisure satisfactions here.

Now, how does anyone presume to estimate the relative importance of this set of persons—and the nature of what they do in their leisure time—against a figure of 18 millions who fished in 1953 or the 25 millions who attended boxing matches? It would take a wisdom greater than our own to achieve grandiloquent and definitive readings of these facts. Yet the new age of leisure is one of the realities of American life; if it is to be taken into account in the many ways in which its influence as cause and effect is felt, then interpretations are vital.

These readings of the American life through its leisure depend in part on the purposes and backgrounds of specific professional disciplines or concerns.

These disciplines and concerns are many and include such varied persons as the city planner, recreationist, gerontologist, family counselor, clergyman, educator, businessman, hospital administrator, government official, physician and psychiatrist, philosopher, criminologist, publisher, advertiser, disc jockey, union leader, and industrialist, as well as manufacturers of cars, clothes, pills, TV sets, or pleasure boats. The interests represented in this cross section range all the way from selling equipment for leisure, to preaching the message of creative activity, to locating sites for swimming pools.

Many magazines now carry articles about what persons are or are not doing in their free time. Under date of January 1960, a new magazine, labeled *Leisure,* took its place beside such publications as *Holiday, Playboy,* and *Hobbies.* It is common now to pick up magazines of every level and to note articles on how to retire, where to spend one's vacation, the new leisure class, or a survey on how time is being used.[14] One brochure of the many on leisure is titled *What Reading Means to Me* (1959); it includes essays on "Escape from Restrictive Surroundings," "Maintaining My Individuality and Character," and "Reading to Ease Mental Torture"; it comes from inmates of San Quentin. Even they are concerned with the use of time, as well as its passage!

Consider for a moment the issue of leisure for persons who are in retirement. Gerontologists speak of the nature of aging, for age is a relative matter; similarly, time is a relative item in man's consciousness, so that a Sunday evening of three hours is perceived differently if it precedes a Monday of hard work rather than a Monday of completely uncommitted time. In another writing we have noted the following on the use of retirement hours: [15]

The sheer statistics of such time are dramatic. If one retires at 60 and lives five more years, his total of new free time (from 9 A.M. to 4 P.M. Monday through Friday) comes to over 10,000 hours; if he lives 15 years, he faces over 31,000 free hours of time previously devoted to work. But assume an average Mr. American who retires at 60 and lives to 70. To his bulk of actual retirement hours we must add the 48 leisure hours per week which most of us enjoy on weekends and evenings. This American may anticipate almost 45,000 hours of time to do with as he wishes—a quantity of time, indeed, which is more than all of his previous working hours from the age of 40 to 60. In other words, his free time in retirement equals precisely half of his past working life!

We are therefore confronted with a large array of professional, business, and scientific groups interested (or called upon to become interested) in the topic of leisure. There is reason to believe that this interest will increase as the implications of free time are considered with fresh eyes. An example may be cited: the American labor movement has devoted its efforts to promoting the economic welfare of its millions of members. As David Dubinsky wrote in 1950,[16] "No group has done more to create leisure for the majority of the people of the United States than the trade unions. They are, therefore, naturally interested in the best possible utilization of that time which is now free from the demands of mill, mine, and factory." For a time this view went without supplementation on a major scale. Yet in 1959 the education division of the CIO-AFL sponsored a conference in Washington on the theme "Education for Retirement and Leisure," devoted to an analysis of issues, reports of existing programs, information on available resources, and the encouragement of new activity or educational programs.

The assumptions and purposes of the union officer is not that of the city planner, the car salesman, or the television business sponsor. Although there may be elements of idealism in the "grammar of motives," which articulates the approach of each interest to leisure, the total variety of purposes is as broad as man's capacity and ambition.

If we have spoken thus far of the manipulator, organizer, professional leader, educator, and salesman of leisure, it is not to ignore the issues as seen by the consumer. Yet the same observation may be safely made of these consumers. Leisure plays many functions and tunes. The user of time is also a complicated man, for whom generalizations may not apply; he, too, is necessarily tied in his outlook on time and its uses to the social controls of family, education, mental and emotional disposition, income, place of residence, health, age, or other more subtle factors.

The position of the present volume is not to approach leisure as a challenge, a "Heaven-on-Earth," a disaster, or as one historian calls it, "the greatest threat to man." Leisure is all of these things and more. The purpose of the analysis that follows is to free us of self-made prisons of thought, easy definitions, and gratuitous exhortations. From such freedom we may explore issues of leisure unfettered by the need to defend, uphold, argue, or plea.

Leisure as a social relationship in culture 2

Science and kinds of social order

Imagine the infinite variety of activity going on in the world at this very moment. Millions are eating, sleeping, walking, riding in a car or on a camel, praying in some church, mosque, or synagogue, working in a factory, repairing a farm fence, plowing or harvesting, bathing a baby, just sitting, drinking at a bar, catching fish, watching television or listening to the radio, writing a book, felling a tree, washing dishes or clothes, fighting, combing hair, and so on and on. A mere recital of the activities in one small community the size of Bangor, Maine, or Bandar, Iran, would be enough without conceiving the vast list for a Chicago or a Paris!

The challenge to a social science is to bring some order out of all this. Where can it begin? We can, for instance, look at a set of clocks hanging in an airport and find that although it is 12 o'clock noon in New York City it is 7 P.M. in Athens, 10 P.M. in Calcutta, 1 A.M. in Shanghai, and 11 A.M. in Winnipeg. Already this simple clue suggests some patterns. At this hour, or hours, we can expect to find more Greeks at work than Indians, more New Yorkers at lunch than residents of Shanghai. The time element is one of man's accomplishments, one of his many devices to bring order into his existence. We say, then, that time, since it means something in relation to human activity, is part of the *culture*.

Yet before other clues to order in the infinite variety of human activities are examined, a question must be asked in answer: what kind of order is meant? For the way in which a scientific answer is brought about depends first of all on the nature of the problem, and, since there are *many kinds of questions*, there are various disciplines of human understanding. Ultimately the difference between philosophy,

14

biology, psychology, chemistry, history, anthropology, and sociology is that although all may be interested in one or another aspect of man each emphasizes a particular kind of problem. Each formulates its own approach.[1]

The philosopher might consider the infinity of actions noted earlier and ask which of all these countless intentions and patterns is good or bad or moral or beautiful. The biologist might try to isolate such a problem as the relationship between speed of muscular reactions and food content. The historian may want to know how the cultural patterns observed in this one moment have come down from past generations in the course of wars, political upheavals, famines, and migrations.

The order sought by the sociologist is that which exists between broad patterns of group life. He assumes that behavior patterns can be seen as uniform wholes. He speaks of "social organization" or "social structure." Like all other scientists, he does so either to understand or to be able to predict that, given conditions A and B rather than D and E, a certain result X may be expected.

All of the disciplines follow two main steps in the scientific method: first, to establish a problem, that is, *the kind of order to be discovered*, second, to establish some concepts and categories of material that begin to unify observations and enable the discovery of relationships *between the* categories or kinds of data.[2]

The problem set by the sociologist is to explain those aspects of human life that consist of patterns of conduct handed down the generations *within systems of meanings*. This over-all part of man's life is called his culture.

Culture

As a sociologist, Joyce O. Hertzler notes, "Culture, as the precious common heritage of a given group or society, *functions as a solidarity-producing factor*. It *is* the common way of life and enables its adherents together to solve the problems posed by the total environments." [3] Or, as an anthropologist, A. L. Kroeber states, "Culture might be defined as all the activities and non-physiological products of human personalities that are not automatically reflex or instinctive." [4]

An example of categories within this vast range of culture is this famous "culture scheme" by Clark Wissler: [5]

1. Speech, languages, writing systems, etc.
2. Material traits
   a. Food habits
   b. Shelter

  c. Transportation and travel
  d. Dress
  e. Utensils, tools, etc.
  f. Weapons
  g. Occupations and industries
 3. Art, carving, painting, drawing, music, etc.
 4. Mythology and scientific knowledge
 5. Religious practices
  a. Ritualistic forms
  b. Treatment of the sick
  c. Treatment of the dead
 6. Family and social systems
  a. The forms of marriage
  b. Methods of reckoning relationship
  c. Inheritance
  d. Social control
  e. Sports and games
 7. Property
  a. Real and personal
  b. Standards of value and exchange
  c. Trade
 8. Government
  a. Political forms
  b. Judicial and legal procedures
 9. War

Herskovits provides this characterization: [6] culture is (1) learned and constantly created; (2) made up of elements from the biological, environmental, psychological, and historical "components of human existence"; (3) structured; (4) constantly changing; (5) exhibits patterns and regularities; (6) the instrument by which the individual adjusts to his social setting and gains the raw materials for creative expression. Culture is the basic conceptual tool for all the social sciences, from the daring task of comparing whole cultural systems (Sorokin, Toynbee, Benedict, Mead, Gorer, etc.) to the humbler and more tractable research on the development of personality.

The following extended quotation is presented to illustrate the relevance to such understanding of the whole culture for our special purpose of understanding leisure. It is taken from the volume, *Cultural Patterns and Technical Change*, a report prepared for UNESCO and edited by Margared Mead: [7]

Spanish Americans have gone to work in the larger economy but they have not absorbed the pressure to keep busy. They do not look forward to "Time off," but incorporate their leisure with their labour. They work by the clock only when they work for Anglos; and if they have "leisure," they spend it in visiting: the men on the job, in streets or at bars, the women at home. Anglos consider Spanish Americans "lazy" and hence in large part responsible for their own difficulties; Spanish Americans consider the economic pressures of Anglo society responsible for them.

Spanish Americans react unfavourably to impersonal employer-employee contacts. "In Albuquerque, the boss would come along and say 'Hey you, get to work.'" They choose to work for someone they know, in preference to jobs of higher status by Anglo standards. And higher status is gained for the Spanish American by working for a locally prominent *patron* rather than by climbing the Anglo ladder of unskilled, semi-skilled, skilled, business and professional work.

The idea of higher pay does not immediately interest the Spanish American. . . . His status in his own community may be lowered rather than raised by achievement—and he has no other community. It is much more important to be than to do; to be a good son, or a good Catholic, or a good member of the village.

Radio, with its continuous programming, is well suited to Spanish Americans, who like listening to Spanish American "folk" music and campaign speeches. In the larger communities, there are now few or no major events which bring the whole group together. This is a striking change from village life. At home, radio is a welcome addition.

Young people have taken over Anglo recreations, but with certain differences. At dances, there is still formality in boy–girl relationships and it is not quite right to ask directly for a date. Boys and girls may go in separate groups to a "show," as before; but they will pair off in the dark—a situation defined by the culture as permissive. From there on the new pattern takes over; it is a date and couples come out together.

The foregoing example relates to a group in transition. Even clearer, in contrast to our American, industrial-minded way of life, is this picture of a primitive people, the Memba of Northern Rhodesia, a picture drawn in 1939 by the anthropologist A. I. Richards: [8]

We, after all, can hardly conceive of time except in terms of energy expenditure and, to many of us, a fixed money value as well. But the Bemba, in his unspecialized society does different tasks daily and a different amount of work. . . . I do not think the people ever conceive of such periods as the month, week or day in relation to regular work at all. A man says he has to cut trees between such-and-such climatic changes, but not that he has so many hours of work to get through, and daily work, which has become from habit almost a physiological necessity to many Europeans, only occurs at certain times of the year. The whole bodily rhythm of the Memba differs completely from that of a peasant in Western Europe, let alone an industrial worker. For instance, at Kasaka, in a slack season, the old men worked 14 days out of 20 and the young men 7; while at Kampamba in a busier season, the men of all ages worked on an average 8 of 9 working days. The average working day in the first instance was 2 3 hours for men and 2 hours gardening plus 4 hours domestic work for the women, but the figures varied from 0 to 6 hours a day. In the second case the average was 4 hours for the men and 6 for the women, and the figures showed the same daily variation.

We turn, finally, to Switzerland, a contemporary European society, to note how its leisure time also grows out of larger cultural attitudes and organization. In a report to the *Christian Science Monitor* for August 11, 1956, Constance S. Sammis writes of the strong Swiss family and attributes it in part to the few outside amusements available to the child. She notes that TV sets are scarce and few teen-agers have cars. Strong religious training, writes Miss Sammis, has led to an honesty that "seems bred in the bone." Comic books are almost nonexistent. Heroes for young people, such as the criminal, are not played up in newspapers. Outdoor facilities are easily available to everyone. Another view is found in *Switzerland in Perspective,* by George Solovey-tchik.[9]

> Of course there are scores of thousands of happy and united families; of course the number of successful marriages by far exceeds that of the failures. Nevertheless it is obvious that something is fundamentally wrong not only with family life, but with the relation between the sexes in general. Marriage advisers, psychiatrists, and experts of all sorts are busy trying to straighten out this unhappy situation, but nobody can any longer deny that it exists. To ignore this painful subject would result in a serious distortion of Switzerland's present-day realities.

> Perhaps the tradition of excessive concentration on work, the inability to relax, and a curious incapacity for leisure have something to do with it. Men and women who get up at six o'clock in the morning and who are on the job all day long have not much energy left for enjoyment at night. Nor are they in the mood for it. . . . At the end of the day men and women alike have little to offer to one another beyond their irritability and their indifferent or hostile boredom.

> This is one of the reasons why the Swiss male spends so many of his evenings at the inn or else attending meetings of the innumerable associations to which he belongs. In the associations—whether it is a matter of choir-singing or target-shooting or playing skittles—things are made easier for him by written statutes that tell him how he has to comport himself. At the inn playing "Jass" or drinking wine does not necessitate much conversation, or at any rate does not entail the discussion of one's private affairs. Though he is none too fond of people, he has an instinctive urge not to be alone—there is greater safety in numbers. . . .

There is little or no neighborhood life in Switzerland as it is known in England and in America. People cooperate with each other when duty or common interests demand, but they have no great urge to continue such relations beyond these contacts. They are not in the habit of "dropping in" on one another. Women meet at tea shops, and social life does not center around one's own home or that of one's friends.

We have seen how attitudes toward leisure are closely related to the culture of contemporary Switzerland, a primitive group of Africans, and a marginal culture of Spanish Americans. Of further illustrations there is no end. The problem is to establish a generalized analysis that relates leisure to the organization of the particular culture. Only by doing this can we arrive at a concept of leisure, for it is a term and a phenomenon that elude easy definition. A study of Wissler's listing, for instance, impresses one with the definiteness of its items—religion, family, and so on. Each has been widely studied, defined, and limited. The term leisure, on the other hand, suggests a wide variety of activities and attitudes. It has barely been treated in the scientific literature. Basic concepts need to be hammered out. Its informal nature seems to throw further difficulties in the way of scholarship. We turn more directly to this issue of clarification.

Concepts and definitions

Among the 39 related topics [10] listed at the end of an article on leisure in the *Encyclopedia of the Social Sciences* are

Recreation	Education
Public amusements	Art
Sports	Women's position in society
Luxury	Theory of the gentleman
Holidays	Culture
Vacations	Play
Amateur	Industrialism
Class	Commercialism

Some of these topics are discussed later; it is important that several be examined immediately: recreation, play, leisure.

Recreation

This term comes from the Latin *recreatio*, to restore or refresh; "To restore to a good or normal physical condition from a state of weakness or exhaustion; to invest with fresh vigour or strength." [11] "Refreshment of the strength and spirits after toil." Used as an adjective, "Equipped so as to provide diversions or amusements." [12]

The essence of the term is *alternation* of light, re-creative, pleasant activity—or inactivity—with heavy, energy-consuming, obligatory activity. The psychological element of pleasant anticipation seems warranted. Recreation is a renewal or preparation for the continuance of routine and necessary work. Using the philosopher's term, it is teleological, from the Greek term *telos*—purpose. In its first sense recreation has the purpose of re-creating or revitalizing us so that we may more efficiently go back to activities that are not recreational but fundamentally of a work nature.

Play

According to the Murray reference, the term play comes from the Anglo-Saxon *plega*, a game, a sport; and this usually meant a skirmish, fight, or battle. In the Bible, 2 Sam. ii.14, to *play* really means to *fight*. Similarly, to "play an instrument" was to strike something. The Latin *plaga*, a blow, stroke, or thrust, is thus a forerunner of the term "plague."

The term "play" is currently used in one of two senses: (*a*) a light, informal, make-believe action, such as the play of children; (*b*) a more formal, stylized, intense, and even serious presentation of some aspect of life on a "stage." In the first use our popular knowledge of psychology has made many people increasingly aware that in "play" the child is doing more than keeping busy; he is, in fact, learning and exploring the world, developing his body, setting attitudes toward himself, toward others, toward things, and toward ethical or social precepts included in the *thou shall* or the *thou shall not*.[13]

Thus as parents have acquired more understanding of the way in which a child grows up, they have begun to see play as a serious thing. The evidence is in educational toys, the large literature for children, concern with the playmates of their children, lessons for parents on how to play with children, and the development of a core of professional workers in recreation whose job it is to make play for children contribute to personal and group welfare.

Thus the change in the conception held of play has in the last few decades reverted to the original concept of play as something significant.

Going even beyond the limited view of play as representing struggle, a searching theory has been presented by the historian John Huizinga in his book *Homo Ludens: A Study of the Play Element in Culture*.[14] He speaks of the play-order and finds in it five characteristics:

1. Play is a voluntary activity, never a physical necessity or a moral duty. It is not only a matter of leisure and free time, it *is* freedom.

2. Play is not ordinary or real life, but this is not to say that play may not be intense or serious; it is not necessarily the opposite of seriousness, and it is further outside the realm of such dichotomies as wisdom and folly, truth and falsehood, good and evil. It is marked, in-

stead, by "disinterestedness," by being an interlude in our daily lives, an end in itself.

3. Play is secluded and limited, containing its own course and meaning: it begins and is over at a specific moment. Yet, since it becomes a tradition, it can be repeated. The dual elements of repetition and alternation are contributions to the independence of play, which further functions within limitations of time and space. Play thus constitutes a temporary world within, and marked off from, the ordinary world.

4. Play creates order; in fact, it *is* order. It is inside a "playground"; slight deviation from the rules spoils the game. Since order has a tendency to be a thing of beauty in and of itself, we have the affinity of play to aesthetics. Order within play contains all the elements of beauty, such as tension, poise, balance, and contrast. *Tension* demands a *solution*, a basic cycle to aesthetic experience. Rules become all-important, for deviations threaten the very existence of the play-community.

5. Last, the play-community tends to become permanent after the game is over, for in the course of playing it has become an "in-group," having already shared a common experience within an atmosphere of some secrecy, some "dressing up," some disguise or identification.

Leisure

In seeking a concept of leisure that can be useful for his purposes, the sociologist may do one of two things: either he may accept leisure to be what people *say it is or what it means to them;* [15] or he may seek an *ideal construct*.

As to the first, if he asks several persons at a baseball game, what brought them there, he will receive a variety of answers: "to enjoy the game," "to get the sunshine," "to get away from home," "to rest." If asked what leisure means to them on a more general level, the same persons are likely to consider it as "time off from work," "free time," "my own time," "doing what I like," "rest," and so on. A more sophisticated audience or a categorical-minded observer might attempt to classify such views in still other ways:

Leisure as a *bulk of time*, qualitatively distinct from other time, such as the evening.

Leisure as *freedom* from those activities that have to be done, such as work or household chores.

Leisure as an *end*, distinct from work as a means.

Leisure as a *minimum of obligation* to others, to routine, even to oneself.

Leisure as *re-creation,* to prepare for better work, to store up energy or knowledge.

Leisure as *self-improvement,* whether in study, seeking new friends, or new experiences.

Leisure as *social control,* using the time of others to win them over or influence them; i.e., Roman games, German youth.

Leisure as a *social symbol* of class position, age, or success.

Leisure as *sets of attitudes or motivations,* not a content.

Leisure as *physiological or emotional necessity,* such as therapy or physical rest.

The second approach is to construct a general picture or concept of leisure that will avoid the narrowness of any one type of subjective interpretation and at the same time permit of both *subjective perception* and *objective analysis.* The terms "ideal construct" or "ideal type" are sometimes applied to our use in conversation about common speech when we speak of "English society" or "communism"; these analytic tools were systematically used by the eminent scholar Max Weber when he analyzed Protestantism, the Chinese literati, and capitalism.[16] As used by Weber, the ideal type is a general, not a specific, picture or a statistical average. It contains the important elements of the situation, against which a real situation can be assessed. As a *typical* picture of leisure, what is sought is something "applicable to the analysis of an infinite plurality of concrete cases." [17]

The essential elements of leisure, as we shall interpret it, are (*a*) an antithesis to "work" as an economic function, (*b*) a pleasant expectation and recollection, (*c*) a minimum of involuntary social-role obligations, (*d*) a psychological perception of freedom, (*e*) a close relation to values of the culture, (*f*) the inclusion of an entire range from inconsequence and insignificance to weightiness and importance, and (*g*) often, but not necessarily, an activity characterized by the element of play.

Leisure is none of these by itself but all together in one emphasis or another. We examine each element briefly:

ANTITHESIS TO WORK AS ECONOMIC FUNCTION. Engaged in leisure, I can dig a ditch in my yard to make way for some landscaping project; this requires energy, more than my economic job. It is, however, outside the economic system in the usual way in which I relate myself to that system.[18] It is, obviously, not altogether unrelated to economics per se, for my "labor of love" may deprive a professional worker in these lines of employment.

PLEASANT EXPECTATION AND RECOLLECTION. With this element we eliminate all enforced leisure, such as unemployment, imprisonment, or sickness, and we include a psychological attitude moving both forward and backward in time. It is impossible to divorce "vacation," for instance, from the expectation, planning, daydreaming, savings, packing, or excitement of going away. Such looking ahead often makes the routine of life more bearable, for then work periods are seen as *means* toward life and living. Similarly, the recollection of the vacation or leisure activity is often inaccurate, colored by the idealization fostered in the preparatory stage. Research would probably show that many persons on vacation enjoy themselves and look back favorably upon their experience because they cannot emotionally afford to contradict their past hopes and projections. As a matter of fact, attitude and expectancy do influence the actual experience itself.

MINIMUM OF SOCIAL ROLE OBLIGATIONS. Social role, to be discussed more technically later,[19] distinguishes John Smith *as* John Smith from the many positions or obligations he has achieved in his society or that he has been given by it: citizen, father, friend, carpenter, Protestant, Mason, and so on. He is only *one* John Smith who plays or possesses *many* roles. Part of the adjustment, maturity, normality, or personality he is credited with by everyone else is defined by how he behaves in each of these roles and, more important, how he combines or synthesizes them all into the one social being known as John Smith. In each of the many circles he touches Smith has rights and obligations (voting, supporting his wife, etc.). Leisure activity, too, may have many obligations, from making toys for his children (every father *should*) to going on trips with his wife (a good husband *should*). These are obligations, however, that he is more likely to assume voluntarily, and with pleasanter expectations, than, for example, going to work on January 2, to which he is formally committed and for a long period of time. Theoretically, he has greater freedom in deciding whether to be with his family in his off time. The observer from the outside can, in specific cases, question such self-deception; yet John Smith, himself, is the one who perceives his relative freedoms and acts in accordance with his perceptions.

PSYCHOLOGICAL PERCEPTION OF FREEDOM. The perception of freedom *by the person who participates in leisure* is an important factor.[20]

Thus there will be considerable variety in the definitions that people give of leisure or of free time. Further, time as a physical element is measurable, but amount of leisure is not, if one mother perceives herself to be heavily weighted down when she feeds her infant, whereas a second finds it a delightful experience. Thus freedom is as much an issue for the social psychologist as for the economist and political scientist. The student of leisure deals on both levels, that is, with absolute quantities of time free from economic functioning and with time that is perceived as free.

CLOSE RELATION TO CULTURAL VALUES. If the concept of leisure is equated with re-creation, it has no value in itself except as a supplement to work. As developed in this book, leisure has moved further and further from subordination to work; increasingly, leisure is an end, a life of its own. As with all human ends, leisure is bound up closely with moral, ethical, and thought systems and with all social institutions.

ENTIRE RANGE OF SIGNIFICANCE AND WEIGHTINESS. Old associations of work with seriousness and leisure with lightness are now outdated and theoretically indefensible. Leisure activity, as we shall see, can include interests covering the whole gamut of human life; hence the degree of seriousness or significance is irrelevant to a concept of what leisure is or should be.

OFTEN, NOT NECESSARILY, CHARACTERIZED BY PLAY. Play, as viewed by Huizinga, penetrates many human activities. In this broad view several of the elements of play, as he defined them, are synonymous with leisure: voluntariness, play as freedom, play as an interlude in life. Leisure, as we are characterizing it here, differs from Huizinga's scheme for play in that leisure is not necessarily secluded and limited, starting and stopping at specific times; it is unlimited in time and space, and as a system of order it is less limited by rules and norms. If we leave Huizinga and revert to the vernacular (historically inadequate) concept of play as an activity that is light, associated with child life, or an objectified slice of life on a stage, then, of course, leisure is a much wider and inclusive concept in which play is only one type.

This ideal construct of leisure is not intended to indicate a *content*, although we will speak later of types of leisure activity. Our basic assumption is that anything or any specific activity can become a basis for leisure. Further, it is evident that the construct has incorporated the subjective listing of views about leisure that were summarized earlier. We are now saying that there will be a variety in the perceptions by which people will see or understand their free time. However, this element of perception can hardly be reduced to only one of a set of elements, for in actual cases one or another of the elements will be emphasized.

Two issues of method demand discussion: the use of this construct in (a) observing and (b) judging specific forms of leisure.

Since we proceed on the assumption that leisure is not definable as a given activity but is rather a characteristic social relationship, how can a classification be derived? As all scientific classifications are: by the creation of typological tools sharpened to meet certain kinds of issues. For example, one difference between a bridge game and a party is that the first requires traditional equipment (cards) and is limited to a set number of players. Equipment and numbers are therefore two ways of classifying or distinguishing activities. Additional types can be invented easily:

1. *Self-directed:*
   Other-directed: } read; visit a sick friend

2. *Participatory:*
   Receptive: } play in a string quartet; listen to a concert

3. *Terminal:*
   Continual: } go to a lecture; enroll in an adult class

4. *Individual:*
   Group: } lie alone under a tree; join a picnic party

Other groupings could be distinguished in respect to expense, amounts of time, degrees of skill, time of year, indoor-outdoor, ad infinitum. (A classification does not have to be limited to two items.)

The problem is not to find classifications but to isolate those issues that seem to be most relevant for understanding behavior. A typology is then a primary set of tools, to be judged solely on its utilitarian value. As a demonstration, three issues are selected here:

1. To what degree do persons relate themselves to other *persons as values,* as distinct from interests held in common with other persons?

2. To what degree do they require activities that are fixed by *rules* and well-ordered *traditions,* as distinct from *creative* or *relatively free* activities?

3. To what degree do they seek to go *to the world* for direct and new experiences, as distinct from leisure experiences in which the world *is brought to them?*

These respective categories then emerge: *sociability and association, game and art,* and *exploration and immobility.*

Type of Leisure	Distinguishable by the Item of
Sociability, association	persons as interests
Game, art	rules as controls
Movement, immobility	approach to the objective world

Although other students of the subject may arrive at different classifications of leisure activities, all will agree that some classification is necessary and that its items must be functionally interrelated. In the foregoing scheme the assumption is made that three kinds of things are worth looking at: (*a*) the way in which people are or are not the main concern of the activity; (*b*) the importance of rules (and, of course, the origin and sanctions for them); (*c*) whether the participant in leisure goes to the world for the experience or has the world come to him.

Such a typology is not a mere *beginning* for analysis but already the result of (presumably) considerable preliminary examination. Every typology, every theory, every hypothesis is a fruition as well as a starting point.

Hence it is inescapable that the typology, as a somewhat finished product, is a theory in which the selection of items and their relationship is tied up with the social values and academic predispositions of the scholar. If this were not so, there would be no need for a history of sociology to deal with *its* social origins. Thus the sociologist cannot deceive himself (he cannot for long deceive others) but rather takes advantage of his own "social origins" by clarifying and stating them. In a sense roughly parallel to the work of the psychoanalyst, the sociologist becomes objectively more aware of his reasons for approaching a subject as he does. The assumptions of the social scientist, moreover, are presumably based upon systematic *knowledge of the world* as well as *knowledge of himself.*

All this has direct bearing on the present issue. Are any specific leisure activities more desirable than others? Is there no qualitative difference between the gang that, in its free hours, vandalizes property and attacks strangers for the fun of it and a group that goes out to repair homes of the poor? If the effects of leisure are to be measured or judged entirely by the participants, then the gangster mob and the Society of Friends are equally sheltered from the judgment of science.

The criteria used by science, however, must arise from assumptions of our society and our time, not from absolutistic judgments that are

"God-given" or "divine" in origin. Some of the assumptions in this book are stated now: [21]

1. There is a need for a person to be rooted, to be wanted, to belong. This conclusion arises from scientific observation as well as folk wisdom. Wherever this need is apparent in a given case, some leisure activity is more effective than others.

2. Conversely, there is a need for a person to be distinct from others, to have interests and abilities that distinguish him. For this purpose, some leisure activity is more effective than others.

3. There is the possibility of combining leisure functions so that pure rest or relaxation can accompany the absorption of a Beethoven symphony. Some leisure activities, more than others, offer a wide dimension of function.

4. Some leisure activities, more than others, serve additional persons of the society at the same time that they serve the participant. One club is entirely social; another combines a community project with its socializing.

5. Other leisure activities, such as gambling away resources needed for one's family, have objective consequences harmful by standards of indebtedness, mental health, or family solidarity. Still others, such as adult study classes, provide new experience but are accumulatively helpful by standards of personal satisfaction, improved skills, or knowledge of the world.

6. There is also the possibility of putting leisure into the creation of works of art, which, among other activities, provide expression of feelings, projections of self-knowledge, affinity with aesthetic traditions, enjoyment to other persons, and objects or works for future pleasure of the creator himself.

We have then

1. need for belonging,
2. need for individuality,
3. multifunctional purposes in behavior,
4. multidimensional effects of behavior,
5. indices of behavioral consequences,
6. activities and created objects as projections of the person.

Lundberg, in one of the classic studies of leisure,[22] establishes the following criteria:

Leisure has, in a relatively high degree, both its original incentive and its fulfillment in the individual himself rather than in coercions of the social and economic order.

Leisure must possess the capacity of being relatively permanently interesting (variety).

Leisure should involve activities or states as different as possible from those which are consciously forced upon us by our station in life.

Finally, leisure should at least be compatible with, if not conducive to, physical, mental, and social well-being.

It is apparent that whatever criteria one cares to choose one is concerned with two levels or dimensions—the satisfactions inherent to the activity itself and the relations of the activity to external values, or relationships to social well-being, of the participant or of others. Which of these is to be emphasized is a matter of one's assumptions of the situation or circumstance. These, however, are matters that more properly follow than precede a detailed analysis of leisure. And in this analysis, we must begin with the condition of work.

Relations and Variables
in Leisure

Leisure and work 3

On this there must be universal agreement, that the dominant motif among all cultures—no matter how they express it—is self-preservation as a collective group. Segments of the population, such as the aged among the Eskimos, may be culturally defined as expendable. However, it is the whole of society that always seeks to remain as a going entity. This is far from saying that the whole of work is simply a matter of keeping alive.

In work man has gone much further than mere sustenance; in it he has found the core of his life. Work in its largest perspective is closely tied in with his relation to family, to other persons, to nature, to objects, to movement, to concepts of God, and to the meaning of life itself. Its impact is on the state of his freedom and responsibility, his position in the esteem of others, his particular relation in the production of goods, his attitude toward government and authority, his mental capacities and achievements, his material level, his circle of acquaintanceships and friends, his concept of himself as a person, and his "chances in life" or the chances of his mate and children. Hence it is folk wisdom at its best and not idle curiosity that asks of the stranger, "And what do you do?" As one writer suggests, "Work is not *part* of life, it is literally life itself." [1]

That the nature of work and its relation to nonwork have been undergoing significant change can hardly be disputed. The Christian view of work is discussed in Chapter 10, a view well summarized in these few sentences by Adriano Tilgher: [2]

> There is no doubt that the religion of work for the sake of work has given mankind peace, calm, and joy. The methodical discipline of professional work binds into a strong sheaf the scattered forces of the soul, frees men from doubts, anxieties, preoccupations, and sets the soul moving in a fine powerful rhythm which tends to perpetuate itself because of the

31

very joy it gives . . . it gives him at all times the divine joy of creation. . . .

There is confusion in a culture when these familiar values are shaken
and leisure values begin to develop. C. Wright Mills notes the following
in his *White Collar: The American Middle Classes:* [3]

> What is psychologically important in this shift to mass leisure is that the
> old middle-class work ethic—the gospel of work—has been replaced in
> the society of employees by a leisure ethic, and this replacement has in-
> volved a sharp, almost absolute split between work and leisure. Now work
> itself is judged in terms of leisure values. The sphere of leisure provides
> the standards by which work is judged; it lends to work such meanings as
> work has.

Although the present writer inclines to agree with Mills' interpretation—leisure can produce values as well as work—our obligation
here is not to deplore or applaud these developments but to explore
the relevant facts and consequences.

To relate work to leisure, we may consider the *intrinsic* and *extrinsic*
patterns of work: work as work, then work in its widest implications
in the culture.

Relation to the raw materials of work

As the first of these intrinsic matters, consider the impact of materials of work upon leisure patterns. The coal miner stays in the area
of the mines, despite modern transportation services that are available
to whisk him elsewhere in vacation days. His main pattern and style of
living centers about hills and generally crowded small-town life. Likewise, the worker on ships or in some phase of work related to transport
on water is limited to activities that associate his liking for water with
the traditional activities of swimming, fishing, and boating. The farmer
has at hand the facilities for visiting other families and the natural
setting for hunting; and because of rural preoccupation with the forces
of nature we may expect a religious emphasis, with many recreational
activities developing therefrom.

On the other hand, the electronics worker who is a specialist in making delicate parts for radio, telephone, or television may more likely
be found with many other experts near scientific laboratories, larger
factories, multiple transportation, and the heart of other electrical development. All this points inevitably toward the large city and, in turn,
suggests a whole range of leisure activities which the city provides in
a unique way: the museum, the professional baseball team, the symphony concert, the race track, the extensive public library. Here also

are found convenient transportation facilities to distant points or the potential fellowship of persons interested in every conceivable hobby.[4]

Thus the nature of leisure behavior is never entirely a matter of free choice nor the resultant of one set of variables such as income. The pattern may be considerably limited or defined in the location of home brought about by the nature of work. Work, in turn, is located in good measure in relation to the materials. The lawyer, the doctor, and many other professional persons dealing in human services are not so limited. They work wherever other people are to be found, although here again there are such factors as concentrations of people, the presence of special kinds of clienteles, and the location of associated services. There are types of workers—ministers, teachers, policemen, storekeepers—who are found everywhere and will often deliberately move to an area in which the agencies for the good life (as perceived by them) exist.

Whenever we find persons who, at considerable effort or expense, leave their places of work during holidays or off-periods in order to search out the advantages of a wholly different possibility of leisure, there we have a particularly fruitful kind of person or activity to study. For instance, two skiers are not the same for a scientific understanding if one lives in the area and the second has traveled several hundred miles. It is true that transportation has affected the situation remarkably, but research in travel patterns must explore the way in which travel facilities are left unused by some or used differently and with a variety of motivations by others.

Social structure of work

A second intrinsic aspect of work that touches directly on leisure patterns of workers is the type of structure found within a plant, office, or industry.

Almost 11 million Americans were self-employed in 1950 as farmers, businessmen, professional persons, independent craftsmen, merchants, and the like. They are never so closely dependent on other persons who work as are the millions employed by industry. The difference goes deep, indeed, and touches on such issues as how free the merchant feels he is compared to the employee who may make more money but who also has to take orders or punch a clock. Different motivations may be present for the self-employed; perhaps the corner druggist values his security, relying on no one for a job from month to month; perhaps the steel worker values the protection of his union; the military career man enjoys his advantageous retirement plan.

Most studies of social structure in work have come out of the factory, beginning on a large scale with the studies of Mayo.[5] There is no need here to tell the story in detail. The over-all result, however, has been a change in several directions of the attitude toward workers by progressive management. First, a new accent on human relationships has developed, so that the worker is observed in relation to his fellow worker and supervisor as well as to machine. Second, there has been a growing realization that the factory or industry is not only hiring a foreman, electrician, or timekeeper but a Tom Jones who has a family, goes to church, likes baseball, and lives a whole life in which work is only a part; that his other interests and roles affect his efficiency as a worker; and that as a whole man he bases his rewards in work on feelings of security and recognition as well as on material reward.[6] Last, there is a new feeling, quite different from the Christian motive that often marked paternalism among pioneer industrialists, that industry must attract and hold its workers by assuming some share of responsibility in promoting the general welfare of the whole community as a place that is lived in as well as worked in.

These realizations have taken many forms, from profit sharing to baseball teams in industry and from housing units and the construction of attractive villages to comprehensive recreation programs, including symphony orchestras and class piano lessons.[7]

Degree of skill and education

Another factor intrinsic to work that might affect leisure activity is the degree of skill and education required by the job.

According to a survey of the Twentieth Century Fund,[8] several factors indicate that more education and skill are required now than formerly.

> Unskilled workers, including farm hands, industrial workers and domestic servants, numbered less than 14 million out of the 52 million persons in the labor force in 1940. This was less than 26 per cent of the total, against 36 per cent in 1910. The second largest group in 1940 was the 11 million semiskilled workers, but here the trend, reflecting the spread of automatic machinery and mass production, was steeply upward—from less than 15 per cent of the total in 1910 to 21 per cent in 1940. White-collar occupations, comprising professional persons and clerks and kindred workers, grew from less than 15 per cent in 1910 to nearly 24 per cent in 1940.

Other types of evidence could be found by examining the knowledge required to operate machines in today's industry compared to that of a generation ago or the degree to which farming of today is marked by specialized knowledge as compared to that of former days. This need not, and is not intended, to imply that the American of today is a more educated or wiser person than his forefather, for other criteria than those of increased formal education or of know-how enter the picture. Yet the general postulate may safely be submitted that a more specialized occupation has beneath it a fairly broad general background, whereas a general occupation has above it a more restricted background.

Thus a graduate physicist whose work demands a very high order of specialized knowledge and judgment has attended school for a considerable period. Whether he ever gets enough philosophy, history, literature, etc., is now and will remain a burning issue within academic circles. At any event, he gets more of these than if he left school at 15 to go to work as a farmer, general salesman, or small merchant. Any of these persons may very well, as their lives progress, develop far greater worldly knowledge than the physicist and learn to spend their leisure time more constructively. Yet the way in which the physicist has been exposed at an early age to a broad variety of interests, which characterize the world in microcosm known as the university, is likely to provide a type of urbanity that comes otherwise only in occasional instances.

Amount of hours in work

Finally, a most obvious aspect of work as an intrinsic factor is the amount of time the nature of the work permits for off-job living. Here facts are familiar to everyone to indicate that although in the last several generations the American worker and farmer have raised their level of material comfort their hours of work have declined. In 1850 the average work week, combining agricultural and nonagricultural work, was about 70 hours; in 1900, 60 hours; in 1940 it was down to 44 hours. Although 1950 saw a new low of 40 hours, the estimate was 37.5 hours for 1960. This represents a drop of 2.5 hours during that decade and an average drop of 4 hours for each decade since 1900.[9] As one writer notes, the average American wage earner now has about 3700 free hours per year, which comes to 230 full days of 16 hours, in addition to time for sleep.[10]

There are many complications in an analysis of such figures. For instance, the statement is often heard that although hours of work went down our level of living went up; that is, we live better in terms of more goods or more "real income." This, although undoubtedly true, is hard to put into a quantitative perspective. We are told that in 1960 the amount of "private national income" produced was 31 times what it was in 1850. In human terms, this means that with a formula to provide a comparison of prices and money income the average family has available a great amount of electrical energy to run its dozen or more appliances, more goods, such as clothing and furniture, more varieties in food, and so on. It is estimated that each of us has at our daily disposal as much power—as many services—as would in the preindustrial days have required 90 slaves. Yet, for statistical purposes, the growth of goods and services that accompanied the steady lowering of work hours is complicated by the simple fact that much of the additional increment to the worker has come in time, not in material goods—and how can we quantify *time* in statistical units comparable to *things?* In this connection, note this important summary in the Twentieth Century Survey: [11]

> Shorter hours are the cause as well as the result of increased labor productivity. Experience during the war showed that the tempo of work in industry today would probably not permit anything like the 55-hour work week that prevailed in 1910. Nor would the leisure time "left over" after working nine hours a day six days a week permit us to enjoy the added goods and services we could afford to buy. Hence, in order to benefit from the increased output per man-hour we probably had to accept part of the gain in the form of shorter working hours and more leisure time. There is every reason to expect that further advances in productivity will mean a continuance of this trend toward more leisure as well as more goods.

It is clear that two things have gone on simultaneously: we are living better and working fewer hours. Left unsaid in such a summary are these considerations: did the nature of the work carried on formerly (over longer hours) contain in it values, attitudes, or satisfactions that are not present in the work of today? Implicit in the terms "leisure" and "work" is the presence of certain kinds of expectancies, satisfactions, and attitudes. If, for example, our work gives us some creative satisfactions and outlets and our leisure hours are merely boring and unsatisfying, then there is little point to interpreting shorter hours of work as "good" or as "progress."

A second consideration enters when a statistical chart dramatizes our increase in goods and services. Is there a fallacy in assuming that more goods and services are indications of a higher level? There can be no question, of course, about the real fact that we have many more things available to us than did our forefathers. How many of these things, which are now essential, have been the result of the *creation of needs* by advertising, emulation of neighbors, outlet for "conspicuous consumption," and the like? There is perhaps a real difficulty in drawing comparisons between the material aspects of a society in 1850 and the present day, for these material aspects are not absolute facts but exist as meanings, ideas, and concepts; they are therefore cultural in nature.

In summary of some factual materials, which, with all their difficulty of analysis, must still provide the indispensable minima for realistic appraisal of the situation, several simple tables and charts are valuable. Table 7 indicates the average number of working hours per week for ten-year periods since 1850 and a projection for 1960. From this we see that half the number of hours a week are taken for work now than a century ago.

TABLE 7

Estimated Employment and Average Weekly Working Hours: 1850–1960

Year	Employed, Total in Millions	Average Weekly Hours		
		Nonagriculture	Agriculture	Weighted Average
1850	7.4	65.7	72.0	69.8
1860	10.1	63.3	71.0	68.0
1870	12.4	60.0	70.0	65.4
1880	16.7	58.8	69.0	64.0
1890	21.9	57.1	68.0	61.9
1900	26.7	55.9	67.0	60.2
1910	34.0	50.3	65.0	55.1
1920	39.7	45.5	60.0	49.7
1930	45.8	43.2	55.0	45.9
1940	47.9	41.1	54.6	44.0
1950	61.5	38.8	47.2	40.0
1960	69.0	36.5	44.0	37.5

Extracted from Appendix 20–4, p. 1073, *America's Needs and Resources,* 1955.

TABLE 8

Hours of Work on Assumption of a 6-Day and a 5-Day Week: 1850–1960

Year	6-Day Week	5-Day Week
1850	11.7 hr	14.0
1860	11.3	13.3
1870	10.9	13.1
1880	10.6	13.0
1890	10.3	12.4
1900	10.0	12.0
1910	9.1	11.0
1920	8.3	9.9
1930	7.6	9.2
1940	7.3	8.8
1950	6.6	8.0
1960	6.2	7.5

What does this mean if we assume that both now and in the years back to 1850 we had distributed our work week over six days? What if we had worked five days all this time? Table 8 shows that in the first supposition the 1850 worker would have been busy almost 12 hours a day, compared to 6.2 hours in 1960. Obviously, if we project the same total hours on a five-day week, we should be working longer each day. Charts 2 and 3 put this material another way.

A different way of looking at this is provided in Chart 1. Let us assume that in each of the years since 1850 we spread our work week over six days. Let us further set aside seven hours each 24-hour period for sleep, an hour for eating, and two hours for other activities more or less essential. What does this actually permit us in each period for doing pretty much what we want to do? About 2.18 hours in 1850, compared to 7.48 hours in 1960. The proportion of more than 3 to 1 remains the same whether one cares to include more time for eating, sleeping, or other activities.

Yet the hours alone are only part of the story. Today, we can easily make plans for leisure activity by telephone, thus saving time. We can travel faster to a destination. We can consult such printed sources as newspapers to help decide what and where we will do something. Perhaps, at the end of the day, we have more energy as city people

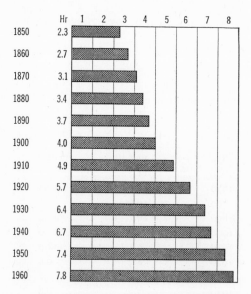

CHART 1. Hours Free After Work, Eating, and Necessities, 1860–1960. Projected on 6-day work week. Includes 7 hours sleep, 1 hour eating, 2 hours miscellaneous.

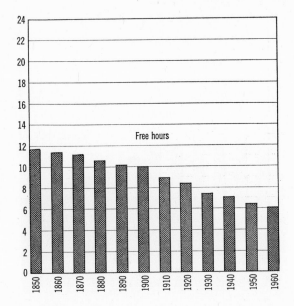

Free hours

CHART 2. Work and Free Hours per 6-Day Week, 1850–1960

than the farmer (a difficult and by no means a clear-cut case, however). Our wives are perhaps freer of household work to join with their men in family activity. There are fewer children around to consider in family planning. We have better light in our homes if we want to read. We have better police protection for night walking. Food is more easily available during or after our leisure activity, often from the home freezer. We enjoy better health and spend less time suffering from serious ills or recovering from them.

There are undoubtedly other differences, and they all strongly suggest that the mere numbers of hours of work alone are not the whole story.

Extrinsic aspects of work

Work as work—its intrinsic aspects—led us into brief discussion of the relation of leisure to the raw materials of work, to its social structure, to degrees of skill and education, and to amount of time spent in work. By *extrinsic* aspects of work are meant all those characteristics that relate a person as a worker to his social role as a nonworker. In the first case we concentrate on Bill Jones as he performs his job in a store, factory, school, or mine; we consider how certain things about

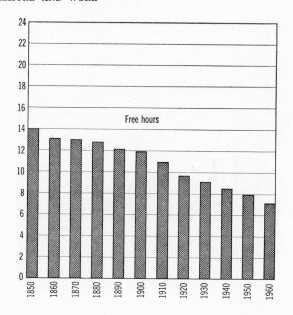

CHART 3. Work and Free Hours per 5-Day Week, 1850–1960

the job itself affect his leisure behavior. But as we look about we see that the job is only one color on a larger canvas of community or society; Mr. Jones brings some ideas, some behavior habits into the job. Further, the job has, in the community "mind," associations of significance, importance, or limitation. This relation of social roles as worker and nonworker is approached from three points of view: type of work, participants, and termination. In each case emphasis is placed on changes now observable in American life.

Types of work and participants

The first purpose of work organization in any society is to provide each person with enough food, clothing, shelter, or other necessities to keep alive in the amount and type defined by the society itself. When to this fundamental purpose is added the phrase ". . . and in some comfort," then the range of needs and desires becomes formidable. For instance, when American engineers have gone to foreign lands as employees of oil companies or other industries, they have sometimes found that the natives will work just long enough to get money for the next day, then walk off the job until they have spent what they had paid to them. The American, used to the idea of allocating his savings to pay rent or to meet other needs, finds it hard to believe that day-by-day living is anything but primitive mentality.

Some societies know no more, or have no other possibility in their access to economic goods, than to reach for the barest fundamentals of keeping alive; other societies go beyond this. Yet, even in the first case, as we know from archeological findings, men always seem to decorate their pots or houses or other objects with designs or shapes that are nonutilitarian. This seems to indicate that mere animal existence as a purpose of human group life is almost impossible to conceive. In most simpler societies every adult person is supposed to be occupied in a task directly related to getting food, making clothes, or caring for children. There is no time for the preacher as a preacher, for the artist as an artist, for the thinker as a thinker, or the story-teller as a story-teller. These special functions are done on the side.

The East African area illustrates the nature of such comparatively small societies. Here we have the Massai, Zulu, and Kaffir peoples. The economy is built around cattle, and there is little trade with other areas. Communities are small. Only iron workers exist as specialists, and, as we may expect, their graphic and plastic arts are crude. Their music, dances, myths, and tales are perpetuated by the general population. Even in Dahomey, to the west, where such specialists are found in good number in iron working, pottery making, brass casting, silver and gold-smithing, appliqué cloth making, wood carving, and calabash decorating, these specialists till the soil. Further, much of their product is made for the chiefs and is not for wide consumption.

This kind of society, of course, contains a considerable variety of activities that we might today talk about as leisure; at least, they are done outside work time and without direct relationship to raising crops, hunting, or fighting. For instance, John Weeks, in his volume *Among the Primitive Bakonga*,[12] describes the amount of dancing that goes on for all kinds of social occasions—at a time of serious illness, start of a journey, or at births and deaths. ". . . and if there is no such ostensible reason, then they will find one or dance for the mere love of it."

A second type of economy, in respect to our issue of leisure, has specialists *outside the immediate productive realm*. Further, it has a sizable bulk of workers in jobs that embrace a relatively cosmopolitan rather than a local view of life and the world. American society since the middle of the nineteenth century illustrates a transition into the second kind of economic situation. The trend away from unskilled to skilled worker, even since 1910, is more than 35 per cent of the total workers at that time to about 25 per cent in 1940. In 1870 about half the workers were on the farm; in 1950, only 12 of every 100. Six in 100 workers in the year 1870 were in some trade; by 1950 it was three times that percentage. Three in every 1000 workers in 1870 were in some enterprise connected with finance or insurance; now it is over three in 100. Government work of some kind employed two in 100 workers in 1870; by 1950 this had gone up four times. Those workers defined as professional men went up from two in 100 workers in the same period of time to six in 100. In the mid-twentieth century almost one of every five American adults working was his own employer, in retail business, farming, or as an independent craftsman.[13]

These figures suggest that even within the last few generations in our own part of the world important changes have been taking place in the kinds of work done by the bulk of our people. With this goes the stream of change in family life in attitudes toward church, personal ambitions, class structure, and many other facets or patterns. In relation to leisure life, several results of the occupational change can be noted:

1. *The professional man and government worker, and others who are increasing in number, are men whose work permits a wide choice in nonwork activities.* Such jobs require persons with broader backgrounds and some awareness of what is going on around them. More important, the shift is toward jobs in which a man's success grows out of his skill in manipulating other persons or, at the very least, working with other persons as his raw materials. Work with other people, rather than with the soil or with the manufacture of things, makes one sensitive to aspects of their lives other than simply their purchasing power. My father was a hand tailor; I am a teacher. Can there be any doubt that my necessarily greater contact with people and the nature of the work itself almost forces me to become more sensitive to the lives of others, to be concerned with others, to learn from others?

2. *In the newer kinds of work suggested above it is more possible to bring values or ideas or attitudes from the nonwork life into the work sphere.* I build a house as a carpenter, I bake cakes and breads, I till the soil, I deliver the mails, or I curry horses; in each of these cases, although my work has in it some aspects coming from the society, fundamentally the job can be objectively outlined on paper. Trousers are pressed about the same way for whites and Negroes in Chicago, and a twopenny nail is the same size in Omaha as in Oshkosh. All this is quite different if I am a psychologist, a teacher, or a government administrator. Then my biases and past experience, my associates, and my professional "orientation" (as a Freudian or Adlerian, as Democrat or Re-

publican) enter into the way in which I give legal advice, propose laws, or teach my classes.

This is the reason why leisure in our own society is a far deeper issue than a relationship of free to work hours. The point is that we are heading, by and large, toward a kind of work that we cannot arbitrarily, by hours, divide from the rest of our lives. It is not enough to say that we work harder at our play or that work is becoming more like play. This is only roughly true. We must begin to think of a society in which the lines between such concepts as work, play, family, individual, group, state, religion, education, and entertainment have faded. Children in the family now learn how to sleep and eat, in part, in the primary grades. For a long time now preparation for trades and crafts has become the responsibility of the vocational school, not the factory or the craft itself. Although the church may have weakened as an influence, moral teachings are an integral part of the school. Other examples of institutional cross functionings come to anyone's mind.

This might be interpreted to mean that we must expect to find increasing numbers of changes in the functions of institutions. In a very broad sense, industrial society has gone so far into the specialization of jobs and social responsibilities that a countermovement has set in. And the whole effect, if we can get back far enough from it to observe, is to create a rough parallel to primitive society, in which there are no clear-cut lines between economic, religious, and family activity, for the same people have social functions to perform in all of them.

A clear-cut definition of leisure is therefore made difficult by the very fact that the shades and lines between religion, work, family, etc., are thinner—as students of leisure, we feel frustrated because we cannot deal with the concept more concretely. Actually, we should turn our frustrations equally to other, more familiar concepts in social science, for we cling to outworn insights when basic changes in our lives require a revised and bold inquiry. For example, as men move about more easily and informally between such places as home, office, church, and playground, the values from one blend into the values of the other. Consequently, attitudes that we formerly associated with work (industriousness, perfection, rewards, response, gratification, etc.) can now be found in nonwork activity. The usefulness of this proposition is essential in an understanding of problems of retirement and old age.

3. *A third result of the change toward new types of jobs in this country is a break in traditional social class lines.* More of us these days have direct contact with people in other types of work, with other social backgrounds, and of other degrees of wealth. Add to this the fact that more of us live in cities, that public recreational facilities are

on the increase, that appeals over the mass media are aimed toward the masses, not elites, and the conclusion is clear that in spite of all meticulous statistical systems by which some sociologists delineate six social divisions within the structure of American life a very considerable freedom exists for Jones and Brown to think or play or study or watch sports together in their own time. New categories and theories are now needed in social science to replace the increasingly dubious label of "class." [14]

4. *One fourth of our total working force now consists of women.* This increase in women as workers is due to several factors. Family life has changed, with organized activity for children more prevalent outside the home, labor-saving devices in factories and better working conditions as a whole in manufacture and business, demand for more workers in wartime, a general movement toward equality of the sexes, and so on.

This means, for those women who work, a clearer concept of leisure than they had before. How is anyone to define the difference between free and unfree time in housework, when the vacuum cleaning may suddenly be punctuated with social phone calls or when bathing the baby is both an obligation and a delight? In interviews with housewives in one community study, some women thought that leisure, for them, came when all the household chores were out of the way and the children were in bed. The woman who works is more likely to have someone come in to help clean the house or wash the clothes; she is more likely to buy prepared foods. She has little time to make an art of keeping her home and, like her husband, is readier to desire rest, relaxation, or play, however she defines them.

According to recent estimates by the Bureau of the Census, it should be noted that the proportion of women who will work in the next several decades will go up sharply. *The New York Times* for November 25th, 1956, summarizes this trend:

If women keep taking jobs at the rate they have been for the past five years, 17,460,000 married, widowed or divorced women between 35 and 64—about half the women in this age group will be working by 1975. In the age group of 45 to 54, about 60% will be working. Part of the demand for these women in the labor force has come in the past five years from the relative shortage of workers 18 to 24 years of age—a shortage due in the first place to the small baby crop from depression days. Ten years from now, as the *Times* report indicates, the post-war baby rise will begin to flood the labor market with about 900,000 young people annually seeking work. What this may mean for the number or the kinds of jobs open to older women then will have to be seen. Automation, for one, will probably most affect women in clerical work with little advanced schooling. Projections of leisure attitudes and patterns among women will be directly affected by all of this.

It is doubtful whether quantitative studies along these lines can get very far into the picture. Careful observations and depth studies are still to be made. Hypotheses can be advanced on several levels: (a) leisure will be more clearly defined and perceived by women who are employed outside the home than by other women; (b) the home as a center for leisure activity is more desirable among women who are employed; (c) a considerable degree of leisure activity by the family, which depends on direct expenditure, is now made possible by the earnings of women; and (d) women who work outside the home will be found to emphasize the value of freedom for themselves—a perception that will be carried over into their leisure activities. These points need to be examined systematically, for they lend themselves to the combined empirical and *verstehen* approach mentioned earlier.

Termination of work

A third approach to extrinsic aspects of work and leisure concerns retirement. Two issues concern us now: the tendency for workers to step out of the productive system (to retire) at an earlier age and the new developments in automatic processes that may cut across all ages and many skills and types of production processes.

As to the first, retirement, the rough facts have received much attention in the last few years. The Federal government has provided a social security scheme that now covers millions of persons. The general age for retirement has gone down. Technological work demands more skills and fewer workers per unit of expended energy, both leading to less demand for older workers. Length of life has increased remarkably. In 1890 two thirds of all men over the age of 65 were working; by 1940 this proportion had gone down to one half. Such are the simple facts.

With a growing recognition of such facts has come a deeper understanding of the adjustments required by retired persons in our kind of society. Only a few need be mentioned here. The nature of our family life, including the growing importance of freedom for children and the equality of wives and husbands, leads to less desire to have grandfather or grandmother in the home of their children. And when they do live as one family, the issue of being needed becomes important: for the transition from being an active member of society to one who is economically unnecessary and socially in the way is at best a difficult one. With the lowering of retirement age, more and more men leave their work when they feel that physically, mentally and emotionally they are at the height of their powers. Thus the change into a completely different social role comes often with no preparation and with fear.

A new kind of question has been raised more frequently in recent years by social scientists, counselors, psychiatrists, and even by some progressive employers. What is the continuity between the personal values (drives, goals, attitudes, and interests) that one has during work years and retirement? Do these drives need to be of the same quality? Should there be a conscious attempt to relate them? Can a businessman or an executive in industry be urged or taught to develop activities that will be important to him later while he is still in his work phase of life? In fact, can the last years of work be organized to "inch toward" retirement? Perhaps, as a result of such questions, big industry may in time approach some system whereby its employees are not retired in one fell swoop but a few months per year at a time. Whatever the actual plans in detail, the problem of a continuity between work and postwork years is an important one.

An increasing portion of the recreation program under tax funds has to do with serving aged citizens; Milwaukee, for instance, has a full-time consultant who works closely with a large number of "senior citizen" groups, offering help in organization and activities.

In general, this over-all issue of retirement has grown in proportion with the development of labor-saving devices, with urbanization, and with the popularity of pension plans (private or public). Yet the issue is not qualitatively different than it was a generation or two ago. We are, no doubt, more conscious of psychological and social aspects than we were in the past, and this has led to more open discussion and action.

The second aspect of termination of work is a more dramatic and recent one: the growth of automation. We need not enter into a dramatic narration of the capabilities of present automatic machines and those of the future.[15] One real concern over automation is unemployment, for although we are as talented in inventing new needs and products as we are new machinery, employment opportunities cannot be expected to persist when the labor force continues to grow and automation processes are increasingly adopted.

The second impact of automation on the worker will be a further depersonalization in relation of man to product. This process has already gone far as the worker has become engaged as a specialist on a fractional part of a total operation.[16] Pride in work, to the degree that it is a fact, is less the satisfaction in the specific product than in being a functional and psychological part of a human group that is sensitive to its interdependency.

In this kind of production milieu, infinitely compounded by automation, the worker can scarcely obtain values and lessons. He continues what he has already succeeded in good part in doing: searching
for ways to shorten his days, weeks, and years in the factory; inversely,
to lengthen his consecutive periods on nonwork activity. In a previous generation the old person had no worry about being wanted as a
responsible and functional part of the economy; he worked to the end,
even if that amounted to simple chores on the family farm. At present,
a major effort in dealing with the "senior citizen" is to present him
with opportunities to engage in productive human—not industrial—
activities in which he is responsible, then to convince him that here he
can obtain values that he was once taught were to be found only in
economic work.

Automation will hurry this transition. The implication is that work
in our society is undergoing a profound change. Although work is
still the most important element in man's interdependency with other
men, it becomes less so.

The factor of earlier retirement and the growth of automation suggest a dual level of enforced leisure, even in an age of high employment
and prosperity. Good times are no longer synonymous with maximum
work levels for all ages. The four types of free time or leisure that have
concerned man hitherto have been (a) permanent, voluntary leisure of
the rich, (b) temporary, involuntary leisure of the unemployed, (c)
regularly allocated, voluntary leisure of the employed on holidays or
vacations, and (d) temporary incapacity of the employed, permanent
incapacity of the disabled, and voluntary retirement by the aged. We
must now expand the fourth group into an ever-increasing number of
involuntary retired who are named as "unneeded" or "unable" by others
but who themselves still feel capable and needed by the economy. To
these, automation may add a fifth group with perhaps the greatest
adjustment to make: those to whom increased automation will mean
cycles of work and nonwork with no stipulation or psychology of unemployment, with continuing pay, and with a dramatic interweaving of
free time and work time.

The generalizing of this chapter has concerned broad issues. Can the
subject of leisure be focused with *people* more directly in view? How
do they, as people, relate work and nonwork? What leads them into
watching an outdoor game of football, baseball, or soccer rather than
into a library, a concert hall, pub or tavern, a movie, a gathering of
friends, a cock fight, the family parlor, or the bosom of female companionship for a price? This is our next area of discussion.

Leisure and personality 4

L ast night, at 8:00 P.M., many millions of Americans were watching
television. Others were in theaters. If it is summer, many thousands
were at baseball games or watching other sports. Some were reading.
Phonographs were being played. Many couples were dancing. Thousands of social and fraternal clubs were in session. Perhaps you were
walking with your dog along a mountain stream.

How were these activities selected? What kinds of people were involved in them?

Free will is one explanation: you *chose* to walk with your dog; the
other fellow chose to see a baseball game. A partial answer has already
been given to this explanation in Chapter 3. If your work kept you in
a logging camp in Canada, you could not have gone to see the Giants
play the Braves. Yet even within the camp there were alternatives: a
dance, a card game, books, radio, walking, sleep. . . . Why did A do
this, B do that . . . ?

A variety of answers is available. People have different needs, dis-
positions, tendencies, desires, tastes, habits, upbringing, goals, and so on.
In a later chapter, as we explore the social process by which persons become involved in activities, we examine such concepts in action. The
purpose of this chapter is more limited. The writings of three authors
are summarized as illustrations in the social science literature of approaches to (*a*) influence of groups on our actions, (*b*) a typology of
persons, and (*c*) the basic needs of man in his culture. These are seen,
respectively, in Howard S. Becker's study of marihuana addicts, David
Riesman's *Lonely Crowd*, and Eric Fromm's *Sane Society*.

Becker: man, group, and pleasure

Why do some persons choose to smoke marihuana? The explanation
one hears frequently is on the basis of some traits or characteristics

within them. After the drug is once taken, we are told, the habit takes over. Howard S. Becker put this theory to the test in 50 interviews as part of a study of the Chicago Narcotics Survey.[1] He indicates that traits that cause the behavior need not be identified and, indeed, cannot be, for some persons who do not possess the traits commonly listed are marihuana users. Further, persons who do use marihuana display variation as to their uses: at one time the drug may be used, then rejected, then used again. Thus Becker states that the real problem is to describe the set of changes in "the person's conception of the activity and of the experience it provides for him." [2] Wanting or the need for marihuana does not precede use of the drug; *one learns to like it by smoking it.*

Becker's first observation is that the novice does not usually get "high" the first time he tries marihuana; several attempts are needed. The smoker must learn the proper way of smoking by direct teaching or imitation. Learning includes the recognition of symptoms caused by the use of marihuana *and their connection by the user with his use of the drug.* Becker notes, "The user must be able to point them out to himself and consciously connect them with his having smoked marihuana before he can have this experience." [3] The element of *anticipation* is present, for if the user does not get "high" he worries about it. He learns how to smoke correctly from more experienced persons:

I didn't get high the first time . . . I don't think I held it in long enough. . . . So he told me to sit on a stool . . . and he said "Let your feet hang," and then when I got down my feet were real cold, you know. And I started feeling it, you know. That was the first time I got a big laughing kick, you know. Then I really knew I was on.

It is this important association of an anticipated—and learned—experience with smoking that leads to pleasure from marihuana. The element of *perception* of the experience is basic. Becker observed that when this perception of the relationship between the anticipated experience and the drug was lost the smoking itself ceased.

Finally, the smoker must *learn to enjoy* his experience with drugs:

The taste for such experience is a socially acquired one, not different in kind from acquired tastes for oysters or dry martinis. The user feels dizzy, thirsty; his scalp tingles; he misjudges time and distances, and so on. Are these things pleasurable? He isn't sure. If he is to continue marihuana use, he must decide that they are. Otherwise, getting high, while a real enough experience, will be an unpleasant one he would rather avoid.[4]

Said one man:

It was offered to me, and I tried it. I'll tell you one thing. I never did enjoy it at all. I mean it was just nothing I could enjoy. [Well, did you get high when you turned it on?] Oh, yeah, I got definite feelings from it. But I didn't enjoy them. I mean I got plenty of reactions, but they were mostly of fear. [You were frightened?] Yes. I didn't enjoy it. I couldn't seem to relax with it, you know. If you can't relax with a thing, you can't enjoy it, I don't think.

In summary of Becker's study: no one becomes a user of marihuana without a learning process that consists of three steps: "(1) learning to smoke the drug in a way which will produce real effects; (2) learning to recognize the effects and connect them with drug use . . . ; (3) learning to enjoy the sensations he perceives."

Riesman: character types, society, and pleasure

The origin and the change of character types, according to Riesman, is related to the population curve.[5] Societies with a high birth and death rate (India, China, Egypt, and Central and South America) develop a *social character*, which early in life is taught to conform to tradition. *Tradition-directed* people result.

Other societies have learned to control the death rate and are in a period of transitional growth (Europe from 1650 to 1900). Here internalized life goals become the standard of conformity, producing *inner-directed* people. A third type of society passes through both phases, bringing a net reduction in population as in the present United States. We produce *other-directed* persons who are sensitive to the "expectations and preferences of others."

Two quotations from Riesman's own summary of his work will help clarify, first, the significance of his approach to the relationship of character to society and, second, the terms applied to his types. As to method,[6] he notes that he began in *The Lonely Crowd,*

> not with the individual, but with the society. And, with respect to the society, our focus was on certain changes that many people have observed in contemporary social organization, particularly the important degree to which modern metropolitan society, in classes and areas boasting high economic abundance, has presented people with agendas for living—and with an accompanying ethos—which are different from those characteristic of the nineteenth-century middle class. And then our effort was to proceed "inward" from these large social developments to study the demands made on individual character. These demands might be traced "outward," in turn, through the subtle channels by which character is formed. Working in the neo-Freudian tradition of Erich Fromm, Karen Horney, and others, we looked for the consequences of social change in the individual, rather than looking, as psychoanalytic characterology did in an earlier day, for the social equivalents of the "family romance" in the society at large.

Riesman's meaning of his terms for character are thus summarized by him:

> In other words, inner-direction and other-direction are abbreviated ways . . . to describe two not incompatible tendencies of which people are capable: one tendency is to find the source of direction in aims which one has held affectively before one from an early age; and another tendency is to find the source of direction in those among whom one is thrown at any given moment in one's career.[7]

These types of character represent attitudes toward both work and play. The inner-directed person organizes his work experience around nonhuman objects; he reacts to and respects organization rather than people. The other-directed, on the other hand, hurries to bring glamour and artificial friendliness into the work situation. A "compulsory nature of personalization" (Riesman also calls this a "false personalization")[8] is sought between bosses and employees. A gamelike spirit is introduced into the factory, with the line between work and play constantly diminished by the increasing power and presence of other-directedness as a standard and goal in work.

Patterns of pleasure and leisure are also related to these types. When to play is decided for the tradition-directed person. Indeed, he is aware of sharp distinctions between play and work: work is long and arduous by its nature.

The inner-directed person, moving from an age of tradition into one with an abundance of things, becomes an *acquisitive consumer*. He engages in an externalized sort of rivalry akin to the process described by Thorsten Veblen.[9] As an *escaping consumer*, the inner-directed person may escape to a " 'higher' level than that of business or professional life or onto a 'lower' level!" The arts represent one example of the first. "Even more perhaps than plumbing, amateur musical skills mark the boundary of middle-class aspirations to respectability."[10] Escape *downward* is found in cheap novels, in races, in barbershop song, in "hootchy-kootch on the midway." Further, this man in business or the professions will exploit his leisure to make contacts, thereby bringing his work into his play.

The other-directed person uses leisure and entertainment as an adjustment *to the group*. He has a large literature to orient him to the noneconomic side of life and all the mass media as his tutor.[11]

> Entertainment today, far more than in an era of inner-directed modes of conformity, takes up the task of telling members of large groups of mobile people what they can expect of each other and what they should expect of themselves. The inner-directed man learned what he needed to know of these matters in the primary group, or by a purposeful internalization

of his schooling and reading. The mass media today are expected to perform ten-minute miracles of social introduction between people from a variety of ways of life and background. The entertainment fields serve the audience today less and less as an escape from daily life, and more and more as a continuous sugar-coated lecture on how to get along with "others."

Although our popular culture stresses group-mindedness as a virtue, it does not serve the purpose of escape because the other-directed person has no clear core of *self* to escape *from*. He can draw no sharp distinction between production and consumption or between work and play.

Fromm: man's needs, the sanity of society, and leisure

Riesman, if not always with success,[12] does not seek the good or the bad man or the good and bad society; he sets out to describe how each type of character develops with population and social changes. Erich Fromm's task is more ambitious.[13] He deals with no less a problem than man's needs. He then asks whether a society can be sane unless it meets these objectively ascertainable needs: "the need of relatedness, transcendance, rootedness, the need for a sense of identity, and the need for a frame of orientation and devotion." [14] Unlike Riesman, who began his analysis with the nature of a changing society, Fromm begins with an immutable man, then searches the capitalistic society to see how the needs are met. They are not. The pleasure of possession and property that came with nineteenth-century capitalism produced a character with a "hoarding orientation," [15] "the use of man by man," and an inherent conflict between two principles of value, "that between the world of things, and their amassment, and the world of life and its productivity." [16]

Capitalism of the twentieth century is marked by important features. Gone are feudal traits. Industrial production increases. Capital concentrates and business becomes big. There are more people who manipulate other people. The worker rises economically and politically. New methods of work develop. What kind of men does such a society need, what "social character arises?" Fromm answers:

> It needs men who cooperate smoothly in large groups, who want to consume more and more, and whose tastes can be easily influenced and anticipated. It needs men who feel free and independent, not subject to any authority, or principle, or conscience—yet willing to be commanded, to do what is expected, to fit into the social machine without friction.[17]

The single concept that Fromm uses to analyze this relation of character to present-day society is *alienation:* a mode of experience in which the person does not feel that he is the center of his world or the creator of his own acts. He is out of touch with himself and with other persons. Man becomes to himself an impoverished thing, *"dependent on powers outside of himself, unto whom he has projected his living substance."* [18]

Other social scientists have called attention to this uprootedness, flight from freedom, depersonalization, or what Lowenthal and Guterman call "a sort of eternal adolescent uneasiness." [19]

We are interested in Fromm's approach because he draws specific relations of alienation to leisure in the contemporary industrial society.

> If a man works without genuine relatedness to what he is doing, if he buys and consumes commodities in an abstractified and alienated way, how can he make use of his leisure time in an active and meaningful way? He always remains the passive and alienated consumer. He "consumes" ball games, moving pictures, newspapers and magazines, books, lectures, natural scenery, social gatherings . . . he wants to "take in" all there is to be had. . . . Actually, he is not free to enjoy "his" leisure; his leisure-time consumption is determined by industry . . . entertainment is an industry like any other, the customer is made to buy fun as he is made to buy dresses and shoes. . . . In any productive and spontaneous activity, something happens within myself while I am reading, looking at scenery . . . I am not the same after the experience as I was before. In the alienated form of pleasure nothing happens within me; I have consumed this or that; nothing is changed within myself, and all that is left are memories. . . . [20]

Implications of Becker, Riesman, and Fromm for our study

Three ways of approaching personality and leisure have been sketched through the writings summarized above. Becker begins with group, Reisman with society, and Fromm with basic needs of man. Whatever the specific contributions of these writers in their respective treatments, the *approaches* are not new. Much has been written, for instance, about the impact of group norms on individual behavior. The technique of looking at the culture as a whole in order to discern or predict the behavior of its people, and even to set up types of characteristic behavior, is found in a growing body of anthropological literature. The famous sociological study, *The Polish Peasant*, long ago proposed three types of persons (Philistine, Bohemian, Creative).[21] Fromm's attempt to begin with human needs and then to see how the society meets them is, of course, a primary position of much psychology, both clinical and theoretical. This does not minimize the worth of the specific writings we have examined. They were selected because they typify such approaches to the problem and because in these writings an attempt is made (most explicit in Riesman) to relate their findings to leisure activities.

The over-all conclusion to be drawn from these approaches to personality is that the leisure-time actions of man somehow stem from one or a combination of three chief sources:

1. *The groups to which we belong and whose controls and norms bear upon us.*

2. *The culture into which we happen to be born, whose interlocking and complex pattern of groups, institutions, and prevailing ideologies sets a climate of opinion for all of life, including our attitudes toward unobligated time and its uses.*

3. *The limitations and potentials of our bodies and minds that influence the selections we make within groups and society and our own creative contribution toward new patterns of organization and thought in them.*

Each of these contributions in turn raises questions. As to the influence of groups on leisure activities of the individual, we must ask how the group itself happens to find certain leisure patterns more acceptable than others and whether the controls by the group over the person are the same in leisure areas of action as in others. In the matter of types of persons, are we actually explaining anything by identifying a type by its behavior and then crediting the behavior to the type? As to basic needs and cultural demands, do we not have to develop a cross-cultural approach that is still the bane of comparative anthropology?

We can go no further in these directions until a fourth approach has been briefly outlined, one that provides a theoretical tool to deal more adequately with the fact that complex society, as Professor Robert MacIver notes, is a *multigroup society*.[22] Each of us belongs to many groups. This fact is fundamental in understanding *how* we relate ourselves to conflicting ideas and norms in society. The analysis shifts attention from our *needs* to that of our *positions or social roles*.

Man is a member of many groups. He quickly moves about from a situation in which he is a hero or a leader to one in which he is a follower and a "nobody." Sorokin provides examples: [23]

> In general, each of us has as many "social egos" as there are social groups to which we belong. . . . When we interact with our family we think, feel, and behave like father, mother, sister, brother, son, or daughter. Our ideas, standards, emotions, volitions, as well as our overt actions, are of a certain kind well known to all of us. When we . . . go to our place of work with our occupational group, our "family ego" disappears and our "occupational self" takes its place . . . and there accordingly result the actions of a professor, engineer, doctor, senator, plumber, carpenter, or farmer. . . . If one should try to assume his family self in his occupation, he would quickly be fired, to say nothing of being regarded as "queer."

A systematic scheme by which this network of "social egos" can be observed is found in the theory of Professor Florian Znaniecki.[24] The scheme is to view each person as a composite of several "social roles," which are played in as many "social circles" as groups to which one belongs. These circles—home, club, factory, church—consist of values or purposes. They have a set of norms and controls by which they judge their members. They train the members and expect certain types of action from them. Thus the church consists of a number of persons who act out established patterns of the priest, the sexton, the congregant, the treasurer, the usher, the organist, and the choir member. Each of these roles sets a way into which people fit, and if we can put together these roles or patterns we have a comprehensive view of the church as a whole.

The second component of each social role is that of function—what is expected of each of these roles.

Third, in accord with the training required in the role or other factors of the situation, the role player gets something in return, whether in actual money or in less tangible rewards, such as honor, a place to sit during services, personal satisfactions, or verbal praise.

Fourth, the prestige of the circle, the feeling of doing what one is expected to do, and the esteem that results all together provide the person (as distinct now from the role) with a consciousness of what others think of him and a sense of personal belonging. A self-image results.

This type of analysis is a way of observing action that is going on at the moment. As Tom Brown steps from the church into his recreational group (poker as well as golf), he finds that their norms are different. In the church he may be a high officer, in the poker group he is one of the "boys." His social position in the congregation is high, yet he may conceal or underplay the club in conversation with the minister. While in the church he has a feeling of "doing right." In the small hours of Saturday night, if his luck at cards is bad, he wonders why he ever got into it.

Leisure activity, among its many other changes in the last quarter century, has produced new kinds of social circles. We can ask if there is anything distinctive about them as groups? Further, is there a continuity of values from leisure groups to those of work, church, and family? Are leisure groups unique in the way in which they create new social roles? Such questions as these, since they are asked in a theoretical way, may appear divorced from "real life." One example is given to illustrate their force in practical situations.

The mental hospital: theory in action

As occasional consultant to the Special Services Division for the Veterans Administration hospitals, the writer has often watched mental patients play such games as baseball, bingo, and volleyball. In baseball games all boys are taught by their childhood peer groups that one runs from first base to second to third to home; that one has three strikes and is "out"; that the catcher stands behind the batter; and so on. We have never observed mental patients who played differently. In every game they went from first base to second. Why?

The question is pertinent because the same men had also been taught other rules about many things no more complicated than baseball and certainly done more often in the course of the week. For instance: do not talk out loud to yourself; talk politely to women; sleep in a bed, not on the floor; you are "you," Sam Jones, and not Napoleon; when someone speaks to you, usually you will say something in response. Yet as soon as the Sam Joneses left the baseball field at the VA hospital, they were "patients," each suffering from some form of maladjustment: some were withdrawn and would talk to no one; others talked a blue streak to themselves; a few required hydrotherapy to calm them down; some were Napoleon, Christ, or Lincoln; and so on, through the range of schizophrenic behavior patterns.

We have in this situation, first, a considerable validation of Huizinga's theory of play,[25] that it is a world of its own and *perceived as a world of its own*. Yet in that world, with its own grounds, its moral order, and its own beginning and ending time, we see these elements. There is group pressure, for the patients definitely seem to care about the impressions they make on their team mates. Some of them are influenced to appear in the game more by fellow patients than by staff members. Second, as in similar games with normal persons, types of personalities are recognized by the players—the "show-off," the "cheater," the "scared," the "gambler" type—type-names that are often exceedingly perceptive. The needs for response and identity for the player, as discussed by Eric Fromm, are easily apparent in the cases of those who do not play in fear of personal defeat as well as in those who achieve reputations in play denied to them elsewhere.

In respect to Znaniecki's analytic scheme of social roles, we immediately face the crucial issue of the Special Services Division in the mental hospital: how can a transfer of behavior be made from the play circle to other groupings? Can the patient who knows that he must run from first to second base, not the reverse, learn that similar observance of social controls brings response? If the medical man says that it is not at all a matter of social learning, that illness is something inside the man, then why is baseball conformity *outside* the same man? This problem touches lightly upon an approach to the hospital that is in fact receiving increasing attention—the hospital as a human laboratory in which treatment and diagnosis become a synthesis of medical knowledge and social science insights.[26] It is in the theory and research of choices and methods of play that some of the clues may be found.

There are other important aspects of personality that must be considered later in this volume, such issues as personal wants, desires, and choices.[27] To obtain a further insight into the broadest areas of leisure, we turn now to the family.

Leisure and the family 5

The family is directly related to leisure in many ways. This chapter considers relationships to work, internal role changes, the community, sex, attitudes toward play, and expenditures.

Relations to work

The life pattern of the family rotates, first of all, around functions of its members in the economy of the society. As seen in Chapter 3, the nature of work may determine where the family lives, its income, the hours in which the working members are gone (both in total number and in the pattern of succession).

In the farm family all members—children as well as adults—may be in the fields or, if in the house, busy with tasks directly concerned with the farming business. Yet this family has greater control over its time in some ways than the urban family in which the husband works on a more rigid schedule of hours.

When the point is made that the line between work and play is declining in the city, we must not lose sight of farm life, which has combined both elements in many different types of societies. The long hours of work, especially on the preindustrial farm, made this blend inevitable; else there would have been much more emotional and mental breakdown than was the case.

In the farm situation, further, the entire family is involved. In a real sense, the family is close as a unit because it is related functionally as well as biologically. The "good" family is in part the family that works well together. The man and the woman see much of each other, but as fellow-workers. They have much to discuss of common professional interest: health of the cattle, weather, crops, prices, and so on.

Interdependence, emotional as well as economic, takes shape in spite of the conflicts and tensions that can also take root.

As long as the city family is engaged in a small business, such as a grocery, a close parallel exists with the farm family. Hours are long, and the wife and children are business associates. However, the trend in American economic life has been toward fewer small private businesses. Increasingly, the city employee, man or woman, goes *from* the house and returns *to* the house. In respect to location, surroundings, time, conversation, associates, presence of children, and opportunity to "take time off," dramatic changes occur.

The number of women at work will continue to rise. Even now, about one third are gainfully employed, and half of these are over 40. Of every five women among the more than 20 million employed, three are married, and four of every ten have children of school age.

When the wife does not work, she has less and less contact with the husband's professional activity. Indeed, as he works with less of the whole product in a factory or with only portions of a process in an office, there is little of interest he can tell her. If he has a more complex professional job, he does not bother with long explanations of what he is doing, and ethics sometimes prevent him. He approaches his home and family as a change or an escape from work. The children know almost nothing of what father does. With this goes the fact that his hours of work decline each decade by about three per week. Now he is or can be home more hours than ever before, with less of a functional economic nature to tie him to his family and with fewer economic interests to share with his wife.

This means that the family solidarity must come from sources other than work; even when the wife works also, her job is seldom the same as his. The contemporary city worker has more energy at the end of the work day than he had in days of less machinery, longer hours, and poorer transportation to his home. Thus, with more energy, more time, fewer household tasks, and a higher economic level, the family achieves whatever strength it has from relatively free time.

Play or leisure then becomes more than a mere diversion. *It becomes a cause, a clue, and an index of sources of respect, love, interdependence, and knowledge about the other.* Thus leisure activity in the family functions in part as the agent for developing a common outlook and attitude.

In the following illustration, reported by a student, note the variety of activities, the give and take between family members, the contribution of the children to the choice of activities, and the spontaneity and informality. The father manages a furniture store in a large Midwest city; the mother does not work. J- and B- are the informant's sisters.

> In the winter we watch television, play games, visit around the fire, pull taffy, pop popcorn, visit relatives and friends, and become a spectator at many events. The girls have more physical activity with their friends than their parents during these winter months. As the summer rolls around, the family becomes more physically active. We always try and get some sort of family vacation in, no matter how short it may seem. We usually have to wait until August because J- and I are working. We go to the baseball games, Starlight Theater, plays, etc. Many times at night J- and I have dates; therefore, the family has to plan many of their activities around us. When we were younger, the folks always played baseball and basketball with us. Now that we are older, Daddy and I help B- to learn the games. Daddy, J- and I play tennis quite a bit on Sunday mornings. We are a family who loves the outdoors and therefore we like physical activity. Many a Sunday we go on picnics, and sometimes take friends or relatives along. Often we use the grill and eat out on our porch. Sometimes after dinner we go in the living room and do something for fun like practice dancing. Since Daddy works every day but Sunday, we usually plan our leisure activities around him. For about a month in the summer all the stores stay open until 9:00 P.M., so when Daddy comes home we just sit around leisurely and talk.

This kind of family life, in which free time rather than work is the central factor, presents a more difficult situation than the rural type of life. More emphasis is put on what people *are* than that they do something useful. Conversation moves away from such topics as weather to the level of human actions or ideas. Children, husband, and wife have moved in different universes during the day. Friends have come from a variety of backgrounds.

In such a milieu the mass media come into the living room, introducing new images of life, new models of family living and happiness. Children go to school longer, more often away from home. These factors serve to lead the family members further into differing interests and a larger variety of activities outside the home. Under these conditions, family life can be dynamic, exciting, ever-changing, growing. It is no longer a monolithic, well-controlled type of life, regulated in large measure by the "radar" inside which Riesman's *inner-directeds* are produced. On the other hand, this family is also characterized by many nuances and subtleties, many more opportunities for division, loss of control and stability, and independence of its members.[1]

Relations to community

As the American family has become smaller, more comfortable in physical goods and available services, more urban, secular, and dependent for its unity on common interests and respect outside the economic, it has also become more involved in community activity.

This tendency could have been forecast at the turn of the century only if the social scientist of that time could have visualized such developments as women's new role, discussion of social issues over an emerging mass media, great wars that produced political-mindedness, or the move to suburban areas in which group life is more controllable. Alexis de Tocqueville, as far back as the 1840's had written: [2]

> As soon as several of the inhabitants of the United States have taken up an opinion or a feeling which they wish to promote in the world, they look out for mutual assistance; and as soon as they have found one another out, they combine. . . . Nothing, in my opinion, is more deserving of our attention than the intellectual and moral associations of America. . . . In democratic countries the science of association is the mother of science; the progress of all the rest depends upon the progress it has made.

This assessment is brought up to 1956 by a perceptive American sociologist, William J. Albig: [3]

> The pervasiveness of voluntary associations in the United States is evident and formidable. . . . The urge to improve the world is persistent and especially endemic in our culture. It is based upon a dominant value in our culture, that of the possibility of progress.

We shall return to a more detailed discussion of such groups when association is examined as one category of leisure activities. The issue now at hand is the relation of voluntary interest groups to the American family of today. In briefest form, five can be cited.

First, there are groups not only for almost every interest but for all ages in the family. Some organizations, such as the church-centered, can absorb the entire family. There is the case in Austin, Texas, of a PTA that held six sessions with the objective of "providing fun for the whole family while instructing each member in recreative activities designed for family fun. The workshop was attended by 370 parents and children. The program consisted of discussion and participation in family music, games, handicraft, and dramatics. . . ." [4]

There are other voluntary groups, from Scout troops to "Golden Age" clubs, that are restricted to an age bracket.

Second, clubs or groups are associations of persons that provide a *content* outside personal friendship per se: political action, the collection of butterflies, gardening hints, photography, and so on. Membership, thus involvement with content, is often brought into the home for others to share or taken *from* one home into others *via* the club. A creative family can hardly be separated from a creative community; at least, the issue presents interesting relationships for further study.

Third, it is apparent that although common interests bring family representatives together in the association, adult class, or other institutionalized agency interest or curiosity alone cannot override social patterns of that area. Negroes and whites do not often get together in the same dramatic society in Milwaukee or Chicago, not to speak of Montgomery or Chattanooga. We have noted, in the chapter on association, how social class carries over into volunteer activities even in New Haven, Connecticut.

A fourth conclusion is the pervasiveness and the real power of women's clubs in America. According to *Life* for December 24, 1956 (entirely devoted to "The American Woman: Her Achievements and Troubles"), about 65 per cent of the women of the United States belong to at least one group devoted to community service. For instance, in Raleigh, North Carolina, the Women's Club alone has over 750 members. It has taken on responsibilities "ranging from local beautifying (planting a public rose garden) to lobbying a law (banning crime comics) through the state legislature." [5] It is difficult to imagine that these women are meek in the constellation of family power as decisions are made on vacation plans or other leisure activities.

A final commentary here is that clubs and associations provide a moving population with instruments of stability. As the retired couple migrates to St. Petersburg, the Elks, Masons, League of Women Voters, and other groups provide continuations, anchors, and identifiable types of persons. Many associations are national in scope, and precisely because (by deliberate intent or otherwise) they involve similar types of people they are often the difference between easy or difficult orientation into the new community.

Aside from voluntary associations, other aspects of leisure in the community relate to the family: the nature and use of commercial and public facilities, the status of amateur and professional art, the attitudes of the school system on work and nonwork goals and skills, geographical assets and debits of the area, and so on. Several of these are discussed later.

Family change, cycle, and crisis

A static view of the family is being increasingly discarded in realistic studies. "The family" is many families as changes take place in the ages of the children, father's career, or retirement. A general *style* of family life may prevail and is perhaps established early in the family's history. Market researchers and economists, for instance, are now concerned with the family cycle; the changing roles of the growing child affect consumer habits.

A recent publication of New York University [6] contains papers on "Family life cycle analysis in research on consumer behavior," "Consumer finances over the life cycle," "The life cycle and buying patterns," and "The life cycle and consumer behavior." An introductory paper by David Riesman and Howard Roseborough approaches style of family life as a succession of roles.[7] These writers speak of the life style as the "standard package" of the large middle-majority: the furniture, radio, TV, refrigerator, food, and clothing. Around this theme are many variations in style, depending on home and neighborhood, region, subclass, ethnic group, and occupation. The roles of children are discussed, especially in reference to "anticipatory socialization," a preparation to play roles even their parents have not had by learning about domestic arrangements and equipment from parents and about styles and moods of consumption from their peers. From other places, such as the modern school, the adolescent is further prepared for a kind of home his parents have not provided. Thus he starts life early in his marriage at the point at which his parents leave off and with their help in money and services (baby sitting).

Research into leisure and family life exists on several levels. The static view inquires into what is done, by whom, how, when, and even why. It is a still picture—this moment in the family history—a moment extracted from the larger process of life. And, of course, such research is important.

A more dynamic type of concern with family leisure adds to the foregoing by inquiring what the present picture has to do with the *changes* in the family that (*a*) can be normally expected in the life cycle or (*b*) may have been unique to *this* family. Examples of the second group might be the family that migrated from another country or from another region of this country, a family in which the husband changed jobs, or one in which a divorce and remarriage took place. An extract from a student's study of her own family illustrates the effects of crisis upon the leisure of one family.

The family consisted of mother and father, two sons, and a daughter. Father operated a gasoline station and repair shop. Although he lacked a high school education, he became well read, with special interest in current affairs. Before the war there were three boys. The daughter describes the family style of life then as essentially unintegrated. The children went their own way in their own circles. Mrs.

N. would "often listen to the radio, and while doing so would either bake or knit. When Mr. N. was home one would usually find him in the basement using his machinery and mechanical devices to make or invent things. . . ." The car alone brought the family together, to visit friends on Sunday evening or to take a drive. This pattern changed sharply within two years, with the death of the middle son. The student writes:

> At first the N's obtained a television set, and through this entertainment media, the family as a whole was more united. Everyone watched the same programs, and discussed them together. Then the N's purchased a "hi-fi" phonograph for their daughter; through this media the family became interested in classical music and as a result attended concerts. Mrs. N. then became active in charity work and more of her time was spent outside the home being integrated in different organizations. As a result, her interests immediately became more diversified. Now that more time was spent away from home, more money was spent on electrical appliances and "gadgets" to make house work easier and faster.

> The function of the automobile as a means of pleasure was greatly expanded. Mr. N. became greatly interested in travel. He still took an active interest in his hobbies, but more of his time was spent with his family. At first only short trips were taken, for Mr. N. was only able to take a few days off from his business at a time, but eventually he was able to secure more time and as a result a trip was taken once a year for an entire month, and a different part of the country was seen each year.

> A family pet was also acquired and no one could express the amount of pleasure she brought to the entire family. . . . Everyone watched the dog perform the tricks that they all tried teaching her at the same time, and the response from the entire family was tremendous.

> In the earlier years of the N. family one can notice from previous facts mentioned that their leisure was more individual than grouped. This can be due in part to the size of the family and the age difference between the children.

> With the marriage of the oldest boy, the family was somewhat more unified in their leisure patterns, but this became more prevalent after the death of A.

> When this tragedy occurred they looked to entertainment as a means of therapy. They didn't like to stay home and think of their misfortune, and thus they participated in things they hadn't done before. Religion, although it had always been observed to some extent, was now more prevalent in the household. As a result of the increased church attendance, their social contacts were increased and more social activities were attended by the family. . . .

Family as source of play attitudes

Just as the family provides a setting in which attitudes are developed toward work, other people, religion, or "good" and "bad" ways of behaving, additional views are found toward play: when and how to play, with whom, and what to do.

The family helps to achieve some perspective of the relative weight of activity around us. One of the ways is by outright sanction. The parent urges the child to practice his music lesson, for music is "good," it will be an advantage in the future, and so on. Never mind, the child is told, that practice is tedious, hard, time consuming: think of the future.

So strong is this sanction in terms of reward in the future that some authors apply the term DGP (Deferred Gratification Pattern) to middle-class families.[8] The arts serve as excellent examples of this, and a reversal of the usual life pattern for children is present: the child is persuaded (or forced) to work methodically so that in adulthood he may enjoy his leisure in music. This is one reason that children, at a period in American life when they are in considerable command of their own lives, do not react well to concentrated application to the arts, as seen in the manner in which the private tutoring system ("taking lessons") has given way to the pleasanter social experience of the public school class period.

Here might be an example of Riesman's anticipatory socialization. The child is given an advantage that the parents did not have. Yet Riesman's insight applied more in previous generations than it does now. The parent of today has gone so far already that there is less need for his children to move beyond. The writer's parents, raised in Russia with no schooling, came to this country determined to provide their children with the things they had missed; and the lone violin shared by the three sons in weekly lessons was an important symbol of this promise. The gap is considerably closed in the third generation, and indeed it is one vital clue to the so-called tightening of classes argued by some authors. We would agree with Riesman that class lines (also age and sex lines) are less than they have been,[9] in part because the children of immigrants, perhaps "marginal persons" in their youth, now feel at ease at concerts, art exhibits, and other former symbols of exclusiveness. Persons like this are now very little if at all concerned with music for their children for the reason that it will open the doors to future acceptance. They are concerned with values in the art itself and its relation to personal growth. One evidence is provided in a study made in 1948 by Bennett and Associates for the American Music Conference.[10]

A total of 1847 persons replied to this question, "Some people study and learn to play an instrument, then give it up. What would you say are the chief reasons you continue to play?" Answers, in percentages, follow: [11]

TABLE 9

Reasons Given for Study of Music

Personal pleasure, enjoyment	82.1%
Interest in music, love of it	38.6
Relaxation, hobby	23.1
Play for family, friends	22.8
Natural talent	19.3
Social asset	7.7
Professional aspirations	5.4
Parental insistence	2.1
Miscellaneous	4.3
Don't know, no answer	1.0
	206.4% *

* Total exceeds 100 per cent; some persons gave several answers.

It should be noted that many of those responding to this question were parents being questioned on a large number of matters relating to the musical raising of their children. It is thus safe to assume that these attitudes are passed down to the children.

A second crucial issue on family attitudes toward leisure is the matter of television. Yet aside from quantitative studies of the number of hours and listeners, no reliable conclusions exist on its impact on family life. Roughly, we tend to assume at this point that parents and children have some influence on each other as to (a) general attitude toward TV, as distinct from other leisure choices, and (b) specific attitudes toward certain types of programs. It is too early to estimate the effect of television on the future family life of today's children.[12]

A third issue on attitudes is the subtle one of *inner resources*. Current social science, which stresses the continuity of person and society, is hesitant to use such a term. Riesman has revived it with his own. Can *inner-* and *other-directed* be applied to a whole family? Consider the possibility in reference to television.

The time to have studied television impact was earlier in its history.

An ex post facto guess is that the previous leisure resources and habits of the family were important factors in amount and kind of TV acceptance. The family that in the past had chosen its reading, movies, and radio carefully was less likely to display a minimum resistance or maximum acceptance. The family that in the past had to be entertained by outsiders simply followed through with TV. At least the facts on participatory leisure activities, including activity in the arts, go very far to destroy the myth that TV has taken over American life and snuffed out whatever creativity might have been expected.[13]

Finally, the attitude toward sex is a major type of teaching within the home. "Sex as play" is a proper phrase to describe changed attitudes toward (a) the sex act itself, which is no longer an "act of sin," and (b) the general relationship of man and wife, which is observable by the children.

> As our advertisers imply daily in a thousand ways, the attractions of sex make it the favorite form of play for millions of Americans. Why do not our thinkers go on from there to contemplate the kind of social life which might result from formal recognition of this fact, rather than implicitly or explicitly reverting to the prejudice that sex as play is bound to be sinful or at best amoral? Is it because to grant its status as play is felt to legitimize its pursuit without restraint? If so, the thinker does not understand the nature of play.[14]

These rules within which sex is a part of family life arise out of the social. Here, indeed, is the importance of sex in a consideration of leisure. When, as in the United States, the family is a unit based on equality of persons, not interdependence of economic partners, this equality extends after midnight. Contraceptives, of course, have freed the woman of unwanted childbearing; her role as companion has freed her of "legal prostitution." Sex is approached as a natural climax of the equality that permeates many contemporary families.

The general atmosphere of the home is, ideally, a relaxed one, so that sex as one fulfillment of companionship is prepared for by the nature of the whole relationship. Consequently, the sexual relationship as such can be as satisfying for the woman as well as the man. The general atmosphere, when this is the case, is reflected in attitudes toward the children.

A theory has been going the rounds of both professional and popular writing to the effect that male and female have lost some of their identity in our society. Leaning on some contemporary psychiatrists, Robert Coughlan writes that there is a "natural" relationship of the sexes,[15]

For women, the sexual act itself implies receptivity and a certain passivity. . . . For the male, the sexual role requires aggressiveness and a certain degree of dominance, even of exploitiveness. . . .

and that therefore these qualities are natural in all relationships of man and woman. Current life violates this condition. More authoritatively, Margaret Mead puts the issue in the very first paragraph of her *Male and Female*: [16]

How are men and women to think about their maleness and their femaleness in this twentieth century, in which so many of our old ideas must be made new? Have we overdomesticated men, denied their natural adventuresomeness, tied them down to machines that are after all only glorified spindles and looms, mortars and pestles and digging sticks, all of which were once women's work? Have we cut women off from natural closeness to their children, taught them to look for a job instead of the touch of a child's hand, for status in a competitive world rather than a unique place by the glowing hearth? In educating women like men, have we done something disastrous to both men and women alike, or have we only taken one further step in the recurrent task of building more and better on our original human nature?

It may well be that the problem exists; it may be that it is exaggerated and exists more in the minds of the scientists than of the husbands who shop with their wives in the supermarket without the slightest disturbance or concern.

However, the overlapping of activities that formerly were identified with one sex or the other has been marked, whether or not emotional or sexual problems have arisen. And leisure has been an important area in which the process has gone on. Men are changing diapers, dabbling on the kitchen stove, and going to art exhibitions and concerts. Women are wearing men's clothes in public without hesitation, playing golf, fixing home gadgets, helping to build the extra bedroom, and taking vacations alone.

It can be pointed out that patterns of dominance, submissiveness, femininity, and the like are socially derived, that these differences in meaningful conduct must be sought "in the unlike expectations, constraints, demands, incentives. . . ." [17] But that is to miss the point. Of course, the concepts male and female have social histories and are undergoing some change in the perceptions we have of them, both in areas of work and play. The important issue which is relevant here is that it is in leisure activity that men and women can with some impunity select activities removed from former norms of propriety. She can fish as well as he; he can sing in the community chorus as well as she. An element of freedom, a release from past traditions has thus come in this age of leisure.

We see that leisure relationships in culture are more than a simple reflection or incorporation of norms and conditions from spheres of work and social life. Leisure provides a source of values, a stepping stone for creativity, individuality, and personal exploration. An issue of first importance thus develops: leisure in relation to conformity, leisure as an opportunity for social invention. Changes in roles and legitimate domains of the sexes is only one illustration.

The family in consumer economics

Thus far we have discussed general issues: leisure as the new basis for family solidarity, family and community, attitudes toward play, and changes in sex roles. We turn now to the matter of expenditures for leisure. These expenditures are not mere financial transactions from which economic deductions alone are in order. They are integral parts of living experiences, perceptions, and cultural meanings. Seldom, even when a confirmed bachelor purchases a movie camera or a hi-fi set, are these actions taken without relevance to other people. The best setting within which to observe economic action related to leisure choices is in the family. The family also provides an observable comparison of expenditures for various types of needs: house maintenance, personal care, food, and so on. Leisure consumption then acquires some depth and perspective.

At least three approaches can be made in a study of family expenditures for leisure. Inventory of equipment in and around the home provides one clue. A second is the study of direct expenditures for activities or events (travel, theater, etc.), which would not show in an inventory. The third is to examine such indirect but important aspects as food, clothing, and housing styles as indices of a general way of life.

Equipment inventories

There exists no systematic study of leisure inventories—the possession and use of things. The functionalist approach sets up a chain of explanations, which may start with a tennis racquet and end with a history of the family.[18] As a method, it seeks relationships by starting with the present. Two random examples are given below.

FAMILY A. A student couple at the university. He is 25, she is 20 years old. A two-and-a-half room apartment.

TABLE 10

Leisure Equipment and Uses—One Family

Leisure equipment	Estimated Time and User	
Radio	3 hr	
Television	28 hr	
Oil paints	5 hr	
Hi-fi phonograph	15 hr	
Musical instruments		
String bass		He, occasionally
Trombone		He, occasionally
Ukelele		He, occasionally
Harmonica		He, occasionally
Bongo drums		She, occasionally
Cards		Seldom
Magazines	1 hr	
Bicycles		On warm days

The hi-fi is explained in part by the fact that he is a student in electrical engineering who developed a musical interest in high school. She is an art student. Since their marriage less than a year ago, he has become interested in painting. His family had not been very close; her family, well-to-do, had traveled together considerably. In spite of these differences, husband and wife appear to have a common perspective on leisure, she defining it as "time in which a person is free to do anything she finds relaxing, entertaining and fun," he as "a time when I can do whatever I feel like doing, and also whatever we do together."

The present activities of Family A are explainable, in the immediate sense, by these factors:

1. Both are students with limited time. (The interviewers did not check on the time when TV is used or how carefully it is watched.)

2. Limited income (note absence of a car).

3. Newly married, so that we can expect some individual activities (musical instruments), plus some teaching in new-found joint activity (painting).

Hidden from view by the inventory of goods is the fact that the couple goes with a group of young married people for visiting and occasional partying.

FAMILY B. Family of four: father, 50; mother, 45; daughter, 19; son, 11. Father is a C.P.A., with an approximate income of 8000 dollars per year; completed college in Italy, born in Hungary. Mother, some college work in Vienna. Daughter now a university junior. Six-room apartment of a Chicago interstitial area (rich and poor, Negro and white).

TABLE 11

Leisure Equipment, User, Time, and Expenditure: One Family

Equipment	Primary User	Approximate Time per Month	Approximate Expenditure
Piano	Mother, daughter	M., 4 hr D., 8 hr (when home)	Initial cost $5 yr upkeep
Guitars, 2	Mother, daughter	M., 2 hr, D., 8 hr	Initial cost
Violin	Father	2 hr	Initial cost
Recorder	Son	2 hr	Initial cost
Ukelele	Daughter	Rarely	Initial cost
Banjo uke	Son	2–3 hr	Initial cost
Harmonica	Father	1–2 hr	Initial cost
Music, songs	All	3 hr	$8 per yr
Victrola, records	All	12 hr	Initial cost, $5 yr $25 yr records
Radio	All	2 hr	$0–5 yr
TV set	All (especially son)	16–32 hr	Initial cost, $10 yr
Books	All	Varies	$40–50 yr
Newspapers, magazines	All	15–20 hr	$50–55 yr
Enameling kiln	Daughter	3 hr	$10 yr
Camera	Mother	2 hr	Initial cost, $10 yr films
Picnic equipment	All	Summer week ends	?
Swimming equipment	All	Summer week ends	$10 yr
Ice skates	All	Winter week ends	Initial cost
Garden seeds, tools	Mother	10 hr	$10 yr
Tennis racquets	Mother, son	Summer, 4 hr	Initial cost
Bicycle	Mother, daughter, son	M., 3 hr; D., 1 hr; S., 6 hr	Initial cost
Toys and child's equipment	Son	Often	?

Activities not revealed by the inventory include family vacations, family attendance at movies, and talking. The father's family had fled from anti-Jewish Hungary and settled in Vienna. The mother came from a Roman Catholic home but converted to Judaism upon marriage. The daughter comments as follows on the general leisure pattern of the family:

> The fact that my parents were raised in a European country has had a great effect on how they spend their leisure time. Americans place great emphasis on sports, football and baseball (to watch) and golf and fishing. My parents were never raised with this kind of sports enthusiasm and have never learned to like them. Their educational and occupational milieu has also had an effect on their leisure activities. As an accountant and highly cultured man, my father gets little intellectual satisfaction from his job, and therefore turns to his leisure time for intellectual stimulation and relief of tension from his working day.
>
> The same is true for my mother regarding her job as a housewife. When I am home we all like to spend time together doing things as a group. . . . Lack of relatives and few close friends because of displacement from a social circle in Vienna, and having to start all over as refugees during the depression, has made our lives (especially those of my parents) very centered on our close family unit. Also, having to start afresh here . . . has left little time till lately for developing social contacts. My father (and the rest of the family at certain times) has joined various religious organizations without too much success because our interests and personalities differ widely from those of the average club joiner.

It is interesting to note, first, the range of the activities that serve to bind this family together—activities used by individuals as well as by the group. Compare this list with that given earlier for a newly married student couple. Further, a pattern of family independence of outsiders was established in the 1930's and still remains. Because of the absence of relatives there might have been a greater interaction with friends. Yet the judgment of others in respect to their personal and intellectual qualifications seems to prevail even in the choice of religious circles. This suggests that the family feels it does not need religion, as such, but only within a favorable social climate.

The foregoing cases, although selected at random, illustrate several points. A study of family leisure can profit from the inventory, using the kind of insight that the archeologist applies to objects as cultural manifestations. As long as we are in the favorable position of being able to talk to the owners and users of these objects, we can add considerable in depth to understanding. Indeed, by starting with a list of leisure equipment for one family, we could provide a beginning in which the full analysis of each object—how it was selected, by whom, why, how it is used, etc.—could easily lead to a large book on the whole subject of leisure in American life.

Objects, things, equipment, and gadgets are, of course, vital to some leisure activity: photography, some games, reading, and so on. The *building* of things, such as furniture, is the use of leisure to create new objects, which may be functional in the home, or, like the building of a boat, tools for further leisure activity. Yet, like objects used in religious practices, *anything* can become useful for purposes of leisure, so that to identify some objects more directly than others with leisure is not to minimize or preclude the consideration of other objects. Is a stove such an object when it is employed in the "fun" of making cookies? Can clear lines be drawn between reading materials that are used for education, stimulation, self-improvement, or recreation?

Use of leisure equipment

It is further obvious that the type and degree of use made of such inventories is an important aspect of leisure study. Conceivable sources of friction, as well as harmonizing factors, must be noted. In the families described, the closeness observed was due to different reasons. When there are children in the family, as in the second case, the effect of such items as tennis racquets, musical instruments, kilns, and bicycles can be to involve parents as participants (even as pals in the equalitarian family), as observers, as listeners, as policemen, judges, public relations agents, critics, teachers, students, and so on. The *fact* that mother and son play tennis together may be a major source of irritation to him, and it is therefore the *process*, the *setting*, the *spirit*, the *manner*, the *reasons*, and *effects*—however these are measured or observed—that must become the nature of the issue. In such an approach, the equipment of leisure leads into issues of its place in the family life; and this, in turn, explains the presence or absence of certain types of leisure equipment.

Some illustration of the possibility of such family study of usage is to be found in a national study of musical instruments made for the American Music Conference by A. S. Bennett Associates in 1948.[19] The study covered 12,815 persons in 4537 families living in 74 cities, towns, and rural areas. These are some results pertinent to the present chapter:

About 30 per cent of the families have one or more members who now play a musical instrument. ("Now play" was defined arbitrarily as playing at least six times during the year.) Twenty-five per cent have one or more former players. No one has ever played an instrument in 45 per cent of the families.

The proportion of present players goes up with size of family; it is higher among native white families than among the foreign born or nonwhites. Proportionately more musical participation is found among executive, professional, and white-collar occupational groups than among wage earners. In cities with over a half million population 24 per cent of families have "musical members"; in rural families, 32.3 per cent.

One of every four persons in the rural areas (of all ages and groups) now plays or has played an instrument, according to the sample of this study. Analysis of age groups indicates that as age levels are younger more musical participation is found; that is, 22.7 per cent boys, aged 10–14 compared to 7.6 per cent men in their forties.

The piano is by far the most popular instrument. More guitar players than violinists were found in the survey. Where guitars are more likely to be found among wage earners and farm families, white-collar families are inclined toward the piano and bowed stringed instruments.

In the survey from which these summaries are drawn this question was raised: what relationship exists between radio listening and record playing and the active participation of the family in instrumental music? The general conclusion to which the findings draw the researchers is that "the more radios a family owns, the more hours they listen to the radio; the more records they own, the more likely they are to own and play musical instruments!" [20] This correlation is especially high among persons owning the largest record libraries.

This type of survey is valuable because it does more than ask how many prefer this or that. The Bennett study relates its figures on ownership and use of instruments to age, sex, occupation, geographical region, income, and other factors. A notable finding is the high proportion of *players* whose *listening* is high. This raises havoc with a pet comment of many who fear the mass media and who apparently view time in a mechanistic sense: more time for X activity leaves less for Y and Z. Yet time, as we note in a later chapter, is a flexible and malleable organization of activity in culture; it is not a bottle that is emptied or filled with frozen items.

A second approach to family expenditures on leisure is to look at the *indirect inventory:* things that are related to leisure life as clues to activity or as accessories. Clothes, food, and the house itself will provide examples.

General consumption as clue to leisure trends

Food preparation in the home has been affected by the development of frozen foods. The first phase of this process was the bulk purchase of foods, such as meats, for keeping in rented lockers or in home freezing units. Recently a large variety of products has been marketed in grocery stores, supermarkets, and delicatessens. With this has come the development of more convenient carriers to keep and transport food for outings and family trips. Even if there were some doubt that all this actually takes less time for the wife in preparing her meals, it has released adolescent daughters from this part of home duty. The total time gained for the family is probably considerable over the past generation.

Clothing habits have also accented leisurely living. Factory clothing replaced home sewing by the 1940's. One result was standardization in dress, commercially inspired fashion changes, and a wider range in the kinds of clothing owned by individuals. Although men's clothes had been more conservative, a shortage of suits after the war led to a trend toward sports shirts of increasingly bright colors. The three main stylistic tendencies, according to David L. Cohn, were [21]

> . . . first, a steady trend toward uniformity, with the clothing worn by people of moderate income coming to approximate the appearance and materials of the clothing worn by people of high income; second, a decline in the number of frills, reflecting a movement in the direction of greater simplicity; third, and most recent, an "accent on youth."

This tendency toward casual dress was encouraged by television and has spread even into offices, especially in large centers such as New York City. The fact that the middle-class purchaser led his wealthier neighbor, as in the case of men's sport shirts, provides an interesting clue to the relation of leisure symbols to social class (with dress as one of the most important).

Housing provides a dramatic index of new family patterns. The move to suburbs and the planning of the modern home itself are serving to break down the distinction between inside and outside. This trend is helped along by automatic heating devices, by excellent lighting, and by the design of rooms and window spaces. Urban decentralization rested in the first place upon the ownership of the car to take the husband to his work and the wife to her shopping. Now, however, both work and shopping centers are rapidly moving out to the suburbs. Consider several pertinent observations by George Nelson, an architect.[22] Noting the trend toward 20 or so electric motors that now run home units for heating, cooking, air cooling, dishwashing, refrigeration, washing, and so on, Nelson says, "This trend is so pronounced that you do not have to be a science-fiction fan to envisage a house that takes pretty complete care of its occupants with no effort on their part beyond servicing the machinery involved." With filter systems, houses can be designed to require virtually no cleaning. Bedmaking could be eliminated by getting rid of bedclothes through electrically warmed pads and radiant-heated ceilings. The home would in time reflect the leisure-time interests of its members. Take golf as an example. Writes Nelson,

> Golf is more than a game, it is a way of life. It involves joining a club of some sort. Clubs multiply social contacts. Social contacts, when expanded, can translate themselves into an interesting variety of things. New dresses for parties (new hanging rods for the new dresses, new closets for the new hanging rods). New clothes and shoes for the golfer. More cocktail and highball glasses. An ice bucket. (A better refrigerator?) New porch furniture for father's new friends. . . . Are you acquainted with the man who was given a power drill for Christmas and is now equipping a complete workshop?

Commenting further on the need to accommodate the ever wider range of free-time activities—without causing conflicts between those in the family who read, watch TV, and collect records—Nelson observes how

> . . . the living room becomes a multipurpose room, bedrooms double as sitting rooms, playrooms and so on, a new type of room (the family or activities room) emerges, and, as the physical shelter becomes inadequate for the demands made on it, living tends to spill into the outdoors.

The contemporary house itself is a clear clue to the functioning of leisure as a basic aspect of family life. We turn, however, to direct expenditures for leisure activity by the family.

Family expenditures

The chief source for statistical data in this section is Volume IX of the 18-volume *Study of Consumer Expenditures*. This large study by the Wharton School of Finance on materials collected by the U.S. Bureau of Labor Statistics is "the most comprehensive information in consumers' economic behavior available and virtually the only detailed information on the pattern of consumers' expenditures in the United States in the period after World War II." The number of families and individual consumers who reported their detailed incomes and expenditures for 1950 came to 12,489. They came from 91 cities ranging in size from 2000 population to New York City:

> 13 urban areas with over 1,000,000 population
> 42 urban areas with 240,000 to 1,000,000
> 216 urban areas with 35,500 to 240,000
> 2527 urban areas with populations under 30,500

Three broad regions were studied (North, South, West) and, under each, three types of cities (large, suburban, small). It is to be noted that

"North" includes communities generally known as the East: New York City, Hartford, Connecticut, and others.

Volume IX, *Expenditures for Recreation, Reading and Education— 1950*, comes to 500 pages of statistical tables. No interpretations are provided. Thus an adequate summary is impossible here. We interpret one of the 15 tables as an example of the data.[23] First, an explanation of the headings that remain uniform for each table. At the top is given

Number of families
Family characteristics
   Average
      Money income after taxes
      Family size
   Per cent
      Nonwhite
      Home owners
Average family expenditures
   Recreation
      Total recreation
      Purchase of radio, TV, and musical instruments
      Admissions
      Other recreational expenses
   Newspapers, magazines, and books
   Education

The 15 tables of data report these expenditures as they are sorted out for all families combined, all families of two or more persons, annual net money income class, family size, race, sex of family head, age of family head, education of family head, occupation of family head, number of earners in family, tenure, residence in city, family living arrangements, family type by family size and income class, and race by family size and income class.

The items under each of the table headings are defined as follows:

Purchases of radio, TV, and musical instruments includes phonographs and recording equipment, musical cases, racks, repairs, and parts.

Admissions includes movies, plays, concerts, sports, and other spectator events.

Other recreation expenses include toys, sporting goods and athletic clothing, phonograph records and sheet music, cameras, films, and photographic supplies and equipment, purchase of pets and pet food, licenses and supplies, collection and craft hobbies, dues to social and recreation clubs, and other recreational expenses.

The analyses that follow do not include expenditures for reading and education, since these items are tabulated separately in the Wharton study; nor is it feasible to consider the spending under "other recreational expenses," since far too wide a range of items is included for any meaningful interpretations.

Regional and community-type differences for recreational expenditures are indicated in Table 1 of the Wharton study. From it the following comparison is extracted:

TABLE 12

Recreational Expenditures by Regions and Community Types

Place	Number Families	Net Income	Recreation Expenditures	Percentage of Income
North				
Large cities	3853	$3958	$179	0.045
Suburbs	1242	4690	208	0.044
Small cities	629	3666	148	0.040
South				
Large cities	1923	3514	145	0.041
Suburbs	503	4124	186	0.040
Small cities	443	3071	93	0.030
West				
Large cities	2192	3887	172	0.044
Suburbs	638	4066	194	0.045
Small cities	1066	3895	150	0.038

According to this table, the average expenditure for recreation among the large sample studied is 4 cents per dollar. This is quite close to the figure of 4.3 cents for 1950 arrived at in another major source, the Twentieth Century Fund survey. Projected upon a national consumers' expenditure of about 215 billion dollars for 1950, the 4 per cent comes to well under 10 billion dollars and is a very conservative figure next to the estimates given by various authorities and used in Chapter 1. The differences, of course, come in large measure from the items listed as recreation.

The question arises, how does recreation expenditure compare for richer and poorer families? Before examining the Wharton figures, we shall look at prevailing thinking along these lines. For this purpose, we refer again to the important Twentieth Century Fund's study, *America's Needs and Resources* (1955).

According to this source, "It is common knowledge, of course, that when a family moves from a lower to a higher income level it will spend less of the increase on necessities with which it was already well supplied, and more on luxuries that it could not previously afford." [24] One approach to determining this process has been to study the degree to which specific items are affected in sales as the income varies. Three *income-elasticity groups* of items were studied by the Department of Commerce in the period 1929–1940: the *insensitive*, the *somewhat sensitive*, and the *sensitive*. The first group took about a third of the total consumption expenditure in 1952; the second, about one half; the sensitive items took one sixth of the total of 218 billion dollars.

Insensitive items are the most stable or essential, varying the least with income: housing, fuel, house utilities, drugs, hospital care, education, tobacco, religion, legal services, and beauty parlors. The somewhat sensitive items are food, liquor, clothing, personal care, and so on. Sensitive items are home appliances, cars, jewelry, and recreation.

Within recreation, some items are more variable than others. Items that are the most stable are motion pictures, college and professional football, horse and dog racetracks, magazines and newspapers, sheet music, and fees to organizations. Some of the recreation items, which change somewhat with income, are photography, fees to social clubs, golf, and commercial amusements. Highly sensitive items are radio and phonograph purchases, instruments, toys and sports equipment, flowers, books and maps, gambling in coin machines, and pari-mutuel betting.

As evidence, in part, of rising levels of expenditure for recreation in the period 1909–1950, we have already seen the comparative increase for recreational items as a whole in Table 2 (see page 7).

Returning now to the Wharton study, data on recreational expenditures by net family income are given in percentage form in Table 12 (see page 78). Contrary to accepted conclusions, the table indicates that *as family income goes up the proportion of recreational spending does not go up*. Where many families spend only 2 cents per dollar on recreation, as in the small cities of the South, recreational expenditure is low for *all* income groups; even families with incomes averaging about 11,500 dollars spend only 2 cents on the dollar. And the largest single expenditure for recreation, 9 cents of the dollar, is found among the poorest families in suburbs of the West. Further, expenditures for TV, radio, and musical instruments, among the largest items within recreational spending, are also highly sensitive, so that all the more we might have expected a considerable variation between the poor and the rich families.

A second interesting fact in the Wharton study is that, with the exception of small cities in the South, there is a remarkable uniformity in recreational spending within all sections and sizes with incomes of 3000 dollars or more. This is not to compare the *style* of life between income groups. But looking ahead to a later analysis of social class, it does indicate, within the facts given here, that family spending on leisure is no longer a criterion of class division. For example, if all the percentages in Table 12 are averaged for incomes of 1000–5000, 5000–10,000, and over 10,000 dollars (for an arbitrary division into lower, middle, and upper classes), they are, respectively, 3.8 cents, 5.0 cents, and 3.6 cents. According to this, the *middle class* spends a fourth *more* than the *upper class* for recreation.

Yet these figures must be tempered with other observations. For instance, a family with a relatively high income is more likely to have in or around the house such facilities for leisure-time life as recreation rooms, garden, tools, and games. Further, it is unrealistic to accept the report of amounts spent on recreation unless to them are added the sums spent for travel and vacations. In a Curtis Company study noted in Chapter 16 it is reported that, for the year ending March 1953, 8.5 *billion* dollars were spent for vacation travel or again as much as the Wharton study reports for all other recreation combined. The annual expenditure for travel reported for families with incomes of 5000–6000 dollars was 256 dollars and for families with 10,000 dollars, over 600 dollars. If these are added, we get

Income: $5000–6000
Recreation: $343 (Wharton, average for all sections)
          256 (Curtis study)
          ─────
          $599 for recreation, including travel
Income: $10,000 and over
          $565 (Wharton, average for all sections)
          724 (Curtis study: an average figure derived from $627 for the $10,000–15,000 group and from $821 for the $15,000–25,000 group)
          ─────
          $1289 for recreation, including travel

It is therefore suggested, in summary, that these totals are more nearly what is actually spent for recreation per year by families in these income groups.

These pages have barely tapped the materials in the Wharton School study. Only one of 15 tables has been used and this only in part. The interpretations of the materials, as we have seen, must never be limited to statistical techniques alone. If we would understand people, it is to the people we must go; the quantitative data opens up questions, they challenge old conceptions, they may confirm impressions, but always they remain a *means* of analysis and a tool of thought.

This chapter has ranged far into family life, relating the family's leisure aspects to work, community, family "cycle," play attitudes, leisure equipment, house architecture, clothes and food, and, finally, expenditures in money. Close to family study is that of social class, for families are indeed more than units unto themselves: they reflect and influence who does what with whom *outside* the family circle. "Who does what with whom" in a total community suggests some such analytic tool as social "class."

Leisure and social class 6

Historically, no one factor has been so closely related to leisure as social class. To see why this is so, we need first to examine the concept of class. Of the direct relations of class to leisure, Thorstein Veblen's *Theory of the Leisure Class* is the most famous and important and is therefore summarized. Finally, a contemporary summary is presented.

The concept of social class

About the only general agreement among American sociologists on the concept or the analysis of social classes is that there is no agreement. In a summary of the matter one writer comments: [1]

> All concur that the concept of class deals with the horizontal stratification of a population, but whether it is based on economic power, occupation, status feelings, cultural differences, or their combination, and to what extent separate group life is indicated by the term, are questions on which there is no substantial agreement. Class is being used increasingly as a research tool but too often in a grab-bag fashion: the researcher knows that there is something in the bag, and when he pulls it out he then labels it, with some correctness but little precision, as class.

There is no need here to review the various "labels" that have been extracted from the "bag" by Warner and his associates and by Davis, Hollingshead, Chapin, Guttman, and Lynd.[2] Criticisms and criticisms of criticisms seem to have found their places in the professional sociological journals and monographs: illustrations will be found in recent writings of Gordon, Hatt, Gross, Cox, Page, and Pfautz and Duncan.[3] Pfautz and Duncan, in their blunt evaluation of the most famous of the class typologies, that of the Warner group, note [4]

(1) that the type of study which Warner and his associates have developed is to a considerable degree not relevant to their announced objective of portraying the stratification structure of American society; (2) that technical deficiencies in the execution of their studies considerably weaken the support claimed for their findings; and (3) that their conceptual formulations are inadequate to account even for their own findings, are theoretically uniformed in relation to existing literature on social stratification, and further, are ideologically suspect.

The essential problems encountered in this important area of research are so great that dissention is understandable. They are first of a theoretical nature, then quantitative. It is basic to any scientific analysis that the elements of a system be abstracted from the whole, studied, and then put back into their proper relationship to other elements. It is evident that an infinite number of possible groupings could be drawn from what is called society but that when we concern ourselves with a *ranking* or a *consensus* a lesser number remains. It is, for example, possible to see the elements of a whole society in terms of men and women, age divisions, years of schooling, income, and so on. Depending on the special problem with which the inquirer is concerned, he can draw arbitrary "classes" to his own liking and fill his notebook with elaborate countings. However, that conception and use of class, although peculiarly apt in the natural sciences, is fallacious in the social sciences because we are dealing not with the groupings arranged by the scientist but as they are arranged by the people who are being studied. We want to know how *they* rank themselves and to what degree *they* attain consensus. As MacIver and Page state,[5] "Whatever objective criterion we use, we do not have a *social* class until class consciousness is present." Similarly, when social scientists refer to *status*, they speak not of individuals but of a person in relation to other persons, that is, relations in respect to a common ranking and a consensus.

The main theoretical problems that arise in determining social class are not far to see: how do we know that the ranking given to a group or to a person is real to *them* rather than just to the observer? Further, can we be sure that there *is* agreement or common feeling on important matters among the "we-group" or the specified class? Quantitative difficulties enter the picture as efforts are made to measure distinctions on one or a combination of criteria and then to place real people on the ranges or scales that are created. The immense number of problems incidental to exactitude in measuring and to conceptual clarity within a given situation may be grasped from this comprehensive definition that E. T. Hiller has given to social class: [6]

Briefly stated, a social class is any comparatively permanent division in society which is differentiated by relatively persistent dissimilarities in rank and separated from other strata by social distance. When a class system is well established, it has the following characteristics: an assumption of superiority and the appropriation of certain rights by a portion of the population; the acceptance of inferiority by another portion; standards of conduct recognizing the place or status of each class, and rationalizations to explain and justify the existing arrangements.

The question whether the familiar classification of upper, middle, and lower classes and the double subdivision within each does not in fact yield groupings "which are too heterogeneous to be at all significant" has been raised by Wilbert E. Moore.[7] If wealth, for example, is used as a criterion, any number of arbitrary divisions is available; if a college degree is used, several possibilities exist. We may turn next to a brief consideration of the one aspect of social class about which there has probably been the most agreement among sociologists, namely, occupation as an index of status.

As Moore points out, occupation is especially useful because it combines many of the important criteria of class membership, such as economic income and worth, achievement levels, social affiliations, and intermarriage. Speaking as a research worker, Professor Moore is frank in noting also that occupational distribution and mobility are more available and utilizable than other types of class information.[8] On the other hand, when we get behind the data in order to see interrelationships of occupational to nonoccupational behavior or, as one sociologist phrases it, between "occupational specialization and social differentiation,"[9] relatively little has been done. Indeed, claims Carlo L. Lastrucci, of all the interactive relationships between individuals and their culture, "probably the most important is that of occupational adjustments and the influence of that adjustment upon one's total way of life. It is this field that remains practically a closed book to the social scientist."

General conceptions have always existed among men of various occupations. Thus, our society has stereotypes of the minister, the politician, the teacher, the burlesque girl; ancient Rome had mental pictures of the soldier, the prostitute, the slave; medieval Europe had its farmer and its tradesman. An illustration of personality profile, as related to occupation, may be seen in this statement from David Hume: [10]

A *soldier* and a *priest* are different characters, in all nations, and all ages; and this difference is founded on circumstances, whose operation is eternal and unalterable. The uncertainty of their life makes soldiers lavish and generous, as well as brave: Their idleness, together with the large societies, which they form in camps or garrisons, inclines them to pleasure and gallantry: By their frequent change of company, they acquire good breeding and an openness of behavior: Being employed only against a

public and open enemy, they become candid, honest, and undesigning:
And as they use more the labour of the body than that of the mind, they
are commonly thoughtless and ignorant. It is a trite, but not altogether a
false maxim, that *priests of all religions are the same;* and though the
character of the profession will not, in every instance, prevail over the
personal character, yet it is sure always to predominate with the greater
number.

Although it is true that the "eternal and unalterable" circumstances
have been somewhat shaken by the fact that huge armies taken from
civilian reservoirs may have here and there affected Hume's soldier, the
general outline remains fairly reasonable. Truer yet, for our purpose,
is the fact that some picture is held by all societies of their occupational
types and that these pictures at the same time *place* each type within
its social circle in a position of relative desirability. The resulting prestige is related in good part to the importance of the value represented
by the occupation, such as health or education, and also by the totality
of feelings and attitudes toward the kind of life lived by those who
engage in the activity.

The difficulties described above should make us aware of too glib
use of the term "class" in reference to leisure in this country. Yet the
discussion need not deter us from several basic observations.

Societies, even democratic ones, do stratify themselves on any number of items. Of these, the most important in our country are occupation and wealth, which often, but not always, go together. These strata
of American society—the "country club set," the "upper-lower," "my
kind," or however they are referred to—attain reality outside statistical tables only when such people *act basically alike, think alike, are
treated alike by others, and are fundamentally motivated by similar
values.* Joseph A. Kahl makes a contribution to the subject in his excellent summary of five "ideal types" of class, associating each with its
most important value emphasis: [11]

Upper class: graceful living
Upper middle class: career
Lower middle class: respectability
Working class: get by
Lower class: apathy

These represent respective attitudes toward life. Kahl cautions his
readers against taking these types too literally. However, most families
have incomes that permit a style of life and a network of associations
that bring them prestige, and they have a class identification and a set
of values that harmoniously integrate their social lives—they know who
they are and their neighbors know who they are, and they have beliefs
that are appropriate to their position.

Yet in addition to these general criteria, the term "class" in European and oriental life has contained an additional element of great importance to the issue of leisure: the upper class was free of productive work *and spent its time in leisure activities.* There was no compulsion toward work, as often found in American families of wealth. They were not expected to work, as opposed to the traditional American suspicion of the idler. There were, throughout Europe, elaborate resort centers in which the rich gathered; the American resort is an imitation by comparison. And the European rich had a "place" that the poor respected and, revolutions to the contrary, one that was part of a system the poor accepted as natural.

In America the problem of the rich group, socially, is always that it must remain open to new devices to identify itself, hence there is no time for an aristocracy to develop a conservative tradition.[12] In no way is the contrast more apparent than in a primary issue of the rich businessman here, namely, *how to learn to play when he retires.* This business class has not learned the first lesson of the aristocratic life, that learning how to *work* should be a problem! When leisure activity becomes a full-time preoccupation among *men,* then we have the European concept of a leisure class. This was perhaps Veblen's greatest difficulty: that his great book was written in America and that by the time his perception was recognized by a large segment of the informed reading public even the limited class divisions here had already begun to appear fuzzier with each passing decade.

Thorstein Veblen: theory of the leisure class

Whereas Marx had argued that each social class develops its own way of life(its own culture and morality),[13] Veblen sought to demonstrate that the lower classes emulate the higher.[14] Of what, then, does the upper class consist? To be one of the upper class means more than the possession of wealth or power; these must be made visibly evident for all. What results is a high self-evaluation based on esteem from others.

In our discussion of personality [15] the elements of social role were indicated. The circle, according to Veblen, is clear-cut, for the wealthy associate with each other, living a life in which leisure becomes purposeful activity; their purpose: to give to other circles of men a public accounting of their time. Their function: to become expert precisely in those skills and arts that go beyond spare time, that go on during the working day of the working class, and that require dress or other equipment beyond the spending power of the workers. Their status, and consequently their conception of themselves as persons, comes from the ease with which they undertake such (productively useless) activities. Part of that ease is wrapped up in the manners that characterize the rich in social intercourse. All together, "these are the voucher of a life of leisure." [16]

The publicly noted waste of time, then, is the principle on which good breeding is evidenced. The visible male servant—the larger and more powerful the better—is one such tangible evidence: servants to do physical work and to exhibit an obvious example of luxury spending.

Yet not all of one's time can be spent in playing polo, riding to hounds, or being driven through Central Park. The year is long and the lower class is not always there to see. Some accounting must be given of private time by the rich. *Immaterial goods* and *quasi-scholarly* or *quasi-artistic* activity form such public evidences of continual and substantively useless activity. Others are the study of dead languages, cultivation of the arts, games, sports, and "fancy-bred animals," or activity in charity organizations, drives, and clubs.

If all this is *conspicuous leisure*, then *conspicuous consumption* is another side of the picture. Time is spent on productively useless activity and money on a superabundance of things.

The guiding motive behind all this is self-satisfaction and position through esteem accorded by the have-nots. But is this all a mythology, a fantasy created by those in power? Clearly, it is a motif deep in the life of all, says Veblen, for the poor themselves seek to emulate the rich. Here, perhaps, is the core of Veblen's sharp irony, for, unlike Marx, he offers no solution.

Veblen made the public aware of waste, as Riesman notes.[17] Veblen's contribution to institutional economics was to outline the latent functions of the system. In relation to leisure, a parallel can be seen between Riesman and Veblen. Both (more explicit in the case of Riesman) are telling us something about groupism, about conformity. To Veblen, one *class* seeks to emulate the other and is sensitive to judgments by the other. To Riesman, one *person* seeks to be like the others and tunes in his "radar antennas" to the judgments and behavior of others. In the largest sense, both authors speak out for freedom of person and group, that they may be true to themselves. In contemporary America it is indeed a paradox that on the one hand the individual tends to conform to what *others* do, thus surrendering some freedom, and on the other hand, judging by the possession of things as well as control over leisure time (which can, indeed, be uselessly spent), *all* classes are now potentially free.

Contemporary leisure and social class: servants and gadgets

A comparison of *servants* and *gadgets* provides our first insight into the issue of this section. Two parallels are immediately obvious. First, both are methods of doing work for us. Second, both provide symbols of status.

Servants are alive, and both as persons and as workers they can be classified as males, females, weaker, stronger, younger, older, attached to the head of the house, attached to the wife or children, door openers, butlers, valets, and so on. Yet with all these differences the servant has been the key symbol and appendage of class division. The number of servants, the housing facilities available to servants, their skill, and their length of service—these and other marks of respectability are familiar in history and literature.

This had to be in the days when work was fundamentally muscular for both animals and men. Servants, unlike field or factory workers, were domestics, hence thoroughly familiar with the manners and habits of the rich. Being people, not machines, they reacted as a trained class (Veblen called them a subleisure class) with traditions of faithfulness, protection of the master from gossip, participation in house or court intrigues, disdain for other types of workers, and physical fighting when necessary. Thus, in a crisis such as a revolution, the servant was counted as part of royalty or upper classdom and charged with responsibility, with treachery, or with acts of accomplice, as the occasion warranted.

Gadgets, operated by the pressing of a button or the turning of a switch, range from the air conditioner to the ironer, from the clothes washer to the deep freezer, and from the radio to the food mixer, and are divided into two major types: (*a*) mechanical aids that turn the typical home into a consuming factory, supplying the family, it is estimated, with services equivalent to those of 90 slaves per day; (*b*) machines, such as radio, television, and phonograph, that relieve no one of work but take up the attention of persons who have been freed (by the other gadgets) to watch, listen, and enjoy. Thus mechanical aids provide a *form* of contemporary family life, reducing motion, sweat, discomfort, and effort; the mass media provide a *content* of contemporary family life, whose intent lies in the realm of ideas, symbols, images, and patterns of life in small glimpses.

As the servant is the key symbol of class division, the mass media are instruments of *classlessness*. Their success depends on large audiences, on standardized rather than specialized programming, and on the creation of stars who are known to all. The movie, now made available in the living room through TV, has always been one of America's notable counterrevolutionary agents and provides a powerfully direct glimpse into the lives and fortunes and homes of the wealthy and the glamorous. This medium provides topics of conversation and chit-chat that cut across all levels and backgrounds. If a series of topics were to be drawn up, ranging from politics to foreign aid, to philosophical issues, to books, to the field of entertainment, there would simply be no question of the area in which there is the largest body of common interest, agreement, and close acquaintance.

It is safe to assume that the breakdown of classes in the United States led to the purchase of many gadgets for removing work and producing contentment; it is just as safe and as important to recognize that once the process began the cycle was under way and that the gadgets hurried the breakdown of classes.

Gadgets, art, industrialization, and classlessness

Mass media came at the same time and obviously from many of the same social and economic causes, such as the growth of widespread participation in the arts that is due in large part to the American public schools. The arts, about which there will be more to say in a later chapter, have also contributed to the fading of sharp class lines. In a previous writing, we have had this to say: [18]

> In this multi-group society, each of us has views, tastes, and leisure-time activities which are only loosely connected with so-called upper, middle, or low class. In the class societies about which Bernard Shaw and Karl Marx wrote, art was one of those interests which used to peg people. Today, this is not true. Today, as poetry, painting, theatre and music have become widely practiced and understood, their value as distinctive symbols of respectability has faded. The factory clerk might not afford an original Rouault, but he has a copy. The banker might still buy his books in buckram bindings, but anyone can provide himself with paper-covered literary masterpieces at 35¢ each. The Higginson children in Boston may have had box seats at the concerts which Papa subsidized so lavishly, but the kids all over now go to concerts, hear records, or make their own music.

The interesting point facing us therefore is that the current vitality in the arts comes in large part from either the influence of the mass media directly or from those same social causes that produced these media as well as other aspects of technology. With this the case, the issue of creative, constructive, or aesthetic leisure has become one of noting how these "good" types of leisure activity have come about *because* and not *in spite of* increased industrialization and gadgeteering.

Further, the thought that gadgets, both work-saving and contentment-producing, break through class divisions is now reinforced by a democratized art in this significant development.

Veblen's major thesis falls on the simple fact that this country has grown so wealthy, and that the wealth is less marked in the accumulation of money with which to buy things than in the accumulation of things that conceal monetary inequality. This means that the department store, another highly important contributor to classlessness, sells goods that are designed to minimize the differential of rich and less rich: fashion designs, for instance, have achieved a point of quality that a woman of considerable means will not apologize for purchasing a ten-dollar dress. The goods in that store can be bought on the installment plan, another highly important classless device. This provides everyone with the opportunity of buying against his own tomorrow, and, as often as not, not the tomorrow as it will be but as it *should be* or as it is *hoped that it will be*. The worst that can happen is that the goods will be repossessed, and this is not a great shame. There is then no need for the lower classes to sit in envious meditation of what the rich possess and to cherish the possibility of someday imitating them. This is entirely unrealistic and unnecessary when an escalator will take anyone in a few moments from the "bargain basement" up to lingerie or furniture on the fifth floor in the *visible* melting pot of classes, the amazing department store. Thus Riesman speaks of the new revolution as the consumers' revolution and uses as his illustration that other purchasing paradise, the supermarket.

As American sociology attempts to define and conceptualize the American class structure, it finds itself in a quandary because it is often prone to follow European models of division based on income or possessions of money, land, animals, or servants. Yet, class, or (more accurately) group level, in our own country is distinguishable in *how* these groups spend, with whom they enjoy their possessions, including time, what they like to do when they are not at work, and what they are willing to do without in order to reach certain goals. Not income, but *style of life*, is the basis for a realistic understanding, and this matter of style is based in part upon choice, in part upon "obligations recognized, and the conditions for making the choices or recognizing that the obligations exist in the individual's subculture." [19] There is something significant in the fact that about half of the 300 million dollars spent in 1959 for motorboats was spent by persons in skilled and semi-skilled working groups.

Some studies and final observations

Several studies illustrate this point. Alfred C. Clarke took a category of five occupational prestige groups and related them to such items as who engages in spectator activity and who in commercial activity.[20] Only 25 per cent of the top level (professional persons) as well as level V (service, semiskilled, and unskilled workers) engage mostly in watching similarly, a minority of each is involved in commercial recreation.

Clyde White studied 1740 boys and girls from the ages of 6 to 18 in Ohio.[21] Dividing them into four categories (upper-middle, lower-middle, upper-lower, and lower-lower), he found that UMC boys use the phonograph, radio, TV, books, and movies more than other boys in proportion to their available time, whereas children of the ULC have three hours more per day to do with as they wish and therefore engage in the activities listed more hours per week.

The study by Leonard Reissman measured two aspects of leisure activity in relation to class.[22] Having first divided a number of families in Evanston, Illinois, into three groups characterized by differences in occupation, income, and education, he found that no matter which class variable was applied these differences in choice of leisure activity could be seen: more time was spent on radio and TV by the lower classes. Whichever of the three variables was applied, the others read more books, attended church more often, and held membership and attended more organizations. "In general, the picture that emerges is a consistent one of greater potential community control and dominance and of greater possible awareness and appreciation of community affairs by individuals of the higher class." Reissman also asked a number of questions designed to reveal the degree to which these persons would "sacrifice their personal views" in order to move up the social ladder, such as giving up leisure time, leaving the family for some time, working harder, and keeping quiet about political and religious views. He found that the lower-class person was more willing to surrender on these grounds in order to advance.

As the subject of leisure in America becomes increasingly important to American sociology, as certainly it must, it will be unfortunate if the dynamic nature of this fertile field for study leads only to the same suppositions and methods dominated by "the clatter of IBM machines." In that event, as indicated by Karl Mannheim, from the ideal "of narrow exactitude nothing will remain except statistical data, tests, surveys, etc., and in the end every significant formulation of a problem will be excluded. Instead of attempting to discover what is most significant with the highest degree of precision possible under the existing circumstances, one tends to be content to attribute importance to what is measurable merely because it happens to be measurable." [23]

The general conclusion of this chapter is that in no area of American life more than in its leisure activity is the outdated concept of class made apparent. The chapter began with a discussion not so much to confound the reader as to indicate how the class concept has already confounded American sociology. In relation to the present subject, then, there is justifiable need and opportunity to experiment with other types of social factors and groupings. The one we shall explore is that of the subcultural group.

Leisure and subcultures 7

Chapter 6 indicated that leisure, as a symbol of position in society, has been a significant aspect of social class. To deny that this is still true in part, even in the United States, would be to shut our eyes.

Yet, in a very real sense, the days are past when the life of a family in its vacations or in other free time is a close reflection of the kind of work done or of other *class* criteria. Travel, use of the mass media, the arts, education, and other forms of leisure have been brought within the psychological and economic reach of almost everyone by installment buying and a general rise in material comfort.

The tables on expenditures (Chapter 5) indicate a deep-seated mental change in types of consumer purchases; the relatively poor family spends about the same as the rich for recreation. Rather than forcing these changes of attitudes and subtle behavior into a scheme of analysis that arose out of other societies, we can do better by finding other classifications. More pertinent to current American life than a quantified approach to social class—whose dynamic is imitation and avoidance—is an inquiry into *styles of life* whose characteristics meander in and out of the stream of income differences, education, family origins, sex, and color. One such category is *subculture*.

A subculture is a somewhat homogeneous or identifiable group within a larger and more comprehensive culture. Such groups may be large or small. They may be bound by ties of religion, ethnic origin, historical accident, significant location, or occupation. To be a Roman Catholic, Seventh Day Adventist, "bobby soxer," Negro, Jew, Southerner, New Englander, Bostonian, or New Yorker means that in these identities one may have motives of attitude and behavior that cut across traditional indices of class.

For example, the division of faculty and town may be a very real one in the mind-life of the college community. The intellectuals within this town-gown structure are generally less rooted in the region. They are cosmopolitan in outlook, critical of material values, and subdivided into specialties and social strata that lack intercommunication. Yet these campus and noncampus groups do not imitate or envy each other; they may shun one another; they exist side by side, dependent on one another and independent as well.

Subculture can be distinguished from *minority group* or nationality. Minority refers to social power. In terms of number, the minority may be an actual majority.[1] With its limited power, the minority is kept out of favored positions or denied access to facilities or opportunities taken as a matter of course by the majority. This minority may possess very little cohesion within itself. In subcultures a "we" feeling is more than a reaction to treatment and results from self-recognized elements of identity.

Similarly, the term "nationality" has lost considerable validity as a classification in the United States. It has referred to a state of "belonging to or being connected with a nation or state as by nativity or allegiance."[2] Yet today we are a third-generation country in the perspective of 1880–1914, when the bulk of immigrants came. Thus most of the "second generation" was born in that period; by 1930 they numbered over 26 millions. By 1950 only *seven* of every 100 residents of this country had been born abroad, and only 15 of every 100 were children of immigrants. Most Americans today do not know what to answer when they are asked their nationality.

The importance of the third generation to our subject is that assimilation on one cultural front or another was taking place just at the historical time when work was declining as a focus of life, when leisure thinking was becoming significant. Had the waves of immigration come at another time, the children and grandchildren would have simply taken their place in the class structure. But as class lines were crumbling, the new generations took on new ways or introduced more. In the case of such groups as third-generation Jews, Italians, and Germans, the leisure pattern provided symbols of escape from the family. In the case of the Negro (second generation of free man), the need for commercial entertainment created an opening for him as musician and comedian. In the first case, especially the Jew, leisure helped to provide a bridge from the subculture to the larger society. With the Negro, whose hope of escape from his group was impossible, leisure activity brought him closer to his group by creating symbols of belonging.

We consider first the Negro in a very brief discussion, then follow with a more detailed inquiry into Jewish subculture.

Negro expenditures and patterns of leisure

In considering the leisure of a subculture, the basic questions are two: what is the evidence that its leisure patterns are sufficiently distinctive to be recognized as one pattern, and how are these differences from other groups explainable in terms of its "inner life?" We turn again to the Wharton study for light on the first issue.[3] Basic information on income, family size, and education of the head of the family is seen in this adaptation of Wharton Table 5, pages 30–32:

TABLE 13

Recreational Expenditures by Negroes—Family Size and Education of Family Head *

Place	Number Families	Income	Family Size	Education of Head
Large cities, N				
White	3417	$4080	3.0	10 years
Negro	424	2992	3.0	9
Suburbs, N				
White	1207	4740	3.2	11
Negro	35	2970	3.2	9
Small cities, N				
White	625	3675	3.1	10
Negro	3	2944	2.3	8
Large cities, S				
White	1384	$3994	3.0	11
Negro	539	2970	3.2	8
Suburbs, S				
White	442	4354	3.2	11
Negro	61	2456	3.8	8
Small cities, S				
White	326	3516	3.2	10
Negro	117	1831	3.6	8
Large cities, W				
White	2081	$3920	2.8	11
Negro	81	3337	2.9	10
Suburbs, W				
White	624	4086	3.1	11
Negro	9	3594	3.2	10
Small cities, W				
White	1030	3943	3.0	11
Negro	25	2440	2.9	8

* Based on *Wharton Consumer Study*, 1955, Vol. IX, Table 5.

In each case the white family head has had one or two more years of education. Family sizes for the two groups are much the same, with a slightly larger Negro family in the South. It is in family income that the wide difference is seen. In each of the areas, for every 100-dollar income in the white family, the Negro family has

large cities, N $74 ⎫
suburbs, N   63 ⎬ or average income $75
small cities, N   90 ⎭

large cities, S   58 ⎫
suburbs, S   57 ⎬ or average income $55
small cities, S   52 ⎭

large cities, W   86 ⎫
suburbs, W   90 ⎬ or average income $82
small cities, W   70 ⎭

Yet, with these differences in income, the white group has 87 mouths to feed compared to every 100 Negroes. How, then, are their recreational expenditures affected? The following data provide a basis for interpretation:

TABLE 14

White and Negro Family Expenditures for Total Recreation, TV, Instruments, and Admissions *

Negro	(a) In-come	(b) Total Recreation	(c) Percent-age of Income	(d) TV, Instru-ments	(e) Percent-age of Recreation	(f) Admis-sions	(g) Percent-age of Recreation
Large cities, N	$2992	$129	0.043	$61	0.47	$37	0.28
Suburbs, N	2970	120	0.040	66	0.55	35	0.28
Small cities, N	2944	37	0.012	—	—	25	0.70
Large cities, S	2280	65	0.028	22	0.33	21	0.32
Suburbs, S	2456	61	0.024	20	0.32	16	0.26
Small cities, S	1831	43	0.023	12	0.28	19	0.67
Large cities, W	3337	137	0.041	29	0.21	48	0.35
Suburbs, W	3594	126	0.044	35	0.32	33	0.30
Small cities, W	2440	109	0.044	35	0.32	33	0.30
White							
Large cities, N	$4080	$186	0.045	$79	0.42	$43	0.23
Suburbs, N	4740	210	0.044	84	0.40	42	0.20
Small cities, N	3675	149	0.044	41	0.27	42	0.28

Negro	(a) In-come	(b) Total Recre-ation	(c) Percent-age of Income	(d) TV, Instru-ments	(e) Percent-age of Recre-ation	(f) Admis-sions	(g) Percent-age of Recre-ation
Large cities, S	3994	176	0.044	69	0.39	42	0.24
Suburbs, S	4354	203	0.050	80	0.39	38	0.13
Small cities, S	3516	111	0.031	21	0.19	43	0.38
Large cities, W	3920	174	0.044	56	0.32	41	0.27
Suburbs, W	4086	195	0.047	67	0.34	43	0.22
Small cities, W	3943	151	0.030	24	0.15	46	0.30

* Based on *Wharton Consumer Study*, 1955, Vol. IX, Table 5.

Column (b) indicates, in actual dollars, how much these families spend for recreation (as defined in the Wharton study). Since this figure means little without reference to total family income, column (c) puts this expenditure for recreation into percentage figures. Reading downwards, the Negro family in large cities of the North spends a little more than 4 cents of every dollar for recreation, the Negro family in the northern suburb, 4 cents, in small cities, 1.2 cents, and so on.

As far as the Negro is concerned, it appears clear that as his total income goes down he not only spends less in dollars for recreation but even the proportion that he spends on recreation per dollar of income is less. Perhaps the most surprising number here is his small recreational expenditure in small cities of the North. We can ignore this difference on discovering that only three Negro families were studied for such communities, compared to 625 white families. It is clear also that the Negro family in the North and West has a pattern of spending that is substantially different from that of the white family.

Of the total dollars spent for recreation, how much of each is spent for radio, TV, and musical instruments? Column (e) indicates (reading downwards) that the Negro family in the large northern city spends 47 cents of each recreational dollar for these items, 55 cents in the northern suburb, and so on. The difficulty for an adequate interpretation of this item is that such purchases can scarcely be written off against expenditures of the particular year being studied. If a TV set were purchased in 1950, in most cases it was on payments extending into part of 1951. Even if paid for within the year, such an item is not a typical expenditure for every year. Qualitatively, the difference between listening and watching to a mass-media gadget and making music is of the greatest importance for an understanding of family life.

Since the white family spends about 32 cents per dollar of recreational money for TV, radio, and musical instruments, compared to 37 cents for the Negro, the share that goes into musical instruments alone would be revealing.

Chart 4 visualizes these comparative expenditures. Of 11 types of communities or regions seen there, the Negro expenditure for TV, etc., is higher in seven, especially in the suburbs of the North and the West. The regional average, to the right side of the chart, indicates that he averages slightly over half his recreational spending for instruments or TV and radio. White and Negro spend about the same proportion in the South, and the Negro again spends slightly more in the West. White families, it can be noted, uniformly spend less for these items in small cities.

Chart 5 visualizes the relative expenditures for admissions. Of twelve types of communities and regions shown, the Negro exceeds the white family in each case except in suburbs and small cities of the West, where he spends about the same. This raises several interesting questions. It is recognized that the problem of discrimination is less in the West, an area to which the Negro has only recently begun to move in some number. Other minorities, such as Indians, Mexicans, and Orientals, have been the objects of segregation here in one form or another. The critical place for such behavior patterns is in small towns, and it is here that the "admissions" picture is so dramatically different. In the South the Negro has a clearer, more distinct community life of his own. Leisure patterns are a part of this life. Going to "live" performances in his social and church groups is part of the pattern of mingling, visiting, and being out of the house. The Northern Negro community may have retained some of these elements.

The West is new to the Negro. The generation of Negroes it attracts may have already experienced more of the majority ways around it. This may account for the data seen in the chart. Closer research needs to be done; statistical data on family expenditures must be related to case studies and to more qualitative types of research suggested in Chapter 5. For example, further explanation of these leisure patterns might explore relationships of Negro life here and in Africa. It is to be noted that the Civil War occurred less than four generations ago; African influences might be clearly evident in areas of play. However, specialists disagree on the issue of African-American continuity. A few scattered observations on his life will suggest connections between socioeconomic factors to leisure.

The Negro in the South is generally barred from public play facilities. He has inadequate private facilities. He lives, often, in relatively

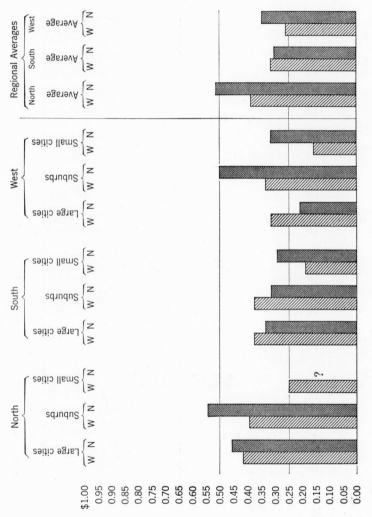

CHART 4. Expenditure per Recreational Dollar for TV, Radio, and Musical Instruments: White and Negro Families

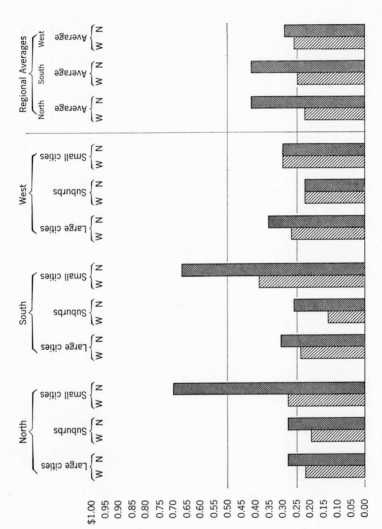

CHART 5. Expenditures per Recreational Dollar for Admissions: White and Negro Families

isolated rural communities. Life in the Southern rural or semirural area is largely uneventful. Frank Tannenbaum found, in 1924 (when going to dances was more popular than now), that 90 per cent of the population had not been to a dance in the previous year.[4] In one county only one family had gone to a movie in a neighboring town. Between cotton-picking seasons, reported Charles Johnson, a common answer to what children do was, "We don't do nothing, mostly just sit and talk." [5] There is some fishing, hunting, and use of commercial amusements among adults. A favorite pastime is going to town to shop, meet acquaintances, sit in the railroad station, or walk. The church is the center of social activity.

Urban activities center on the street corner, poolroom, and barber shop; in recent years there has been more use of playgrounds and settlement houses, social clubs, athletic organizations, and lodges. Clubs often meet in private homes, and their content includes discussions, dances, style shows, music, and dramatic productions.

There is much gambling on the job, often in moments between duties in the case of waiters, porters, and bellhops. There is little vacationing because of poverty, travel difficulties, and treatment during the trip or at its destination. Pseudo-vacations are found by Negroes who work in resort areas such as Miami and Atlantic City.

In summary, Gunnar Myrdal says: [6]

> One of the most wholesome aspects of Negro recreation and amusement is that it is not a separate part of their lives, but is well integrated into the daily routine. Part of this seems to be that Negroes, having little time free from hard work, devised relaxing accompaniment to their work. Singing, for example, accompanies all work, even on the chain gang; gambling while working is another example. Part of it is that so many of the recreational forms were denied them that they learned to enjoy the everyday things they did. Whatever the cause, this integration of fun and work has undoubtedly made life possible for many Negroes under the difficult situations they face.

We turn now to the Jew as a subculture. Comparisons with the Negro await the close of the chapter.

The Judaic ethic: flesh and spirit

We discuss, first, some philosophy of the Judaic way of life; second, the application of these elements in the life of the Middle Ages; third, Jewish assimilation patterns in the United States; finally, the Jew's current position as an accepted member or leader in leisure trends.

Ahad Ha-'Am begins his essay *Flesh and Spirit* with a discussion of true asceticism—the tendency "to turn from the pleasures of the world with hatred and contempt, as something evil and degraded, to be avoided by him who cares for his soul's health." [7] There are material reasons for avoiding levity and play, such as health and conserving energy. In true asceticism there is no further end in view, "there is no higher victory for man than the killing of the flesh, the extinction of its desires, and the refusal of its pleasures."

Examples of this attitude are found in India and in European Christian culture from the fourth century on. A historical principle was involved in this approach to life: all of history is testament to the selfish desires of man and nations. The end of life must be placed in a world beyond nature; emphasis must be shifted from the body to the soul.

> This flesh, condemned to suffer and finally to rot, is but a temporary external garment of the real, eternal Ego, that spiritual essence which lives independently of the body, and does not die with the body; this spiritual self alone is the real man, with a future and a lofty purpose in a world where all is good.

The natural consequence of this thought, says the essayist, is that having assigned to his body a transitory, inferior position man then begins to see his body as his *enemy* in the way of the "true life."

Two extreme theories then arose from troubled times. On the one hand, make the flesh supreme, live while you may, and indulge in momentary pleasures. On the other, free the spirit from its natural foe and live only for the next world.

Judaism went to neither extreme. It is in this fact that we find the source of its attitude toward the good life, hence its unique relevance to a discussion of contemporary leisure.

Man is indivisible, according to Judaism. His full existence is in this world. Instead of the dualism, body and soul, there is man in his group and community. Inner union exists between the physical and the spiritual, not inner tension. The spiritual purifies the material, but it is not degraded in doing so. Rather the spiritual "uplifts the flesh, which is irradiated by the spirit's sanctity; and their joint life, each linked with and completing the other, brings man to his true goal."

Judaism wavered from this philosophy in the Middle Ages, when the Cabbalists converted many to asceticism after the expulsion from Spain. Yet the view of the Prophets—synthesis of flesh and spirit—persisted; it found its way even in the interpretation of the corporate community as a natural union of state (material) and Judaism (spiritual). In sum, the Judaic philosophy is not a doctrine of original sin or of a human nature that is depraved and needs to be suppressed. As a contemporary scholar notes, "The carnal is something to be surpassed rather than annihilated. . . . The enemy is not in the flesh; it is in the heart, in the ego." [8]

This creed of living does not lie buried deep; it is alive in the Talmud, which has directed Jewish life among the believers for the last two thousand years. Indeed, that life cannot be distinguished from the Talmudic commentaries written by many scholars in the period 500–200 B.C. In these writings the Rabbis assume that God wants his creatures to be happy. It is sinful to shun good things and joyful ways: "There is no sadness in the presence of the Holy One, blessed be He . . . Strength and gladness are in his place" (Chron. xvi.27); "Where there is no meal, there is no Torah" (Aboth. 111,21); "Worse is poverty in a man's house than fifty plagues" (B. B. 116a).[9]

On the other hand, accumulations of riches or objects for themselves is also to be avoided. Temperance in drink provides one example: "One cup of wine is good for a woman, two are degrading, three make her act like an immoral woman, and four cause her to lose all self-respect and sense of shame" (Kith. 65a).

Applications in daily life

This philosophy of the whole life proved of practical value in the unique conditions of life imposed upon the Jew throughout many centuries. The Middle Ages provides clear examples.

It was a life set apart from the Christian majority, a life of the Ghetto or enforced Jewish community life within a larger community. Legal, social, and religious controls in the Ghetto were clearly defined, uniquely Jewish, generally conservative. It was an earth-bound life, not too concerned with a Hereafter. The individual-community relationship in ethics rather than the person-soul dichotomy of the non-Jewish world was felt on every hand. Historians of the idea of "progress" often date that concept from the 17th century; Jewry had emphasized the future long before, a "future good" connected with a coming Messiah.

"Life was consequently cherished as a supreme value in itself." [10] Helping others, Gentiles as well as Jews, became a cardinal virtue. The Jewish community, counterpart of the Christian Heaven, was sternly controlled by law as interpreted by Halakah, or Jewish self-government. Social welfare activities were prominent, a strong family

life persisted, prestige was ascribed to the aged, and education prescribed for the young.

Israel Abrahams documents the life of play that grew naturally out
of the Jewish position on the oneness of flesh and spirit. As he notes,
"The stern, restraining hand of religion only occasionally checked
the mirth and light-heartedness with which the Jew yielded himself
to all the various pleasures of which his life was capable." [11]

The Sabbath itself was a happy day, with much walking about; it
was even a day for weddings and feasts. Singing and dancing were
encouraged, and many indoor games were played. This day was "strict
but not sombre; it was Judaic and not Puritanical. . . ." [12]

Counterbalancing this lightness were religious prohibitions, especially against gambling and free relationships between male and female.
"Men and women shall neither rejoice nor mourn together," wrote
the Rabbis. Wives could dance with their husbands, brothers with
their sisters, father and daughter, mother and son—but that was all.
Violations occurred, of course, even in community dance halls on
the Sabbath.

Gambling continued through the Medieval period in spite of constant exhortations. Song and poetry inveighed the demoralization of
card playing when money was involved, whether the player won or
lost. For in gambling, wrote Maimonides, "the player always loses.
Though he may win money, he weaves a spider's web round himself." In one of the most famous of Medieval documents on the pros
and cons of gambling, Leon of Modena wrote that gambling trespasses
each of the Ten Commandments. . . . "Consider and answer now,
whether the evil of this wicked pastime is not monstrous enough to
reach unto Heaven. . . ." In the same document, this writer predates
much of our own personality studies in his refutation, as he suggests
a concept of "integrated personality": "To sum up the matter: a perfectly righteous person will be as upright in commercial pursuits as
in sport or anything else; whilst a wicked person will act wickedly
in one matter as in the other." [13]

Until the sixteenth century, Jewish educational supremacy was
indisputable. At a time when only the upper classes and clergy could
read, nearly all Jews were reading books, and many were writing
them. When the Christian and Moslem worlds were ignorant of each
other, with the Moslem the more advanced, the Jew served perhaps
his most important function in the Middle Ages as intermediary between these cultures. Many Jews had traveled or were in close contact with travelers; further, they were at home in the mind-life of
the East.

This sophistication and intelligence was reflected in the nature of some games found in Jewish life. Arithmetical tricks were based on numerical values ascribed to Hebrew letters. Word games were common: in one the contestants chose the letter Samech or Pe; a page of the Pentateuch was opened at random and the winner determined by the number of times the one letter or the other appeared. In the "Rabbi game" boys satired their teachers and included laughter at sacred objects. Riddles were common. Says Abraham: [14]

> In their origin, riddles were an attempt of early races to solve the mysteries of life; they were pieces of primitive science dependent on the discovery of somewhat remote analogies. . . . In the Talmud and Rabbinical literature, a large number of famous sayings are put in the form of riddles. Who is mighty? Who is a fool? Who is happy? . . . It goes without saying, therefore, that many Hebrew riddles of the Middle Ages were serious intellectual exercises. Riddles were the most characteristic of Jewish table-amusements in the Middle Ages.

Other aspects of leisure activities can be briefly summarized. Chess was well established among Jews by the twelfth century, first among the women. Dice was played, although frowned upon by the leaders. Cards were taken up in the early fifteenth century, behind the rest of Europe, but this became the most popular of leisure pursuits. Hunting was always strongly condemned; cruelty to animals as well as an aversion to carrying arms were major reasons. Foot racing was common.

Thus, altogether, we find in the record a people whose leisure activities were an integral part of life, reflecting both its religious and community prescription. A wide range of physical and mental activity was enjoyed. Festivals and holy days were often happy occasions. A sense of drama and satire was there. High literacy, rich home life, a love for abstraction, strong educational traditions, considerable free time—these served the Jew as he applied the theological ethic that synthesized the "flesh and the spirit."

Finally, a separate point must be made of the time and care given to community service. This grew out of the basic view that "poverty had rights as well as disabilities, and the first of those rights demanded that the poor need not appeal for sympathy by exhibiting their sorrows." [15] Individual begging and public giving were therefore discouraged; [16] the highest form of charity was that which helped reestablish the receiver's economic base. Widows were pensioned by the community; orphans were given dowries. Special organizations arose to systematize aid-giving to poor residents and travelers. Congregations would appoint a committee of charity overseers, whose function it was to raise funds by regular assessments in accord with ability, and donors included every man, woman, and child. In the sixteenth century this businesslike procedure entailed even a public financial accounting. Meanwhile, private charity continued.

It is apparent that a considerable time went into communal activities, if the summary were extended to include the self-government that had to be established in the Ghetto to facilitate life for its residents and to maintain orderly relationships with the surrounding community and law. The expertness and ethical views that characterized such community institutions were passed down into the new societies in which the Jew found himself in later generations. The United States was the most important of these new homes.

Some historical and contemporary developments

Accustomed to cities, Jews for the most part became urban dwellers in the United States. They went into small business, needle trades, and middleman services and often lived in voluntary population pockets or "Ghettoes" among their own. Most of the two million Jews who migrated here after 1900 came from Russia and Poland. They were conscious of themselves as laborers as well as Jews. Having seen the fruits of Czarism, they were thoroughly idealistic, democratic, liberty-loving, and militant. This group was more secular in many cases than the medieval Jews pictured above, a secularism not unrelated to their Socialist orientation.

The leisure patterns of these people were distinctly purposeful and based on a two-fold objective to become successful in the new country and to further their ideology as workers. Classes on Americanization were popular. Social visiting often ended up in political discussion. Clubs and informal groups carried on long evenings of drama, poetry, literary essays, concerts, debates, and folk dances. Zionism—the movement for a homeland in Palestine—was a constant theme for debate and action. The Yiddish press was strong; in the newspaper, *The Daily Forward*, this subculture had one of the finest journals on the American scene.

The occupational shifts among Jews during the last half century indicates their rising economic importance and tells much about the present generation. The 1900 Census showed the following distribution of occupations among those who had migrated from Russia (virtually all Jews); it covered 140,000 persons in seven large cities: [17]

TABLE 15

Occupational Distribution among Immigrants from Russia—U. S.
Census of 1900

	Percentage of Total (M and F)
Manufacturing and construction	60.6
Trade	19.9
Domestic and personal service	7.9
Clerical	6.7
Professions	2.6
Transportation, communication	1.6
Agriculture	0.4
Public service	0.3

Although this group comprised less than 4 per cent of the total persons employed in those cities, they made up 27 per cent of all the shirt, collar, and cuff makers, 29 per cent of the tailors and seamstresses, and almost 35 per cent of the cap and hat workers. A very small number was in the professions. Some saved enough to open small stores and businesses. An expanding economy for everyone, combined with the traditional Judaic stress on education and the group's ambition to better itself led to dramatic changes in this picture of occupational structure. Only one example is needed to suffice: by 1937, 64 per cent of all dentists and 56 per cent of all physicians were Jewish. . . .

Interpretations: current leisure patterns of Jew and Negro

1. Note first some major differences between the Jewish and Negro groups. For the American Negro there is a sharp break in his history, and an aversion against repairing that break. He is not interested, for the most part, or even aware of the riches in the Negro life of the Yorubans, Dahomeyans, or other areas from which his forefathers came. His total effort in the United States is to be accepted like others and to accept majority values. The distinctive Negro patterns that exist in arts or in communal life are reflections of status and social circumstances; they are not based on a positive, accepted ethos. Beginning his life in America the Negro was an illiterate. Conditions of slavery and its attendant economy produced broken families or weak familial ties. Religious continuities with African tradition were inconsistent with the life of America's South. The Negro's leisure time,

in short, is tied up with life *as it took shape in a new culture, its great climax coming with the end of slavery.*

The Jewish immigrant came here voluntarily, even though the element of "push" was prominent in Europe, often with exaggerated notions about "streets paved with gold." Once here, he was a free man, anxious to adjust, politically and legally able to make his own way. Yet he had had a long and proud tradition and history upon which to draw in a practical way. Minority status at its worst was slavery. The Jewish community found itself quite at home; it prospered, became *other-directed*, and conformed eagerly to dominant patterns.

2. Both the Negro and the Jew, especially the ambitious peripheral or marginal members of each group, found careers in new economic niches that had been undiscovered or undeveloped by the white Gentile. Jews became the pioneers of motion pictures. Both minorities rose to leadership in the entertainment business, for among other reasons, "good" families in well-established segments frowned upon such careers for their children. In the field of jazz the Negro and Jew found a common ground, for the jazz band is the most democratic and colorblind of all musical groupings.

3. Weak family controls, among other factors, led to considerable drinking by the Negro. Strong family controls plus religious connotations attached to liquor resulted in light social drinking among Jews; heavy drinking of the kind that leads to serious illness is extremely low.[18]

4. Such factors as race relationships, the normal isolation of rural living, poverty, religion, lack of education, and love of display—enter directly into the leisure life of the Negro. Such behavior serves to identify its members symbolically with the group, thus becoming a source of group solidarity. On the other hand, the life of the entertainer tends to remove the individual from his own group. The minstrel show, once popular among whites and acted out by Negroes, has become recognized for what it obviously always has been—a caricature of the simple, uneducated Negro—and is now discouraged or banned in many white circles. Similarly, the Jew is often very conscious of himself when, as an entertainer, he tells "Jewish" stories. In both cases, then, the hesitation in making fun of one's own group results from a maturity: there is no further economic need to engage in such self-destruction for the edification of outsiders. And both Negro and Jew have found more universal themes for their humor. Leisure then, for both minorities, will be a clue to their respective degree of acceptance on the American scene.

5. An appraisal of the trends in leisure patterns of the Negro and

the Jew are closely related to their relative socioeconomic positions, but, in the case of the Jew, to his inner ethic as well.

The Negro can be expected to migrate in increasing numbers from the South and more than before into the West and the Southwest. His full energy is going into the struggle for civil and economic rights and the sheer burden of getting out of the educational and social shackles that have been his lot. Assuming that in the next half century he continues his upward climb in these respects, the Negro may turn more consciously to his African past in order to develop a characteristic art and ethic. Or, being drawn further into the stream of mass culture in his effort to adjust, the Negro of tomorrow may continue to deny that there is any difference between him and others and, indeed, become an over-conformist. The pluralists of our society who hope to see each subculture retain a balance of uniqueness and integration will find disillusionment in this prospect. For, certainly, if the Negro is to interpret his life in his literature, art, and thought, its positive themes must go beyond the motif of social protest.[19] Increasingly industrialized, both in the South and elsewhere, the Negro will find himself with a higher material base, more time away from work, more mental life, and a wider state for social action. Negro leaders will continue to ponder over their assumptions for the good life of their group after the struggle for life itself has been largely won.

Issues other than these face the Jew. His economic, social, and educational struggle is almost won. As much, if not more so than others who are successful in business, the Jew has substituted business and industrial values for the spirit of his theology and ethics. In the metropolitan area he has adopted *in toto* the style of upper middle-class life, including the country club. On the college campus his fraternity is like everyone else's, perhaps "more so."

Those elements of his free-time life, which might go on the left side of the flesh-and-spirit formula, are in abundance: good food, homes, cars, furnishings, social life, gambling, resort vacations. Those elements that once made him unique and found reflection in his leisure pursuits during past centuries are on the decline: study, intellectual games or activities, contact with nature, civic and social welfare participation (he still gives generously), acquaintance with foreign cultures.

The close student of American Jewry, Professor Oscar Handlin, sees no better prospects for the future. Writing on "What Will U. S. Jewry Be Like in 2000?"[20] he notes that with other Americans they will live in the ring of remote suburbs in vast megalopolitan areas. In one generation Jews have become professional people and eagerly adjust to their new status. In this respect "the suburb permits them . . . to make a fresh social start." The large city, presently being deserted by the Jews, at least offered "relative anonymity and consequent freedom . . . a variety of choices." Group activity and identity among the Jews—among all groups—had meaning precisely because they were the product of free choice. Conformity, says Handlin, is the characteristic of the suburb. Here all variety and diversity is engulfed: "He can visit his neighbors or be visited by them, drop in on a meeting at the Center, go to a local movie, watch television, or read the latest *Life* or Book-of-the-Month selection." Two features of Jewish life will be lost:

> The long tradition of intellectuality that gave a peculiar dignity to learning will not be readily accommodated in the suburb. The intrinsic idea and the freely speculative mind are disruptive to the stability and order of a community that cherishes the familiar. An environment that stresses conformity . . . is not likely to produce men who believe in the importance of questioning the common assumptions and tastes.

The revival of Jewish values, now evident superficially in the revival of religious interest, may prove to be more genuine than its present critics suppose. Professor Handlin, for instance, may be underestimating the potential dynamic for diversity in the new suburb, just as he seems to underestimate the degree of conformity, homogeneity, and social pressure in the urban center.[21]

It may be said, speaking entirely outside a theological ideology, that many persons in the United States are seeking in their leisure time a synthesis of material and nonmaterial, of means and ends, of "flesh and spirit." It would be unfortunate if the balances found for many centuries by the Jewish community were to be lost just at a time when the country as a whole is searching for this synthesis.

6. Finally, the relation of minority status to leisure patterns may be summarized in this manner:

a. Leisure is often used as a device for social mobility. One method is for contact with majority persons in *their* leisure (as by becoming an entertainer).

b. The minority, illustrated by the Jews, may employ play-forms as symbols of integration. This may be overdone; it may lead to undue oversensitivity to the opinions of others and thus to a self-censorship or withdrawal. Witness the sizable number of second- and third-generation Jews who play golf, a game totally strange to all their grandfathers and to most of their fathers.

c. The mass media, especially movie and television, cater to ideas and images of the national total culture; they provide a damaging counteraction to families of minorities that attempt to maintain some ethnic or subculture integrity.

Subculture and leisure

This chapter has examined only two groups in a nation of multi-groups. No doubt there are significant differences even within these groups. For instance, Franklin Frazier devotes a whole volume to the middle-class Negro.[22] As a method of study, the analysis of these groups as vertical wholes can yield insights by providing historical focus. Other groups need to be examined: the teen-ager, the older person, the young business executive, the working woman, the sub-urban population. In each case we may find something characteristic of these groups for an understanding of the group as a whole and its connection with other groups.

Subculture, whatever its content, is understood only in relation to the full culture or *total culture.* Here arises an interesting problem in semantics. In general history and in the layman's vocabulary culture usually refers to the amenities, the good things of life, the arts. Thus a man is cultured, as distinct from the man who is unlettered, unedu-cated, or ignorant. From this use comes the distinction between the two terms, "elite culture" and "mass culture." The first is the posses-sion of the finer things of life by a small privileged group, distinct from a democratization of the good things.

In strictly sociological terms, *all* groups are part of a culture, but within a social structure there are persons who are given access to greater or to lesser benefits and opportunities. Subculture, in this sense, has no reference to the use groups make of art, travel, or education. It refers to a kind of integration, to a possibility of a somewhat com-plete existence, to the presence of an *enclosed system* of values. In the foregoing discussion, for instance, it should be clear that in sci-entific language both the Negro and the Jew are part of a culture. In lay terms, the first is less cultured for the most part than the sec-ond. It is perhaps unfortunate that writers in the social sciences have begun to use the term "mass culture," for they are confusing the lay and the scientific concepts. If we need a referent for the totality made up by the sum of all the subcultures in a society, we can easily talk of larger culture, total culture, or simply *culture.*

A complete picture of leisure in our society can begin only with analysis of segments. The larger problem is to examine the total cul-ture in which many types of groups, institutions, individuals, and ac-tivities are going on at once. The community is one such major setting. We turn to it now.

Leisure and community 8

On July 11, 1957, many thousands of people attended major-league baseball games in Chicago, Kansas City, Detroit, Cleveland, Brooklyn, New York, Philadelphia, and Pittsburgh. On the same day some women went to a rummage sale at the Church of Good Prophesy in Peoria, Illinois. At 2 P.M. the St. Louis zoo held its monkey show. At 1 P.M. there was a meeting of the New Orleans Women's Auxiliary, Volunteers of America. That day thousands of streams, rivers, bays, inlets, lakes, and both ocean shores were visited by fishermen of both sexes. In San Francisco some people must have spent several hours watching the harbor sights and the Golden Gate Bridge. Across the continent, over 18,000 persons listened to Billy Graham at Madison Square Garden. Meanwhile, some readers of the *Dallas Morning News* worked on a crossword puzzle on page 11 and, just below it, on a "Test Your Horse Sense" self-evaluation by Dr. George W. Crane. And that evening the writer of these lines was debating whether to work on this book or see an Italian film, *La Strada*, at the "cooled-by-refrigeration" Illini Theatre in Champaign.

It has been said,[1] "Every man is in certain respects

a. like all other men,
b. like some other men,
c. like no other man."

Every community, too, is in some ways like all others, in some ways like some others, and in some ways it remains unique. What its people do with their leisure is an important clue to its state of uniqueness. Almost all American communities now have television; many have harbor boats to watch; only New Orleans has a Mardi Gras. Similarly, in every community (excluding sick persons or the imprisoned) one can take a walk; in many, a baseball game can be played or watched on a week end; only Holland, Michigan, has a tulip festival.

112

Many issues arise as we consider the relationship of community and leisure. How does leisure activity contribute to the picture of a particular community held by its residents in their minds? Has the community, as a political unit, a responsibility to contribute to the leisure of its people? Can we establish a relationship between various types of communities and types of leisure? What effects have the mass media had in erasing uniqueness? What changes are taking place in population movement that are influenced by or that affect the free-time life of the people? Does one community more than another lend itself to such characteristics described in earlier chapters as the "play-oriented family" and the "gadget-class democracy"? Can a new category of communities be established on the basis of its internal leisure life?

Gemeinschaft-Gesellschaft

We can get underway by relating leisure to two terms that are important to sociological thinking: *Gemeinschaft* and *Gesellschaft*. These terms were the basis of a theory of social relationships developed by Ferdinant Tonnies (1855–1936), a founder of the German Sociological Society.[2] Tonnies used them as "ideal constructs" of traits or kinds of relationships. *Gemeinschaftiche* (the adjective) refers back to *Wesenwille*, an inner relationship between people that arises out of common adherence to certain values. Rough analogies were drawn by Tonnies between *Gemeinschaft* as organic and *Gesellschaft* as contractual relationships. The commonest translations of these terms —always admittedly inexact renderings—have been *community* and *society*. The reference is not to a specific place but to a source of solidarity and thus at best to a type of place. The broad distinction can be listed in sets of descriptive analogous terms: [3]

Gemeinschaft	Gesellschaft
Community	Society
Simple	Complex
Rural	Urban
Organic	Contractual
Homogeneous	Heterogeneous
Sacred	Secular
Wholistic	Segmented
Integrated	Unintegrated, differentiated

In other words, by *community* we mean a way of life in which people are values or ends. They know much about each other. They need each other. A solidarity is built on common interests, values, and symbols. There is cooperation between people. Creative sources come from within the group. When conflict arises between the old and the new, tradition prevails. In the complex type of life opposite conditions prevail: each for himself. Laws rather than traditions dominate as controls. Distrust is common. People are known as fragments, as customers, landlords, or clerks. People are "used." Competition is favored. Loneliness and alienation exist, even with the crowd. Mental and emotional disturbance is prevalent.

Some elements of both types of social relationships may be found in the metropolitan center, the village, or the rural area. With these distinctions in mind, however, we proceed to correlate them with elements of leisure, not as a series of hypotheses—community A will always go with leisure types A₁, A₂, etc.—but simply as a basis for more systematic thought:

GEMEINSCHAFT	GESELLSCHAFT
CHARACTERISTICS OF LEISURE	
Outdoor	*Indoor*
More use of large yards, streams; outdoor games.	More use of special buildings or rooms in the home; indoor games.
Participation	*Observation*
More self-reliance in leisure; more talk and visiting.	More reliance on entertainers; more mass media; more reading.
Noncommercial	*Commercial*
More activities in schools, homes, and community buildings.	Willingness to pay for entertainment; theaters and other establishments.
Group-centered	*Individual-centered*
Family activity; church groups; leisure close to group norms.	Tolerance of individuality; less dominance by family.
Few choices	*Many choices*
Relatively small range of interests among residents.	Larger variety of interests and types of persons.
Generalized activities	*Specialized activities*
Less opportunity to develop or use special play skills.	More specialized training and outlets.

GEMEINSCHAFT	GESELLSCHAFT

CHARACTERISTICS OF LEISURE

Utilitarian-orientation	*"Cultural" orientation*
Leisure as outgrowth of household or work skills.	Wider interest in artistic activities.
Spontaneous	*Organized*
Little need for formal organization of play-life.	Dependence on recreational specialists.
Body-centered	*Mind-centered*
Games of strength; play in setting of physical work (communal home building or harvesting).	More reading; creative activity.
Classless	*Classbound*
Activities cut across social stratification.	Leisure as symbol of status.
Conservative	*Faddish*
Slow to change play-ways.	Follows newest fads and crazes.

The foregoing correlations may be used as an ideal construct [4] against which we can examine several real communities. A series of focal points has been presented and, to the degree that the relationships exist in observable fact between types of communities and characteristics in leisure, a number of useful hypotheses will result for more empirical controlled study. Our first case is that of Cisco, in the heart of Illinois.

Cisco

Cisco: population, 334 in 1950, 23 less than in 1940. Aside from homes, the town contains a general store, two service stations, two hardware stores, an implement company, pool hall, barber shop, post office, grade school, grain elevator, restaurant, agricultural service company, and two churches (Methodist and Baptist). Many workers commute to towns that are 8 and 18 miles away. High school students go to nearby towns. Median year of completed schooling for the county: 10.6. No more than 10 native residents have had any college; those from the area who go away to college generally never return to live there. Boys who marry immediately after high school tend to remain in the area. The population is all white; one family is Roman Catholic, the others are Protestant.

The majority of older people look upon drinking and smoking as a sin, an evil, or, at least, as "cheap." Both are much worse for women than for men. Younger residents accept the same judgments, having grown up with this training. Our student-informant notes:

> The younger generation has no desire to instill drinking in their parties or bridge clubs. Although I was almost positive no drinking was done at these parties I did ask a friend. The expression on his face was one of complete amazement. . . . The "no" which then followed was inevitable.

Activities in the community that take up leisure time are concentrated on various clubs. Most are either for men or for women; few include husband and wife, and none exists for entire families. Many elderly women are prominent in church and Eastern Star activities; older men, in church and the Masons. However, much free time is spent in the home, reading, watching television, tending flowers, sewing, and playing with children.

In the middle-aged group about ten families provide the leadership in such groups as the Home Bureau, the church, PTA, Women's Club, Eastern Star, the Guild, the Auxiliary, and the 4-H. Men take part in the volunteer fire department, grain elevator meetings, the American Legion, and the Village Board. A few play in the unit school band. A group of 20 leaders attends the same social gatherings, seldom inviting others. They play bridge together.

People from the farm area nearby are easily drawn into town activities that involve their children. The band provides one such meeting place.

One set of persons—not the leaders—plays pinochle regularly. Consuming a glass of wine before play begins is one of its customs. One woman explains that this is the only drinking she and her husband do; she thought they would drink beer if it were offered. "But it is never offered!"

The student informant, a native of Cisco, made this observation on the power of gossip:

> The town is controlled by gossip. . . . In the city you can go out and get drunk and no one cares, just as you can here on campus. Everyone thinks you're really funny and as long as the crowd is being amused it doesn't matter what condition anyone is in. In a small town where everyone knows you, everyone also seems to think they have a moral obligation to help you. So what do they do? They tell everyone they see about you and what you did last night. . . ."

For commercialized leisure Cisco residents go outside the community: bowling, dancing, and theaters are available in Monticello, Decatur, or Champaign—8, 18, and 25 miles away. Tennis, softball, or basketball can be played on the Cisco schoolground.

Considerable loafing is done by the men who farm, especially in the winter months. Favorite centers are the grain elevator, a hardware store, and a gas station.

The leaders or local upper class do not bowl, play golf, or bridge with the middle class. Each class may contain both Cisco residents and farmers who live nearby. Little visiting of homes is done for the purpose of talking. Getting together means playing bridge or going out as a group to another place. Little driving is done for relaxation; generally, a purpose or destination is clear.

Interpretations

Cisco, with a population of less than 400, has in it elements of *Gemeinschaft* and *Gesellschaft*. Gossip is a strong control; conservative concepts color such actions as drinking. On the other hand, note these factors that would not have been present in this community a half century ago:

1. Residents who want to leave the community for several hours or a day have easy escape via good roads and cars to the outside world.

2. Equally important, the presence of radio and television brings the outside world into each living room in Cisco, thus relating people in this small community to currents of entertainment, information, and thought in major cities.

3. Classbound leisure groups exist; further, if the information is correct, there is little visiting between Cisco homes.

4. The kinds of leisure activities in Cisco cut across the *Gemeinschaft-Gesellschaft* dichotomy. On the one hand, we can note club and church activity, loafing among the men, and adults being drawn into activities by their children. On the other hand, there is the presence of many choices because of the availability of other communities, wide use of the mass media, and patterns of social stratification.

Just as farm families around Cisco are drawn into its social life, the same social and technological developments have affected rural life as a whole and lessened the gap between rural and urban communities. In a United Press dispatch of April 24, 1956, economists of the Department of Agriculture predicted that the old tradition of isolated, independent country life is crumbling and will be replaced by

1975 by "city life, widely spaced." Closer social as well as economic ties will have set in among the cities. For example, the predicted 30 per cent decline in farm population will mean that the remaining farm families will have more members working or living in urban areas. The Washington report notes that the living standards are already narrowing: "More and more rural residents will be going to urban schools, churches, shopping centers, and to recreation and entertainment facilities."

Additional factors affecting farm life will be the anticipated urban shortage of labor about 1975 and the increasing mechanization of the farm. In the Far West (California, Washington, Oregon) farms of 1000 acres or more are 6 per cent of the total, compared to 3 per cent for the rest of the country. Hence more tractors, trucks, and cars are found here than in other rural sections. In a review of western rural life the *Christian Science Monitor* for July 13, 1956, reinforces these observations:

> . . . "more farmers are living in cities out here, either farming part-time or letting the work to managers. The trend is making slowly and surely, but apparently inexorably, the whole and spacious Far West into a sort of supercity, where people think in terms of convenience, television, and fast traffic.

Thus the Cisco picture fits into the national trend. This community in the midst of a rich farm belt provides an example of what is happening everywhere to a greater or lesser degree—a blend of rural-urban elements or types of social relationships, a general style of living for which a new name needs to be found.

Westchester County

Lundberg, Komarovsky, and McIlnery's *Leisure, A Suburban Study*, published in 1934, remains a major contribution to the field.[5] The area studied, Westchester County, is 15 miles north of New York City; it covers 445 square miles and in the early 1930's had about 520,000 persons in and around the several suburbs. Although references may be found to various parts of the Lundberg volume in the present work, a general summary is presented here.

An introductory chapter sets broad issues and defines leisure as "the time we are free from the more obvious and formal duties which a paid job or other obligatory occupation imposes upon us." [6] Another preparatory chapter describes the community: its population, history, economic and political characteristics, and the types of suburbs in the county.

The topic is met directly in a discussion of organization of leisure as specific types of leisure activity are described—hiking clubs, radio listening, reading, sports and games, and so on.[7] The authors note a high degree of organization in an area of life "usually regarded as relatively spontaneous and free." This is interpreted as a loss or departure from "the essential nature of leisure," since participation becomes an obligation. In the case of club activities, membership becomes "instrumental to ulterior ends of various sorts"—usually social status— and participation is not even regarded as part of one's leisure life.[8]

An important empirical contribution is made to studies of leisure in a chapter devoted entirely to measuring the amounts of time given to various activities.[9] A total of 2460 diaries (mostly for a period of three days) were kept by school children, club members, employees of a large utility, housewives, and some unemployed persons. About 10,000 schedules and questionnaires, as well as about 200 formal interviews, were tabulated and interpreted. Additional observations "frankly impressionistic and anecdotal" were used. Social class differences were correlated with expenditures and types of activities. Ninety per cent of all leisure time among all classes (except students) went into eating, visiting, reading, public entertainment, sports, radio, motoring, and club activities. The more time people had, the higher the figures for visiting, reading, and clubs. Differences between social classes were more qualitative than quantitative: an example would be that the upper classes listened more to symphonic music than to jazz.

One half of all adults in Westchester had no club affiliations at the time of this study; yet in the cases of upper-class women participation in organizations was often the principal form of leisure.[10]

The suburban family was studied and its play patterns were recorded.[11] For instance, in lower-class families leisure was associated with "going somewhere" or with "spending money." As one woman said, "I do not want any more leisure because I have no money to go anywhere." Such families, if given an additional 1000 dollars per year, said they would spend it on payment of debts, furniture, and other necessities. Upper-class families had more time, educational background, and a larger range of leisure likes and habits. However, such activities as club membership, which takes on heavy obligation, was not perceived as leisure. Given an additional 1000 dollars each year, this group would use it for recreation: vacations in Florida, more dinner entertaining, more time in New York City, and so on.

The suburban Church "has perhaps more of an interest in leisure than any other suburban institution."[12] This conclusion of the investigators is confirmed by the 45 of 50 ministers who agreed that leisure tendencies have provided a new challenge to religious life. Indeed, say the authors, the alternatives are whether the Church will provide a wide program in leisure within its own doors or whether it will cooperate with other agencies of the community. To ignore the new horizon of free time is out of the question. Differences in viewpoints among Roman Catholic and Protestant clergy in another eastern community, discussed elsewhere in this volume,[13] indicate that the issue is even more challenging to the Church a quarter century after the Westchester study.

Since leisure choices, skills, and attitudes are much a matter of training, the American school has been a significant contributor to present practices. In 1934 the Lundberg group concluded that the Westchester public schools directly dominated the leisure and work of about one fifth of the population and played a highly important role in the style of life taken up by the rest of the community.[14] A trend in the schools was the range of extracurricular programs; to the former interest in games and sports had been added the fine arts and crafts. In respect to the arts, growing interest was noted for the adult community as well. The recreation commission had taken active leadership in such activities as an annual music festival.

The final subject treated empirically in the Lundberg study was the extent of reading and adult education.[15] About 500 persons were taking extension courses; another 4000 to 5000 were enrolled in evening classes at the high school.

The volume summarized is a landmark for its time. It has in it a good amount of moralizing about what the community should do; the writers did not hesitate to take stands on what is a better kind of leisure activity and what is less desirable.[16] Yet the total community was examined in reference to the one strand of leisure, vital theoretical issues were recognized, and some objective techniques were employed to dig out the facts. The two decades of sociological advancement since this volume was written are notable for research into social class structure—an area of methods in which the 1934 volume is weak. The presence of television since World War II has revolutionized the entire leisure picture in counties of New York State and elsewhere. A contemporary account would undoubtedly find travel a more important item than it was. Taking the volume for its value to an understanding of the 1930's, its chief weakness is perhaps its shortage of historical materials.

Interpretations

As in Cisco, rural and urban elements are blended in Westchester County: visiting and reading, hiking and intensive club life. Yet the differences are striking, of course. To be 15 or 20 miles from a Decatur or a Champaign, Illinois, is not the same as being that short a distance from the largest city in the country. Ideally, one author or team of authors should undertake to study several communities at once, so that generalizations could have perspective, even at the expense of empirical depth.

A wide variety of leisure choices is available in any of the Westchester suburbs. Many more specialized persons live here than in the Illinois community, and they represent a higher educational level. The "escape" into New York City is not simply for those activities that are entirely absent (there are *no* theaters or night clubs in Cisco); New York offers attractions possessed nowhere else. The kinds of occupations found in Westchester County include a variety of skills —medical, legal, scientific, marketing, and advertising—which are taken into the big city in the morning and out in the late afternoon but which affect the quality of home life before and after work hours. The commuter from Cisco is neither the "Man in the Gray Flannel Suit" nor the "Exurbanite."

These differences need not detain us. The overriding similarity is the combination of indoor and outdoor living in both communities. In their leisure, if we take the liberty of updating the Lundberg study, the two most important changes were brought about by equipment: the car and the TV set. One takes us inside, the other takes us away from home. The Ciscoans, percentagewise, are probably better traveled than New Yorkers; the TV fare is about the same for both sets of addicts. The Illinois town is about a half hour from a major state university and thus has access to nationally important athletics, art exhibits, concerts, and lectures. The same community (Champaign), like almost a thousand others in the country, has its amateur symphony, theater, painting, chorus, and contemporary dance groups. Does this mean that the new leisure implies an equalization in the style of life available to communities that are small or large, urban or rural in their economic orientation, less or more educated? Have the advantages of a New York become decentralized? As people leave the metropolitan area for the suburban, is the increased conformity, which is bothering some observers, a matter of only temporary adjustment to a less dynamic type of life and neighborhood or is it one price that comes with the adoption of a semirural life? Is the distinction between a Cisco and a Westchester County as great now at it was two decades ago?

Muncie

A most important community study in the sociological literature is the two-volume work by Robert Lynd and his assistants. *Middletown* (actually Muncie, Indiana) is a report on many aspects of the community in 1925; *Middletown in Transition*, in 1935.[17] The ten-year interval therefore provided an opportunity to observe change, in this case the impact of the depression. Each of the volumes has a chapter on leisure. Our object is to point out the major observations of both volumes, moving back and forth in time.

In the middle twenties Middletown delighted to pass the time in "talking or listening to talk." [18] There were still many speeches being made, although this characteristic of life was already noticeably declining at the turn of the century. Printed matter was taking over. By 1935 the changeover was complete. For instance, book circulation in the public library between 1925 and 1929 had gone up 15 per cent, whereas the population jumped 25 per cent; yet from 1929 to 1933 the population rose 5 per cent and the circulation of books rose 108 per cent. This increase is attributed by Lynd to time made available by the depression. "Adult reading, therefore, responded more markedly than did children's reading to depression conditions, rising more steeply and further with the onset of 'bad times' and falling off more sharply with business recovery." [19] This printed matter originated outside the community and was purchased by a relatively small number in the business class; the bulk of books read by others was borrowed from the library. But even in 1925 the content of books was discussed very little.

Musical activity in the twenties had become a prominent school subject. Forty-one of 124 working-class families indicated that one or more children had had music lessons in the preceding year. The phonograph and radio were on the way up. For adults, music was almost entirely a passive experience and, even at that, of considerably less interest to men than to women. There were no singing societies for adults in Middletown. Leaders complained of the lack of support for concerts, although they insisted that the town was "music hungry." Little spontaneous singing took place. There were few if any local painters, and home art was as standardized as the furniture. Like music, "art seems somehow to drop out of the picture between the time boys and girls sketch in their high school classes and the time they become immersed in the usual activities of Middletown's adults." [20]

Decided changes took place in the arts during that decade. In the second volume evidence is given of the changes in kinds of artistic activities as well as in sponsorship. The local college had already begun to assert its influence. A civic theater, in part the result of stimulation by the college theater, was created in 1931 for amateur performers. In 1925 there had been only a high school dramatics society. Plays were presented as part of the F.E.R.A. program during the depression. A combination of W.P.A. funds and contributions from a wealthy family built an Arts Building at the college; this encouraged the formation of painting classes among businessmen, some of whom who have held exhibitions.

Musical life developed. High school music increased in popularity, and choirs were formed. There was an F.E.R.A. orchestra and a Municipal Band. Again, sponsorship of many concerts by the college was evident, and a question was raised in the minds of the writers about locus of sponsorship:

> In the case of lectures, art, and music in Middletown, the removal to any considerable extent of the local generating center for these types of leisure from the persons of the city to an impersonal It, the college, along with the holding of these affairs out on the campus at one extreme end of the city rather than downtown in the geographical center, may involve in time a slow attenuation of interest.[21]

Cars first appeared in Middletown in 1900. By 1923 there were two for every three families. In the first volume the Lynds summarize the meaning of this:

> But as the automobile touches the rest of Middletown's living at many points, it has revolutionized its leisure; more, perhaps, than the movies or any other intrusion new to Middletown since the nineties, it is making leisure-time enjoyment a regularly expected part of every day and week rather than an occasional event.[22]

By 1933, as noted in the follow-up study, there had been no decline in use of the car. Filling stations grew from 41 to 70. During the depression it was commonly observed that the car was the last thing to be given up; relief officials made no formal effort to discourage car ownership among clients. Far more vulnerable in hard times were marriages, divorces, babies, clothing, jewelry "and most other measurable things both large and small."

The motion picture occupied about the same position in the thirties as it had in the twenties. One exhibitor felt that with less money at their command people had become more discriminating in their choice of picture.

The amount of listening to radio took a definite upturn in the ten-year period. In 1924, for example, a sample revealed one radio per eight business-class homes and one in every 16 homes of workers. Six years later, 46 per cent of all homes, or 5791 in all, had radios, and the town supported a private radio station.

Clubs persisted in their importance to businessmen. Parties continued to be important as entertainment throughout the decade in Middletown, but more informality was noted with the passing of time. The back yard was rediscovered as a place for neighborliness. Considerably more drinking was observed in the second study. Even with high sentiment against "speak-easies" in the 1930's, such places flourished. Commenting on their meaning, the study notes that a dual function was performed:

> . . . as a physical place of meeting new people, and, psychologically, as an environment conducive to spontaneous human association. The first of these is a relatively more acute need for the working class, who are more sparsely served than the business class in Middletown with institutions facilitating the meeting with and coming to know new people. It is easy for one with a business-class point of view to fail to realize the deterrents to human association, and the resulting isolation, loneliness . . . shabby household furniture, too little money, no place to go and no money to go with, newness in a neighborhood. . . . The speakeasy and tavern, like bridge playing for the business class, help to institutionalize spontaneity. Here one sees a cityful of people, with little chance in their workday lives to be directly personal in a spontaneous sense, finding out a way in their leisure to circumvent the strait jacket set for them by their culture . . . being with people in a mood where one takes people on one's own terms . . . one can sit silent, or one can talk with a degree of animation and intensity that would make one feel silly and self-conscious in the more constrained environment of one's own parlor with one's neighbors about. . . .[23]

Bridge as a highly important device for "putting in an evening" with friends increased considerably over the ten-year period. The significance of this game, with references to the Middletown findings, is discussed in Chapter 14 under games.

As in Westchester County, clubs for women of all classes existed and took considerable time. More important, they helped to define the social roles of women symbolically as those concerned with the finer things of life. "The heavy concentration of 'culture' in the refined, artistic sense in the female side of the community is the result." [24] Ten years perhaps saw a growth of this tendency in Middletown.

The foregoing review scarcely does justice to the materials in the Middletown books. Quite aside from the changes noted over the decade, and especially the impact of the depression, a major contribution of the studies was to show that leisure in the community must be seen as functionally different for the various class segments. Work to the businessmen offers positive values, "The element of exhilaration and adventure associated in our physically unprecarious culture with play activity: one's winnings depend upon one's drive, ingenuity, thrift, and skill, plus a substantial sporting element of luck."[25] Hence little ingenuity is to be found in the play-lives of these men. Women of the business set, on the other hand, with relatively little interest in home-making, throw themselves wholeheartedly into leisure activities. The worker cannot derive status and a sense of achievement from his job. You work because you must. "Someday you're going to die. Mean-while, leisure assumes a simple, direct, and important place in your scheme of things; *it's* when you *live*, and you get all of it you can—here, now, and all the time." [26]

Yet whether leisure is a means or an end, the question of its quali-tative content remains; for even activities that are pursued as means can achieve unintended importance and become transformed into ends. On this basic point, Robert Lynd concludes his survey with this ob-servation:

> But the summary balance sheet of Middletown's four years of prosperous growth and six years of depression experience suggests decidedly that the community has not discovered with the help of its "new leisure" new designs for living. In the overwhelming majority of cases, the community has simply in the fat years bought more of the same kinds of leisure, and in the lean years made what curtailments it was forced to make and just marked time pending the return of the time when it could resume doing the familiar things.[27]

Interpretations

In Chapter 5 the point was made that leisure patterns may be affected by crises and cycles in family life. Similarly, it can be said that a com-munity, regardless of size or type, also meets crises and goes through a community cycle. This is one implication of the Middletown books. The Lynd research illustrates the meaning of ex post facto research, that is, conditions not set up by the investigator but examined by him only "after the fact." [28]

It must be remembered that the Lynd studies, too, are now outdated. The second volume, published in 1937, purported to describe effects of the depression; yet there are many persons who would insist that the depression was not over until the late 1930's, when defense spending came into the picture. From our historical vantage point we can see three phases of change: (1) from the 1890's to 1925 (covered in the first volume); (2) 1925–1935, the second volume; (3) 1935 to the present, which includes World War II and the war's aftermath. These, therefore, are the questions we can ask:

1. Were the changes in Middletown from the first to the second period already under way, with or without the depression; if not, what specific changes seem more closely related to the depression than to other factors?

2. Does the first historical phase offer some clues to reasons why the depression affected this community the way it did?

In answer to the first question: the distribution of reading went up noticeably in the period 1929–1933, and this is attributed by Lynd to depression free-time; this seems to be a reasonable inference. A rise in artistic life was clearly marked, whether more from the stimulus of the college or the relief program in the arts is not clear. Subsequent developments in other communities lead us to the conclusion that it was the college program, with its high status and its more permanent leadership and curriculum. The use of cars was somewhat slowed by lack of money in the depression as it was later by gasoline rationing in the war period. Consistent growth in the use of radio was perhaps inevitable, with or without the depression, just as TV has boomed in good times. We might roughly characterize the sequence as

talking	(1890–1925)
reading	(1925–1935)
listening	(radio: 1935–1945)
watching	(1945–)

Television, like the movies, is, of course, a combination of the last two phases of the sequence, but it is the watching that provides its uniqueness and attraction. This sequence has been universal in the country, and therefore the second question asked is difficult to answer: what was there in the quality or history of Middletown's life that affected this sequence? Lynd's description of the "spirit of Middletown" is a portrayal of a generally uncreative, conformist community, in which behavior patterns and mental attitudes are closely tied in with business-class and working-class status. Indeed, as we go down the list of types of leisure activity in relation to the *Gemeinschaft-Gesellschaft* construct, much of leisure seems to exist on a dual level in which the *Gemeinschaft* (more rural, unorganized, etc.) is associated with the working class.

Another question can be explored in the Lynd study, one in which the historical materials are relatively rich: how might such a community have been expected to use or perceive the mass media? Is there anything fundamentally unique or independent about this community? If the community has been overwhelmed by the images and symbols and barkers of Madison Avenue or Hollywood, was this (*a*) because the impact was sufficient to overwhelm anything in its way—all communities everywhere—or (*b*) because there had been insufficient "inner resources" before the TV era in Middletown? To our knowledge, there has been no scientific study or statement of the problem in this form. Yet it would seem that if there had been a differential acceptance of television, causes for this could be traced.

To develop this train of thought for research, perhaps a continuum could be worked out, from extreme "local orientation" to extreme "mass orientation." The first implies a full development of indigenous resources, such as knowledge of regional folklore, self-reliance in recreation, local writers, amateur painters, and so on. The second would be comparable to Riesman's *other-directed*, the willingness (now on a collective not a personal level) to react to external forces, people, and images. If a Middletown were rated heavily on the mass oriented side (before television), then TV could be interpreted as simply a *replacement for previous kinds of noncreative activity*. Indeed, out of this might emerge the clues for a classification of cities in reference to types of relationships to the mass culture.

High Wycombe

High Wycombe, a town of over 40,000, is situated 30 miles from London and 28 from Oxford. Over 200 factories are there, most of them for the making of furniture. Of these, 24 have recreation facilities for employees, including sports grounds, fishing clubs, theaters, billiards and concerts.[29]

The Town Hall seats almost 1000 and is used for dances and meetings as well as concerts. There are many social clubs in the community; the British Legion, with 1200 members, is the largest; a Liberal Association Club numbers over 300; a Trades and Labour Club has over 250. There are special clubs for young people, as well as the Boy and Girl Scouts. A social center is open to persons over the age of 17; run cooperatively, it provides socials every month, and there are athletics, theater, and other activities.

The four theaters sponsor football teams that play other theater groups from neighboring cities; they have also introduced community singing as part of their regular cinema showings.

Many educational activities are available in High Wycombe. A Technical Institute for young people and adults offers commercial subjects, enginering courses, chair making, art, and languages; its extra-mural program includes dramatics, choral singing, folk dancing, and photography. A Workers' Educational Association, which is part of a national movement, offers lecture courses. The city also supports a Young Farmers Club, a chapter of the National Book League, and a branch of the National Council of Labour Colleges.

Its many musical groups include the Oratorio Choir of 60, a Symphony Orchestra of 40, and an Operatic and Dramatic Society. Four grounds for outdoor recreation, with facilities for football, cricket, net-ball, hockey, tennis and golf, are to be found in High Wycombe. There is also a chess club.

Betting and gambling is prevalent, as it is throughout England. There are six race tracks within 30 miles of the city and five bookmakers in the community itself.

Interpretations

Although a short report, the present summary of High Wycombe is placed here to remind us that the variety of communities is immeasurably increased as soon as we step out of our immediate culture. English life is not sufficiently different from our own to be called strange or incomprehensible. Primarily, the language is our own. Yet we note some interesting differences: a social center run on cooperative principles, an apparently wide use of clubs for leisure purposes, a high interest in sports and betting, and a rather full amateur artistic life. These suggest the futility of trying to understand a community unless one has full knowledge of the national or regional culture in which it finds itself. This must be kept in mind as we turn next to an American community, the giant of Midwestern America.

Chicago

A major community study of recreation was issued in Chicago in 1937.[30] The first volume covered public recreation, the second, commercial recreation. The research had a long history of "on again-off again" because it was originally undertaken as a work-relief project. At no time, even when funds were available during an "on again" period, could more than 10 per cent of the staff consist of professional administrators; the remainder, totaling several hundred, were persons without research training selected from relief rolls. The books issued represent the cooperation of the Sociology and Anthropology Department of Northwestern University, the Chicago Recreation Commission, the Works Progress Administration, and the National Youth Administration.

A summary of the considerable data and observation in the work would take more space than is warranted here; serious students of leisure should become acquainted with this material. Volume 1, after an introduction and history of public recreation in Chicago, deals with administrative aspects. The following facilities and programs are next examined in some detail: parks and playgrounds, public school facilities, museums, state and county forest preserves, golf and tennis facilities, swimming facilities and harbors, the public library, and miscellaneous facilities.

Volume two begins with two introductory chapters: the scope and significance of commercial recreation and the regulation of such facilities. Treated in detail are the following: motion picture theaters, the legitimate theater and concerts, billiard and bowling establishments; baseball, basketball, football, boxing, and wrestling; commercial health clubs, gymnasiums, and natatoriums; horse racing, riding, polo, and horse shows, bicycling and automobile racing, golf and tennis, ice sports and roller-skating rinks; miscellaneous activities, such as excursions and annual shows, radio, ballrooms and dancing schools, liquor establishments and cabarets, and commercialized vice; and a number of activities found in amusement parks, such as riding devices, penny arcades, games of skill, shooting galleries, circuses, and endurance contests. A hundred charts and maps contribute to the content of these important books.

Material from the introductory chapters of both volumes is briefly summarized here: the history of public recreation, to describe some of the factors that are unique in a metropolitan community such as Chicago, and the chapter in the second volume that discusses the general scope and significance of commercial recreation.

Chicago was incorporated in 1837. Its first park was established two years later, and for more than a decade parks were the only form of public recreation facility. Two museums were opened in the 1850's. Music and physical education were introduced into the public school system in the 1860's. The Public Library was built in 1872. The first public playground in the country was created by Jane Addams at Hull House in 1894; five years later the Mayor of Chicago opened a campaign that led to other playgrounds and small parks throughout the city. Forest preserve land was provided by Cook County in 1916.

Implicit within this development was the work of many citizens' groups, a recognition of the effects of crowded city living upon personal lives, and the great effort by individuals who became leaders in the community. For example, the model playground established by Hull House consisted of less than an acre of play space, a sand pile, swings, and building blocks. It was a natural part of the total philosophy of a settlement house but provided a stimulus for the movement toward playground provision under tax auspices.

It can also be expected in a large community that opposition to the expansion of functions will be organized. For instance, music became part of the Chicago school curriculum. It was attacked as a "fad and frill" and the question whether it was constitutional for a child to sing in a public school had to be fought out in the state courts. Further, since a municipal recreation program develops in fragments, a lack of coordination developed. It took almost 20 years for all the parks to be consolidated into one administrative unit. Even now, more than 20 years after the 1937 report was issued and more than a century since the public recreation development began, Chicago's municipal recreation program is administered by three agencies, the Chicago Park District, the Department of Public Works, and the Board of Education. The Board provides the facilities and programs for social centers and recreation in school areas; the others fulfill similar functions in park or playground areas under their control.

In its opening chapter the 1937 report on commercial recreation defines its scope as "more or less highly organized amusement enterprises engaged in primarily for profit making." [31] In respect to the content or form of recreation, there is a broad parallel between public and commercial recreational facilities. "The difference between the two, therefore, is not primarily in the nature of the recreation provided, but in the motive, and likewise the method of financing, management and control." [32] The estimate was made—as of 1937—that the total amount spent per year for all commercial recreation in Chicago is about 80 dollars per capita, or 250 million dollars; roughly, half the total spent for public, private, and commercial recreation combined.

The reporters were forced to qualify many of their findings in light of their difficulties in obtaining trained investigators, but they were able to come to these conclusions about the relative use and expenditures. About one third of all recreational expenditures went into motion-picture attendance; billiards and bowling, about 5 per cent; dance hall, 2 per cent. These remarks were made about the effects of the depression on nation-wide leisure patterns:

Theatres were severely hit. Even motion pictures suffered. Opera languished. Declining football revenues disappointed many colleges which had gone heavily into debt for stadia. Hotels, not by any means the least important of commercial recreation centers, were notoriously frostbitten by the drop in business temper. Many minor amusements hobbled uncertainly or became completely paralyzed during those lean years. Thousands of workers in these fields were added to the ranks of the unemployed.[33]

Chicago shared in these depression effects. Between 1920 and 1936 licenses for amusement places were cut to half.

In respect to vice, the 1937 survey concluded that conditions in Chicago were decidedly better than in "certain other large American cities." The "policy" racket placed 350,000 bets daily for about 20 million dollars a year. Relationships between gambling and other illegal activities with municipal politics was a "matter for general knowledge." Gambling devices to appeal to children were known to exist near about one third of the city's elementary schools. "As to sexual vice," the report asserted, "the situation is usually determined by local industrial conditions, the business trend, race or national composition in the population, proportion of the sexes, age divisions, local police administration and the activities of private welfare or reform agencies." [34]

An estimate of the number of prostitutes in Chicago at any one time was about 5000, and the total income of the 400 houses in which they operated came to about 10 million dollars a year. This represented a drop from about 3500 such places in 1913. In respect to this problem, the last paragraph of the Chicago survey emphasizes a view important to this chapter—the integral way in which recreation is a part of the whole community way of life and its interests:

In Chicago commercialized vice is concentrated and thrives in certain areas known to every health and social welfare worker . . . centers of taverns, dance halls, and the like. But their full significance comes to light only by the addition of other social facts from those areas, facts of congested housing, juvenile delinquency, under-employment and social insecurity. Irrational recreation, therefore, can only be attacked by an enveloping strategy of raising the whole level of community well-being. Thus we reach the significant conclusion that planning a city's recreation including such controls as may apply to commercial recreation can only be attained as it becomes an integrated part of comprehensive planning for the totality of a city's living conditions.[35]

Interpretations

The history of recreation in Chicago reveals several unique characteristics of a metropolitan center. One, its overcrowded condition produces a natural demand for public play space. This overcrowding is most marked in areas in which families are poorest, streets are busiest, and home facilities for recreation are the barest. Even so, those persons with most political influence do not live in such sections, and the interests of the heaviest taxpayer are fought for by business associations. Since the residents of overcrowded neighborhoods are neither organized nor in positions of power, volunteer groups and political leaders sometimes step in. Across the country there has been a gradual victory for zoning of land use and for park and recreation provision. Such agencies as Hull House took some of the initiative in Chicago in establishing playgrounds on a very small but significant basis.

In a large city the development of public recreation goes on side by side with the growth of commercial facilities. Some, such as a professional baseball team, are entirely outside accepted municipal functions. Others, such as private golf courses, are duplications of public parks; they generally delineate economic classes and relieve the public of this additional burden. There are varieties of private facilities, such as theaters, which are accepted as legitimate businesses, that are "built into" the large city and live off residents as well as transients. Gambling, prostitution, etc.—often exist only with the protection of law enforcement officials and political figures. This type of "destructive leisure" is therefore characteristic of certain sections of cities more than others; it is encouraged by huge profits for the businessman; it is fought by one arm of municipal government while in partnership with others.

The large city is the natural center for such agencies as art institutes, museums, athletic stadia, specialized theaters, and important educational centers. Its shopping centers may be counted as leisure areas for many persons. These facilities can be supported only by large populations. In 1957, for instance, Chicago obtained state legislation to authorize the construction of a huge convention auditorium. The city's population growth before and since the 1937 study has been referred to by a leading population authority as "fabulous": "In the brief span of a century and a quarter, a swamp and onion patch around the junction of a river and a lake became a major world metropolis." [36] This growth is seen in the facts:

1840	4,470 population
1860	100,000
1870	250,000
1880	500,000
1890	1,000,000
1910	2,000,000
1930	3,000,000
1950	3,600,000

Many questions arise when growth of community is related to its leisure patterns; for the size is only one index of a very wide range of social change. As Chicago grew in population, and even in geographical limits from 10 to 213 square miles, there was an important exodus to the suburbs. The question then arises, do suburban residents make use of neighborhood leisure-time facilities or do they go into the central city for the large facilities? At a conference on city planning in April 1957, sponsored by the Cook County League of Women Voters, the writer issued a questionnaire in which the women present checked off facilities that they or someone in their family had used in the preceding year and those that would probably be used *more* by the family in the succeeding five years (Chart 6). Of the 432 women, the largest number, over 270, checked off the central shopping center as most useful, followed by

Loop theater, concert, opera
Neighborhood library
Art institute
Neighborhood theater
Museum of Science and Industry
Neighborhood park
Beach
Brookfield zoo
Cook County forest preserve
Neighborhood sports field
Neighborhood recreation center
Comiskey Park
Soldier Field

Note in this list that neither a neighborhood nor a central facility predominates in the order of popularity. In the order of facilities, which these women expected would be used more by the family in the succeeding five years, the first three were the Art Institute, loop theaters and opera, and the Museum of Science and Industry. The women were asked for the ages of their children, and a clear relation was observed between the expected future use and the ages of children five years from then. This was in no way a "sample" of population. It seemed clear, from a study made in the same questionnaire, that most of these families lived in suburbs to the northwest and the southwest of Chicago.

The issue of relative use of recreational facilities in the central area or of those that are decentralized is of increasing importance to planners and political leaders. For, already, Chicago and seventeen other urban regions of the country total over 60 million people. Each of these is defined as a center in which two or more metropolitan areas (50,000 population each or more) overlap or adjoin. The largest of

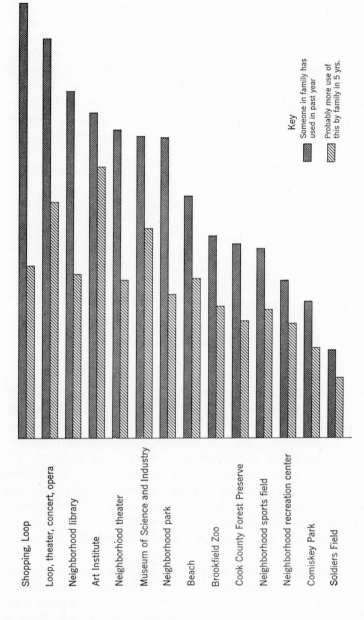

CHART 6. Recent and projected use of some Chicago recreational facilities, April 1957. (Indicated by 432 Members, Cook County League of Women Voters.)

these regions extends from north of Boston to below Washington, D. C.; this 600-mile stretch includes almost 30 million persons.[37] Such regions or "megalopolitan" centers have resulted from vast internal migration.

The moving of large populations has always been a mark of American life: first the broad moves to the West, then to the large cities, and more recently to the suburbs. Twelve million persons changed states between 1940 and 1947. In 1850 about 5 in every 100 Americans lived in cities of 100,000 or more; a century later, 60 in every 100.[38] One of every 10 Americans lives within commuting distance of Broadway and 42nd Street in New York. Every year from 1940 to 1945, one *million* farm families, particularly Negroes, moved to cities. In 1850, 85 in every 100 Americans lived on the farm; this number had gone down to 36 a century later.

Much of the city population has spilled out into suburbs. More than 9 million persons moved to the suburbs of our metropolitan areas. Of course, this urbanization trend has gone on in other countries as well. For instance, in 1800 no city of the world had as many as one million persons; by 1950 there were 46 such cities. Nowhere has the trend toward city life been so pronounced as in the United States.

The general significance of these population moves for leisure analysis is that the clear distinction which may have existed between country and city a generation or two ago does not hold today. Rural life is more like city life; suburban life is closer to open spaces than to the large central city. The *Gemeinschaft-Gesellschaft* contrast appears to have decreasing importance on several levels of inquiry: first, the physical location of our people; second, the influence of the mass media in standardizing thought and interests; third, the trend among students of city life to discern more primary and informal groupings; fourth, the higher level of rural living. And leisure activity, the very area of our lives that at one time was highly important in distinguishing rural from urban, is no longer a safe criterion. TV is viewed by all; many of us, wherever we live, are traveling. Such factors as education and wealth are important, but they cut across rural-urban lines.[39]

However, it is possible to summarize from the studies in this chapter those aspects of "pure" city and "pure" farm or village life that still color leisure. To some extent, it would be a mistake, in view of the foregoing paragraph, to assume that these distinctions have been *completely* eliminated. If we take the long-range view and consider trends, the generalizations made are truer than in the specific lives or histories of all persons and communities today. The city has at least these distinctive facets for leisure:

1. Such facilities as museums, made possible only by very large tax structures.

2. Parks and play areas with excellent facilities and often with expert leadership.

3. Volunteer citizens organizations whose function it is to work for recreational facilities in the community.

4. Many homes without sufficient play space or facilities within them for children or adults.

5. Large commercial enterprises for recreation that depend on concentrated populations.

6. Many businesses devoted to advertising and selling equipment for leisure use.

7. Transportation facilities to other play spaces, either in the region or across country.

8. Educational institutions to meet almost every kind of interest.

9. Many kinds of persons with specialized interests who can be called upon for the creation of clubs and hobby groups.

10. Creative centers in the arts, with persons highly skilled in producing works for enjoyment of others and in teaching amateurs.

The rural life, in its "pure" form, has these distinctive aspects:

1. A generally less hurried pace, so that even with considerable physical labor in farm work there is less psychological and emotional need to relax for therapeutic reasons.

2. A family that is closer together in the sense of awareness of what others are doing and is therefore in less need of leisure as a stabilizing or solidifying factor.

3. With the presence of cars, often the ability to take advantage of city facilities in addition to the ever-present rural patterns and benefits.

4. Longer periods of consecutive free time, as in August on some farms or the winter months.

5. The development of such organizations as 4-H in which programs contain both educational and recreational activity.

6. The use of the church as a social center for many purposes.

7. Freedom from fads and crazes in leisure.

8. Less class-leisure and therefore less reliance on it as a symbol of distinction.

9. More reliance on local and "natural" leaders, rather than professionals.

10. Fewer choices in entertainment provided by professionals or other persons and therefore more development of resources in the area.

These items, perhaps more accurately than the list presented at the opening of this chapter, characterize city and noncity leisure. Residents of Cisco are not limited to one set of items or the other but are more likely to fit into the second group than are persons in Chicago.

Developments since World War II may have reduced some of the distinctions between rural and urban areas. It is also important to bear in mind that great differences exist between one city and another. Writes the sociologist Jessie Bernard,

> Sometimes we hear that American cities are all alike, completely standardized, cut of one pattern. Nothing could be farther from the truth. Because we all speak the same language, see the same motion pictures, read the same national magazines, newspaper features, and comic books, study the same traditions, hear the same radio programs, absorb the same advertisements and propaganda—because Americans move about so much that it seems impossible for any community to set its stamp on them or to crystallize its own personality—we are likely to overlook the very real differences in community personality.[40]

It is not a far cry from a study of community to that of the state. Yet in the case of the state, other issues arise, to be noted in Chapter 9.

Leisure and state 9

A ll governments are directly and indirectly concerned with the leisure of their people. There are many grounds for such concern, including the control of masses by the distraction of large-scale amusements; laws regulating hours of work and the minimum wage; laws that prohibit some people from mingling socially with others; the provision of leisure-time activities or facilities in tax-supported schools, parks, or playgrounds; tax income from admissions or other aspects of the leisure business; building of strong bodies for military preparedness; and the use of playlike activities for developing loyalty to the state.

Indeed, a moment's reflection indicates that the attitude of the government toward leisure is a fundamental clue to its whole political philosophy. At least four issues bear on this: (*a*) the continuity of personal-communal values, (*b*) relations of private to public rights, (*c*) the functions of government, and (*d*) the uses of leisure as mass control.

Continuity of personal-communal values

We have seen, in the Lundberg study in Chapter 8, that as persons become obligated to some activities in their free time—women's organizations, for example—they often cease to define those situations as leisure. One of the elements of leisure discussed in Chapter 2 was psychological perception of freedom. The chief element in the freedom of leisure is the choice of getting into it and getting out of it. In between these steps is the continuum of lesser to greater obligation and commitment:

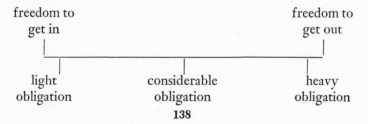

When I join a club, but in the course of time I hold no important office, or in other ways the organization does not depend on me or I on it, the likelihood is that this relationship is relatively free for me. Election to office is often a precise point at which increased commitment is observable and is one technique for involving potentially valuable members. An important and perhaps unique characteristic of American government, from local to Federal, is the large number of voluntary associations. De Tocqueville's comment on this point was noted in Chapter 5. It arises from personal need for obligation that is satisfied in such activity, quite aside from the merits of the action program; such needs can be met in the educational activity of the League of Women Voters or the effort of a local citizen's committee to obtain a municipal swimming pool. Almost all voluntary civic activity of this kind is done on one's time off from work. Deep convictions and significant social issues are often involved.

The key concept here is "voluntary." *Volus* is Latin for *will*. Many thousands of Americans comb the skies several evenings each week for the Ground Observation Corps. Their Russian counterparts in Moscow during the 1940's also "volunteered" for a task of national significance in helping to construct the beautiful subway. What kinds of pressure or intimidation existed in the American or the Russian actions? To raise the issue of "will" is to have stated the issue of this section. If the Russian action means simply that these people saw no distinction between their personal and their social or collective welfare, they were indeed acting freely. Several observations are proposed:

1. A high level of continuity from personal to communal value will lead a person in his leisure time to activities of a public service nature.

2. As he becomes communally active and committed, the participant perceives this *decreasingly* as leisure.

3. A moral issue thus arises: to what degree *should* persons with more time be encouraged to enter public service on a voluntary basis? For retired persons, many of whom fear empty time, will involvement become a substitute for leisure, as they perceive it? Given the present association of leisure and uselessness in the minds of many persons, it may be a wise policy to urge older persons into activities that will, in effect, be so meaningful as to eliminate the problem of large amounts of free time.

4. A conclusion of recent social science, long ago noted by writers and dramatists, is that more important than over-all slogans or principles of government in motivating men is our respect for opinions held about us by small, primary groups.[1] These are the pressures that prompt per-

sons to devote much free time to civic or patriotic duty; it is therefore advisable to apply such terms as "exploitation" or "propaganda" with care to such situations.

Public—private

In the history of our political system the concept "public" has been widened steadily by (a) explicit enlargement of the scope of the public right, welfare, or domain or (b) implicit enlargement by limitations on private rights. An example of (b) relating to uses of leisure is a series of laws in the South that prohibits sociability between the races. Ordinarily, segregation is analyzed for its effects on the minority. In fact, it restricts those white persons who would fraternize with Negroes if the law permitted. The very necessity of such a law in Louisiana is evidence that the possibility and desire for commingling exists in some white quarters.

The danger to custom from the association of majority and minority groups is peculiarly present in leisure-time relationships. For when Negro and white communicate as economic persons—customer, worker, employer, etc.—these are defined roles in harmony with the larger social system. However, as we note in Chapter 12, sociability is characterized by the temporary suspension of functional roles. Segregation rests on the assumption that there are qualitatively different kinds of social relationships, that the play relationship is potentially more dangerous to established order than that of work. Private choice is therefore limited in favor of the eventual public (majority) "good."

Another illustration of the private-public relationship is the history of the Boy Scouts movement. Youth movements—as in the case of the Hitler *Jugendbunde*—are often unique in their multiple functions and in the pressures that are exerted in their direction.[2] The Scouts organization was launched in 1906 in England as a direct outgrowth of a book, *Scout Training* (1899), by Robert Baden-Powell, a British soldier then stationed in India. The application of this book to peaceful purposes was its attraction to teachers in England, for its philosophy was based on ideals of manliness, endurance, resourcefulness, and truthfulness, all to be developed in an outdoor setting and with the military symbols of status and achievement. Thus there were present the dual attractions of personal development for youth and a powerful instrument for nationalism.[3]

The movement was quickly endorsed by state, church, and military groups. It proved useful to England during World War I; by 1909 it had been well received in Germany, Sweden, France, Canada, Chile, and South Africa. A new political complexion entered with the foundation of an international unit in 1920, dedicated, according to Powell, to "the worldwide spirit of scout brotherhood," a development encouraged by the League of Nations several years later. In 1947 scouts from several Communist countries came to the Paris conference.

The history of the Boy Scouts in America illustrates the conflicts in which such a dynamic movement inevitably becomes involved. After 1910 the Boy Scouts of America won a court injunction to prevent use of their name by three existing groups, all ultramilitary. To meet Roman Catholic objections to some vows taken by initiates, scout dedications were instituted instead to the concepts of bravery, cleanliness, and reverence. American labor leaders objected to reactionary political implications as well as to military emphases.

This picture was further complicated by the pattern of mixed sponsorship, so that even today there are few independent scout units. Units, for the most part, are organized by or related to churches, settlement houses, schools, nationality groups, and so on. Thus the ideologies of each type of parent group are protected, or at least not violated. In the Polish scouting movement we have an illustration of open conflict in the matter of dual loyalty and the use of the Polish language as part of scout life. This division over assimilationism versus pluralism led to the split represented by the youth department of the Polish Roman Catholic Union and the Polish Boy Scout Association.

To young boys who are the objects of all this current, these historical facts hardly exist or they seem far away. The single member is most influenced by the fact that his own friends are involved or by the awards, activities, and the feeling of belonging. Yet the lesson is important: first, that the leisure activity can serve many functions, that the same activity can be viewed differently from several quarters, and that the seemingly simple objectives of a free-time activity may simultaneously include a larger array of significant social values. Further, in Boy Scout history we see governments directly concerned with a movement that is not private (a concern only of its members and sponsoring groups) but a public concern on the highest levels of international goals, religions, and political animosities.

Functions of government

Another positive approach by government to leisure is found in the notable expansion of tax-supported activities and facilities.

For example, more than 200 million acres of recreation land are owned by the state and Federal governments. These parks were visited by more than 210 million persons in 1952. In addition to the park areas, the Federal government has fish and wildlife refuges; it also maintains museums, historic sites, and monuments. Taxes from leisure activities are major items: about 915 million dollars in 1952 in Federal and state taxes were levied on recreational goods and services; state collections totaled 138 million dollars in the same year as taxes on pari-mutuels at race tracks; and more than 70 million dollars were realized from hunting and fishing licenses.[4] In subsequent discussions of tourist travel, we note that governmental activities, here and abroad, have attracted substantial income: for instance, 22 per cent of the annual income of New Hampshire comes from tourists, and in one half of the states of our country revenues from tourists rank among the top sources of income.

During the depression of the 1930's the FERA, WPA, CCC, NYA, and PWA—all work projects—included the construction and leadership of leisure-time programs in a way that, according to some authorities, advanced the recreation movement by perhaps a quarter century.[5]

An example of government expenditures is the arts program. From 1935 to 1938 about 35 million dollars a year went into the Federal Art Project, whose activities included music, theater, painting, writing, and historical surveys. By 1940, when the war began to wipe out the need for work projects, relief programs were supporting 15 symphony orchestras, 75 concert orchestras, 65 dance bands, 49 concert bands, as well as numerous chamber-music ensembles, choral groups, opera units, and teaching groups in 40 different states. The 11,000 so employed [6] were, or were supposed to have been, professionals in their fields. But the area of the arts is one in which many millions of persons are interested, either as participants, watchers, listeners, or promoters. The financial assistance provided by our national government exceeded anything done before or since. Other governments have gone far in one way or another to take a direct part in art activities.[7]

The technological basis of modern war has shifted the attention of military planners to the recreational ("morale") needs of civilians as well as of service personnel. During World War I the WCCS (War Camp Community Service) was organized in 600 communities adjacent to camps and industrial centers to bring recreational services to men in uniform. In World War II a Division of Recreation was created within the Federal Security Agency. Its 65 field representatives helped communities near military posts or those swollen with industrial workers to make the best use of their recreation facilities and to train local leaders.[8] The impact of this program on civilians during the war and upon the professional recreation movement after the war was immeasurably large.

Debate on the proper functions of government has been especially pointed in the area of recreation facilities and program and leadership provision. Many persons have argued that the home is primarily or wholly responsible for providing play facilities. However, opposition to public parks comes from many quarters. Robert Moses indicates some sources of opposition from his long experience as Park Commissioner of New York City:

> Everybody with an axe of his own to grind. Every vested selfish interest. Politicians who endorse the program but don't like its application if some votes may be lost in the process. Arthritic toes which get stepped on. Ultra conservatives who like almost everything near and dear to them as it is, but would go along with change elsewhere. Special groups for this, but against that. Nature fanatics. Hunters and fishermen who want 2,000,000 acres of the Adirondacks to themselves. Taxpayers organizations which welcome progress if it doesn't cost anything. Real estate boards which concede that parks raise surrounding values generally but not at this particular location. Civic organizations which demand another exhaustive survey. . . . Pundits with their "on the one hand, on the other hand" opinions. . . .[9]

On the whole, the acceptance of the zoning philosophy in cities has affected the entire range of local thinking about the future, which recognizes the essential need for parks, playgrounds, and neighborhood areas. City planners have reached general agreement on minimum requirements; property owners have recognized the financial benefits of open space to surrounding property; the policy of taxation for public parks has been accepted generally by a wide segment of opinion, notwithstanding Mr. Moses' frustrations, owing in large part to persons with his persistence and vision.

In retrospect, a remarkable historical development has been that the new leisure now upon us finds a solid preparation in the contemporary acceptance of leisure facilities as a proper responsibility of government. Illustrations for these statements are to be found in the annual reports of hundreds of American cities and in the increasing number of state and county commissions.

The next major development for tax investment in leisure will serve adult needs. Adult education has already made giant strides in the last century and a quarter. Malcolm Knowles, then Executive Secretary of the Adult Education Association, was quoted in 1954 as saying, "I predict that the education of adults will become accepted as a public responsibility, just as the education of children will eventually exceed the total expenditures for childhood education." [10] Present figures and activities are impressive. About 50 million adults in our country are enrolled in some educational course, about three times more than a quarter century ago, when the AEA was formed. More than 100 member schools belong to the Association of University Evening Colleges. A report from *Time* for November 15, 1954, notes:

> The Nation's new school masters range from the U. S. Department of Agriculture's Extension Service, which reaches 8,000,000 students, to the Y.M.C.A. with 70,000, to I.B.M. with 16,000, and to the International Ladies' Garment Workers' Union with 12,700. More than 15 million adult Americans are attending Sunday schools or classes under the auspices of various church groups, nearly 2,000,000 are taking courses from various U. S. libraries, and an estimated 5,000,000 are going to school via TV. At the same time, the foundations are stirring up the field as never before. In 1952–53 the Ford-sponsored Fund for Adult Education spent more than $9,000,000 on every sort of project from the American Library Association's American Heritage Program to promote the study of basic American documents (6917 students) to the Great Books Foundation's seminars (21,000). In 1954, indeed, the U. S. has become one giant classroom.

Leisure as social control

The most dramatic or the most publicized relationship of leisure to government has always been the use of circuses, pageants, festivals, or large displays by totalitarian rulers to distract their people from more important issues. Familiar to every schoolboy are stories of Roman festivities, in which Christians were thrown to the lions in the Colosseum. Hitler, a master in applying controls, developed careful techniques for his shows.

Russia provides important examples of direct state interest in the leisure time of its citizens. This is evidenced in several directions: a major program in physical education and sports, state-owned resort centers for free or low-cost vacations for workers, a vast output in literature, and an apparently genuine interest in all the arts, on which Mr. Howard Taubman concludes a first-hand report to *The New York Times*.[11]

> The spreading of culture in the Soviet Union is pursued with unflagging energy. The arts are the great highroad to the minds and hearts of people, and the Soviet authorities are well aware how powerfully books, songs, films, symphonies, plays, and ballets can aid them. But it would be a grave error to assume that everything in the Soviet Union has no purpose but propaganda.

The arts flourish because they are also prized for the laughter, warmth, dignity, exaltation, and insight they bring to life. They are supported with unparalleled government generosity because they are acknowledged to be a great good in themselves.

U. S. S. R., the official Soviet publication distributed in the United States, often carries articles on state-supported leisure activities.[12]

According to one of these articles,[13] the Soviet Constitution guarantees an annual paid vacation of at least two weeks. Many categories of workers get more. (Three or four weeks are given to those in mining, iron and steel, nonferrous metallurgy, transport, oil, and chemicals.) In some industries those with more than two years of service get an additional two months every three years.

In addition to time off, the Soviet worker has access to vacation and health resorts "at very reasonable prices and in some cases without cost." This is financed by a combination of government and trade-union funds. The worker pays nothing into these funds.

The author, Ivan Kozlow, traces an example of the plan in operation. A textile worker decides to go to a Black Sea resort in the Caucasus for his vacation.

> There will be a variety of sports activities if he cares to participate, a library and game room at his disposal, theatre and motion pictures, dances, concerts, excursions to points of interest. . . . If he needs it, he can have a special diet arranged or get medical treatment or mineral baths, all without extra cost.

Having made his decision, the worker appears before the trade union committee of his shop, which will arrange for his stay. Cost for two weeks is 300 rubles; in the past he paid 30 per cent, with 70 per cent coming from union funds. This year, because of his good work record, he will be sent at no cost to himself. Indeed, we are told by Mr. Kozlow, vacations or reduced rates go as a matter of policy to old workers, low-incomed groups, large families, and to those in poor health. Free accommodations come to about 20 per cent of all persons attending health resorts and to 10 per cent of those at vacation resorts.

The foregoing Soviet account is, then, an illustration of direct governmental interest in leisure for general purposes of control but in a positive way that uses the device of winning loyalty through a significant benefit to the person. This is quite in contrast to the large-scale spectacles designed to distract the masses from central issues of the society. In a similar way the recreational programs of American industry attempt to win loyalty, reduce transiency in work, and cultivate favorable attitudes toward the plant. Critics of the Soviet Union will emphasize the propagandistic or ulterior purposes of the state as it "captures" the worker. Suspicions of the welfare programs in American industry are similarly held by labor unions on much the same grounds and, indeed, have led some unions to establish their own recreational programs.

International good will and travel

We bring this chapter to a close with an important development in leisure with which all countries, especially the United States, are involved. This is the potentiality of international travel in creating cross-cultural and ideological good will. Chapter 16 presents a picture of the extent of travel abroad. There is hardly need to belabor the economic importance of travel. For instance, in his report to President Eisenhower Clarence B. Randall finds that,

> For many countries, earnings for travel represent the largest single source of foreign exchange . . . travel constitutes the biggest single items of all dollar earnings for the United Kingdom, France, and Italy. Canada earns more dollars from the United States tourists than from any Canadian export other than newsprint.[14]

Mr. Randall makes the further observation that "travel makes back-fence neighbors of nations . . . as we seek the political goal of world peace, therefore, we should make the strongest efforts to promote international travel." Yet, concludes the report, it is discouraging to find a lack of interest and coordination among Federal agencies.

Perhaps a small case to illustrate the last point is the present fate of a practical plan to make foreign travel available at reasonable costs. Several years ago, a New York owner of hotels, Mr. H. B. Cantor, was struck by the possibility of operating ocean vessels as floating hotels; food, for instance, would be purchased separately by the consumer, and the administration would proceed on the up-to-date principles of the hotel business rather than on nineteenth-century practices common in the country inn. His plans took the shape of two 90,000-ton vessels, each to transport 6000 passengers, many of them for 100 dollars round trip, from New York to Zeebrugge, Belgium. (In war 12,000 to 15,000 troops could be carried on each voyage.) Estimated costs are 135 million dollars per ship. Great interest in this project has been displayed by many Europeans, by many organizations that would shift their conferences to shipboard, and by individuals who cannot afford to pay the usual fares.

If we assume that government controls or influences in leisure patterns can be positive, to encourage welcome developments, one would expect that the United States government would be concerned with the full utilization of ships now that jet plane travel is here: now, indeed, is a ripe time to enlarge the total framework of all types of transportation and a larger traveling public. It was therefore surprising, at hearings on the Cantor proposals in the summer of 1958 before the House Merchant Marine Committee, to find opposition voiced by the Chairman of the Federal Maritime Board.

If, indeed, the Federal government, in some plan under the aegis of the United Nations, were to undertake a systematic and serious interest in leisure travel as part of its foreign policy, effective steps could be visualized. A division of recreation in the Department of Health, Education and Welfare has already been proposed. In relation to travel, such a division could help establish adult education refresher groups in geography; special scholarships of financial aid could be devised for those who took suggested courses in languages, European or Oriental history, and politics; funds could be granted to the Council for Student Travel or to similar agencies that expedite the exchange of students; programs of assistance could be worked out with colleges offering credit for study abroad. We could, without chauvinism or propaganda, see that the many Americans who travel abroad are more adequately prepared to represent their own culture and to obtain insights into others. With the long tradition we have of subsidizing many aspects of our industrial, labor, and farm economy, as well as special groups, there is a precedent for the present proposal. The only objective should be a step for peace; for unless the peace is maintained, all other considerations, including leisure, fall by the wayside.

The foregoing paragraph was a recommendation. In spelling out a "good," the ideal took over from the real. This moves our study into the relation of ethics to leisure. We turn, therefore, to the consideration of religion and values.

Leisure and religion 10

With the present chapter we come to the heart of the discussion on leisure. As religion is based on such ultimate questions as the meaning of life and the nature of the good life, so we need to consider the *meaning* of leisure, its goodness and badness. More specifically, we seek here to indicate that the attitudes toward leisure are in part derived directly from the philosophy and the practice of religion itself.

Religion and work

Work is divine. God is revealed as the great worker and it is through work that men become like God. It is through work that man finds his life, and his life is measured by his work. Business is a means by which men exchange usefulness. In the exchange of commodities and services both parties are benefited, both parties profit. The more a man is given the more he receives. To run away from work is to run away from life. To repudiate work is to commit suicide.[1]

This statement, written in 1939, is an excellent summary of a view that in one form or another has dominated fundamentalist Christianity since its beginnings. Its preachings said, and had to say, that in work man can serve his God and from work derive those values of the good life that prepare man to ascend to Heaven. In this Heaven all men will be alike, for Heaven has no class structure, no factories, no poverty. If then, life on earth is a preparation and man's entry into Heaven is determined by his quality of life on earth, it is man's destiny to work hard, to accept the situation even when its injustices are apparent. With the expected coming of the Messiah, there is no need for revolution. Improvements can be sought, of course; churchmen have always followed a variety of policies as to the nature and degree of change that should concern the Church. More important

148

has been the Church's concern with the way in which such changes are brought about. Since the Church must be based on stability and conservatism, it is to be expected that a parish in a Mexican village today or in a Polish village of five centuries ago would accept the feudal conditions of their respective societies as God-given.

If the good life on earth as conceived by the Church is based around the acceptance of work, work itself has to be a source of social and moral values. Work is more than a necessity, it is a good. Work is "divine." Characteristic of the duality that penetrates much of Christian or other religious thought, the opposite of divine is therefore declared to be imbued with human faults, frailties, and, indeed, with antireligious potential. It follows that both elements of life, work and nonwork, are the proper concern of the Church and subject to ethical precepts.

There is no purpose for the Church to insist on continuous work. This is contrary to biological and psychological need. What attitude could the Church take? Some of the free time could be turned toward a religious activity. Whole days or hours could be declared as holier than others and therefore more subject to control. Further, specific types of leisure activities could be blessed, tolerated, discouraged, or banned. All of these approaches were used. Consider, briefly, the creation of sanctified time.

Sanctification of time

The sanctification of time can be illustrated in Judaic thought. One position is stated by a contemporary scholar and mystic, Dr. A. J. Heschel. He writes: [2]

> Judaism is a *religion of time* aiming at a *sanctification* of time. Unlike the space-minded man to whom time is unvaried, iterative, homogeneous, to whom all hours are alike, qualitiless, empty shells, the Bible senses the diversified character of time. There are no two hours alike. Every hour is unique and the only one given at the moment, exclusive and endlessly precious.

> Judaism teaches us to be attached to *holiness* in time, to be attached to sacred events, to learn how to consecrate sanctuaries that emerge from the magnificent stream of a year. The Sabbaths are our great cathedrals; and our Holy of Holies is a shrine that neither the Romans nor the Germans were able to burn; a shrine that even apostasy cannot easily obliterate: the Day of Atonement . . . Jewish ritual may be characterized as the art of significant form in time, as *architecture of time*.

Time in this case is accompanied by strong ritual whose strength arises from repetition and brings continuity between past, present, and future. As we have indicated, the naturalist reasons that the holiness has been *read into* time by the faithful of the church. A sociology of time is based on this very fact; that just as space, persons, objects, or concepts are given meanings—some are profane, some sacred, some important—so time receives meaning in every society. Associations arise from usage. The night is related to romantic actions, noon to eating, 8:30 to the opening of a play, dawn to the start of a new day, Sunday to rest. So powerful are such associations, that we *feel* different in such hours or times and are expected to act differently. One way of being different from our neighbors would be to invite them to a party at 8 A.M. next Saturday.[3]

Since we set aside special times in secular life, holy times have strong connotations, even to the nonreligious who have grown up in the shadow of the Church. All religions have their holy days or periods. Moreover, all societies, primitive or sophisticated, have conceptions of holidays. A pertinent problem is the relationship of time that is officially sanctified by the Church to time that is not devoted to work but is also not sacred.

Of all nonwork time, that devoted to play is the most perplexing to the Church. In the sphere of play we can forget social rules and prescriptions, for here is a world within a world, with its own concepts of right and wrong, good and bad. How can religion put morals into something that at first sight seems far removed from the central stream of daily life? Obviously by calling attention to the fact that all of life is one, interrelated and inseparable, if not on social or economic levels, then on the psychological. An example is drawn from the religious magazine, *These Times*, for January 1955. The editor is replying to the question, what about dancing as a recreation for Christians?

> If the Christian friends are also Christians—and none others should be his chosen intimates—they will enjoy only those things with which Christ can share. Can you invite Him to your dances? Can you imagine the Lord Jesus dancing the modern social dances? Rhythm—that is, organized motion—is not sinful in itself; for all the motions of creation are rhythmic. But rhythm and music in the dancing of men and women together serve only one purpose—the gratification of the sensual passions. This is always vehemently denied by the proponents of dancing. But the denial is either ignorant or hypocritical, as can be tested. Would anyone go through all the physical and emotional efforts of dancing without the stimulation of the partner? At once someone will say that this is done in solo dancing, chorus dancing, interpretative dancing. But in that the audience is the stimulated or stimulating partner, and the sensual effects may be mental. The Bible plainly teaches that impurity is a matter of thoughts. Can the thoughts be pure in the atmosphere of the dance hall? At once someone

will say, "Confine the dancing entirely to the home." But here, as with home drinking of alcohol and playing games of chance, there is a very short step from home to hell. The young person who has been taught to dance at home is sent out into the world without moral armor. Does dancing conduce to holiness? Can the Christian continue instant in prayer while dancing? Will the Holy Spirit dwell in his heart while his body sways to the rhumba or other "hot" music? To ask is to answer the question.

A second example, this from early American history, illustrates how the Church can attempt to assume control over all time.

Virginia originally enacted laws fully as restrictive as those of New England. The Assembly in 1619 decreed that any persons found idle should be bound over to compulsory work; it prohibited gaming at dice or cards, strictly regulated drinking, provided penalties for excess in apparel, and rigidly enforced Sabbath observance. There was, for example, to be no admission of actors "because we resolve to suffer no Idle persons in Virginia." Court records show that offenses against these laws were dealt with severely. It was only as conditions of life became somewhat easier that enforcement grew lax. Once the colony was firmly established and the need for incessant work began to lessen, Virginians were more generally permitted to make the most of whatever opportunities for recreation their expanding life presented.

In New England, where the stern rule of Calvinism condemned idleness and amusements for their own sake, the tradition that life should be wholly devoted to work ("that no idle drone bee permitted to live amongst us") held its ground more firmly. The magistrates attempted to suppress almost every form of recreation long after the practical justification for such an unrelenting attitude had disappeared. The intolerance of Puritanism was superimposed upon economic necessity to confine life in New England within the narrowest possible grooves. Massachusetts and Connecticut banned dice, cards, quoits, bowls, ninepins, "or any other unlawful game in house, yard, garden or backside," singling out for special attention "the Game called Shuffle Board, in houses of Common Interteinment, whereby much precious time is spent unfruitfully." They listed "comon Coasters, unprofitable fowler, and Tobacco takers" as idlers subject to immediate punishment. No smoker in Connecticut could "take any tobacco publiquely in the street, nor shall any take yet in the filds or woods." His indulgence in a habit generally condemned as time wasting was limited to the "ordinary tyme of repast commonly called dynner."

Throughout New England, local ordinances further ordered the constables to "search after all manner of gameing, singing and dancing" and to report "disordered meetings" even when they were held in private homes. John Cotton had condoned dancing under certain circumstances, reserving his disapproval with possible justification for "lascivious dancing to wanton ditties, and in amorous gestures and wanton dalliances," but his successors admitted no such subtle distinctions. The Devil was responsible for all dancing and especially "Gynecandrical Dancing or that which is commonly called Mixt or Promiscuous Dancing of Men and Women." When the Massachusetts General Court learned that the custom of dancing at weddings was growing up, it flatly decreed that there should be no more of it, then or at any other time.

The theater was, of course, absolutely prohibited. Connecticut was prepared to adjudge as common rogues and serve 15 stripes on the bare back to any one who should attempt to "set up and practice common plays, interludes, or other crafty science." Boston on one occasion refused permission for an exhibition of tight-rope walking "lest the said divertisement may tend to promote idleness in the town and great mispense of time." [4]

The uncharitable view of this history is to declare that these Church leaders were narrow, bigoted, inhuman, and fanatic. A more understanding view is to note that life is raw in a frontier society; men who guard the religion must be strong men, commands must be stark and sharp. There is no "intellectual" in mass and little need to qualify precepts. Clear dichotomies exist between work and play, good and bad, the life of good works and the life of sin. Only as society becomes complex do the grays arise between the blacks and the whites. Huizinga's attempt to reconcile play and religion would have been impossible in the philosophy of the Puritan day.[5]

The first common quality between play and religion, according to Huizinga, is the possibility of seriousness. As work becomes lighter and shorter in our society, play becomes more intense and imbued with ideals of perfection. Second, it is the separate space that reminds the player or the prayer that he is momentarily in a world of its own rules and sanctions. This physical space is real and finite but unbounded in the imagination. Special spaces exist within the larger area, such as the altar of the church or the ten-second line on the basketball court; each has its special significance, to be used only in particular moments by special persons. Third, the holy and the make-believe have pretense and illusion in common: symbols of light and darkness, colored windows, pageantry, ornate vestments, special language. Thus religion and ritual are both play, and this analysis, notes Huizinga, does not bemean the one but elevates the other. For Plato saw this when he asked "What, then is the right way of living?" and then answered, "Life must be lived as play, playing certain games, making sacrifices, singing and dancing, and then a man will be able to propitiate the gods, and defend himself against his enemies, and win in the contest." [6]

Leisure as integral to religious thought

The final step for the Church to take toward leisure is to deny that leisure is an outside force altogether by incorporating it completely into theological and philosophical thinking. This was done in 1952 by Josef Pieper, a brilliant Swiss Catholic philosopher, and in 1956 by a conference on leisure held in Boston by the Jewish Theological Seminary.

Pieper asserts that "one of the foundations of Western culture is leisure." [7] Its proper understanding requires that we set aside "our prejudice that comes from overvaluing the sphere of work." [8] This overemphasis had come from Kant's conception that the good is normally difficult. Pieper adds to this, "the highest moral good is characterized by effortlessness—because it springs from love." [9] Contemplation goes with leisure and may therefore be spoken of in the same breath with play. The divine wisdom, according to Proverbs VIII is "always at play, playing through the whole world."

Pieper draws on St. Thomas Aquinas to show that effort is not a necessary cause of knowledge but may be one of its conditions. As further argument that effort can be separate from value, we see that even the Christian concept of sacrifice or discipline is not based on suffering *qua* suffering but is concerned with "salvation, with the fullness of being, and thus ultimately with the fullness of happiness."

Then Pieper considers leisure in relation to the liberal arts, for here is to be found the true function of the intellectual worker in his social system. Again Aquinas is brought in: "The liberal arts, then, include all forms of human activity which are an end in themselves; the servile arts are those which have an end beyond themselves, and more precisely an end which consists in the utilitarian result attainable in practice. . . ." [10] Not everything is useless, notes Pieper, "which cannot be brought into the definition of the useful." [11] Work does not exhaustively define the world. Man is more than a worker if he leads a full human existence.

Approaching a positive conception of leisure, Pieper begins by distinguishing it from acedia (A-Kedos, or not care), since *sloth* is one of the seven deadly sins—a capital sin from which follow despair and other conditions. Idleness is the utter absence of leisure; indeed, it renders true leisure impossible. Real leisure is, first, "a mental and spiritual attitude," not simply a result of external factors, such as spare time, a holiday, a week end, or a vacation. Its characteristic attitude must be one of nonactivity, inward calm, and silence: not being "busy" but "letting things happen." Other qualities are given for true leisure: "a form of silence," a "receptive state of mind," the capacity for "steeping oneself in the whole of creation," a certain happiness that comes from recognition of the mysteriousness of the universe and the recognition of our incapacity to understand it.

Second, true leisure can be viewed as a contemplative "celebration," for it leads man to accept the reality of the creation and thus to celebrate it. Consequently, feast days and holy days "are the inner source of leisure." [12]

Third, leisure is opposed to the ideal of work as social function. A chronological break in work time is still part of the world of work. Leisure is not considered a "restorative, a pick-me-up, whether mental or physical. . . ." Following Aristotle's view, then, leisure steps beyond the ordinary world, touching upon the superhuman life-giving power.

Finally, Professor Pieper deals with the practical question, how can man be brought to this view, how can he be saved from work as his exclusive interest? For his answer, Pieper goes back to his conception of "celebration" as the source of leisure. Here all of its elements combine. The basis of celebration or the feast is "divine worship," and thus we arrive at the ultimate attainment of leisure. There is a divine *time*, as there is of *space:*

> In divine worship a certain definite space of *time* is set aside from working hours and days, a limited time, specially marked off—and like the space allotted to the temple, is not *used*, is withdrawn from all merely utilitarian ends.[13]

In more contemporary tones, but arriving at much the same conclusion, is the report of the *Conference on Leisure*, March 14 and 15, 1956, sponsored by the Jewish Theological Seminary.[14]

In a preliminary memorandum to the Boston conference it was argued that there is a *moral* factor in the uses to which one puts his free time. This might be defined as

> . . . the recognition that life is not without purpose; and that one should, therefore, discriminate between those pursuits which help oneself—and others—become better, and those which do not.

In fact, we *are* our time. "To waste time is to waste ourselves." If man is his own master, then each act requires a moral decision. In every act man makes his own choices. For his is a universe, "a complete and whole world." Body and spirit are indivisible in a union that can maintain and develop only by "proper modulation of his *rest, recreation,* and *creative time.*" The memorandum examines each of these briefly.

Rest is more than abstinence from activity; it is a "positive decision to advance toward perfectibility." The moral function of *recreation* is to insure "the full exercise of the gifts given to each personality." This requires self-discipline. Most difficult and rewarding is the *creative* use of time.

> It involves not only the utilization of those powers and talents the individual already possesses, but the exploration and adventure of *extending* one's self into new dimensions, new situations, and new challenges.

In a section called "The Human Revolution in Work and Leisure in America," the decline of work as a source of human values leads to the question, can the values of this leisure really function as a major vocation of man; can freedom be realized in leisure? The attempt to answer leads to statements on the meaning of freedom and the relation of freedom to mass entertainment, individualism, and independent action and choice.

Several "modes of leisure time" are presented in a classification that judges them in reference to freedom:

1. Least adequate is *mass entertainment,* whose two types are "those based on tactual and gustatory feelings such as erotic experience and the pleasures of eating and drinking; and those based on the distance senses of sight and hearing, such as mass spectacles and shows, exhibitions, sports events, movies and television."
2. Handicrafts or hobbies are somewhat better (knitting, carpentry, gardening, photography, etc.). In these, man obeys no higher command. He has pride in his product, for it has values of its own.
3. Still more preferable is *play: sporting and gaming.* These have satisfactions of their own. In sporting, a force of *nature* is the obstacle; and "joy is taken in the free expression of spontaneous action."
4. Finally and most preferable is *recreation,* which consists of three groups: artistic creation and appreciation, study and discourse, and prayer and worship. All these have intrinsic values of their own. In performing these acts, we are engaged "in the very reformation and recreation of ourselves." This is freedom *par excellence.* Worship is placed above the rest, for in addition to the element of freedom, worship "Seeks the aid of the transcendant."

The conference took up these preliminary comments written by a planning committee of ten. In a summary of the first day's discussion, one of the planners, Professor Kenneth Benne, noted,

We came back again and again to this question. How central is the importance of free and rational decision and choice for the individual within this whole process of spending leisure time? Most of us affirmed the general value of rational choice.

Free choice, he added, implies criteria of values; and the danger exists that we impose a fixed external standard rather than allow the person to be active in developing his own value system.

The statement of final consensus asks a series of questions that indicates the hopes of the conferees:

> We are faced with a new dimension of freedom—but freedom to do what? Is it to be for millions the freedom to be bored? Is it to be the freedom to feel neglected, rejected or abandoned by one's fellow men? Is it to be freedom to use one's leisure time and tastes as so many counters in a ceaseless game of social competition—a game of status and career pursued beyond the point of no return? Is it to be freedom, in short, for more self-induced pressure and anxiety?

> Or could there be freedom to stop and rest, to feel and to think? Could there be for all a leisure that would come as a new breath, as a pause for recollection and renewal? Could we plan to make our cities more spacious rather than more tense; our roads leading to fewer billboards and more trees; our hours of play more a source of reassurance and of liberation; our lives directed to intellectual and spiritual values and our moments of thought more a sense of awareness of the eternal and the infinite?

Finally, the conference proposed the formation of a national "Commission for the Study of Creative Uses of Leisure Time" for five purposes: to obtain facts on time and human resources potentially available for creative leisure; to assess those areas in which time and resources could best be applied; to disseminate information to interested groups and agencies; to propose necessary public policies and legislation; to facilitate and encourage the most fruitful use of free time.

Another illustration of the relation of religious thought to the evaluation of a specific type of activity is seen in reference to gambling. In gambling a unique situation exists in which two or more persons "bet" against each other; that is, they back up a prediction with a sum of money or some other guarantee. Anything can supply the content or object of the bet: the winning horse in the next mile will be Rabbit Ears; the winning team will be the Yankees; the next car to pass this spot will be a Ford; ad infinitum. Thus a game is made out of any situation in which a coming event or act can be prejudged. Gamblers may or may not be directly involved in the act or in the content itself. The gambler relies as much on luck as he does on prior knowledge, and therefore he is strongly inclined to attach himself to symbols, from a rabbit's foot to a person. Thus gambling runs head on into the heart of religion. Why is this so?

We may recall the analysis in which Huizinga discerns common elements in play and religion. In gambling, as one form of play, there is a continuity with age-old formulas of magic. As David Allen notes,[15]

> The gambler is essentially a passive person who responds to an often harsh reality in a primitive and magical way. In his efforts to control the chance factors in life . . . he is attempting, symbolically, to supplicate the powers that deal out good and bad fortune with ruthless indiscrimination . . . he is asking of fate the question, "Am I one of the favored, or am I one of those to be cast down?"

Gambling is common everywhere in the world today, and evidences of its practice are found in early excavations. The conquering gambler is a motif in many tales of the North American Indian. For the United States at present, Table 1 in Chapter 1 shows an estimated rise in pari-mutuel receipts from 400,000 dollars in 1929 to 419 million dollars in 1952. According to an Associated Press story of December 5, 1955, a total of more than 2 *billion dollars* was bet on horse racing in the 24 states in which betting is legal; the revenue to these states came to almost 149 million dollars.

	States Betting	Total Bets	Revenue
1952	19	$563,579,895	$44,005,278
1955	24	$2,086,638,242	$148,888,403

In 1934 state revenues from betting were only 6 million dollars. These figures apply to thoroughbreds; add another 31 million dollars in revenue for trotters. Thus it is clear that a staggering sum is involved in gambling and that this leisure-time activity, which has always attracted mankind, is now a firm aspect of American economy. The Kefauver Crime Committee's estimate was that *illegal* gambling of all kinds totaled 20 *billion* dollars a year, or twice the gross turnover of the automobile industry, the country's largest.

Of course, the religious opposition to gambling is only part of its larger attitude toward games as a whole.

The morality read into games [16] is perhaps in part due to the interesting fact that a game is inherently a secular pursuit; hence it is in conflict with religion. With its morality, the game becomes, in a real sense, a substitute for religion. American and European history is replete with illustrations. The Church has, over and over again, either condemned games outright or at least sought to control them. Why this attitude?

In games like bingo and cards luck is involved, but luck is by definition uncontrollable. Yet, in contrast, God is not fickle, for he establishes an order with cause and effect. There is systematic—even if
mysterious—reward and punishment. Thus religion provides methods
by which this mysterious power can be supplicated, as in prayer and
sacrifice. It is the Church, especially under Roman Catholicism, that
provides the instrument of revelation, liaison, or understanding, so
decidedly so, that even the miracle announced by a nonauthorized
layman (as a Joan of Arc, or a Wisconsin farmwife in the 1950's) is
carefully investigated with gravity and considerable doubt. Such an
ideology cannot permit luck to become a powerful counterideology.
In quite a similar vein a university is based on the idea of just rewards
for work done and cannot, for instance, logically permit gambling
devices on its premises.

Games of skill are based, not on luck, but on calculated controls.
Yet it is not man's place to control his destiny. The game, notes religion, is indeed a world of its own, in which one's destiny can be made
explicit in a short time; let no man make the analogy to real life, in
which man's destiny is known only to higher powers.

Given this antagonism, the religious ideology seeks either to eliminate or to control games. To incorporate them, even in raising money
for the Church (as bingo has in recent years), is to create a division
of opinion within the Church.

Leisure in the Church as a local institution

The discussion to this point has dealt for the most part with religion
on a broad level. More specifically, we can view the place of leisure
in the Church as it deals with the community on a day-to-day basis.
We have already referred to the inclusion of much more activity
called *social* and *recreational* in the Church of today. Some large
churches employ professional recreational leadership. One of the
writer's students was a young man from the Mennonite Church who
had been sent to the university to seek a reconciliation of contemporary
thought and trends with the previously rigorous practice of his Church.

Holyoke, Massachusetts, provides a case study of the ways in which
churches use leisure activities to further their views. The study is
one chapter of Professor Kenneth Wilson Underwood's *Protestant
and Catholic: Religious and Social Interaction in an Industrial Community*.[17]

This New England community of 54,000 is now predominantly
Roman Catholic. That Church considers social and civic clubs of

great importance and has sought "with considerable diligence" to relate their program and thinking to the Church.[18] Church members are encouraged to belong to lay associations created or recommended by the Church. Such groups as the Catholic Veterans and Catholic Scouts are engaged, according to the author, in adding the "supernatural to social and occupational organizations."

The Knights of Columbus, as "militant Christ-bearers," is the most important lay Catholic organization. The Protestants have nothing comparable. In a comparison of the Catholic Girls' League and the Protestant Girls' Association, Underwood notes that a chaplain is usually present at the formal meetings of the league and speaks when he is there; very few clergymen ever attend the Protestant meetings. Joint meetings of the groups are not permitted by the Roman Catholic clergy. Roman Catholic speakers have addressed the Protestant groups but not vice versa. A similar story is told about the Scout groups. In all mixed religious groups in Holyoke the Roman Catholic clergy seek to "avoid having the mixed association become a place for the exchange of religious ideas."

> The Catholic official position is that the nature of societies is specified by the avowed ends. If the society "has an essentially spiritual end," then it is a spiritual society and "is dependent upon the supreme ecclesiastical authority." If the society tends to promote some temporal good, then it is dependent upon the civil power. The church decides what are temporal and what are spiritual ends, even if the "temporal seems to predominate, insofar at least as the religious end is concerned, the society is dependent exclusively upon the ecclesiastical authority." [19]

The Holyoke "Y" has increasingly de-emphasized reference to religion. The YWCA has 83 per cent Roman Catholics, 17 per cent Protestants and Jews. Seventy-five per cent of the YMCA are Roman Catholic youths, and 90 per cent of its summer-camp boys are from this religious group; one third of the Y's finances for a new building came from Roman Catholics; according to Underwood, the Y has recently gone more often to this church to check on its policies. The official policy of the priests on the Y is neutral; they neither support it nor oppose it.

The Rotary, Lions, Kiwanis, and other businessmen's groups have no programs with religious content and, as in the case of the Rotarians, no pre-meal blessings. The Rotary Club is the "men's club of the most influential Protestants" in the Massachusetts community. Of its 142 members, one is a Jew and only 15 are Roman Catholic.[20]

Although the Protestants thus have shown increasing accommodation to the Roman Catholic point of view, since their own churches have no well-developed attitude on leisure, there seems also to be some reappraisal by the Roman Catholics. Underwood believes that there is some revolt among their young members: "The people sense the profound pluralism of American culture and have in the newer ethnic fellowships and school alumni associations been asking for less Church direction of their activities." [21] The author predicts that the real troubles of the Roman Catholic and Protestant Churches over associations in the area of recreation lie ahead. Because of the mass media, former religious controls over leisure are breaking down. In view of this, Church leaders of all denominations are at the moment uncertain what to do. However, in November 1957 the Roman Catholic group announced a program, on a national level, to study what it can do about improving the content of TV. On a local level, it may be noted that in the same month Holyoke elected a Jew as its new mayor.

Summary

It is the function of religion to establish its moral codes in terms of universal truths as the particular branch or ideology sees the truth. Its strength is its conservatism. As the centuries have passed, churchmen have seen their members increasingly influenced by the products and values of industrialization. Time, both in its use and perception, has been severely affected by economic changes. As work has been taken less for granted, the Church has had to revise its own teachings, for it could not square its position with the reduction from a 16- to a coming 4-hour day. The importance of Joseph Pieper's contribution is that he establishes a point of view by wiping away the Calvinist position on work. He illustrates the new position of the Church, which is to accept leisure as a potential source of significant living. The Church has, in addition, often appropriated the psychology and the technique already developed by the rising profession of the recreationist. Yet ethics and evaluations of behavior are not necessarily precluded in the world outside the Church. Early in this chapter we related leisure to the nonreligious view of life. Chapter 11 pursues this theme in bringing to a close the discussion of social factors that affect our leisure in America.

Leisure and value systems I I

In secularist philosophy and discourse, too, the issue arises: what is a "good" use of leisure and how can people be brought to such uses? The whole of this book will be misunderstood unless the topic is examined in its relation to social science. To begin with, we must be clear as to what social science can tell us on the one hand and what our personal philosophies, group norms, and social trends can tell us on the other.

The phrase *good leisure* cannot make sense without a prior conception of the *good life*. There are sociologists who state that social science can or should attempt a definition. The general position in contemporary social science is to the contrary.[1] Examples of three positions are quoted below. Bierstedt writes:[2]

> Ethical neutrality . . . means that the scientist, in his professional capacity, does not take sides on issues of moral or ethical significance. . . . The scientist, *as such*, has no religious, political, literary, philosophical, moral, or marital preferences. That he has these preferences as a citizen makes it all the more important that he dispense with them as a scientist.

In sharp contrast is this comment in a report on the World Congress of Sociology (Amsterdam, August 1956) by Norman Birnbaum, a sociologist of the London School of Economics and Political Science:[3]

> Many Westerners at Amsterdam were themselves not free of ideology. It took the form of supposing that the laws governing social life lie very near the surface, just awaiting discovery. One more inquiry (and one more grant) and there they'd be . . . lacking only suitably simplified packaging for freshman courses. Part of this is simply a professional attitude: sociologists need to convince themselves and university administrators . . . that they really are entirely distinct from economists, historians, political scientists, and, above all, philosophers.

161

A middle position is perhaps presented by a third sociologist, Jessie Bernard: [4]

> A past generation of social scientists, lacking testing devices and influenced by the so-called scientific schools of historians of the nineteenth century, used to argue that scientists as scientists make no value judgments. They simply present facts. . . . Both the scientist and the layman make value judgments, whereas most of us tend to make subjective or emotional value judgments. . . . But in all cases we are making value judgments. It is a question of kind.

Does this mean that, as a consequence, nothing can be said by social science on the issue of meaningful leisure? Not at all. *Given the generally accepted values and norms of our society,* we know with some reasonableness when someone is a criminal. We can, with some objective support, distinguish a somewhat happy or successful family from one that ends in divorce or the throwing of dishes. With plenty of room for confusion of terms and error in objective measurement of normal, subnormal or pathological personalities, we can still be fairly sure that the majority of mental patients belong in their hospital rooms and the majority of us do not.

Given the generally accepted values and norms, it is unwise to assume that the effects of leisure are entirely beyond the reach of social science. The first requirement in this task is to see whether the many subjective conceptions of leisure can be generalized to permit (*a*) observation of uniformities and (*b*) careful—even experimental—observation research to pinpoint effects and processes. Chapter 2, taking the position that a single definition will not do, demonstrates an attempt of this kind. Leisure is not this or that; it is a certain type of social situation in which several characteristics are most likely to appear. Thus not all free time from making a living is leisure; and some of us have jobs that are, to *us,* more leisurelike than the other man's vacation.

However, in order to investigate its effects, types of leisure must be established so that qualitative effects can be recognized. Expectations enter here; one looks for something different in art than in athletics. Potentials also enter, for art and athletics contain different elements, exist in different situations, appeal in different ways, and require different standards of success as leisure activities.

What have we, then? One, a concept of characteristics—an *ideal construct,* not a definition of leisure; two, a set of conceivable social situations and factors; three, a category of types of activity; and four, the application of criteria from the given values and norms of the society. Let us apply this process of analysis to a specific case.

Jim gambles on horse races. *Good* or *bad?*

Step 1: Is this leisure?

Let us assume it is not his source of livelihood. Even if he loses, Jim perceives the activity as pleasant, before and after. He sees nothing wrong with the ethics of gambling. He is relatively uncommitted and has chosen it among other activities open to him. Thus the activity follows our earlier construct; it is a leisure activity.

Step 2: Type of leisure.

Gambling falls naturally into our later category of games and sports. It combines some knowledge, inner "gossip," and luck. Jim may have recourse to forms of magic as he tries to control his luck. The money element also makes playing the horses a part of a very large business enterprise.

Step 3: Relevant social factors.

Section 1 of this book examines work, personality, family, class, subculture, community, government, church, and value systems. Assume, arbitrarily, the following combination of factors. Jim's work in no way suffers from his gambling. His personality is *other-directed*, and most of his friends, whom he respects, also gamble. His family does not mind; they are well provided for and thankful that he is not a drinker; his wife goes to the track with him. Members of his social class in his culture and community also gamble or, if not, do not look upon it with disfavor. As to church, he seldom goes; if he thinks about it, he does not care what the minister might say, and, besides, "doesn't the Church have bingo games?"

Step 4: Criteria of successful leisure.

It will be recalled that in the course of Chapter 2 six criteria were presented to help judge successful leisure:

(*a*) It provides a "belonging."
(*b*) It helps one to be different from others.
(*c*) It can combine several functions for the person.
(*d*) It can serve the society as well as the person.
(*e*) It has no objectively measurable negative consequences.
(*f*) It provides for creative projections of oneself.

Most relevant in the present case are (*a*), (*c*), and (*d*) (if one accepts the social benefit of tax income to the state from gambling).

Point (e) seems demonstrated; there can be serious doubt about points (b) and (f).

The case has been deliberately drawn so that nothing in this activity interferes with Jim's life. Science could apply detailed evidence by an analysis of his home life, his finances, his social set, and so on. The situation becomes much more complex if the case involves conflicts of interest, sentiments, values, or attitudes. What if Jim's wife objects to gambling, and he loves her? What if he loses money that is needed in the family? What if he steals money to cover his bets? These situations are still capable of analysis on an objective plane. Generalizing roughly, *the leisure activity becomes decreasingly successful on a continuum as the points of conflict increase and as the intensity of conflict deepens.*

Continuum in evaluation of successful leisure:

Activities in complete conflict with relevant social factors and criteria	Activities relatively unaffected by social factors or criteria	Activities completely consistent with relevant social factors and criteria

The intensity factor is the crux of much difficulty in contemporary social science. It seems, on first contact with the subject, that the problem of measuring the effects of an activity is simple. Yet even in the area of the mass media, this has proved far from simple. We know how to measure the size of a TV audience; measures of its impact are still in their infancy. More complicated, perhaps, is the measurement of a behavioral pattern implied in leisure activity.

Assuming even that social science will in time have more to say about measures of conflict and intensity, its judgment of leisure is possible only on the condition that one bring to each case (a) a complete acquaintance with all the facts and (b) some outside yardsticks, ethical formulations, or opinions, such as "this is better than that."

Basic to (b) is the fundamental awareness of social scientists that there can be no society, no social structure, no developed way of complex life without rules, sanctions, or educational or legal prescriptions. A study of *social control* may well be considered the chief preoccupation of the sociologist, under whatever topic or title. It can be a most serious misreading of a discipline to confuse its *analysis* of law, precepts, or moral codes with *criticism* of them. Nor does its tradition of cultural relativism mean that one system, order, or value is on the same level as another; but although the origins of a value system are to be found within the natural historical-social system, the system appears to be supernatural and obvious to its participants.

It is on this point that the rationalist and the religious views begin to part. Consider the following statement in *The New York Times* of September 30, 1957, reported to have been made by a Congregational minister in that city who was opposing a move to legalize bingo for church or other nonprofit uses: [5]

> No institution has the moral right to exploit the cupidity of its fellowmen for the church or any other cause. Gambling is a sin against man, against society and against God. It perverts a noble instinct, the spirit of adventure; it vulgarizes and exploits the spirit by a spirit of thievery—one man's gain is another's loss; it's a fool's game; it makes man a parasite.

The humanist might well criticize bingo in the church or elsewhere, but for other reasons, for he knows that some men do not mind being fools, gaining from another's loss, or enjoying parasitism; more, that the fear of sinning against society or God has long ago lost its hell-and-damnation power for many persons. But the gambler may be approached in respect to his motivations and expectations, his need to conform or to be different, and the direction in which his "spirit of adventure" is satisfied. He can be exposed to other kinds of adventure. The community can create other possibilities for his use, such as libraries, clubs, other games, parks, travel facilities, and the like. The "infection" of gambling, as we note in a later chapter, has been with man from his earliest recorded history. If bingo is not the particular game, any other game or human activity lends itself easily to gambling in some form. The reasonable approach of society, it would seem, is not to seek by legislation to deny activities that, like gambling, cannot be eliminated but rather to enlarge the range of possible activity and then to acquaint its people that they exist and are tasteful.

A more difficult issue than laws or precepts is that of developing attitudes about whether leisure time is to be considered a time for meaning or for insignificance. In this regard, a humanist-social scientist can examine the position of Louis Kronenberger with considerable doubt.[6]

> The quintessence of leisure, clearly, is freedom rather than pleasure . . . to be completely ourselves. . . . We owe no apologies for the hours when we do exactly as we please. . . . There may be an art to leisure, and even an ultimate morality, there shouldn't be an uplift movement; . . . though this age has given human beings far more leisure than they ever had, and made leisure far more respectable than it ever was, it has also coated leisure with a certain purposefulness, and made it, too often, a mask for self-advancement.

And what might be an example of the ideal leisure, uncommitted to anxiety, a complete expression of unlimited choice? Kronenberger continues,

> How salubrious to expend one's competitive instinct on something value-less, to get intense over something trivial. I once knew a fellow who was gloriously happy trudging up and down railroad yards collecting the names of Pullman cars. Heaven knows what he did with them afterwards, but for a long time now I have envied him.

An assessment of the humanist-social scientist puts him somewhere in the middle between Kronenberger and the Church: with Kronen-berger he agrees that leisure must in essence offer freedom; with the Church he agrees that leisure may have a rich meaning. Opposed to Kronenberger, he works on the assumption that a reading of the classics may be entered upon freely and with no motive of self-advance-ment. He disagrees with the Church's notion that the highest or the only content of pure leisure must be mediation, church activity, or celebration of God's work.

Finally, making the circle back to Jim the gambler we may note a folk wisdom and an intellectual-educational tradition that holds that a nation with 50 million happy gamblers is not as desirable as one with 50 million Jims creating works of art. There is a common-sense judgment, statistically apparent, that if Jim has activities A, B, C, and D available to him—and is aware of the fact—he is more likely to become involved in more than one than in a situation in which only A exists. Further, there is sense as well as science in the statement that if leisure activities A, B, C, and D are qualitatively different, of-fering different kinds of satisfactions, a more ideal situation exists than if they were variations of one type. Finally, the ultimate em-phasis is placed on the kinds of training and atmosphere provided for Jim and in the situation around him: that is, he is most ideally placed as a member of a society (a) when that society makes available to him a wide variety and range of leisure activities, from the least to the most meaningful and significant, and (b) when that society has prepared him to choose with discrimination and taste those activities that fit his mood, use his skills, supply his emotional and psychological needs, enlarge his value to his social groups, supplement the nature of his work experience, and fit well into the family pattern.

Summary

1. Social scientists themselves take various positions in their ap-proach to values, to judgments of good and bad. The dividing line

between social scientists and laymen is that (*a*) social scientists are sensitive, by training, to their own assumptions, (*b*) they subscribe to a scientific method in which even assumptions can be challenged and reshaped, and (*c*) their judgments involve, whenever possible, the presence of facts or data upon which interpretations are based.

2. An objective evaluation might, as in the case of Jim the gambler, find that no objective basis exists for judging his behavior as bad. Other interpretations could easily emerge, provided that one took either (*a*) a moral position that gambling per se is bad or (*b*) the view that Jim's activity is a poor one when compared with alternative activities —a situation for which both he and society share some responsibility.

3. The writer submitted the generalization that success of the leisure activity might be observable and perhaps measurable by studying the degree of *conflict* created by the choice *within the given situation.*

A blanket position that tries to cover all situations is precisely what we propose is impossible by methods of social science and unwise by canons of common sense. In Chapter 15 we examine the assumption that the mass culture is worse than the elite or aristocratic art; in Chapter 17 we continue this discussion in relation to the use of television, radio, and reading. Chapter 22 summarizes the writer's personal position on creative values in leisure.

Thus this central issue is examined from several contents.

We enter now upon an examination of several types of leisure. We may recall, from Chapter 2, that these "types" grow out of raising three concerns:

1. The degree to which *people* or *interests* are a source of leisure (types: sociability, association).

2. The degree to which *rules* or *creative traditions* are sources of leisure (types: games and sports, art).

3. The degree to which, in leisure activity, we *go* to the world or *bring* the world to us (types: movement, immobility).

In each type we are further concerned with its essential nature and its relation to one or several of the social factors discussed in the preceding section. Sociability is our first type.

Types and Meanings
of Leisure

Sociability as leisure 12

The concept

Throughout world history, some people have liked some other people—members of their families, sweethearts, or friends. It is conceivable that no other element is present in a specific social relationship than this "liking." No consequences, no rewards, no material gains, no favors need be in the offing. This relationship is called sociability.

Sociability may be found in a large variety of situations. Its model is the family. True, in the family one obtains security, protection, response, or economic support. However, the relationship is not consciously maintained on this level of interlocking functions and statuses, although the roles are often structured. A *quality* of family life is sought, which provides an atmosphere that rounds out and dramatically affects the selection of roles. This quality is a liking of others in the group. It is tested occasionally when crisis comes, as in the sickness of a member, and regularly when the functions of "mother," "father," and "child" are finished for the day and sociability takes over.

A party provides a second classical example of sociability. Here meet persons who, for the duration of the party, freely shed their normal roles as policeman, clerk, teacher, or minister. Conversation turns quickly from one topic to another. No discussion is prolonged or, if it is, not beyond a certain point of seriousness in which excitement or offense can prevail. For, aside from a purposeful lack of content, there are factors of manners, good taste, and tact that are observed.

We have in sociability both a decided freedom and a consciously observed limitation or control. It is a control that arises out of consideration for persons *as persons*. The host's chief function is to create the group, then to maintain this quality of sociability. One technique he adopts is to select members of the group by mentally matching them, anticipating who might force his opinions or favorite topics of conversation or who might simply not like other guests.

When a content is provided—entertainment, song, serious discussion—then the informal and unorganized group takes on, no matter how momentarily, the aspects of a political group, an audience, etc., with such role functionaires as debaters, entertainers, group fools, jesters, sages, or teachers.[1] However, there are devices used by the host to insure a successful affair, although he is not necessarily aware of what he is doing. He will provide refreshments to break down reserve and make extended conversation more difficult or liquor that at once dulls the mind and stimulates spontaneity.

The concept of sociability revolves around three terms that will receive only passing attention here: "intrinsic person," "friend," and "informal structure." [2]

As to the first, Professor E. T. Hiller's sociological analysis of persons as values provides a focal point for an understanding of sociability. By *intrinsic valuation* we refer to the respect, accountability, and inviolability with which our mores invest each person. These are inseparable from the person. In general, the person is to be treated as an end, never as a means. *Respect* "implies deference of one person to another in terms of self-feeling . . . upon one's actual or imagined standing in the estimation of other persons. . . . To be respected is to be a person, a social self, not a thing or convenience." [3] *Accountability* implies a "trust bestowed on the agent," for in this sense the person is considered as a moral being, responsible for his actions. By *inviolability* is meant that our mores prohibit "degradation or profanation" of the person.

The term "friend" has as one of its fundamental meanings a relationship based on mutual recognition and continuing expectation of intrinsic value in the other. One of the issues in a study of sociability is whether some types of society are especially favorable to the development of, are indifferent to, or, indeed, are hostile to close friendships.

Finally, *informal social structure* is that which, in contrast to a maximum of explicit statutes and power recognition, is flexible in its role relationships. If leisure as a whole signifies a minimum of obligations, then for the most part leisure is one of the contexts in which informal groupings can well be observed.

The process of sociability

People search out other people in leisure because informality provides a psychological and emotional release from conscious, normal social roles. As a banker, father, mayor, or lawyer, our professional or functional behavior is based on actions and ways of speech expected of us and for which we have been trained. These patterns are either grown into gracefully, and the way of life becomes natural, or (in part, at least) the lawyer, undertaker, and others pose in gesture, style of conversation, and general deportment. Thus in a social situation with no functional or productive significance we purposely expose ourselves in terms of our "real" selves and "break through" others, seeing them for what they "really are."

The relation between these psychological and sociological realities of functional and nonfunctional roles can be a delicate one and sometimes difficult to disentangle. We recall the story of a friend, a teacher of music in a private boys' school. After a dinner to which he had been invited by the parents of one of his wealthy students, the family and guest sat and talked. Then the musician was invited to play on his violin; he did so. (Note that he had been asked to bring the instrument on a "social" call.) The host was a lawyer; a while later the violinist brought up a matter of some property trouble. When asked for advice, the lawyer stiffened and told his guest to call for an appointment, that he never did business at home. Apparently, one of the parties was expected to merge his roles; the other would not permit this.

What, then, are the obligations to others within the ideal construct of leisure? To say there is none—that normal roles have been completely suspended—is seldom true. Among the obvious reasons are that persons react differently to the opposite sex and that one seeks to turn conversation to topics in which he is somewhat secure, often stemming from his usually defined role. Yet, in sociability the obligation to behave in expected ways is relatively less than in other situations. The expected pattern in this regard varies among groups and bears a relation to such factors as age, sex, and social class. The aristocracy of Europe, the wealthy landowners of Argentina, or the "upper-uppers" of Philadelphia and Boston exhibit differences among themselves but display a uniformity when set against social gatherings of friendship patterns within the same cultural areas among peasants, workers, or *petit bourgeoisie*.

Georg Simmel's insights into sociability still remain the classic in the field and have formed the basis of our discussion.[4] The key to his analysis is found in this observation:

Inasmuch as in the purity of its manifestations, sociability has no objective purpose, no content, no extrinsic results, it entirely depends on the personalities among whom it occurs. But precisely because everything depends on their personalities, the participants are not permitted to stress them too conspicuously. . . . Tact, therefore, is here of such peculiar significance. . . .[5]

Simmel introduces the term "sociability threshold" as the point at which content or subjective aspects enter the scene. We have here a relationship in which each person acts *as if* all were equals; this is not a lie, any more than art or play are social lies. It becomes a real lie when the ostensibly self-contained phenomenon is a deception played for ulterior purpose.

It would seem possible for empirical research to construct scale measurements or observations of two factors: first, one's interest in people *as people,* apart from their extrinsic valuations; second, one's level of personal security when confronted with verbal thrusts and explorations. With these it may then be possible to predict, hence to check, the behavior of types of persons in an atmosphere of sociability. Kurt Lewin's comments on national character types will be recalled; he notes that the stranger can break through to the American person quickly but then finds it hard to get at his core, his deeper thoughts or feelings; the German person is more difficult to know at first, but once rapport is established he will bare his inner thoughts.[6]

A relationship exists between sociability and our American value of "individual personality." There exists a general feeling that individuality is something of an assertiveness. To be "one's self" is not easy, for it implies "standing up" against pressures for conformity. To have individuality is to be relatively free, either in leading or following, in originating action or responding to someone else's prior action. Yet individuality comes not out of self-isolation but exactly the opposite: its test is among other people.

It is, of course, true that many feel a lack of independent thought, or of the "inner resources," fundamental to individuality. They may be at home in the momentary or fragmentary relationships that are proper at a party but quite lost in the open scrutiny of person in this situation. Although, as Simmel noted, there is no *content* in sociability, no content is needed between two people for one to uncover the second as shallow or dull, which even small talk may reveal. It has often been remarked that Americans have lost the art of conversation; if so, it is both a result of less sociability and a cause of it. Lewin's observation of our ease at getting to know other Americans on the surface, but seldom going very far, would seem to result naturally from concentrations of population, from persons rubbing shoulders with many others, but never for very long.

The presence of the mass media in America is a second factor in producing a paradoxical situation. For although listening or watching movies, radio, and TV does reduce the actual time in which people may need to talk to one another, it also serves to provide topics of conversation that are safe and inconsequential, hence not threatening to the conversants. Leo Bogart makes this observation: [7]

> The mass media provide a natural source of such conversational material. They are by nature impersonal, there being no direct interaction between artist and audience. Their heroes, symbols, and themes are part of a common universe of discourse. They are familiar to all; their meanings are clear and stereotyped. They interest people without threatening them. Since they belong to the world of imagination, they are not obviously value-laden. Nonetheless, they are close enough to unconscious fantasies to permit identification and to create interest. Thus the newspaper comic strips, and the press generally, with television, radio, the popular magazines, and the motion pictures all provide grist for the mill of conversation in America today.

A third factor touching upon sociability is the ease with which one can make of himself a stranger. Urban numbers make it possible for the Chicagoan to be lost in the crowd or lonely on State Street and Madison. The same factor, large numbers, makes it possible to find persons with similar interests, ranging from enthusiasm for flying to collecting bugs. The second aspect of numbers is that here one is in a position to make an adventure of new friends, of sorting them, matching them, rejecting and accumulating them. This romance in friendships, quite common in a transient area such as Los Angeles or Washington, D. C., is both a cause of complaint and of freedom. Like other freedoms, this wide choice in friendships is interpreted by some participants as a source of superficiality. To others this means a welcome release from the lack of alternative friendships within the small town. Recent study tends to recognize more than before the presence of strong primary groups in the metropolitan area. It also casts suspicion on the statement that the large center is capable only of preserving cold and tenuous human relationships.

Several variables discussed in Part 1 are now briefly related to our present type of leisure: work, family, and religion.

Relations to work

Riesman has made a telling point that we work harder at play and play harder at work. Certainly the contemporary factory or large business is laid out and managed to achieve maximum social freedom consonant with productivity. *Fortune* describes the careful planning that went into new quarters for the Connecticut General Insurance Company, in which every level of employee contributed to the plans for social as well as work needs.[8] This situation is not the rule. Yet personalization in work has gone far. Coffee breaks, more women at work, more use of machines, well-organized recreational programs in the plant, a pleasanter physical environment for work—all of these must be taken into account as we consider the apparently lesser degrees of sociability in the American home.

One of the issues, therefore, is the *quality* of sociability *within* a work situation. Does it offer as much choice in selecting one's friends as in a nonwork situation? Do class lines exist in the large factory or office building, so that typists, secretaries, junior and senior executives, accountants, and clerks (or foremen, time-study men, watchmen, skilled craftsmen, unskilled workers) are clearly defined in coffee breaks, factory picnics, industrial choruses, or baseball teams? As a consultant in 1954 to SPEBSQSA, Inc. ("barbershoppers") an organization whose general principles deserve great respect, the writer put this question: how much overlapping of ranks is found in a quartet that emerges from a work situation? Very little, he was informed. Yet, in his *Fortune* studies on the expected social life of young executives and their wives [9] William Whyte indicated that there is a considerable degree of intermingling of social ranks in the evolving industrial pattern.

Family

We have already referred to the family as a classical model for understanding sociability. The subject can center either on sociability patterns within the family or between families.

Within the family we refer to interrelationships between members *outside* their functional roles as parent or child. Clear lines cannot be drawn between the quality of a relationship in which a mother feeds her child or plays with it. But such relationships exist in fact. The point was made in Chapter 5 that the contemporary American family is less unified on a functional basis, more unified on a leisure-time basis. Another way of saying this is that today more conversation in the home can be eliminated without disrupting the essential economic, social, or sociability patterns needed to keep the family intact. This is so because in a situation in which persons are true values a larger symbolic range of communication takes over: little things, gestures, small motions become clearer as there is closer rapport.

There is a deep-laden assumption in much of our thinking that because we can talk, we should; that husband and wife who constantly converse, even in "small talk," are somehow happier than the couple who may be silent together for many minutes. If it is true that television has cut out much conversation that might otherwise take place, it may also have cut out much small talk on a level no higher than the mediocre material in the mass media. And TV has relieved many of us of the burden of going beyond small talk.

Since we are in the realm of observation and common sense on much of this until science has more to offer on the effects of the mass media, we dare go even further: perhaps a respectable form of sociability is that in which two or more people can be together, quite silent, reacting to a common stimulus—someone in the room (alive or on a screen), reading, acting, making faces, or trying to be funny. There are no statistics, if these be the *sine qua non*, to show that couples who divorce have talked less to each other than other couples. Perhaps they talked more, and intensely!

There are stereotypes of the old days when families visited one another and everyone, parents and children together, talked, played games, and sang around the piano. It will be recalled that former generations had fewer choices of activity. If they were together more, it was a situation largely defined for them by circumstances. There has been, further, considerable evidence of increasing sociability since World War II, brought about by such factors as suburban expansion, a higher birth rate (children help create friendships among adults), and greater ability to escape from TV.

The back-yard movement that accompanies suburban life creates interfamily visiting. The outdoor trend noted in figures on fishing, camping, motoring (see Chapter 1) brings us into contact with families from other styles of life. When over 100 million Americans visit the national parks in one summer, a tremendous informal sociability has taken place. No one can tell or measure the net result.

Religion

As a community institution, the Church has taken on elements of a social center. We have seen that this has been one of its accommodations to the realities of present life. We have also noted, in Mt. Holyoke, the pattern in which a religious content is brought into a social situation. The Protestants, also, but in a less direct fashion, seek to insure that their young people will meet with other young people through the Church. Thus the sociability of this group is "wholesome," somewhat planned, and the content of meetings is consonant with Church teachings.

On the theological level, many references are found in the Old and New Testaments on friendship: "Faithful are the wounds of a friend" (Proverbs xxvii:6); "This is my beloved, and this is my friend" (Song of Solomon v:16); "Make to yourselves friends" (Luke xvi:9); "Greater love hath no man than this, that a man lay down his life for his friends" (John xv:13). In the matter of conversation, there is deep concern for the ills that can follow irresponsible talk: "Be ye holy, in all manner of conversation" (1 Peter i:15); "Let no corrupt communication proceed out of your mouth, but that which is good to the use of edifying, that it may minister grace unto the hearers" (Ephesians iv:29).

Possibilities and prospects

A full development of sociability is difficult to envision in our type of society. We live hurriedly; we move our residences often; there is much to see, many places to go. It is perhaps reasonable to assume that we can hardly expect the comforts and efficiency of industrialism while still maintaining the deepest values of a pretechnological era. Just as in the exchange for socialization the child surrenders some of his imagination, so the price of atomic energy is a world of change and impersonalization.

The intimate history of this country, with its generosity and ideals in what Gunnar Myrdal has called The American Creed,[10] also has some chapters of ruthlessness, inhumanity, personal and community coldness, clear divisions of "we" and "they," and inhospitality to stranger and immigrant. What would the Fromms and the Horneys of former days have written? Nor can one find a one-to-one relationship between preindustrial society and a respect for personality, friendship, or *Gemeinschaft*. If historical factors are taken into account, one becomes more cautious before making sweeping condemnations of the lack of sociability in present-day America.

Finally, what are the potentials in sociability as a form of leisure? In Table 4 of Chapter 1 no person had checked "with family" as a form of preferred leisure. This may mean only that few people think of time with the family as *leisure;* such action falls under *love, responsibility, expected behavior, good family life,* or *obligation.*

The purpose of this chapter has been, in one sense, to submit the proposition that, *notwithstanding change in family and community life, sociability is still a persistent form in which people meet basic social needs to belong, to assert themselves, to explore others in depth;*

in which the person learns more about himself, how to communicate, how to bring tact into social relationships. At the same time, it is a difficult form of leisure for some who are unsure of themselves and devoid of anything to communicate.

We turn, in Chapter 13 to a form of leisure in which communication is more purposeful, for it centers on a common interest.

Association as leisure 13

The concept

Sociability is a relationship with a minimum of content other than interest in persons. Association is characterized by content, by a common interest that is more important than people. Hence more structured roles will be expected. The interests, with accompanying sentiments about them [(a) dogs; (b) be kind to dogs] may center on almost anything from a shared hobby such as collecting stamps to a shared political belief.

Contrary to many who assert that most Americans are lonely, living anonymous lives removed from the interests of others, the facts point to a nation of joiners. As a shrewd observer of American life, Donald Bell points out: [1]

> There are in the United States today at least 2,000,000 voluntary organizations, associations, clubs, societies, lodges, and fraternities with an aggregate (but obviously overlapping) membership of close to eighty million men and women. In no other country in the world, probably, is there such a high degree of voluntary communal activity, expressed sometimes in absurd rituals, yet often providing real satisfaction for real needs.

Arnold Rose points out that, although no international comparisons of membership exist for voluntary associations, if the United States does lead, there may be a legal reason: [2]

> The First Amendment to the United State Constitution specifies the right of all citizens peaceably to assemble and the courts have always interpreted that to mean the right to form free associations. On the other hand, democratic countries like France and Italy have had a history of restrictive legislation with respect to voluntary associations, and still other democratic countries, like Great Britain and Switzerland, have never put either encouragements or restrictions into their laws.

It must be noted that a sociability can easily arise (or the reverse) in an association. Millions of persons who met during World War II through a joint interest in civil defense, as volunteers for Red Cross activities, or in the military itself have remained friends on a purely social basis. The Ku Klux Klan serves as an example in reverse, a case in which a program for social action resulted when bored young men, sitting around, looked for a source of excitement.

Functions and roles

Voluntary associations provide many functions, quite aside from their contributions vis-à-vis the explicit interest. It is here, for instance, that millions of microscopic political structures are created, so that agencies for leadership and for "followership" are achieved. An army of "presidents," "sergeant-at-arms," etc., is to be found in every town, city, village, or hamlet. Millions of cards are mailed every month by "corresponding secretaries," and perhaps millions of dollars are collected by treasurers across the land. These are offices created partly on a functional basis, of course, to keep the group machinery going and partly as a device for involving many persons. As much as we must say that these offices find the men and women to occupy them, so, too, men and women deliberately create these responsibilities in order to have something in which to become involved, to achieve some status, to exercise power, to feel important. Within the perspective of the Tuesday Study Club, decisions that are taken by officers or members are as important and dramatic as those made by the President of the United States and the Congress and, indeed, occupy more of their attentive and anxious interest. Matters of fame, significance, drama, importance, or reputation must always be seen against the respective mental world that is involved. Certainly, the leadership experience to be found in decision making or in the small political manipulation within leisure time associations is an important training center. From such political "sandlots" come the "big leagues."

Another function of voluntary associations is to provide a meeting place for people whose ideas or interests are similar. Thus, especially in a large city, primary groups are made and vicinal proximity becomes less significant than in a smaller community.

Third, as a member of a club or group with a goal, one's leisure takes on direction and the perceptions of constructive living. This is especially needed by persons who feel guilt at wasting time or doing nothing. A deep psychological, perhaps even a religious, sense of duty or ethics enters here.

Personal growth and information are found in voluntary associations. Yet it needs to be added that in the arguments, bickerings, intrigues, electioneering, and enmities, which also characterize such groups, is to be found the nourishment that makes life interesting to many people. Leisure activity, in this sense, is also constructive, if that word is used generously. Shared struggles and defeats, as well as common victories, provide solidarity as well as factionalism.

In summary, the association as a form of leisure goes far beyond the stated objectives of the group. The organization or role grows largely out of the tradition and circumstance of the group. A local Masonic lodge has its hierarchical pattern already established for it. Elaborate study, followed by tests and probationary periods, is prescribed to graduate its members into various "degrees." [3]

In many associations, perhaps less in the Masons than in others, there is a correlation between role position in and out of the group. A member is more likely to be elevated within the association if he has, in "normal" life, proved successful according to general societal standards. Persons are members of several groups or social circles; although these circles do not provide a uniform status across the board, the key role that is recognized by the society (examples: banker, teacher, millionaire) does often find its way or its reflection even in the world of play and associations.

Several important studies of associations in American life cut across the variables we have discussed in Part 2 of this book. Professor F. A. Bushee of the University of Colorado examined 268 social organizations for adults in Boulder.[4] Although 29 per cent of the population belonged to no groups in 1945, 71 per cent of all adults belong to one or more, many to 16 groups. Women there join more than men and attend meetings more regularly. Most popular are the religious groups, followed by educational, social, and recreational. Best attended are the luncheon clubs; poorest attended are the fraternal groups. The average group has 65 members, or one for each 48 persons in the community (compared to one per 73 persons in Middletown). Motivations for membership, writes Bushee, are religion, followed by self-improvement, social recognition, and reform.

Several years later Professor Stuart Queen of Washington University found in another community that the more education there was among club members, the more participation could be expected in the club. Lower economic status went with lower participation. Negroes did more "neighboring" than whites.[5]

Relations to social factors and work

A later study by Floyd Dotson verifies Queen's findings: those with higher incomes join more groups.[6] Mirra Komarovsky studied 2223 adults of New York City with incomes of 2000 to 15,000 dollars.[7] She divided them into five categories in order to observe the percentage of each belonging to a "voluntary association," excluding church:

Unskilled   32% belong to one or more associations
Semiskilled   44% belong to one or more associations
White-collar   47% belong to one or more associations
Business   67% belong to one or more associations
Professional   68% belong to one or more associations

Contrary to Bushee, Komarovsky found more men than women in organizations, even among higher-incomed groups. She emphasizes that not all urbanites are joiners; indeed, that many are cut off from channels of power, information, and growth.

Several general comments are made on an impressionistic basis of general developments. It is not a simple thing to define or to tabulate the number and variety of clubs even within one medium-sized community, much less the entire country. In 1956–1957 the writer was one of a group seeking to build a public building in an Illinois community of 70,000. A survey was conducted to measure the need for such a building. Our list of organizations came to more than 400; among them were auxiliaries and offshoots, especially among patriotic and fraternal groups, organizations created to hold a dance once a year, and groups whose functions it was impossible to determine even from their officers.

In relation to work, these kinds of issues arise: if in the decades ahead it develops that work does not provide a synthesis around which lives are organized, can voluntary associations become, more than in the past, an area of commitment that will (as in the case of Westchester) remove it from the mental realm of leisure?

Personality

As a basis for needed research, several questions can be posed:

1. Do certain kinds of associations attract certain kinds of persons?

2. Within the formal structure of associations, what is the process through which leadership is discovered or asserted and what is the relation of such leaders to the roles they take outside the association?

3. How do associations provide innovators, creative persons, and

"good neighbors" to make themselves felt or to be, in the words of Sorokin, "creative altruists"? [8]

In each of these questions direct bearing is to be found on major issues of leisure: the directions it takes, its relations to nonleisure social roles, and its potential for personality expression and constructive meaning. As lesiure becomes a direct topic for social research, personality studies will need to move from the laboratory or the paper-questionnaire contexts to living situations.

A division of the interests of associations, as in Bushee's classification, is an index to the life directions and goals of its members as well as the character of a community. For research purposes, it should be possible to develop a weighting for each type of interest in relation to types of criteria or concerns. Examples of the criteria would be the degree of obligation, personal commitment, local or national orientation, rational action, personal autonomy, permissive deviancy (tolerance of individuality), leadership posts for the "inner-" and "other-directed" persons, conflict potential, and so on. A guess at the findings, if these concerns were applied to three types of association—political, religious, fraternal—would place each in the respective categories of *most, medium,* and *least:*

P = political group; R = religious; F = fraternal.

	Most	Medium	Least
Social obligation	F	R	P
Personal commitment	R	P	F
Local orientation	F	P	R
National orientation	R	P	F
Rational action	F	P	R
Personal autonomy	P	F	R
Permissive deviancy	P	F	R
"Inner-directed" leadership	R	F	P
"Other-directed" leadership	P	F	R
Conflict potential	P	F	R

Each of the categories needs refining, but already some prediction is implied from such a scheme. For example, personal counseling for retirement or for advisable leisure choices might reveal that Case A, known to be a person who is *locally orientated* and *inner-directed,* seeks to avoid conflict, etc., and is advised to select X type of association in which he is less likely to find himself ill at ease.

This approach may also help in studying how time is used by persons with "talent" for its use. Much of our science has observed the lives of persons in trouble. There is need for a knowledge of their opposites. Sorokin puts the matter thus: [9]

> For decades Western social science has been cultivating, *urbi et orbi*, an ever-increasing study of crime and criminals; of insanity and the insane; of sex perversion and perverts; of hypocrisy and hypocrites. A vast set of special disciplines has been developed for these purposes: criminology and penology, with their subdivisions and branches; psychiatry, psychoanalysis and mental hygiene, with still more numerous branches and proliferations. . . . In contrast to this Western science has paid scant attention to positive types of human beings, their positive achievements, their heroic actions, and their positive relationships. . . .

Just as the disorganized person is viewed as one whose difficulties are a part of the groups and the norms he finds himself with, so we can develop ways of looking at "well" people and find that they are well in part because of a favorable combination of groups.

Family and class

Numerous relationships were drawn in Chapter 5 between family and associations: the fact that specialized community groups exist for various age groups, that groups provide a content outside friendship that can be carried back into the home; the power of women's organizations; finally, associations as a means of stability for mobile populations.

Subcultures

Minority groups will often be found to have associations of two types: one, to provide a positive content to represent and conserve the group's cultural heritage; two, to fight for its legal, economic, or social rights. For example, the N.A.A.C.P., at one time primarily an action group of white persons in the field of civil rights, is now run by Negroes with the second objective. The Jews have such groups as the B'nai B'rith, a fraternal society that spans both purposes. Yet both types of groups are also sources of sociability while serious business is at hand. Our view of leisure has not been to describe it exclusively as light, pleasurable, or only inconsequential.

To restate the matter: to be a member of a social action group may have direct results in the political or social life of the community. At the same time, participation may meet personal needs, such as a sense of belonging, doing, living fully, being needed, making history, and finding personal direction. The combination of obligation to a purpose outside oneself and one's personal satisfactions can provide relaxation that is different in quality from complete withdrawal from meaningful activity.

Community

The continuing trend toward urbanization has had an effect on the way in which associations are used for leisure purposes. On the one hand, the city is requisite in a technical society. One result is the mass media. And the mass media are substitutes for person-to-person communication. This tends to destroy one's need for clubs and their purpose as a setting for sheer talk on a level and in a style different from home, street, or work situations. Middletown studies noted the decline in the spoken word. On the other hand, urban expansion, at least until the World War II period, produced smaller families. The new communities, many of them consisting of homogeneous young families with small children, have seen a renewed interest in PTA's, church activity, and committees for neighborhood and city improvement. In some housing developments such committees or councils are formed as soon as the young parents have their furniture in place and a baby sitter on call. These groups are also marked by an informality that reflects the entire suburban way of life.

In our rural life the last generation has been one of immense growth of 4-H Clubs, Future Farmers of America, the Farmers Union, and other important groups. These groups serve many functions, not the least of which is social. It is doubtful whether their growth has been impeded by television. Rather, the mass media have played a major part in equalizing the cultural "intake" of farm and city families. Transportation facilities now permit a wider geographical world for the rural person. Rural associations have been agencies through which it has been possible to retain some of the basic values of person-to-person contact on a social level and to enliven or deepen such relationships with content of information and social action.

Ritual and ceremony—secular potentials

Chapter 10 contained a summary of the attitude of religious groups to voluntary associations in a Massachusetts community. The study of ritual and ceremony in organizations provides another relationship. Ritual is a repetitive set of actions in which the *doing* becomes an end; ceremony is an irregular set of actions for an important but not a regular event. In both cases the symbols of the group are brought together—important persons, holy books, flags, emblems, oaths, and so on. Although these are not limited to the church, it is in the religious institution that we have classic examples of both ritual and ceremony.

One of the elements of leisure noted in Chapter 2 is a minimum of social role obligations. Play and leisure often establish a precise role for the participant, but they call for a function quite different from that ordinarily performed: the store clerk is a "sergeant-at-arms" for the I.O.O.F. on Wednesday night. Only in sociability does one seek to shed all functional roles except that of friend; in many other activities he is actually in search of roles that spring from a variety of motivations, such as escape, exhibitionism, return to childhood, power, or new friends.

Further, the strength of role expectations in society is that they facilitate social order. As soon as the Twelfth Street Gang convenes in its clubhouse, a fantasy takes place as the boys go through a metamorphosis from Joe to President, from Jim to treasurer, from Tom and Sam and Larry to members. Thus a pattern, social recipe, or behavioral mold is now filled by the human raw material upon the descent of a gavel. In its most complete form this social mold is more than a bare set of rules for procedure. It is enriched by symbolic names for officers, by meaningful objects, and by oaths, words, and songs. This type of leisure action is so serious, indeed, that life as a whole has more than the two orientations, work and nonwork.

We can divide our days into (a) those details of living as a person and family member: eating, shaving, washing, raising children; (b) activities that introduce us to patterns of group and community life not objectively essential to sheer maintenance but essential to personal and social order; (c) productive economic work for maintaining life. A rough comparison of these spheres suggests that work is structured on function, personal and family life on habit and custom, and associations on symbolic relationships.

This leads to the observation that ties both ritual and ceremony to leisure. It is a mistake to assume that free time is spent in seeking freedom from commitment, ritual, or social forms. Man—and child, too— finds security in authority of persons and ways. His "escape from freedom" does not mean that he rejects it. There are many kinds of freedom, including that which comes from predictability—a freedom from uncertainty and choice. This helps to explain why some persons, given time to do with it as they wish, will choose to toil over a game requiring skill and discipline or over an artistic activity that demands great concentration and a "sacrifice" of activities automatically available to the person "free" from self-imposed aesthetic problems. In the game, the artistic experience, or the meeting man does not surrender himself or his freedoms: he finds a new life in the conflicts, the discussions, the sense of accomplishment. And in each case the rituals bring comfort and a recognition of the familiar; from the ceremony he gets a reaffirmation of his world.

Might it be that in an age of leisure—brought about by science—the return to religion expresses a fear of *leisure as freedom*, that ritual and rite are an easier path than rationality? And if the institution of religion itself is not acceptable in its old forms, does the voluntary organization not become a substitute, providing the form if not always the substance? In this sense, finally, leisure that finds expression in associating with other persons can be a deep commitment that is still void of significance. We all know that very often an organization of men and women is very busy, very devoted, very ritual-minded—over *nothing*. But *belonging* is important. *The potentiality of this leisure type is most realized when there is belonging based on substantive believing and a goal-centered becoming.*

As we move into a third type of leisure, a new dimension is added to mere belonging—the dimension of *direction* toward a victory and the rules that control the *style* or form in which the contest will take place.

Games and sport as leisure 14

Games

From sociability and association we move to a type of human relationship that is relatively less concerned with persons and more with structure. A game is a situation in which one or more persons emerges from a regulated series of actions as the "winner" or the "loser." Thus we have, in its most basic form, activity that involves (*a*) more than one person, (*b*) a climax and struggle, (*c*) a consciousness of victory, defeat, or "draw," and (*d*) rules accepted by learning or under certain formalized situations requiring a judge of some sort.

This definition of games cannot insure easy recognition of its elements, for, as Jerome Fried points out, sometimes games "are mysterious matters, closely linked with religious beliefs or customs. . . ." [1]

There are several observations to be made about games in general before we relate them to characteristics of American life.

The rules are supposed to create a fair or just set of conditions. As in norms of social structure in general, an equilibrium of freedom and obligation is established. Thus, by its inherent quality of restraint for the "good" of the ongoing game, the situation lends itself to moralizing and, further, to serving as a *model* for life outside the game. When English society speaks of "sportsmanship," it is referring to a model taken from an upper-class sport such as the fox hunt. But fox hunting is more than one person pursuing an animal; it involves elaborate rituals, dress, and conditions of pursuit. Since it is a distinct phase of human activity to which virtues are *given*, these virtues are then also *taken from* it and appropriated to general life. Teamwork on the baseball field becomes a slogan for the factory; fair play in games is applied in grand fashion to the whole economy. Yet men who run the factory and the economy have in a real sense put these qualities *into* games in

189

order to have a source of sanction understood by large numbers, for
the old sanction or religious teaching has weakened and needs to be
supplemented. We have, then, more than the problem of games as a
moral receptacle. There is also the interesting problem of transference of morality within spheres of the culture.

It would perhaps be fair to say that the considerable justification
given by the recreation profession for its work is the *transference of
morality*, of good qualities, from the play to the nonplay world. Actually, one can be a first-rate "sport" on the playground and a scoundrel
away from it. How one behaves, in part at least, stems from the atmosphere, the values, the controls within the group itself, the behavior
of other people, and one's position in the group. Further, we have
abandoned the notion that skills, attitudes, or virtues are automatically
transferred from one activity to another, although such a possibility
under the right conditions is by no means denied.

A second characteristic of games is that although two or more people
are involved—or one imagines the presence of the others—these persons are not present in their usual capacities. To understand this, an
introductory comment on social roles will take us further into the
theory than was necessary in Chapter 4.

My name is John Smith. I am a husband, a father, a grandfather, a
Protestant, a shoemaker, a member of the Oddfellows, a Democrat, a
citizen of Brooklyn, a friend of Tony, and a bowler in the neighborhood team. Each of these positions or functions means that within a
given relationship (father-wife-children or congregant-minister) I am
expected to do certain things; I get back certain rewards or rights because I do those things (income, right to a church seat, right to vote,
etc.); I get an idea of how important I am and, indeed, even of my "personality" or my "self" in each of those circles or relationships. In the
two most important theoretical expositions of this whole process the
anthropologist Ralph Linton speaks of role as what one does and status
as one's position.[2] The eminent sociologist Florian Znaniecki speaks of
social role as a composite of social circle, function, status or esteem,
and a conception of oneself in the role.[3] Within either analysis, a person has many roles, as he moves from one circle to another.

In a discussion of sociability it was noted that functional social roles
are eliminated. Quite the opposite is the case in games. Each person is
arbitrarily given a new social role, but it is neither social nor occupational. Rather, one becomes a baseball shortstop, South in a bridge
game, guard on the football field, goalie in hockey. Znaniecki's four
elements are present. Each of these titles or positions involves a circle
of players, within which the particular role plays or functions; it de-

rives rights (dealing, batting, etc.) and even a psychological association or prestige and associated "character."

Yet although roles both in human relationships and in games contain all the essential elements, the most important difference is that in games these rules arise not out of *social* but out of *nonsocial* assumptions of the good behavior. Game rules, unlike norms of life, are arbitrary and relatively little affected by cultural differences.[4]

A third aspect of games is their relation to play. To play is to exaggerate, to objectify, to back up and look anew: to play "house," to play "school." The qualities most important here are imagination, pleasantry, and social comment. Play may be present in a game, of course, and ideally the whole game is supposed to be play. Actually, with pressures to win or perform well, a game may be more like work than play. The case is often made that in America this compulsiveness with which we feel we must play and play hard and well robs it of its original intent and thus becomes a deception. The pure model of play comes from childhood, and its essence there is delight and interplay of the real and the imagined.[5]

It is possible for an adult "playwright" to amplify his observations stylistically into a full-length "play," which may, in fact, move so far from its origins as to end in tragedy. Even then, the tragic portrayal may be considered a "good play," for it has used certain devices to make its observations on life effectively, with a proper juxtaposition of reality and illusion.

Games, in summary, are one form of play. Play, for its part, is unlimited in its scope or context and may quickly enter realms of work, sex relations, business relations, or, on some occasions, even religious activity.[6]

Sports

Gregory Stone's insights on sports are in good part devoted to the nature of its audiences. A recent paper reports on his interviews with 127 adults, of whom half were men and more than half were over 40 years of age.[7]

One issue is the way in which *talk* about sports becomes a solidifying force in the society—talk as a "community of experience." This talk need not be about participation, but about *others*, such as Joe Louis or a baseball team. Sixty per cent of the men and one third of the women reported frequent or very frequent talk about sports. Of these men, most come from the middle or lower socioeconomic stratum. However, more women than men discuss sports while *at home*, especially women of the middle and upper-class groups. These women, notes Stone,[8]

> . . . rarely exhibit expertise in matters of sport; yet, their efforts to acquaint themselves with the area were characterized by great self-consciousness and resolve. I have the distinct impression that these women are rather compulsively entering the world of sport—grasping at this among many other straws—to reassure themselves that their marriage is, indeed, "companionate."

We may recall the comment made in Chapter 2 that any specific activity can become a basis for leisure. Stone bears this out even in reference to the activities that people associate with the term "sports." In addition to the recognized games, these included dancing, television, movies, wood working, and sex.

Additional findings by Stone may be briefly summarized: men develop loyalties to teams earlier than women. Interest in golf increases with wealth; not so with baseball and basketball. Middle-class groups appear to outweigh wealthier men as sport spectators rather than participants. Again, turning to the family, Stone judges from his Minneapolis informants, that "a kind of desperate situation is suggested, where the middle-class husband is pulled away from home by sport while the middle-class housewife strains mightily to pull him back into the home." [9]

He presents data to support a hypothesis that "as the professionalization of sport continues, socioeconomic differences in the audience will disappear." Finally, Stone has some sensitive insights on spectatorship.

> With the massification of sport, spectators begin to outnumber participants in overwhelming proportions, and the spectator, as the name implies, encourages the spectacular—the display. In this regard the spectator may be regarded as an agent of destruction as far as the dignity of sport is concerned. There is a tension between the morality of the game and the amorality of the spectator (immoral in its consequences).

> However, spectators are hardly discouraged from attending or viewing the game. I have shown, too, that spectatorship may have important consequences for promoting the solidarity of the larger society and its instituted relations, such as the work relation, the family, and other regularized intimacies. In addition, spectatorship may not be as pervasive as it seemed to one who is a spectator. Finally, the consequences of spectatorship may not be grossly different from the consequences of participation. It seems quite clear that what troubles us about the contemporary state of American sport is its promotion, not its attendance or popularity.[10]

Thus, as Stone indicates, an inquiry into sports can hardly be made without a close look at many institutions of American life. Yet sports have a long tradition in all parts of the world and, similarly, reveal aspects of the total culture in which they find themselves. Contemporary Europe provides an example.

Games and sports in contemporary Europe

The following extracts are taken from a private report by Dr. Seward Staley, head of the Department of Physical Education at the University of Illinois.[11] Professor Staley's report covers conditions in France, Spain, England, Portugal, Switzerland, Italy, Germany, Austria, and Holland, where he visited service and training institutions and facilities having to do with physical education, gymnastic activities, and teacher training.

Dr. Staley notes a steady increase in all areas of sports since World War II, explainable by increased leisure and a widespread sensitivity to maintain "individual and national vitality." The most popular sports in Europe today are hiking, soccer, gymnastics, skiing, cycling, and swimming. Camping is popular everywhere. Paris has 15 judo clubs. Handball has gradually spread. Gymnastics shows signs of declining interest, as does fencing. Basketball and volleyball, introduced by American soldiers in World War I, are now widely played. American baseball has never caught the imagination of Europeans. Local sports clubs are found everywhere, sponsoring one to 20 or more different sports. Some of these are sponsored by churches or political parties. Membership may range from 15 to 5000, with the commonest between 30 and 100. For example, Nice (population 225,000) has 100 sports clubs totaling 40,000 members; Munich (population, one million) has 300 sports clubs with 200,000 members; Paris (population, 2.5 million) lists almost 600 sports clubs.

Dr. Staley concludes his report:

> Most Americans are disposed to assume that the American people are more sport-minded . . . than any other national group. . . . There are no studies bearing on the subject and it would be exceedingly difficult to make one. . . . I came home with a very definite impression that, percentagewise, there is more active participation and more interest in most of the countries visited than in the United States. Portugal, Spain, Italy, and France are the possible exceptions. A difference in climatic conditions, and/or economic conditions, and/or national temperament may explain the difference which seems to exist between northern and southern Europe.

American factors

Games are more than a reflection of other activities of life; they are in their own right a part of the way of life of a people. It might even be said, in view of the great emphasis placed upon games and sports in the United States today, that games form the distinctive feature of modern American life.[12]

In themselves, the available data about games in America are indeed impressive. Retail business in athletic goods totaled almost 310 million dollars in 1948. Almost 66 million dollars was spent on billiards and pool in the same year, 138 million dollars for bowling, and more than 175 million dollars for professional football and baseball. In respect to participants, the following figures appear for that year, in millions of persons: horseshoe players, 5; golf, 4; shuffleboard, 6; tennis, 2; bowling, 16–20; table tennis, 8–10. Similarly impressive are these numbers of spectators, also in millions: softball games, 125; basketball, 105; high school and college football, 65; auto races, 40; major- and minor-league baseball, 63; wrestling matches, 7. Unfortunately, these data do not account for the overlapping of persons nor for the number of times one person watched or participated in a particular kind of event.[13] We must look elsewhere for an understanding of the processes or implications behind such widespread participation or spectatorship.

As in preceding chapters, our procedure is to relate our immediate subject to several elements in the American scene covered in an earlier section of the book.

Work

Stone refers to sports as a "linkage of play and work form." This link developed with the growth of industrialism, for this system of economy brought play and work together. Until they exist on an equal basis, "sport has no major role in social life." [14] But when that happens, some participants convert play into work—for example, professional and subsidized athletes—whereas others make a work function into play—hunters, fishermen, campers, and "do-it-yourself" addicts. Spectator sports, then, rise as play becomes work; and participant sports develop as part of the process that changes work into play.

Thus the professional in sports *works* at the activity, with all the obligations and commitments and the unique contractual relationships of a professional person to a client. The amateur may engage in the same activity, but he is *playing* at it. His skill may be as high or higher. Whatever the origins of the professional player, he serves the audience and the amateur player in one of several ways: as teacher, model, or entertainer. To the middleman or businessmen, he is no more than a commodity, the price of which is based on supply and demand. In any of these roles there is a curious blend of work and play. The professional baseball player, for instance, is supposedly interested as much in winning for the sake of it as for the better salary or the World Series "cut." He falls in the estimation of the public if he displays no "spirit"; a balance of some sort exists between being a "sport" in face of the umpire's manifestly idiotic ruling and of standing up to him with the appropriate gestures of disgust—a worker demanding his due "pay."

What is involved here is a curious dilemma for the professional, but right-minded, player who attempts to minimize the indispensable audience. Gregory Stone treats this problem by noting the relations of "play" to "dis-play": dis-play, for example, means to "dress" for an audience, a symbolic way of "addressing" or playing *to* them.[15] A parallel has been drawn for the field of jazz music, as Howard S. Becker analyzed the jazzman's need of and disdain for his audience.[16]

As before, we are thus led to conceptualize the professional or amateur in games or sports in respect to obligations to the clientele or audience.[17] Whether such play is recreation, also, finds its solution in this analysis: players who are directly part of the economic system are working, not filling free time. The conscious presence of a network of obligations can become overbearing, and the game becomes a confused item in the scale of means and ends. For the worker, the game becomes an *end*, not a means to better work; for the businessman, the game, for example, golf, is a *means* to a "deal." Similarly, to an educational institution, such as a university, football was formerly a minor consideration for its participants, not the major part of their campus careers; now, as everyone knows but dares not always say publicly, the "spirit" of the game is carefully nurtured as a myth among the students and the public, but the "business" of the game goes directly into the matter of attracting victorious coaches and players, soliciting alumni contributions, and competing with other schools who carry on this subterfuge in their own way.

Thus work and play are in a state of flux.

Family

The relations of family life to games and sports are manifold, and the range of thinking is almost limitless. We could consider the *perception* of married life among children as exhibited in their games; we have already touched upon sex as a "game" (Chapter 5); the history of games reveals some that are traditionally for the whole family; the emancipation of women could be traced partly by their entry into the male world of games and sports. A major point of our discussion of the American family is that play or leisure becomes more than a mere diversion. "It becomes a cause, a clue, and an index of sources of respect, love, interdependence, knowledge about the other." [18] Implicit in this interpretation is the assumption that there has been some sort of role reversal: in the past the child played the game of being "mama" and "papa"; nowadays, the mother and father play the game in terms of childhood or for the love of the game.

When we seek to provide a systematic framework for understanding leisure, our task is to search not only for broad generalization and theory but also for some empirical, limited, repeatable kind of study. On the immediate issue, the place of the card game in family life is a limited but a valuable example.

Card playing has a long and honorable tradition. Ancient China and India had card games, and some historians claim that the wandering gypsies introduced cards into Europe about 500 years ago. Everywhere this tradition has been steeped in symbols of the period: the four suits are the four directions of the compass; the chance element in cards becomes interwoven with fortune telling (cartomancy); or, as in Medieval days, each suit represents something—hearts are for love, clubs are for knowledge or fertility, diamonds are for wealth, and spades represent death.

The close association of card playing with gambling led to the restriction of cards among children. Of all the ways in which young people have been encouraged to be like adults, serious card games have not been one. Thus the game of bridge is not firmly grounded in American life as a *family game* but as an *interfamily* game for adults. Poker is generally considered a game for men: it is based on bluffing, bold action, and more often than bridge it leads itself to gambling for money.

Robert Lynd, as part of the Middletown study, noted the increased popularity of bridge over the ten-year period covered in the two volumes.[19] This trend has not abated. One survey indicated that cards were played in 87 of every 100 American homes in 1942.[20] Over 50 million decks of cards are sold annually.

Of the functions served by bridge, Lynd has written,[21]

> Most people have but a spotty fund of knowledge with which to carry on a prolonged conversation without becoming "heavy" or disputatious. All of this tends to make the effort to carry on an evening of talk overstrenuous and likely to be judged in the end as "not having got anywhere." Into this problematic situation has come bridge, the hostess' best friend and the universal social solvent: safe, orthodox, and fun. Men and women who are not interesting talkers can still be good bridge players. Most people's lives involve but a meager amount of sheer fun; they are busy and preoccupied and perplexed as to what to do to make living more fun.

And most people, particularly men, in an urban culture crave more human contacts out of business hours with people they like in an atmosphere that liberates spontaneity. Neither the movies nor reading supply this sense of social participation. What bridge has done is to institutionalize fun-in-small-social-groups, at the same time that it is tending to drain serious talk from Middletown's leisure. It is an unparalleled device for an urban world that wants to avoid issues, to keep things impersonal, to enjoy people without laying oneself open or committing oneself to them, and to have fun in the process.

Again this is confirmed by a study of 1955 in Endicott, New York. Irving Crespi found that 57 per cent of the adults play cards regularly or occasionally.[22] The study of 275 persons sought to uncover significant characteristics of card players and the conditions under which they played. An impressive finding was the large proportion of persons who play at least once a week, yet express only a moderate interest in the game. Games are for the most part among primary groups (friends and family). Less than 25 per cent play for money stakes, usually very small. In another small group are the "skill players." The large majority "like to play cards because it enables them to experience the conviviality that stems from playing a game with people with whom they want to spend their leisure time." The motivations are social atmosphere, friendliness, a substitute for and a source of conversation, an inexpensive way of "going out," and a relaxing activity. On this evidence, Crespi concludes that the popularity of cards is not to be associated with a desire to gamble. It is rather "a group phenomenon and not a manifestation of social disorganization . . . reflects not moral regeneracy, but the struggle of primary groups to maintain their viability in the contemporary scene."

Social class

In Chapter 6 the point was made that in the past leisure activity was a major clue to social stratification; today, leisure is an important contributor to increasing classlessness. We prefer to speak of new styles of life whose patterns zigzag in such a complicated way that any threefold or sixfold subdivision becomes a serious oversimplification. The game is unique in evidence of this, for among the ways in which games serve as a device to separate people is that one or more of these factors may be involved:

Special equipment	horse, golf clubs, boat
Cost of participating	member of a polo club
Cost of watching	varying prices at a professional event

Time of game   afternoon, when most men are working
Special dress   riding habit
Travel costs   ski area
Expendable assets   gambling stakes

Beyond these objective factors have been the less tangible ones:
attitudes that associated a game with a social level. Squash, for instance,
is a game for the "uppers," but so was tennis at one time and certainly
golf. As our middle class expanded in numbers and in its breadth of
life, these attitudes gave way. In part, our level of material comfort
has gone up, notwithstanding the fact that the dollar of today is perhaps half its value in 1900. Our level of normal life, that is, our list
of essentials, has changed markedly: the middle-class professional man
is quite rational and reasonable nowadays in hoping to own a summer
home.

Consider the phenomenal growth in boating as another example.
In one year, 1955, estimated owners, crew or passengers shot up from
20 to 30 million persons. A total of 240 million dollars was spent for
boats and accessories (compared to 200 million dollars for hunting
and 150 million dollars for fishing). Boat designers, following the lead
of auto manufacturers, are now attracting the interest of women with
new styles and colors, and special instruction books are now prepared
for them. Hulls are designed to be carried on the top of a car or pulled
on a trailer. Florida, with its 30,000 lakes and almost 1400 miles of coast-
line, has begun to see long cruises in which as many as 75 boats will
sometimes sail as an organized group for long distances. Canada reports similar growth; about 700,000 sailing craft are registered, or
one for every 22 persons in the country.

Community

Relationships with leisure activity exist on many levels: rural and
urban types of games; geographical conditions, such as hills, warm
weather, outdoor patterns; community traditions and folk materials;
folk games; and the presence of tax-supported recreational professionals
whose function it is to introduce or lead games and other free-time
activities. It is our purpose to deal briefly with still another intercon-
nection: players as *collective* possessions, as symbols of the community
image of itself.

For what is the sense behind the vast psychological fantasy by
which eight cities play against each other in a baseball enterprise called
the American or National League or the dozens of other leagues

throughout the country? Everyone in Chicago or St. Louis or Detroit is completely aware that these teams are operated for profit. Salaries of each player are usually public knowledge. A steady stream of writings keeps alive a minute interest in every detail of "selling" and "buying" of players, of the farm systems, as well as other details of profit, loss, and paid attendance. Few if any of the players come from the community for which they play. No one has illusions on this score, least of all, the owners of the teams. For instance, in 1958 both the Giants and the Dodgers shifted to the West Coast. Attendance at Giant games had fallen from 1,600,793 in 1947 to 629,179 in 1956; Dodger attendance in the same period fell from 1,807,526 to 1,033,589.[23]

There is nothing else to equal this collective delusion of possession. If one looks at the St. Louis Symphony, there is no analogy: the orchestra members are also hired, but they are not traded in a feudal-like arrangement among managements; further, these players have many other roots in the community, as teachers, performers, and generally as older persons with more family obligations and local roots than the young athletes.

It is true that to be a resident of a community is to be more than a geographical datum. A person's total activities, his circle of friends, the quality of his work—all begin to blot out lines between *me* and *us* or between the individual and the total images that identify him with others. And even these "others" are more than a congeries of the many. The collectivity is supraindividual and supragroup; it achieves a common identity in such symbols as its name, a unique landmark, pride in a famous personage, or some historical tradition.

The competitive quality of the game emphasizes its uniqueness for this purpose. We are reminded of the Greek city-states, when physically close cities were proud of local dress or speech mannerisms, songs, and dances. These belonged uniquely to each. The competitive game is superior to these, in that the contest against the other team—actually, the other city—is a harmless way, but nevertheless a clear way, of fighting, struggling, competing with an outside "enemy." The conflict unifies each camp, for competition between groups strengthens the bonds *within* each.

State

Obvious relationships exist between government and games and sports: revenue from admissions to professional events, regulation of hunting and fishing; "blue laws" that prohibit some events on Sunday; the construction of public facilities for play; and so on.

Two topics are developed briefly, both on the theme of morality in or through games. The introductory exposition mentioned the tendency we have to read morals or lessons into the game, then to pull them out at our convenience. The following Associated Press dispatch from Moscow, dated December 5, 1954, provides an illustration:

> The Soviet press for many months has been denouncing drinking and smoking. Now it has begun to condemn card playing as an evil relic of capitalism, a crime breeder and a corrupter of the character of the Soviet man. The magazine *Young Communist* reports that all sorts of crime and character erosion arise out of card playing, including drinking and murder, and that "card playing is incompatible with the Soviet way of life." It says: "You can often find our youth playing cards . . . but lovers of card playing among our youth are found mostly among those young men who have no other cultural amusements and who have nobody paying attention to their training and upbringing. . . . Card playing gives people a light-hearted attitude toward money. Arguments arising during card games spoil the nature and character of people, and arguments lead often to fights, even murder. . . . Furthermore, card playing is harmful to health because it is usually accompanied by heavy smoking and often ends in drinking . . . besides a gambler long over a gambling table is in a nervous state. . . .

Note that the evidences of immorality are not put into the game as such; rather, the game is played by . . . or it leads to . . . or it is harmful. The concept of games as moral agents is not limited to one period of history or one kind of political system. The precise nature of the *reading into* the game or the *taking out* of moral quality is colored by the culture, the period, and the precise purpose or need.

Olympic games provide an unusual example of games whose international symbolism is a curious reversal in morality imputation. Although the spirit of the games has often been violated since the first recorded games in 776 B.C., the intended symbolism has been that of a festival, a dedication to international amity. There was an unbroken period of 1000 years when the games were held every four years, and the supreme act of mutual good will was a truce several months prior to each set of games. Festivals were held before the altars. Animals were sacrificed. Oaths to fair play were sworn. Yet winning was secondary, in theory; the purpose of the Olympic Games was to supersede the nations by placing the competition within the larger social value of cooperation. This is a reversal of the normal philosophy of competitive games. The audience—in the true sense the whole world —is supposed to become *one* in spirit, with the larger theme (dedication to fair play between nations) overpowering the minor theme (individual, team, or national victory). Indeed, team points or victories and defeats are not formally recorded as such.

This is the epitome of the amateur spirit of games and, indeed, is in theory prevalent in *all* contests that are held. Playing *against* each other is *ipso facto* playing *with* each other. The amateur, who plays for love of the game, also plays out a symbol of love for those with whom he cooperates (his rivals) in order to create the conditions of the game. In this sense, the competitive aspect of games is a minor aspect, a means; the larger, all-inclusive end is mutual understanding, symbolized by a score that is first and foremost intended to say in mathematical terms here is evidence that an agreement has been reached by both parties; and the judges are the mouthpiece of the larger values —justice, honor, ability, and just due—which embrace all competing parties, societies, committees, teams, or individuals.

All games are thus cooperative efforts first, struggles or competitions second. And it is this theory of the game as a unifying bond that provides one theme of leisure as a source of symbolism. Essential to games are rules as the criteria of the *manner* in which the game is being played and the *objective score* or result. We turn to art as the prototype of activity in which the emphasis is on *traditional and aesthetic logic* rather than on rules and on *subjective evaluation* of its success.

Art as leisure 15

What is it about art that relates it directly to leisure? What are the functions of art? What is the distinction between professional and amateur, and how is the role of each related to current trends in American leisure? Finally, how is the new leisure influencing the quality of art?

Art as leisure activity

Elements that make art an important concern to the student of leisure are many:

1. Art embraces a wide variety of media—music, theater, painting, literature, dance, and sculpture.

2. Artistic activity is already an accepted "good" in society.

3. Art has the possibility of providing a change of pace, a heightened experience, and thus a form of relaxation in the midst of emotional tension.

4. Much artistic activity can be carried on either alone or with others.

5. Art in some form appeals to almost all persons of all ages, stages of life, and degrees of emotional vitality and maturity.

6. From an economic view, contact with art, as participant or audience, can be cheap or expensive, from a gallery visit to the purchase of a masterpiece.

7. Art provides a common social value that serves to create friendships across lines of origin, faith, creed, color, material possessions, or schooling.

8. Many styles of art and a range of skills from neophyte to master are available.

Further, there is general agreement that the state of the arts is an important index of the level and direction of society. If leisure activity in art has penetrated into the core of basic art developments, issues of the first magnitude emerge. Finally, artistic experience may, according to some psychologists, provide an integration for the personality and a sense of accomplishment, rootedness, and dignity.

Functions of art

The functions of art may be seen on two levels. Its *aesthetic* function is to relate its creators and audiences to materials, forms, or inherent content. An example is seen in rapt listening to a fugal theme as it unfolds in a Bach organ work. *Social* functions of art relate one to persons, ideas, cultural norms, or patterns of behavior that may be connected to aesthetic content but are not central to it. The following are subdivisions of these patterns:

1. Collective experience, as in folk art, which draws persons closer to their groups.

2. Personal experience, which supplies a means of fantasy or escape or brings one into contact with circles or historical periods other than one's own.

3. Social symbol, in which art represents an idea or a social relationship, such as class position.

4. Moral value, or art considered as good, decadent, inspiring, sensate.

5. Incidental experience, in which art is used for purposes completely unrelated in any aesthetic sense: art for political purposes, as a commodity in business, or to help fill a psychological void while one sits in a restaurant booth.

The problem of art as leisure activity is a reconciliation of these two types of broad functions and their accompanying approaches. Putting this in the form of an issue of deep concern to professional persons in the arts, we may ask whether art can be a part-time activity in a leisure context without at the same time violating or weakening artistic standards and respect for traditions. Indeed, can art legitimately fulfill both types of functions simultaneously? One approach to the issue is to examine the concepts, professional and amateur.

Professional and amateur [1]

According to A. M. Carr-Saunders and P. A. Wilson, a profession is marked by "the possession of an intellectual technique acquired by special training." [2] E. T. Hiller goes further and speaks of five variable attributes of professions: [3] (a) long, systematic preparation; (b) the presence of norms of conduct; (c) an "occupational conscience," or emphasis on standards and services rather than on material rewards; (d) recognition by the public of professional authority based on knowledge; and (e) a kind of personal bearing "consistent with the value served by the profession."

The three tasks of the profession, according to another analysis,[4] are to maintain its authority and prestige as a group, to pursue the quest "for new and better methods and processes," and to spread the value represented by the group. But within this pattern there arises the problem of reconciliation of interests caused by the attempt to "fulfill as completely as possible the primary service for which it stands while securing the legitimate economic interests of its members." A code of ethics, therefore, attempts to provide the solution and thus becomes a characteristic aspect of professionalism.

Beneath these distinctions is the primary economic issue: the amateur does not depend on art activity for all or a major part of his livelihood. Several early sentences of Chapter 3 will be recalled: [5]

In work, man has gone much further than mere sustenance; in it he has found the core of his life. Work in its largest perspective is closely tied in with his relation to family, to other persons, to nature, to objects, to movement, to concepts of God, and to the meanings of life itself.

Thus the fundamental distinction is that the professional painter, composer, performer, playwright, actor, dancer, director, sculptor, writer, or architect is entirely committed to his art as *work* as his major objectively identified role in society. The professional and amateur can be compared further in terms of four elements or components of social role: social circle, functions, status, and conception of the person.[6]

First, the professional is accepted as such by his circle of patients, clients, or audience. He has authority because of recognized technical knowledge and not because, like a policeman, he is delegated powers by others. In addition, as Talcott Parsons notes,[7] the relation of the professional person to his client or circle is impersonal, "universalistic." The amateur is not held up as an authority by his circle. He is free to choose his own and can perform—or refrain from performing—as he feels. Dedicated to freedom, yet entering into his activity with enthusiasm, he can be expected to contribute to new ideas. In this sense, the problem of every professional artist is how to find a balance between freedom from his circle as an amateur in spirit at the same time that he is supported by it as a professional in occupation.

This can be illustrated in the case of the serious jazz musician who seeks to balance his love for playing "real" jazz against a flat pocketbook.

Second, the function of the professional is to make his special knowledge available to critical audiences, often under circumstances or conditions set up by a middleman. The performing artist, singly or as part of a group, exposes himself to professional critics, whose function it is to evaluate performance against current standards and general traditions. What the amateur does to the art is not so important, from the long view, as what the art does to the amateur.

Third, the professional occupies a *key status* in his area of specialization. He is a professional banker, lawyer, or teacher. The banker or professor who collects stamps or looks at the heavenly constellations is still the banker or professor to his society; his wife is not the wife of a philatelist or astronomer. To have become established with the key role of artist means to be associated with a history of artistic and economic independence and, indeed, a struggle for such independence that is far from solved in our own society.

Some history is necessary at this point so that these roles in art—amateur and professional—may be seen in their present unique interrelationship. It should be recalled that the artist has seldom derived his status or his economic support as a free artist, but generally as an artist-in-employment, whether for church, royal court, or wealthy patron. In spite of a large literature that draws a picture of the artist as ideally free to produce his own concept of subject, form, and style, in actual practice this has seldom been so.

In the United States the three traditional sources of patronage were missing: the rich had taken up other matters to support, such as education and welfare services. The Church had never been interested in the arts as it had in Europe, and there was no nobility. For a long time, further, the nation was too busy building its cities, factories, schools, and homes to pay attention to the arts in a way practiced in preindustrial, feudal societies. Nor was the frontier a favorable social structure for the independent, patronless artist. As late as 1900 there were only ten symphony orchestras.[8]

Even as late as 1939, a good year for the economy as a whole, fully 24 per cent of the men and 46 per cent of the women who listed themselves as professional musicians in the United States Census earned less than 100 dollars from music all year.[9] Thus the economic difficulty of the professional artist in this country began in the very nature of our social roots. Indeed, a case could be made out for the position that because of the absence of traditional sources of patronage our professional art grew as it did after the turn of the twentieth century largely because a broad substructure was being developed on the grass-roots level, marked by a growing body of amateur participants and, simultaneously, a remarkable growth in audiences.

There were reasons for this dual growth: immigrant parents sought to give their children the advantages, and music lessons fell into their stereotype; the vast majority of immigrants from 1880 to 1910 came from Italy, Germany, and Russia, with their rich peasant arts; and the emergence of a large middle class, interested in helping its youth to rise on the social ladder.

Certainly another direct contribution to the arts was that made by the public schools after World War I. Howard Hanson, prominent educator and composer, writes of this,[10]

> . . . in the field of music education I think that the last fifty years have seen a progress in the United States which is so astonishing that we ourselves do not realize it. . . . Those of you who are old enough to recall what there was of music education fifty years ago, and now go about the United States hearing great symphony orchestras in the high schools, will, I think, agree with me that this is something that would have been considered almost unbelievable fifty years ago.

The schools, however, are confronted with a new problem in ideology as well as in methods of teaching the arts. What is the role they are preparing their creative students to fill—amateur or professional? (a) As musicians, painters, and actors who are to be encouraged for an uncertain but important place among serious artistic circles; (b) for careers as teachers in new leisure-time circles such as adult centers; or (c) as persons prepared to take their places in society as lawyers, businessmen, etc., but who can still enjoy their participation in the arts as an avocation? The larger body, of course, will be consumers of the arts, and in this respect alone the attitudes implanted by the schools are enormously important to the leisure content of the future.

Some evidence of the "cultural explosion"

Quantitative evidence on the present state of the arts is abundant: expenditures in 1957 of 500 million dollars for concert tickets, 80 million dollars for classical records, 166 million dollars for hi-fi equipment and tapes, and 40 million dollars for published concert music and teaching pieces. The total of 336 million dollars compares with 240 million dollars spent in the same year for all spectator sports. In 1934 recordings of Beethoven's Ninth sold less than 500 copies; in

1953 and 1954 Toscanini's recording of this work (at $11.44 per album, or $1.27 per symphony!) was purchased by almost 150,000 persons.

That this interest extends into contemporary creativity is also clear. The leading catalogue of long-playing records (Schwann) was put out 100 times in the period between October 1949 and April 1958. Whereas the first list contained 26 pages, 11 labels, and 674 titles, the last had 200 pages, 303 labels, and 19,380 titles. In 1949, 96 composers were represented, of whom 19 were contemporary and only four were American; in 1958, 718 composers were represented, of whom 330 were contemporary and half (165) were American.[11]

The ten symphony orchestras of 1900 had increased to more than 1000 by 1958. There are now over 700 opera groups in the country. A sampling made for the American Music Conference indicated that 20 million Americans play the piano, 4 million, the guitar, 3 million, the violin and other strings, and half a million, the woodwinds and brasses.

Music is not the only creative area in which the cultural revolution seems to be taking place. We have more than 5000 community theater groups; an estimated 2 million persons paint regularly in their leisure time, and the audience or clientele of art exhibitions runs into the many millions. If to this activity is added the amount of reading about the arts, adult study courses, and the multitude of persons involved in promoting or organizing artistic groups, there emerges the conclusion, in respect to quantity, that amateur participants, as well as the public, have never experienced such a plethora of opportunity to hear or to be heard, to act or to be watched, to paint or to dance.

Qualitative measures of this vitality are difficult. Has the level of art gone "up" or "down"? How does one set up criteria that span comparisons of time and cultures? For example, should one examine America's development from a pioneering society and therefore take pride in her present arts? Should the comparison be made with European traditions of the past that would lead one—fruitlessly, to be sure—to conjure an American counterpart of 50,000 Italians in the funeral cortege of Verdi, singing his operatic melodies? Should the analysis go deeper into the kinds of assumptions and predictions offered by de Tocqueville—assumptions still powerful in intellectual circles? [12]

> . . . the democratic principle . . . induces the artisan to produce with great rapidity many imperfect commodities. . . . In aristocracies a few great pictures are produced; in democratic countries a vast number of insignificant ones.

Clear answers to these questions or positions are not apparent. The artistic profession, including its teachers, is only beginning to face these issues; many quarters of instruction, including many universities, barely raise the questions. Yet even the preparation of professional artists is involved, happily or not, with the revolution in leisure: a larger audience, given the mass media, does not imply a larger body of creators; perhaps the reverse is true. At the same time, a mass audience whose appetite is whetted for artists-in-the-flesh (and, also, artists-in-the-community away from New York) may provide a new kind of patronage whose tastes are catholic and who develop such artistic decentralized ferments as the widespread American college campus.

Relation of art as leisure to factors in American life

Several relationships that will even further pinpoint a discussion of art as a leisure experience are briefly suggested.

WORK. It is clear that although deep implications are to be found in current developments for the professional worker in the arts we are primarily concerned in the present context with amateurism. In quite another sense, intense activity in amateur arts may provide a substitute for values that formerly came from work. As Chapter 22 states, the arts are not alone in their creative value. Yet there are unique elements of the arts (some were delineated at the beginning of this chapter) that need to be studied in special connection with specific groups; for example, retired persons. Successful retirement has already been correlated with such items as health, economic welfare, and attitudes of family. Could the arts—even the playing of instruments—be useful in new ways as constructive activity for older persons? How would success in acquiring new skills be a function of attitudes, past occupation, etc., rather than manual skill or coordination?

PERSONALITY AND FAMILY. In professional circles concerned with changing family life in America an important issue is the goal of balance between individuality or independence from family and identity with family through mutual dependence. The arts serve as devices that may be useful in both directions. Family groups may be observed in community orchestras or choruses, in amateur theater companies and art classes, yet each of these may also serve to take a member from the family. Of the several types of leisure activity discussed in Part 3, perhaps none is more flexible in this regard.

COMMUNITY. A recent survey of 377 cities in the United States of 20,000 or more population indicated that 187 contribute tax funds toward music.[13]

Recognition of European policies in this regard for the arts has tended to ignore a growing American practice. Sample states which contribute directly in tax subsidies to music are Vermont, North Carolina, Massachusetts, Rhode Island, and Arkansas. Some counties which finance music are those embracing the areas of Los Angeles, San Francisco, New Orleans, and Atlanta. A few of the many cities are Philadelphia, Chicago, St. Louis, Indianapolis, Detroit, and Rochester. The City of Los Angeles has its own outstanding Bureau of Music.[14]

Apparently there is a considerable body of citizens who believe that a legitimate function of government is to enrich their lives through the arts by collective action. As leisure becomes a more dramatic issue in community life, we may expect more rather than less interest; but more competition for the tax dollar is simultaneously developing. One emerging public need, for example, is the increased demand for the economic and medical care of older persons. With what success can one equate the use of a dollar to pay a teacher in an adult education class with the use of a dollar for a public housing unit for older people? Such issues will become more insistent with the development of a wider social-welfare philosophy. The answers in a democracy come from the power of pressure groups, on the one hand, and the prevalent ideas that motivate leadership on the other.

The precise process by which such community decisions are made is far from clear. One scholar describes it thus: [15]

Education of the young, support for veterans, expanded medical service, and other general welfare programs in a sense compete with one another for shares of the Gross National Product. The processes by which these shares are determined have not yet been studied. We do not know, for example, whether increases in expenditures for older people actually reduce a community's willingness to build new schools or pay higher teacher salaries. We observe only that a legislature or a governing board of a community chest or united fund gets a vague conception of how much the community, be it city, state or nation, will spend on welfare. It then proceeds to weigh and balance the relative claims of competing interests. After long discussion a balance is struck, each interest receives an allocation. The total amount to be spent may be increased simply because it seemed more practical to enlarge the pie than to reduce the size of any of the pieces. Records are not kept of these economizing proceedings; only the final decisions are publicized. Consequently, one is left with inferences about this conflict of values made from accomplished facts.

Leisure activities as a whole find themselves in an advantageous position in the division of the community tax "pie," with apparent need for adult education, meaningful activity for older persons, and the enlarging interest in free time for everyone. Community school and recreation agencies are among two beneficiaries of this acception. And even within such agencies the arts may anticipate a large proportionate share of allocations in expenditures of time, money, and trained leadership. How large this proportion will be is more than a matter of local circumstance. The artistic circles themselves are perhaps now in a transitional period in which, utilizing all the magic of electronic assistance, they can break through to the masses on a high level of leisure experience; or, ignoring the issues of an emerging American scene, they may live in the past, insensitive to revolutions in thought, community forms, and such technological dramas as the new communications.

We turn now to one of the technological changes that have given rise to the type of leisure called "movement."

Movement as leisure 16

The two most important trends in leisure activity seem at first to be complete opposites: television and travel. The first keeps us home, in a semidark room, near or in front of a tube that is lighted on the average of four hours a day. Travel, on the other hand, takes us away to the next town, to a neighboring state, across the country, and, increasingly, to foreign lands.

Yet both experiences are built around a relationship to the world. In one case *the world comes to us*. It is a quick and inexpensive access to the world. A lesser number prefers to read than to watch. Although the first requires a greater effort, both reading and watching are class-less activities in contemporary America. Education is open to every-one. Libraries and paperback books have almost eliminated considera-tions of cost, and TV sets are now found in 45,000,000 American homes.

The meaning of travel is that now *we go to the world*. In relation to reading or watching, the experience of travel limits us and frees us at the same time. Most of us are somewhat limited in time and money. Our vision is limited to one place as we move from Venice to Florence to Rome to Naples, and the realness of the perception does not in-validate the sheer hour-by-hour succession of impressions that can be telescoped and edited in television, movies, or reading. Meanwhile, however, we are freer *in* Venice than when we read *about* it: freer to explore, to meet the unexpected, to face experiences directly and immediately through our own senses and unedited by other minds. We are freer, too, to rub elbows with travelers from other lands as well as with local populations.

Furthermore, the total experience of travel is larger than the physical act involved and the psychological perception of places seen. A more systematic and rigid analysis could view its dual aspects as form and content. Under *form* might be considered such matters as motivations, expectations, planning and preparation, actual movement, the return, and the use of this experience in post-trip life. *Content* of travel experience might investigate contacts with new people, seen either as masses or as secondary friendships; new acquaintances who become additions to the traveler's vocabulary of types of persons; new physical and natural objects or scenes—cities, landscapes, buildings, paintings, and so on; new experiences or adventures, whether in shopping or coming across an intriguing street in Venice; and direct contacts with the values and ways of other cultures.

Our plan here is not to follow this suggested scheme rigorously but to inquire into several interrelated aspects of the matter. We begin with some facts.

Some facts about travel

A Curtis Company annual survey of domestic travel indicates that for the year ending March 1953 between 7.5 and 8.0 *billion* dollars was spent on vacation travel.[1] Families with higher incomes took more trips for longer periods: of those with incomes between 5000 and 6000 dollars, about 62 of every 100 families took trips of an average length of slightly more than 18 days; about 75 per 100 families with incomes of more than 10,000 dollars, made trips of almost a month. On the whole, we averaged two family trips and were gone about ten days each time. It is true that most trips were in the summer (40 of every 100), but about 17 per 100 were in the winter, almost 18 in the spring, and more than 25 in the fall of the year.[2]

How did we travel in 1953? By far the greatest number of trips (85.5 per cent) were made in our own cars. Trailing behind came

train	13.6%
air	8.2
bus	5.5
ship	1.8
other	.8

Of course, this does not refer to the mileage. Our trips by car averaged 1108 miles, by air, 6521 miles. Thus with the volume of longer trips there is greater use of airlines; from 1929 to 1953 the traffic on railroads between cities fell from 78 to 46 per cent, whereas scheduled airline travel increased from one tenth of one per cent to 24 per cent of the total volume.[3]

Since there is a relation between amount of education to earnings, it follows that the more educated do more leisure-time traveling. Some idea of the vast economic importance of the tourist trade is the Curtis figure of more than 1.5 billion dollars for lodging and food alone. Motels have become the favorite stopping places for the American. An evidence of middle-class tourism is that more than six of every ten dollars spent for vacation travel came out of current income rather than savings.

We cannot forget that all this is a recent development. Many Americans behind an automatic-shift, power-steering car can still recall from personal experience the trips they made a generation ago with less reliable, less comfortable machines bumping along on something less than turnpike roads. Many factors, of course, are responsible for making us now "the most mobile people the world has ever known." [4]

The trends of the last decade have thus been summarized by an expert in the field:

> There is more year-round travel everywhere in the country. Air conditioning has helped develop hot-weather travel to all parts of the country. The summer season in Florida, for example, abetted by air conditioning and off-season rates, is now at least equal in volume to that of the winter-season peak. Snow removal on northern and western highways coupled with the further development of winter sports has created more travel in large areas of the country.
>
> A greater variety of packaged travel programs are available—everything from a bargain weekend in a big city or a resort hotel to trips around the world. Where cost is a controlling factor, these package plans offer the prospective traveler outstanding bargains at a known low price which is very appealing. [5]

Travel abroad

Vacation-time travel of the American is now worldwide in scope. According to John Wilcock, writing in *The New York Times* for July 7, 1957, American vacationists spent more money abroad in 1956 (about 1.75 billion dollars) than this country spends abroad for either coffee or petroleum—our two most important import items. This was an increase of 12½ per cent over 1955.

Most of this travel was by airplane. In 1956 half of the 1,239,000 Americans who went abroad went to Central America and the West Indies, 42 per cent to Europe and the Mediterranean. In 1957, according to the Department of Commerce, of the 1,370,000 Americans who left the country for trips, 885,000 persons, or 65 of each 100, went for pleasure and the remainder for business, study, health, or other purposes. [6] We were told, "Confidence and optimism prevail throughout the travel industry that 1958 will be a record travel year. . . . This in spite of the debate on are we or are we not in a recession . . . and the undeniable fact that travel (domestic) for the first four months of 1958 was down about 10% in comparison to the same months last year. . . ." [7] Reservations for travel abroad in the summer of 1958, indeed, climbed to new highs.

Many are the agencies and publications ready to assist the vacationer to decide where to go. For example, in 38 pages of *The New York Times* for March 2, 1958, there were general articles ("Tourism returns to normalcy," etc.), special articles about one country or another, specific tips (use of a European car, camping, a full calendar of events scheduled in 25 countries and regions, a half page of information on documents and currency restriction, etc.), and innumerable advertisements by travel agencies offering to help the reader to get anywhere. One interesting aspect was the amount of advertising by official tourist offices or agencies in many countries: Austria, Czechoslovakia, France, Ireland, Italy, Japan, Germany, Greece, India, Portugal, Scandinavia, Spain, Yugoslavia.

To assist persons in planning, *The New York Times* and other journals often estimate the cost of sample tours to various parts of the world with an eye to interesting those with limited means. The Kiplinger magazine, *Changing Times,* for April 1960 lists 28 offices in the United States maintained by foreign governments to supply tourist information.

Who is the traveler?

There have been four major types of travelers throughout history: the explorer or adventurer, the businessman, the soldier, and the missionary or religious pilgrim. Their motivations were many—profit, salvation, scientific knowledge, the subjugation of people, or the conversion of the heathen. The poetic description [8] quoted below surely applies more aptly to the bulk of those who had none of these *work-oriented* goals, but who traveled in their free time unobligated to a congregation, military ruler, customer, or government:

> But where do we want to get, and why? What do we seek, what have people always sought when they have left home and embarked on their enchanting errors over earth and ocean? First, I suppose, change, difference, otherness, that alien otherness which forever seeks some new thing, desiring to be where one is not. The seducing pull of the exotic has us in thrall; we seek a country. "Let us," that travel-minded Jacobean Mr. Thomas Coryat exhorted us, "propose before our eyes that most beautiful theatre of the universe, let us behold whatever is abroad in the world,

let us look into provinces, see cities, run over kingdoms and empires." If we do not, he threatens, we shall become rude, slothful, uncivil, outrageous, foolish, barbarous, puffed up with admiration of ourselves, effeminate, given to sleep, banquetings, idleness and dice. Away then we must go, into the delicious pleasure-park of Abroad. . . . Climate, then, and food; after the great Otherness, these are perhaps our chief seductions. There are also Sights, both artifact and natural; some prefer one, some the other. Some will chase after palaces and churches, temples and castles, houses, loggias, spires and towers, the glow of paint on canvas and on walls, the delicate carving of marble, ivory and bronze, the pillared portico, the Roman colonnade, the Greek temple, the Romanesque church with baroque façade. . . . Others will only be perfectly happy in Scenery; they desire mountains, valleys, oceans, islands, forests, rivers and lakes, and, had man never set brush to paper or chisel to stone, they would still be in paradise among these.

A more scientific approach evolves categories of travel motivations for leisure-time travelers: change, conformity, imitation, curiosity, advertising pressures, the purchasing of objects, etc. Among these reasons, the search for *being a somebody*—"status panic," as it has been called—has been of interest to social scientists.[9] Other observers of the social scene (novelists, satirists, culture historians) have long been intrigued with travel as a symbol of social distinction.

Consider the elements of a trip to foreign shores: until World War II, it demanded much in time and money, provided a source for unusual gifts and purchases, supplied unending conversation, required special clothes, and permitted proximity to royalty on their own grounds. The snobbery that resulted grew out of a physical and visible act. The imitator might deal well with other symbols on the less expensive domestic front, or he might turn the challenge aside—my family is as good as yours, my education is better—but the fact was that he had not been to the Louvre nor tipped a ship's bartender. He might have gone to Burton Holmes' lectures and seen many pictures or read books (no magazines were as attractive as today's *Holiday*, not even the *National Geographic*); but even this is not like packing, getting a visa, and finally *being there*.

In the years since the war this has changed. Now the middle classes travel, as they have also acquired other symbols of status, such as air conditioning, retirement and pension plans, long cars with chrome, and access to star entertainers in their private home theaters. Yet is this altogether accurate, this "status panic"?

A common-sense view suggests that the middle classes took to travel and vacations because comfort, curiosity, and fishing are enjoyed as much by one person as another, regardless of pedigree. Similarly, running water, air conditioning, and vacation trips or cottages are self-evident and legitimate goals like owning several pairs of shoes and hanging a picture on the wall. The average American takes color slides with his 35-mm camera—whose price he can now afford—and although he may seem "alienated" to Eric Fromm the pictures will relate him more closely to his friends. If the upper classes saw Paris first, they could afford it first. Simple economics suggests a reasonable explanation of leisure travel over great distances.[10]

The new traveler—his significance

Many words have been written about the behavior of the American tourist abroad. He is sometimes inclined to exhibit a sense of superiority over people with less material advantages. A brief division of all travelers into two rough types will apply to others as well as to Americans.

First there are those we may call "comparative strangers." These persons travel physically, but in reality they never, or seldom, leave their own familiar ideas and judgments. They find security wherever they may be in what is called *ethnocentrism*, the application of one's own standards to other situations: their own are always superior to those of others. They view, but do not understand. As Walter Lippman wrote, these are persons "who do not see first and then define, they define first and then see." [11]

A second group may be called "emphatic natives." These persons seek, as best they can, to put themselves in the place of those whom they visit. They become native as much as their backgrounds, study, and empathy permit. What they take from their own environments are not particulars but universals. They sincerely wish to perceive and to understand. Like the explorer or trader, the soldier or the priest, these travelers depend on preparation and knowledge.

With more and more travel among the middle classes, a larger proportion of empathic native travelers is probably emerging. Travelers as a whole are more educated than a generation ago. Increased use of the mass media has acquainted people with far-off places. War and cold-war tensions have familiarized us with areas until recently outside our consciousness. Millions of our men have themselves been abroad during the war, and are no longer puzzled by the names of strange-sounding islands, peoples, and cities; and their families, too, have learned to look at maps. People returning from trips are expected to know, to have pictures, to recite facts. All this may have had something to do with producing a more mature tourist public in the first decade and a half following the war.

Mr. Abram Chasins, Music Director of WQXR and former concert pianist, describes this change in a statement to *The New York Times* for October 6, 1957:

It was not surprising to encounter hordes of our countrymen during a recent European jaunt. What was surprising and greatly heartening was the constant evidence that their presence was having a vital effect on European minds and hearts. They were winning a new respect for themselves and for our country, they were erasing remaining impressions of the "typical American" as an uncultivated, unilingual money-bag.

These "new" Americans were our average, hard-working citizens and their children. Many of them had obviously made sacrifices to travel, and they had made them because of the inspirational attraction that the centers of humanity's religious and cultural history held for them. They were there not to make impressions, but to receive them and share them . . . displaying what Europeans are taught from childhood to admire—a respect for tradition, an understanding of art, and a reverence for the places of their origin.

One wonders whether the industry devoted to tourism has fully realized the nature of this change. A misinterpretation of what is happening is seen in the type of guide books being published, books with "tips" about what to wear, money exchange, living costs, customs regulations, night clubs, etc. A more substantial type of book, familiar to the wealthy traveler of the past, is almost unavailable. As P. G. Anson concludes after an examination of recent guide books,[12]

Somebody, either the author or the publisher, has a very low idea of the average traveling American, and that idea is that the tourist is nothing more than a consumer: a consumer of food, drink, lodging, tickets and souvenirs. . . . That is why such guidebooks as these avoid the cultural aspects of the countries they describe: monuments, the everyday existence of the people, the countryside cannot easily be made to contribute to the Big Business that tourism has become.

On the other hand, a heartening evidence of leadership that provides opportunity for a blend of recreational experience and learning is the program of the Council for Student Travel. The Council is a clearing house for several score agencies that are interested in sending high school students abroad for a summer of living with a family and bringing students from abroad to live in the homes of American families for a year. The Council arranges the passage and a comprehensive educational and recreational program on shipboard. This program, which cooperates closely with Federal agencies, has been extended to immigrants and adult tourists as well. In the summer of 1958 students were sent to the Soviet Union for the first time. As a ship lecturer one summer, the writer has experienced the meaning of this activity. It gave him a concept of the integration of learning and leisure travel. This project begins to answer, in a constructive way, how international travel can be fully put to effective purpose beyond personal satisfaction. Mr. Chasins had this further note about the travelers he saw:

> In this new zeal to be in other lands, I sensed the will to survive, the need, subconscious perhaps, for the individual to take matters into his own hands in order to build a stronger foundation for a human community based on mutual understanding.

Leisure travel in the future

The facts of tomorrow's travel read like fiction. Yet they can hardly be disputed. At what speeds will the tourist fly into outer space, perhaps before A.D. 2000? How will jet travel, in full swing in the 1960's, affect concepts of distance? How will the Federal highway crossing the continental United States affect domestic travel? How will the new St. Lawrence Waterway influence the destination of passengers from other lands?

These developments, and many others to come, are more than technological advances. Holiday travel has become vital to the dollar-short countries of Asia, Europe, and Latin America. Italy, which attracts a total of 10 to 11 million visitors each year, is providing 25-year loans for hotel construction; it is encouraging an economy plan for off-season tourists (10 to 20 per cent discounts on hotels, restaurants, and transportation to visitors from the United States). Tourism in Belgium has increased 100 per cent in the last few years and was further spurred by the Brussels World's Fair of 1958. Travel to West German health resorts is above prewar years. The Economic and Social Council of the United Nations has been drawn into active plans for coordinating tourist trade across national borders. Ceylon now has 100 tourist inns and has trebled its facilities in a six-year development program. Mexico is planning a network of highways and airlines to encourage more visiting to its interior regions. Japan, among other ways of improving its services, is sending students of hotel management to the United States and Europe. The 100,000 tourists who visited Haiti in 1959 spent a sum in excess of income from sisal, the number two item in the national economy, second only to coffee.[13] Nepal, which prohibited all tourists until 1950, has announced that a bureau has been set up "to lure world travelers to its mountains, jungles and fertile valleys," and guides are provided for tours to Hindu and Buddhist shrines.[14] Russia now has tourist offices, and although costs to the Soviet Union are high discounts are being offered. If the change in official attitude toward the place of tourism in that land continues, we can expect that the largest of all tourist attractions will eventually be in the direction of Russia. Costs can be reduced drastically if the Russian government decides that it wants Europeans and Americans to come.

The economic element is predominant in the planning on top levels illustrated in the foregoing paragraph. However, as the Russians and all others know, the by-products of two-way communication between ordinary persons can have deep political and cultural effects. Planners in official circles of Washington know, in spite of current inactivity indicated in the Randall report, that the United States also has much to gain by this kind of rapport. We are aware of the attitudes about our life that are fostered by motion pictures. Following is a section of the famous Baedeker guide book on the United States, prepared in 1904 to help the English tourist. In some details the Englishman is perhaps better informed today. Yet, some impressions of a half century ago still remain. Incidentally, the description will also indicate real improvement in conditions since that time for the American tourist as well.

> The first requisite for the enjoyment of a tour in the United States is an absence of prejudice and a willingness to accommodate oneself to the customs of the country. (The traveler) will often find that ways which strike him as unreasonable or even disagreeable are more suited to the environment than those of his own home would be. He should from the outset reconcile himself to the absence of deference or servility on the part of those he considers his social inferiors. . . . The average Englishman will probably find the chief physical discomforts in the dirt of city streets, the roughness of the country roads, the winter overheating of hotels and railway-cars (70–80° Fahrenheit being by no means unusual), the dust, flies, and mosquitos of summer and (in many places) the habit of spitting on the floor; but the Americans themselves are now keenly alive to these weak points and are doing their best to remove them. Throughout almost the whole country traveling is now as safe as in the most civilized parts of Europe, and the carrying of arms, which indeed is forbidden in many states, is as unnecessary here as there . . . the traveler should . . . come provided with an ample supply of all the articles of personal use he or she is likely to require.

It is to change this kind of impression about us—on material and cultural levels—that we want people from distant places to visit us. But whether others come to us or we go to them, *movement as a leisure activity is now a major concern of all the world.*

However, impressions of the world *come to us.* This is one of man's new wonders, that he can now remain physically immobile but see the world, hear its sounds, and become exposed to its ideologies and currents of life. This, too, is leisure and our next issue for study.

Immobility as leisure 17

Never has the world been so readily at hand in every room of the house. Images, information, pictures, ideas, art, propaganda —these come to us from the radio at our bedside, the symphonic record in the den, the television set in the living room, the book on the shelf, and the newspapers and magazines that clutter the tables everywhere.

Indeed, so plentiful is this orgy of consumption, so easy is it to watch, listen, and receive this wealth of stimuli that here we come to the heart of much current criticism of leisure for the masses.

It is not our purpose to glory in or to deplore this development. Rather, our first observation is that *these activities include a broad range of mental or emotional activity, from complete boredom, disinterest, and insensibility to complete and exciting creativity, inner struggle, and participation in the affairs of the world.*

It will at once be noted that the degree of involvement can hardly be measured. We may go further: the traditional distinction between "active" and "passive" participation holds little water, since it is based on a rural or physiological criterion of muscular versus mental. Lactic content, as Riesman has noted,[1] is not a proper criterion of participation. None of the media or devices—books, TV, records, radio—is *ipso facto* better or worse, creative or parasitic. Much depends on the situation or "field" in which a particular activity takes place. How is it used? What is brought to it? With whom, when, why, how often? Thus arises a second observation:

Statistical measures of popularity of a single device or leisure activity that brings the world to our home are of little scientific purpose for generalizations. How many hours per week one sits before his TV set means little without a knowledge of further facts. Mr. Jones, the *average* American, spends between 16 and 19 hours per week there. Of Mr. Jones, the *real* one, we want to know what he did before the TV age; has he anything to say before or after these shows; has TV stimulated reading, travel, hobbies; does he spend these hours in company with his family; and so on and on. Until the measurers of TV "watching" are willing to leave the simple statistic of hours and look into these multiple factors, they will not be in a theoretical position to understand intensity, meaning, or perception of the experience.[2] Personal history or longitudinal research is also requisite to such study: it is one thing if our listener has forgone Western motion pictures and poker sessions to make way for television; it is another if he has surrendered his walks or social visits.

In the exhibition of ship models at the Massachusetts Institute of Technology is one model called *The Frigate President*. A marker notes that it was constructed by Mr. Harry J. Garceau of Muncie, Indiana, in a period of 9700 hours. Simple reduction shows that this amounts to a total of 1212 days, 242 weeks, or more than four and a half years of continuous labor at the rate of eight hours per day! To state this is only to raise more questions. How was this labor of love actually spread out in time? Was Mr. Garceau sick, single or married, young or old? What had been his past associations with the sea? These are longitudinal inquiries, which, when answered, give the statistical M.I.T. label some meaning.

Functions

The functions served by the devices of immobility are many: fantasy, information, adult baby sitting, fun, escape, source of conversation, aesthetic satisfaction, mental stimulation, "killing time," being with the family. The same device—even the same program or activity—may have several purposes for one person at one time; it may also serve various persons in different ways.[3] Consider the matter of fantasy.

There are *unorganized* fantasies, rooted in the subconscious, as in the case of day dreams; *productive* fantasies, organized by the person, as in the case of artistic creation; and *consumptive* fantasies, prepared by others for the consumer. Either of the last two can result in the first. So large is the choice of books that can bring the world into the home of the productive and creative person that he is limited only by his speed of reading, his grasp of materials, or the scope of his imagination. He serves in part as his own censor, since his mind is already affected at the moment by previous experiences, tastes, or thoughts. On the other hand, if his view of the world as it comes into the home is determined, selected, or manipulated by others, then he has become the subject, victim, or beneficiary of the tastes and motivations of others. The motives of these middlemen, businessmen, and a whole array of persons involved in the mass-media industry are also varied: they range from pure profit to idealism, uplift, enlightenment, persuasion, information, and sincere service.

Thus there arise several issues for a study of leisure as the motivations or *processes* of consumption and production come together. Is my own version of the world, put together through my own creative synthesis of knowledge and reading, more accurate than the versions brought to me in mass production for the millions? When information or ideas come to me in a context of entertainment or relaxation, is it as lasting as when I seek out such information? Is the *ease* with which I can receive impressions from the mass media a factor in its effect upon my thought? What is the relation between the experience of getting the world into my living room and traveling out to see the world at first hand? To what degree can my sensitivities and discrimination be sharpened so that I can be a better censor of what is permitted into my home from Madison Avenue or Hollywood?

In exploring a few of these issues, we need to look more concretely at several facts and studies. We begin with television.

Television

The number of TV sets in the United States increased from four million in 1950 to over 45 million seven years later. This contrasts with an estimated combined total of 11,726 sets in the countries of Britain, West Germany, France, Italy, Belgium, Holland, Denmark, Switzerland, Sweden, Japan, and Russia.

According to the Nielson research, a total of 1.9 billion man-hours per week are devoted to all productive economic activities in our country; but 2.6 billion man-hours are spent watching television. This is based on an average of at least 16 hours of weekly watching for the average American adult.

This amount of viewing has had its effect on other leisure-time activities. As far back as 1950 John Houseman summarized some of these.[4] Over a period of two years after 400 families in one study had purchased TV sets their movie going dropped 46 per cent, football and baseball attendance was down 30 per cent, book reading declined about 33 per cent. High school students in Stamford, Connecticut, spent more hours before their TV sets than before their teachers. Houseman summarizes:

Television is not just the latest and most miraculous of these media. It is a synthesis of them all. It is radio with eyes; it is the press without the travail of printing; it is movies without the physical limitations of mechanical reproduction and projection.

Similarly, a report in the *Christian Science Monitor* concludes: [5]

Television has had its effects on the innermost core of personal habit. The presence of a piece of electronic furniture in the living room has changed how much people eat (more) and how much they sleep (less). It has transformed the pattern of day-by-day living more than any invention since the automobile. . . . It has fascinated people, exasperated people, and bored people; but it has reached them and, on the whole, held them. Few people who now have a television set will ever be without one again.

However, a closer examination of the effects of television indicates a more complex situation. Since the most intensive research has been on the impact of crime shows on children, we refer to this type of study for our illustration of the point.

The facts leave no doubt of the amount of crime depiction during hours when children watch. A few examples: 1953, seven Los Angeles stations, 692 crimes in one week; 1953, seven New York stations, 3421 violent episodes; 1954, a repeat study of the same New York stations, 7065 acts or threats of violence, or twice that of the previous study; 1954, four stations in Washington, one fourth of the viewing time devoted to violence. During the period of September 13–17, 1954, between 4 and 10 P.M., TV content was studied in Seattle, Denver, Chicago, San Francisco, Kansas City, Dallas, Atlanta, Cleveland, and Philadelphia. Of the total of 192 hours, about one fifth was given over to the crime-violence motif. The trend for such programs seems to have gone up during the years since then.

These are the facts.[6] On the *effects* there is less agreement, for they cannot be so easily quantified. One group of psychiatrists, in testimony before the Kefauver Committee, stated,

Does the vivid, living portrayal of crime by the media have an impact on the mind of a child, juvenile, adolescent, in such manner as to effect delinquent behavior? . . . There exists no data of sufficient scope, either on the basis of clinical first-hand experience or on theoretical grounds, to enable qualified investigators to draw valid conclusions, either that these media are harmful or beneficial.

Nor is there clear evidence that juvenile delinquency has been increased by depictions of crime. Opinions can be found on both sides. For example, children have a new reason for staying home; a well-adjusted child can resist crime suggestions; children are already living in a world of violence, portrayed even in Homer, the Old Testament, Shakespeare, Mother Goose, or the modern novel. Contrary opinions hold that about 10 per cent of school children are in need of psychological help, and these are most likely to seek out violent programs, and that even well-adjusted children become more callous by exposure to repeated violence.

A moderate view of mass-media effects is submitted by Dr. Paul Witty of Northwestern University after his study of 2000 pupils, parents, and teachers.[7] Children sleep about as many hours as they did before TV; there is more parental regulation over TV than is often assumed. There seems to be "little or no decrease in outdoor activities and hobbies." Repeated observation of the same families indicates less concern by parents and teachers in such problems as nervousness, eye strain, meal disturbance, and the like. Where serious maladjustments occurred, teachers found other factors present, such as unfavorable home environment. The average reading of those studied increased in the course of a year, due perhaps to other factors as well as to TV. Many children reported learning much from the media about science, current events, and life in other cultures.

There is no reason to assume that conclusions can be any more clearcut for adults than for children. There is, indeed, more reason to assume that the mass media have been adapted by the adult to his previous way of life. We do not yet have an adult population that had been raised in its formative years by mass media. Such researches may be expected after the year 1975.

We noted in Chapter 16 that the traveler who goes *to the world* is limited in the sense that once he sets his course he becomes totally submerged in his present world, be it Japan or Germany. The recipient *of the world* has a less vivid but a greater possible choice of experience. In both the selection is limited, by itinerary in one and available mass-media offerings in the other. Both admit of fantasy, colored perception, misinterpretation, or the type of experience characterized in Chapter 16 as that of the "comparative stranger." Yet there are several ways of getting the world into one's home. Next to radio or TV, reading is the most important. In this area, too, a marked change has occurred.

Reading

One index to reading habits is the number of new titles published in the year. In 1957 there were 13,142 new titles, exclusive of pamphlets. This was the highest number since the turn of the century. During the same year almost 21,000 appeared in England (including 6000 new editions of older works). Both were far exceeded by publication figures in the Soviet Union.[8]

Not only new titles but the total number of books published is a fact to consider. Of course, the paperback revolution is a dramatic development to note. In this country paper-bound books were known in the middle of the last century. However, they got a real foothold in 1939, when 25-cent originals were issued by Gold Medal Books. The sales since have been astounding. In 1951, 231 million paper-bound volumes were sold; in 1953, 260 million. The best sellers were westerns, sea romances, and science fiction, but the record also shows a sale of more than a million copies each of Homer's *Odyssey* and *Iliad*. It is estimated that about *2 billion* copies of 12,000 titles have been sold in inexpensive editions during the last 16 years.[9] This trend may be as significant as the rise in TV watching for insights into the impact of the new leisure. Apparently we have enough time to increase our reading, our TV watching, our traveling, our gardening, and our chores around the house, as well as our hunting and fishing.

There are similarities in reading and attending to the mass media. Both, for example, provide a function of sociability, the one in auto-biographies or love stories, gossip, and inside information, the other in (declining) quiz shows. Both can provide other worlds, times, and places, but the differences are more striking.

The reader has a larger scope of topics available to him at any hour of the day or time of year, from comics to cosmology; the writer of a book has had more time than the writer of a script to develop a theme; the reader spends more time and effort with his book. It is probably true that the reader retains his experience longer than the viewer. Judging from one research report, to the point that many pleasure trips are completely forgotten, it may even be true in some cases that to read about a place may be as vivid as going there.

Although we may not go so far as Thurber in encouraging day dreams, we may note that television lends itself less well than reading to this kind of fantasy. One cannot halt the action of a TV show to muse, close one's eyes, or go off on a flight of fancy. Television, like the motion-picture house, provides a "world-embracing league of man-kind," but its audience has no unity, as Arnold Hauser notes, for it is an amorphous group, a "very confused social structure." [10]

Since the mass-media experience is easy, those who control it are in positions of great power. This power decreases as the audience becomes more discriminating. As in underdeveloped or preindustrialized countries, the parallel holds here, too: those in control are ideologically opposed to a rise in literacy, for the literate man is the critical one. However, the process that produces the semiliterate of the mass-media TV also produces the paper-bound volumes that are sold in quantity at the drugstore; we are faced, therefore, with a situation that Morris Cohen called "polarity" in social affairs: the same conditions may produce opposite trends.[11]

As adult education becomes an increasing concern in our teacher-training institutions—the concern is just coming over the horizon—its theorists will become more adept at utilizing the mass media and, further, at developing practical relationships with reading or other forms of direct study and knowledge. Quality is their goal; otherwise, as Lundberg and his associates wrote in 1934,[12]

> . . . the principal *raison d'être* for such institutions as the Recreation Commission, the Park Commission and all other educational and promotional services having to do with the raising of recreational standards disappears. The existence of these services is based on the assumption that it does make a socially significant difference whether, for example, children sing "Polly Wolly Doodle" or a Bach chorale.

In Chapter 11, the present author has not spoken differently; he has only cautioned that those in the front line of service know what their assumptions are and be prepared, on the basis of better knowledge or changing social conditions, to rethink them. The social scientist is within his professional limits in providing the insights and data or the unraveling of interrelationships with which the assumptions and correlative practices can be more effectively adopted.

The general conclusion to be drawn from the present chapter is that a great deal of our free time is spent in the home. This, far from isolating us from the world, produces a living room that, as Russell Lynes notes,[13] is a combination "theater, . . . ball park, . . . fight ring, . . . night club, or . . . symphony hall"; also a classroom and a political arena. When to this phenomenon is added the presence of the hi-fi phonograph and the printed page, the old distinctions of active-passive experience become outmoded. Only a few yards away, in the garage, stands another vehicle, this one to take us far afield. This duality, in which we pass from day to day in a most natural way that would have amazed the Utopians of yesteryear, is the dramatic climax of the mass leisure now open to most of us. Its ultimate meaning is still beyond the understanding of those of us who grew up without these pieces of magic. Their present consumers are pioneers, but so are their critics and would-be teachers. It may be that a middle line can be drawn between de Tocqueville's view that the "hypocrisy of culture" belongs uniquely to democracy and Walt Whitman's plea that democracy must develop its own culture, for "the models of persons, books, manners, etc., appropriate for former conditions and for European lands, are but exiles and exotics here." [14]

Comparison of immobility and movement

There is a final comparison between travel, reading, and television that presents fascinating possibilities in the understanding of time. We may speak of three kinds of time—fixed, horizontal, and vertical—and the relations of each, respectively, to television, travel, and reading.

Television relates the viewer to *exact time;* it conditions him to half-hour periods, with abbreviated pauses in between for commercials. One could toy with the thought that part of TV's attraction, especially to the habitué, is precisely this security and regularity in time—a security that comes from alternations of concentration and release or relative confinement and freedom. We might find in this fact a reason for the toleration, indeed, the therapeutic effect of over-long advertising (over-long especially in the eyes of the intellectual). But the intellectual is accustomed to long periods of concentration.

The traveler, in contrast, is related to *horizontal time.* He is free of TV schedules and even of his home and work routines. But even though he may tend to forget the day of the week or hour of the day, he is conscious of his ties to the routines of *others:* times when stores are open, when motels are filled, and so on. Indeed, one of the little joys of travel consists in recalling, "if I were home now this is what I'd be doing."

The reader, finally, is the freest of all, for he is related to universal or *vertical time.* He is free not only of TV half-hours and routine schedules, but, within the content of his reading, free even of his culture, his century, or (if he is addicted to science fiction) the earth, space, and time itself!

It would be unwise, if a pleasant exercise, to carry this comparison too far. Yet, questions persist: could a comparison of science-fiction or history readers versus TV addicts help develop a continuum of more to lesser security in personality? If so, is security related positively to *more* imagination rather than to the common assumption of less?

Surely, the whole field of the mass media as a leisure form, especially when it is studied side by side with other forms of behavior, is far from adequately covered in this or other books. And the further we get into the subject, the more we question whether we have even hit upon the significant questions. The complexity of the matter is such that caution is urged in the face of grandiloquent pronouncements made about the mass media. At the present stage of inquiry and validation, bold questions are as much in order as are humble and qualified answers.

Processes
of Leisure

Leisure and the theory of social control 18

We have set out, in Part 2, several factors that serve to condition the kinds of leisure activities that may be found in a society. Part 3 considered several types of leisure, and in a sort of reverse gear moved informally back and forth among the conditioning variables. The question now facing us is more complex: how are the variables and the activities brought into actual focus?

A simple example: Mary has enough money for a Mediterranean cruise. Money does not explain the cruise, for she might have done many other things. Money was certainly *one* of the conditions that made the trip possible; what were some others? The directions and depth of this inquiry are in part dependent on the discipline of inquiry. The classical economist may be content to go no further than money, price, demand, commodity; the psychoanalyst may concentrate on Mary's subconscious urges and perhaps find her desire to travel in a "death wish." The sociologist stands somewhere between these two: he wants to keep his economic feet on the ground but not to ignore insights into the mind that were given their first (but not their complete) impetus by Freud. If the first is labeled roughly as the "outer" conditions of man and the second as the "inner," the sociological position has been to develop a theory of their unity, justified in part by the falsity inherent in the dichotomy. Money is more than a commodity. It has meaning and is therefore part of the culture, for "the content of an item of culture consists of the significance ascribed to it, what it is supposed to be good for, what can be done with it, the uses and functions it serves, the public expectations about it, and the ideas and sentiments with which it is linked in the history of a society." [1]

Within this patterning, *man* is not the whole, determining by his will the nature of the world, nor is the *world* the whole explanation as a final determinant of the nature of man. The world, indeed, is an

231

interwoven fabric, with man so closely and relevantly a part of the pattern that lines that seek to distinguish man as Individual or Ego exist on paper but in real life are blotted out by the controls and influences of groups, custom, and prevailing climate of opinion. Accepting the dichotomy for its convenience and traditional use, a rough distinction of disciplines might refer to the biopsychological disciplines as those that move from the inner to the outer dimensions of man and the cultural-sociological sciences as those that start with the outer dimensions. Both disciplines will generally subscribe to this paragraph from the pen of the philosopher-cultural analyst James Feibelman: [2]

> The extent to which the human individual is a social product is indeed astonishing. The human individual would not be human were it not for the social milieu. The forms of social effect upon the physiological individual include such practices as cicatrization, tooth-extraction, nose-boring, head-shaping, foot-binding, neck-elongating, lip-distending, ear-boring and -distending, infibulating and circumcising. The psychological individual also changes in relation to the demands of his social group to a remarkable degree. Some of these changes are: in thresholds of pain (ready response and lack of response) and in emotional response (weeping out of sorrow or out of a sense of duty). The social influence is evident likewise in the institutional capacities and performances of the individual. He acts as a father (the family); a taxpayer and voter (politics, the state); a breadwinner (economics, business) etc.

Obviously, the way in which leisure choices are made becomes a central issue in view of the double focus: what man *does* with the conditions *available to him*. To explain concretely how a leisure choice is made, we must therefore broaden our frame of reference. We have, in Chapter 2, examined the concept *culture*. We turn now to the problem of how the person treads his way between the various kinds of controls that exist within his culture. Our next task is to relate leisure to the controls we shall call consensus or conformity, tradition, representation, hierarchy, knowledge, exclusiveness, and imposition.

Consensus and conformity

The source of solidarity between persons may be agreement on common values or a mass pattern of activity *as if* there were agreement. The more explicit the agreement, the more we are inclined to call this consensus; more implicit agreement as covertly projected in behavior is more often called conformity.

The area of agreement may be anything from a liking for risqué stories to belief in fairies or the beneficence of vacations in Florida. Whatever the source of such ideas, the classifications into which they might be put, or their relations to interests and actions, we do know that important ideological constellations such as Communism, Confucianism, Materialism, or Idealism can be distinguished and traced through and into the structures that exist upon each. Their power to their constituents consists in the nature of the training, mythology, or police systems that may be found. To the extent that there is genuine belief, we can expect to find superstitions, myths, lies, revelations, and illogical assumptions as effective in controlling people as are scientific or objective knowledge. Irrationality may constitute the very strength of some beliefs.[3]

The area of consensus, such as the thrill of momentary adventure illustrated in this description of a high school clique, may be only vague: [4]

> The search for something exciting or novel is a major part of a clique's activity. Many hours are squandered in restless, random movement from one public place to another. Early in the evening, a boy may leave home in his car and pick up a pal. They may drive around town for a few minutes, park in front of a hangout, get out and go in. There they meet a third friend, have a coke or a beer, play the pin ball machine for a few minutes. Suddenly one of them suggests, "Let's go over to Diamond City and see what's going on." The others respond, "Yeh, that's a thought." They get in the car and drive to Diamond City, go to Mike's Tavern and have a beer, then start for the Gay Paree to see if they can "find a babe or two." Possibly they will see some girls on the way, drive by them slowly, whistle, and circle the block, but the girls are not interested. They go on, but "nothing may be doing" at the Gay Paree. After a drink, one of the party suggests, "I wonder what's new at Angel's Point." This starts them for Angel's Point, about nine miles away. On the way they pass Piccolo Pete's, and the new "three-way" girl "Pete just brought down from Chicago" is discussed. "Boney tried her last week. He says she's the best in the county." The second observes, "Let's go back and look her over." The driver retorts, "None of that stuff for me; I'm broke. I was out to Paula's the other night." The first boy ruefully remarks, "No cat houses for me; there's plenty on the streets for free." The driver rejoins, "Yeah, but you have to scratch for that stuff. When I want my ashes hauled, I want it now." The car pulls into Angel's Point, drives down the main street, and out to the skating rink. The boys park, go in and watch the skaters for a few minutes, and decide, "No likely meat here; let's go." They drive back to Elmtown on the river road and note that the highway signs they used as targets last week have been replaced with new ones. "Jeez, but they changed them quick this time." "Yeh, we gotta be careful; the state cops are patrolling this road." They park in front of the Blue Triangle upon their return to town and go in for coffee. There they meet three or four other cliques, exchange greetings, talk about where they have been; then the group breaks up as each one starts home about ten-thirty or eleven o'clock.

What is important, then, about solidarity through consensus or conformity is not the nature or truth of its content but the sense of identification in a common mental, psychological, and social climate. Indeed, a group can often be found that has quite forgotten its original motivations or its original needs have been long fulfilled, yet the group continues to find satisfaction in the simple fact of its being; it therefore finds other excuses for justifying itself.

Consensus or conformity are opposites of diversity. Means of control vary: a fear of disbelief in Hell, which is really a belief in the main body of thought; ostracism, social or theological; physical retaliation, as in the Inquisition; ridicule, as being considered "different" or "queer." Types of deviants include dissenters, doubters, eggheads, skeptics, fools, professors, and marginal persons who sway between two or more systems of life and throught.

A common illustration of consensus as a force in leisure choices is the fad, fashion, or craze. One author, describing the rise of the bicycle,[5] notes that "the craze hit all ages. It led to a change in women's styles—skirts became shorter—and it started the movement toward decent roads." The United States Census wrote, "Few articles ever used by man have ever created so great a revolution in social conditions." There were more than 300 manufacturers of bicycles in the five years before the turn of the century. The prevailing price of 125 dollars restricted the craze to about one million adults. This form of travel —called the "safety" in the nineties—did have practical advantages, such as enabling travel to nearby communities or riding to work, but that it became a craze is explainable largely by the temper of the times, expressed in conversation as well as in a large number of stories, advertisements, and articles in such journals as *Harper's* and *Scribner's*.

In our own day there has been a new body of writing on what Vance Packard has called *The Status Seekers*—those "striving, frightened" people who seek to own the right house in the right location, to entertain the right people, or to send their children to the right schools. Russell Lynes writes pungently of conformity in *The Tastemakers;* William Whyte's *Organization Man* and C. Wright Mill's *White Collar* are more serious but equally dramatic discussions in the same vein.

Thus we use consensus in a broad sense, not limiting the term to conscious agreement by a small group but implying unanimity in the larger sense. The term "mores" is familiar to sociology and may be used here. What is *in the air* or *in the mores* may be mah-jongg, the yo-yo, miniature golf, or (1958) the bright-colored hoop. "Crowd behavior," "imitation," and "mimesis" are other terms roughly comparable in the parlance of social psychology.

Interesting examples of leisure as grounded in the mores are the festivals that have long histories in various parts of the world, as among the Aztecs, Peruvians, Teutons, Aryans, Semites, and Egyptian last have three festivals of the seasons, twelve of the month, a dozen relating to bi-weekly periods. According to Strabo, the number of holidays exceeded work days in Greece at one period. The Mohammedans had two major festival periods, each extending three or four days. Hinduism observes a festival time of five days in the Spring.

In all of these cases, as in our own Easter time—and no matter how commercialized such a season may have become [6]—there is a general heightening of excitement and anticipation. As Robert Trumbull reported in a Kyoto dispatch to *The New York Times* of October 8, 1955,

> This month also there is the Festival of Auspicious Offerings, the Dance of Land-Tax Exemption, the Bull Festival, the Festival of Ages and the Fire Festival, so Kyoto, Japan's capital for more than 1,000 years, is bursting at its seams. Its geisha districts, illuminated by thousands of colored paper lanterns, possibly are the merriest neighborhoods in all the world just now.

Under such a mood, perhaps the problem is to explain why some persons are *not* carried away with the prevailing mood.

In some cases, as in fashion—generally defined as longer-lasting than a craze—the origins of group behavior may be calculated. Particularly in Western cultures, as in our own, popular heroes such as motion picture actors may be prevailed upon (or paid) to pioneer a style or a game, to frequent a particular vacation spot, or to popularize smoking. On the other hand, there are leisure activities, such as the game "scrabble," that are available for some years and then suddenly and for no apparent reason became exceedingly fashionable.

Some activities of long-standing popularity are accepted as normal patterns by certain segments or groups; to be taken into the group, one has to conform in this respect as in others. Such activity may range from attending art exhibits, to bowling, to becoming adept at poker. Conformity to the group is visible evidence, in part, of the fact that one indulges skillfully in its fashionable and symbolically important activities.

Reports by William Whyte reveal the prevalence of expected leisure patterns among junior executives. In the work circles of others, as well, there is often a consensus or climate of opinion on the proper free-time activities of the miner, musician, lumberman, farmer, scientist, and other occupational groups. Since the types of leisure mentioned in Chapters 12 to 17 differ in cost as well as connotative qualities, travel is more likely to be in the fashion of businessmen than of unskilled workers. The pervasiveness of radio and television has crossed all community, class, or even educational lines. Only the movie, with its overwhelming audience below the age of 35 has maintained an age segmentation.

To summarize: *one major explanation for some choices is that the leisure activity is "in the air."* Participation assures one that one is behaving as expected in one's own circles.

Tradition

Some groups or social relationships exist over a period of time because they take on a certain righteousness *in the doing.* Here is the basis of "common law." Sumner used the terms *folkways* and *mores* to distinguish various degrees in which patterns of action are accepted as natural by a society.[7] Folkways are acts that, repeated "often by great numbers acting in concert or, at least, acting in the same way when face to face with the same need," become accepted as right. They become habit for the person and custom for the society. Mores, resulting from the larger importance we attach to some violations, are more binding; the sanctions—rewards and punishments—are therefore more explicit. In both classes of importance, folkways or mores, social actions themselves have become normative values.

Many means of control can be cited in this category: obligations to preceding generations, dead and alive; simple habit; fear of ostracism; venerated writings, which explain origins or otherwise seek to justify the going patterns; and taboos, which stand as negative limits on behavior.

Some types of deviants within this category of order are the stranger, unacquainted with established ways, hence a potential or actual danger; the Bohemian, who makes a fetish of nonconformity; the creative person, who refuses to be bound by the past;[8] the cosmopolite, such as the traveler, the soldier, the leisure-class member, who has had contact with other traditions or whose status does not spring from stability within the whole society or even a segment of it.

As to leisure, something is said in Chapter 20 on patterns and repetitions of activities, such as regular attendance at movies or weekly bridge. *The regularity assumes a momentum, a source of security in the familiar.* Any of the leisure types discussed in Part 3 lend themselves to the creation of leisure-ritual.

Representation

We seek constantly to bring experience into our consciousness through such symbol systems as languages, pictures, colors, and artistic forms. We do not abstract a desirable social relationship rationally directed toward the good life; we create and surround ourselves with myths, legends, gods, decalogues, rituals, sacred books and people, holy places, and heroes to represent and justify them. We take oaths and observe holidays. We indulge in stereotypes and address each other via meaningful titles—or lack of them—denoting rank and relative position.[9] We live in a certain section of the city in accordance with its symbolic meaning of position and success. All these symbols, oaths, etc., are not only means of maintaining social distance, power, or orderly human relationships, they often become fused with the "reality" of the relationship itself. Play—games and drama especially—thus become sophisticated mirrors of the society.

Deviants to such representations are found among skeptics, doubters of the gospel, religious agnostics, philosophical pragmatics, cynics in business, or professional social scientists.

The most direct implication for this form or source of control for leisure is its place in social class. As noted in Chapter 6, class patterns are changing in good part because of the possibilities for the masses to adopt leisure ways that until recently were associated with the elite. Leisure as a form of control through its symbolic class image has all but disappeared. Thus, in a real sense, the new leisure is a potent counterrevolutionary force. As a by-product of capitalism, leisure has become its protector.

Of the several important leisure types, the arts are the most important of the new procapitalistic forces. For art was historically an upper-class possession. Elite art, some argue, is inherently superior to the mass culture. As the masses obtained a material level of life worthy of kings only a short while ago, they appropriated the symbols of kings, art and play among them. It may be that the superiority of elite or of mass art will fast become an academic question, for it is no more a matter of either/or. Mass art exists within a whole social relationship that differs in its fundamentals from class society and can hardly be judged by criteria or referrents of the past.

In summary, we sometimes choose a leisure activity not because of its content or inherent worth but because it is associated with the good, thrilling, avant-garde, beatnik, dignified, religious, youthful, and so on. *Leisure activity becomes a means, an instrument for projecting that which we think we are or are expected to become.*

Hierarchy

Power, as expressed in status positions, can be a forceful element in cementing a society. Various types of hierarchies exist: *revealed authority*, a priest or a Father Divine; *bureaucratic*, in which authority is present but elusive; *coercive agent*, such as sheriff or dean of college students; *institutional*, such as father at home or captain in the military; *knowledgeable*, as the editor-in-chief of an encyclopedia staff. *Paternal* control is central in Jerome Dowd's *Control in Human Societies*, ". . . the father in the family, the king in the state, the priest in the religious order, and the master in the workshop." [10] Hierarchy is to be found not only in terms of ascendant power positions among individuals or offices but also between groups: slave–master, Brahmin–outcaste, American white–Negro, business–working class.

Implicit means of control vary somewhat in the foregoing illustrations, but they are generally reducible to techniques or agencies that capitalize on respect, fear, force, or law.

Types of deviants range from the social fool—the Schweik, the court jester, or the village idiot, who recognizes no status positions—to the social climber and passer, the unbeliever, or the lawbreaker.

The appeal of some leisure to some persons is that some special persons have it. The same psychology is at work whether it is the purchase of a cigarette or a car—imitation of a hero or a cultural leader.

Knowledge

Knowledge, whether through knowing, learning, or contact with a variety of experience, becomes an important social factor when it is controlled. Most prominent in the actions of parents toward young children, rationed intelligence implies a limitation on the awareness of alternatives. Science and public education are two important agencies for enlarging and spreading knowledge; hence they compete in the arena of controls with agencies holding special points of view. Knowledge is also the *sine qua non* of the professional person, who therefore occupies a special position within this category. Propaganda, censorship, the exercise of power through the ownership or direction of the mass media, control by direct or indirect measures of the school as an institution or of the teacher as a person—these are obvious means of control.

The deviant may be looked for among those who have access to knowledge beyond that degree desired for them by those in power—persons who are curious, discerning, doubting, discriminating, or who (like the "genius") somehow exceed limits of knowledge hitherto taken for granted.

T. W. Adorno and others have pointed to the use of the mass media as agencies for "soporific controls" over the minds of the many.[11] More recently, techniques of the "hidden persuaders" have been widely popularized. In their leisure hours before television—hours when their intellectual defenses are perhaps at their lowest—millions of persons are thus at the receiving end of images that are planned by some of the best advertising minds in the country.

On the other hand, *many persons are using their leisure by committing themselves to the pursuit of knowledge.* For example, in 1960 there were more adults attending evening classes than the combined student population of all grades from the first through the university. No one can calculate the proportion of literacy, in the larger sense, that is attributable to an increase in leisure time. Further, there is evidence that television is not entirely a passive or unrewarding experience in terms of knowledge.

Exclusiveness

Both the objective of exclusiveness and its criteria vary from group to group. Among the first might be the desire to serve better "our own" (Elks, Rotary), to provide some channel for making a group a power over outsiders as well as over themselves (college fraternity), to create a tighter discipline over one group only to influence others (the underground resistance in France or Communist cells in the United States). Criteria on which a group feels exclusive or defines its membership may be age, family origins, allegiance to a doctrine, wealth (either amount or source), sex, and so on. A feeling of superiority exists, sometimes reaching fanaticism and extreme intolerance. If not the cause itself, *it is the feeling of belonging that is the source of solidarity.*[12]

Means by which such groups control their own members include secret rooms, oaths, elaborate rites, initiations, probationary periods, testing experiences, dress, careful selection of members, provisions for expulsion, and systems of promotions or other rewards. Secret or semisecret societies may exercise control over outsiders by threats or actual violence (Ku Klux Klan), by sabotage or revolution, or by peaceful means through persuasion, teachings, conversations, and community services (Knights of Columbus, Freemasons).[13]

At the other extreme from secrecy are those who assert or purchase exclusiveness in a public way, as outlined by Thorstein Veblen in his theory of conspicuous consumption.[14]

A traitor to one's class is a type of deviant. Another is the disillusioned person. We also find pariahs, parvenus, and the *nouveau riche*, who transgress, who move into neighborhoods or circles in which they were once excluded.

We have already spoken of social class and leisure. The bicycle craze, for instance, moved up from the middle class to the upper class, who found that they could keep their waistlines down by sufficient pedaling, even though they continued to eat rich foods. Other activities, such as tennis, golf, fishing, and hunting, have moved downward in the economic scale.

It is possible to distinguish public from private class and caste manifestations. Only moral force is usually available or advisable in treating of the first. It is, to many persons, regrettable that the fraternity system lends itself to the drawing of sharp lines between the selected and rejected; here the moral principle is applied that secrecy or social discrimination is incompatible with educational tradition. On the more adult level of exclusion from private clubs, the liberal similarly regrets the incompatibility with larger ethe of the democratic society. Indeed, since leisure behavior is based on the presumption of voluntariness and freedom, the admission of minorities into play circles is a more accurate criterion of democracy than is admission into schools.[15]

Another way of looking at it is to approach leisure or play activity as therapy. From this light, such vehicles of exclusiveness to be found in sociability and club activity provide an escape mechanism from an excess of equalitarianism. The semisecret lodge and its ritual may thus be perceived as some guarantee for democracy where democracy counts—in the polls, streets, or political arenas.

Real issues are thus presented to the group leader or recreation worker: to what degree, ethically as well as practically, can or should he look upon recreational organization as a technique for creating new social patterns; to what degree can or should he mix groups that, aside from such possibilities in play, do not mix? On these points there is divided opinion among professional workers. The issue will come to the fore in the decades ahead, as more and more persons become available to the various services influenced or led by those in the leisure professions. A new and important dimension is thereby added to what was said in Chapter 11 on value systems; for now the concern broadens from the judgment of successful leisure, as seen in terms of the individual's criteria and needs, to criteria of group and community life.

Imposition

This, the most explicit and naked form of control, is simply force, violence, and terror. A military system of discipline can be included, since the threat of punishment is close to the surface; however, some account must be taken of the subject's willingness to subordinate himself in respect to larger objectives.

Media for such controls are rigid training in reacting to symbols of authority, outright threat, reprisal, punishment, terror, assassination, spy systems, and the sowing of suspicion; in a prison or concentration camp, constant guarding, the cultivation of absolute dependence upon authority, and the division of one group against another.

Deviants are such persons as the "fifth columnist," the person who works with authority against his fellow-men, and the person who—like Schweik—is a fool and sees only the game in life or the one who finds his own security in his dependence.

Perhaps the clearest example of force as an element of control in leisure is in the gang. The gang is usually a despotism; none of its members wants to defy this authority because it means a beating and ostracism. A gentler but even better disciplined unit is the college fraternity, in which such leisure practices as dating and drinking may be imposed by fiat and, if not carried out as prescribed, are ultimately punishable by expulsion.

Other controls—applications to research

The foregoing discussion has highlighted several explanations for the choice of leisure activities: (*a*) everybody is doing it; (*b*) I have been doing this for a long time, I am secure in it; (*c*) this choice represents what I want to be as a person; (*d*) my idols and heroes are doing this, it is good enough for me; (*e*) this activity will improve me, give me more knowledge; (*f*) by doing this, I will show that I am different; and (*g*) I really have no choice, the gang says I must do it.

Many more controls can be added. For instance, we have already discussed the controls of work, personality, family, community, social class, subculture, state, religion, and value system. There is little point in erecting elaborate systems of analysis in which every type of leisure behavior is catalogued or in which controls are distinguished from motivations, goals, needs, drives, satisfactions, will, and so on. The purpose of systematic thought is in part to seek particularistic, rather than wholistic, or total analytic systems so that hypotheses may be established.

Thus, the foregoing analysis may prove of value in the design of research. Three types of issues are suggested as fruitful, and are noted at this point:

1. Personality types can be discerned by their accessibility to patterns of control.

2. Types of leisure can be distinguished by clusters or combinations of control elements.

3. It is possible to correlate the scattering of personality needs (as seen through controls) and activity, thus arriving at predictions concerning:

(a) Probable choices of activities.

(b) Types of personal needs met by the activity.

(c) Prevalence of controls in relation to work, family, class, subculture, state, religion, and value system.

(d) The resolution of social deviancy in and through play forms.

A series of hypotheses is attempted for some of these in the course of this and subsequent chapters.

Personality types seen through response to controls

Various attempts have been made in the social sciences to develop profiles of character types. We have referred previously to Riesman's *directeds*. For present purposes we use a threefold "value-orientation" taken from a recent study, *Occupations and Values:* [16] "people-oriented," "extrinsic-reward-oriented," and "self-expression-oriented." The authors claim that under the first are persons in social work, medicine and teaching; under the second, persons in real estate, finance, hotels, sales, and promotion; among persons of the self-expression orientation are those in art, drama, journalism, or architecture.

In the diagrammatic hypothesis that follows, each of these types of persons is rated as positive or negative in respect to each type of control on a rough scale of seven points. For instance, a plus 3 indicates the highest respect for or vulnerability to the control; a minus 3 is the greatest degree of rejection. Our hypothesis is that the correlation between forms of control and value orientations is approximately as follows:

	Consensus	Tradition	Representation	Hierarchy	Knowledge	Exclusiveness	Imposition
People-oriented	+3	−1	+1	−1	0	0	−3
Object-oriented	−2	+2	−2	+3	−1	+3	0
Expressive-oriented	−2	−3	−2	−2	+3	−3	−3

If this is diagrammed,

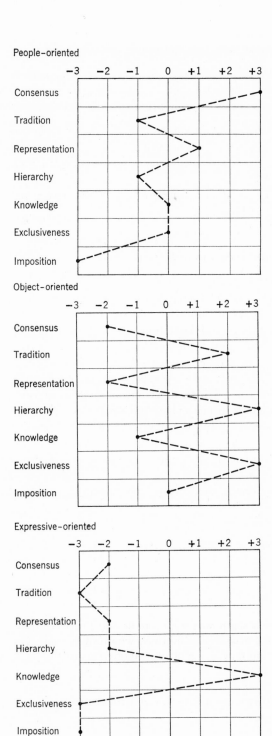

Assuming that preliminary tests were run and scales devised to test the degree to which the person is subject to each form of control, the hypothesis indicates roughly that

1. *The more expressive or creative the person, the more he is controlled or influenced by knowledge.*
2. *The object or reward-orientation is motivated most by status, as in class position.*
3. *Those oriented to people are most concerned with factors under consensus or conformity.*

Leisure type seen through its controls

The second hypothesis is built on the fact that each type of leisure —as, of course, in all other patterns of human actions—contains characteristic elements of dominant control. For instance, a baseball game may be organized (and kept together as a social group) because of the liking of one player for another, respect for a physical education teacher who ordered his students to play, or the economic rewards that go to the professional player. But the *game* itself is primarily dominated by rules, which determine the duties of each position, the number of players, times at bat, and so on.

In the following table, a rough attempt (unverified in any experimental way) is made to hypothesize the importance of each control for each type of leisure. Again, a scale of seven units is employed.

	Sociability	Association	Game	Art	Mobility	Immobility
Consensus	+3	+3	+2	−3	+1	+2
Tradition	+2	+3	+3	+2	0	0
Representation	0	+2	+1	+2	+1	0
Hierarchy	−2	+2	+3	−2	−2	−2
Knowledge	−2	0	+1	+2	+1	+1 *
Exclusiveness	−1	+2	+1	+1	+1	−2
Imposition	−3	−2	−3	−3	−2	−3

* In this case, a sharp difference is to be noted between those who compose audiences of the mass media and those who read or study. Knowledge is obviously less important as a control or motivation of the former. (See Chapter 17.)

From the foregoing, the major control elements dominate the following leisure types:

1. Consensus is most dominant in sociability and association, least in art.

2. Tradition is dominant in association and game, least in mobility and immobility.

3. Representation is most dominant in association and art, least in sociability and immobility.

4. Hierarchy is most dominant in game.

5. Knowledge is most dominant in art, also in that portion of immobility devoted to study and reading.

6. Exclusiveness is most dominant in association.

7. Imposition dominates none of the leisure types.

Hypotheses correlating personality types and activity controls

From the two hypotheses given, we may attempt to combine them in reference to several items:

1. *Those who are people-oriented are most in need of activities in which consensus dominates, that is, sociability and association.* The problem exists whether such persons do, indeed, seek out such activity. The assumption is that they do, since the scientist assumes some consistency between what people are and what they do. Thus the hypothesis may be amplified: those who are people-oriented will seek out leisure of sociability and association.

2. *Those who are object-oriented are most in need of and will most likely choose leisure activities in which hierarchy and exclusiveness dominate, that is, game and association.*

3. *Those who are expressive-oriented are most in need of and will most likely choose leisure activities in which knowledge dominates, that is, art.*

It is possible to employ the analysis of social controls in leisure by applying them to specific segments of the population. Our illustration is drawn from studies of business executives and college sophomores.

Leisure and business executives

Business executives may be called a subculture in the sense of Chapter 7. Several paradoxes in their leisure attitudes and actions emerge from a recent study and illustrate issues of our discussion on social controls in leisure. August Hecksher and Sebastian de Grazia raise the questions, "Are executives beginning to see leisure in a new light? Are they beginning to question some of the assumptions and habits which have led them to work longer hours than their own employees and indeed than almost any other group in the population?" Over 30 per cent responded to an extensive questionnaire submitted to 17,000 executives.[17]

We are not surprised to find that the old notion is strong, "to work is to live," and that for a variety of reasons given 90 per cent of the respondees would go on working even if they had independent incomes. What is perhaps surprising is the *verbal* dedication to the idea of leisure even though the average time spent in work—both in office and at home—comes to 55 hours per week. A large majority—73 per cent—reported that they would like more time for nonbusiness activities. Do they, as bosses in the work situation, take an occasional day off, as one evidence of their belief? Less than half do so, according to Hecksher and de Grazia, who ask whether this fact does not raise a question about "the seriousness of their desire for leisure." Thus we see a clear reason, as suggested in Chapter 1, for taking a hypothetical answer, a statement of attitude, with the traditional grain of salt. The element of control—consensus—which dominates the *verbal* response, is overweighed by the other element of control—tradition, habit—which more effectively guides the businessman's behavior.

What does the executive do with his free time? According to the investigation, he spends on the average only 5.2 hours per week on literary and cultural activities (including good reading) as against 21.8 hours in "hobbies, sports, TV, movies, visiting friends, relaxing, etc." Thus we have empirical evidence of the interests of object-oriented persons, as already noted. Those executives with more college background, especially, indicated that if they had more time they would devote it to self-improvement and civic improvements. A general attitude among executives—perhaps reflecting a philosophy of individualism transposed from business to leisure values—is a suspicion of the guidance of leisure time—their own or that of their employees.

Among these businessmen, who are at the top of the American economic system in terms of financial rewards, only one fourth take as much as a month's vacation; a third, as much as three weeks, another third, two weeks. Almost eight in ten of these men concede that their employees will have more leisure time than they, yet only one half believe that they themselves will gain more free time. Thus a final paradox is noted by the study that the pattern of values for more leisure is more deeply established among *workers*. As we noted in the chapter on social class, the European rich were specialists at play; the American class system is breaking down in this respect, and here (contrary to Veblen's prediction) *the business-rich are learning how to play from those below.* We may add to this observation, supported in the study by Hecksher and de Grazia, the view noted in the chapter on art, that the *content* of leisure is also shifting upward from the middle to the upper economic classes. As their research notes, business executives do not associate leisure with art or other creative activities; their ends in free time are those we might associate with mass culture.

To the degree that leisure, in amount as well as in depth, was once a manifestation and tool of wealth in Europe, leisure is not a symbolic control by or of the elite in our country; the center of control through leisure is in the middle class. Yet the evidence now exists that the concept of leisure is changing among the higher business circles. Today's executive no longer feels that to want more free time for himself is immoral; on the contrary, he feels it is a natural and proper thing to wish for. The authority or hierarchy of the economic system does not function as it might have been expected to for the realization of ends. Conformity is as strong a control among the powerful in business as among their workers. These executives, especially those on the lower rung of the ladder, are in a highly competitive situation in which they are conscious of status and its proper behavioral symbols.

College students and the future

We turn for our second illustrative study to a group of college students with a special problem in mind: how does the student look ahead to his future leisure and his future society? Our rough assumption is that in some degree what he *expects* is a control of what he *wants, works for,* and therefore *receives.*

The report is based on a questionnaire submitted by the writer to his 104 students at the University of Illinois in 1957; most of them were sophomores and juniors. Ten predictions were noted, some taken directly from a volume by Morris Ernst on what we may expect in 1976.[18] The student was asked to check whether he thought the predicted change was "certain," "reasonably certain," or "improbable" for the year 1976 and again for A.D. 2000. The fourth column was to be checked "if you feel that there are too many conditions, qualifications, or 'ifs' which enter the picture to make *any* prediction." The totals are presented:

TABLE 16

Predictions by College Sophomores: Life in 1976 and A.D. 2000

	A.D. 1976				A.D. 2000			
	Certain	Reasonably Certain	Improbable	?	Certain	Reasonably Certain	Improbable	?
1. Most men will work 30 hours per week or less	25	54	21	3	60	26	5	8
2. Week end plane trips to Asia or the Orient will be common	7	38	49	8	41	41	11	10
3. No major wars will have been fought	3	14	39	46	7	9	45	43
4. Polio and cancer will be licked by medical science	13	62	18	10	60	34	4	4
5. Atomic energy will be major source of industrial energy	16	68	17	1	74	29	0	2
6. Symphony orchestras will be found in most communities	10	37	47	11	18	29	36	18
7. Air conditioning will be found in most homes	51	41	8	2	80	17	3	2
8. The United Nations will be a world government with a strong military	0	18	50	34	5	21	32	44
9. Divorce will be very easy to get and quite common	7	30	47	18	10	26	40	26
10. There will be no legal or social division of races	1	16	75	11	10	28	46	19

The most doubt was expressed on the items concerning the probability of wiping out war and enlarging United Nations authority. The most certainty was expressed for the prediction of home air conditioning and lowered working hours. Again, progress in the physical and natural sciences was heavily predicted, as in cancer cures and the possibility of quick transportation to all parts of the world. Five areas that concern social change (war, orchestras, the United Nations, divorce, race equality) were given the least hope, especially racial equality. These probably represent widely held views of the larger public.

TABLE 17

Projections and Record by Students: Leisure Activities 1957 and 1976

Key: Directions to students
In column A check one or more activities you enjoy doing.
In column B check *three* of your favorite activities.
In column C check those you have done since last July 4.
In column D check a plus (+) or minus (−) sign if you expect to do any
of these more or less often in 1976.

Activity	A Enjoy This	B Prefer This	C Did This	D 1976 (+)	(−)
1. Television	90	15	104	70	19
2. Radio	74	1	104	33	51
3. Phonograph	99	26	103	73	20
4. Read a book	87	26	99	88	8
5. Read a magazine	84	4	100	75	8
6. Watch sports	76	13	99	42	33
7. Play in sports	75	26	85	27	55
8. Fish	41	7	27	33	22
9. Hunt	28	7	23	25	23
10. Play cards	61	6	90	55	22
11. Other indoor games	45	1	74	30	29
12. Gamble	25	2	33	15	32
13. Dance	82	20	94	35	46
14. Parties	86	19	97	46	34
15. Ride car	68	4	96	64	13
16. Ride airplane	46	6	35	61	15
17. Be with family	80	15	98	57	29
18. Go to concerts	68	5	64	65	16
19. Walk	60	5	90	28	39
20. Sew or knit	26	2	40	38	22
21. Loaf–sleep	70	5	92	35	42
22. Church activity	33	1	55	46	14
23. Make things, wood	24	2	27	15	36
24. Make things, clay	19	0	16	14	31
25. Photography	39	6	44	37	22
26. Conversation	93	32	97	64	6
27. Work puzzles	30	2	48	19	28
28. Just sit	31	1	63	29	33
29. Visit friends	79	14	97	66	10
30. Club meetings	42	2	74	49	18
31. Go on trips	85	35	88	77	8
32. Shopping trips	44	3	84	51	16
33. Sing, play music	47	7	49	24	11

The same study sought to check what the students themselves enjoyed doing, what they preferred to do, and what they had actually done in the preceding year; in addition, predictions of an increase or decrease of the same list were invited for 1976. The directions given are presented, together with totals.

Many observations can be made by comparing items within this classification. For example, we note the disparity between the number of students who say that they *enjoy* cards (61) and those who have played (90), that a larger number prefer to go on trips (55) than prefer TV (15) or radio (1), that about a third of the college group enjoy church activities (33), and almost 50 enjoy singing or playing music. However, let us play a bit with these figures by sorting the activities roughly into the classification used earlier in the volume:

Sociability

Dance
Parties
Be with family
Conversation
Visit friends

Associations

Church activity
Club meetings

Games and sports

Watch sports
Play in sports
Fish
Hunt
Play cards
Other indoor games
Gamble
Work puzzles

Art

Phonograph
Go to concerts
Sew or knit
Make things, wood
Make things, clay
Photography
Sing, play music

Mobility

Ride car
Ride airplane
Walk
Go on trips
Shopping trips

Immobility

Television
Radio
Read a book
Read a magazine
Loaf–sleep
Just sit

When these items are added to the student replies noted, the following totals appear for each *category:*

TABLE 18

Student Activities According to Classification of Type

	Enjoy	Prefer	Did	More in 1976	Less in 1976
Sociability	418	100	483	268	125
Associations	75	3	129	95	32
Games, sports	381	64	479	246	244
Art	322	53	313	266	158
Mobility	303	53	393	281	91
Immobility	436	52	562	330	161

We note in every category *except art* that students engaged in particular activities more than their indication of enjoyment. Does this suggest that there is more social pressure to engage in activities other than art? If, out of curiosity, we tabulate the difference in the other five areas between *enjoyment* and *activity*, we find that the number of those who did these things *even though they do not necessarily enjoy them* was

sociability 65,	or 13% of participants
associations 54,	or 41% of participants
game, sports 198,	or 40% of participants
mobility 90,	or 22% of participants
immobility 126,	or 22% of participants

Perhaps a hypothesis lies dormant here: *that a scale of pressures seems to exist, which exerts itself most in the area of joining groups and games, least in the area of friendships, and almost not at all in the arts.* (It would appear that much the same holds true for the business executives discussed in the preceding section.)

It is the last two columns of Table 18 that look toward the future. In every category students predict that they will do more in 1976, when they will be about 38 years of age. Yet there are marked differences within these totals. Activity in games will, they suggest, be least affected by changes in the intervening years. Most change of activity will be in the realms of mobility or travel, followed in descending order by sociability, immobility, art, and association.

Were a similar questionnaire given to middle-aged and older persons, we should predict a generally similar forecast of the future. Nor can the social scientist differ substantially in his projections, based upon current trends and increasing impact of technological devices upon our lives. The scientist, further, brings into *his* projections the force of the predictions made *by those who will live into the period being considered in time.*

Yet the nature of our predictions is not a matter of cold fact or cerebration; it is also a projection of what we are as persons. It is to this issue of personality to which we return in Chapter 19.

Personality and social roles in leisure 19

In a study of how leisure choices are made, Professor Robert Havighurst writes,[1]

> The significance of leisure activities is more closely related to personality
> than to the social variables of age, sex, and social class. Thus leisure activity
> is an aspect of personality. It is a response to personality needs, being one
> of the ways by which people express themselves.

The issue remains: what is personality? The various social sciences
have been moving toward a unified theory, which stresses the inter-
relations of several factors traditionally emphasized by special disciplines. Witness this conclusion by a group of psychiatrists: [2]

> Personality and society are viewed here not as closed systems but as con-
> tinuously interacting. Each influences the other selectively toward change.
> While the intactness of personality is reflected in relatively fixed pro-
> pensities of behavior, it is simultaneously in continuous interaction with,
> and is influenced by, the environment. Behavior is determined both by
> stimuli derived from the internal organization of the person and the ex-
> ternal organization of the social environment. Constitution sets limits to
> behavior potentials, but structured behavior is always conditioned by
> social experience. The development of personality is influenced both by
> biological makeup at birth and by the process of internalization of ele-
> ments of the social environment. All behavior, beginning with birth, is
> bio-psycho-social.

The social environment in the largest sense is the culture. Thus,
capitalizing on this anthropological concept, the social scientist now
faces this problem; is there a *core personality* that has constant characteristics across cultures? And within the culture, how does the person relate himself to its unique set of social controls—to its sanctions,
laws, traditions, mores, assumptions, legends, and authorities? Robert
S. Lynd writes,[3]

253

We were all born little animals with unique endowments. We have been "house-broke" in varying ways—gently or roughly, consistently or erratically—by people bigger and stronger than ourselves and able to exercise authority over us. For convenience we say we have "grown up," "become socialized," "been acculturated." What we mean is that we have learned, under the sharp sting of necessity, how to "get by" and get what we want and avoid trouble in terms of the habit systems of our coercive elders, who in turn had picked up their habits from the retrospective habits of their elders.

Another anthropologist, the late Ralph Linton, provided examples of this assertion on the impact of cultural ways: [4]

Cultural influences . . . begin to operate on the infant from the moment of birth. According to the customs of his society, he may be laid naked on a hard plank (New Caledonia), tucked into a padded cradle (Plains Indian), or tightly bandaged from the neck down (southern Europe). He may be carried about constantly (Malaya), or left alone half a day at a time (Alor). He may be fed whenever he cries (Malaya), on schedule (modern America), or simply when it suits his mother's convenience (New Guinea). He may be the petted center of the family's attention (Japan), or receive only the minimum care necessary to ensure his survival (Alor). Training to control his excretory functions may be imposed within the first six months (Madagascar), or may be delayed until he can learn by imitating his elders.

The purpose of this chapter is something less than a summary of the theories of personality, which would explore the complex interdynamics of the biopsychosocial. Indeed, the history of how this scientific trinity was achieved is that of the social sciences since the turn of the century. Our task is to extract several items from the whole that raise pertinent questions for our present study. How are leisure choices made and practiced? Putting the matter in psychological parlance, if the "two main directions of drives are approach and escape or avoidance," [5] can one's leisure behavior be predicted in reference to a given goal or need?

Needs, drives, wishes, and motivations

Two broad kinds of theories have won adherents for the explanation of behavior. On the one hand are those that ascribe behavior to *antecedent* causes, drives, or instincts. William McDougall, for example, referred to instincts as the "prime movers of all human activity." [6] Among those he listed were the exploring tendency, the gregarious tendency, acquisitiveness, and constructiveness. McDougall spoke also of sentiments consisting of a cluster or grouping of instincts around an object or person.

Freud referred all drives to tensions arising from hunger, thirst, or sex, summarized in the concept of the Id. Freud developed the concept of cathexis or investment: a particular form of behavior is an "investment" or structuring of instinctual energies.

A psychological staff of Harvard listed 28 "psychogenic needs," including personal achievement, dominance, exhibition, and cognizance. These types of explanations have gradually given way to, or fused with, a second, more functional or dynamic approach.

The second type of explanation stresses the purposiveness, teleological nature, or awareness of the *subsequent* aspect of the behavior. One classic illustration is W. I. Thomas' scheme of the "wishes" for new experience, security, response, and recognition.[7] Woodworth's "behavior-primacy" theory considers how man "deals with the environment" by purposive behavior that has a definite goal or end "with means adopted to reach the goal." [8]

One of Woodworth's chief contentions is that "the interactions of a capacity with the environment will generate a specific interest . . . an individual who engages in a task will, unless distracted, find himself absorbed in that task, interested in it and motivated to bring it to completion." [9] Woodworth, writing in reply to McDougall, argued that the behavior pattern develops independently of the underlying need or drive. His book (1958) goes considerably in the direction of Gordon Allport's theory of "functional autonomy," which emphasizes the integration of personality around levels of activity that are not necessarily reducible to basic principles but have a life or validity of their own.

A different order of needs is further suggested by those who argue that purpose or end is a basic component of personality. For example, the psychologist Abraham Maslow [10] speaks of the physiological needs, the safety needs, the need for belongingness and love, for importance, respect, self-esteem, independence, information, understanding, beauty, and self-actualization.

The significance of the two general approaches to a study of leisure is that the biological or instinctive school is *mechanistic* and oriented in the *universe;* mechanistic in that nothing can be done about it, universal in that all men everywhere react similarly to the same signals. A given choice in leisure would therefore be, in Freudian terms, the natural resolution of a tension; in McDougall's terms, an activity such as travel is simply a manifestation of the "exploring tendency."

In contrast, the environmental approach to personality emphasizes its *flexibility* and is *culturally* oriented. A more complex explanation, this view calls upon further analysis of learning, conditioning, or what

Gardner Murphy calls the "canalization" of basic needs into specific actions, interests, or tastes.[11] Murphy speaks of three kinds of human nature: (a) raw or original, (b) devices absorbed from the culture that can be transmitted, and (c) the "urge toward discovery," a living curiosity or "freeing of the intelligence" as it "breaks through the mold." [12]

Further reference to Murphy is made in a later chapter as we discuss the malleability of human nature in connection with the modification of leisure.

Several positions on personality, which represent contemporary sociological thought, have already been noted in Chapter 4. Howard S. Becker's marihuana study illustrated the impact of primary groups on actions as well as on perceptions of enjoyment. Riesman's inner-other typology was one of several attempts to summarize personality types. Eric Fromm's *Sane Society* considers the encouragement that a culture gives to certain types of persons. These are all in sympathy with the newer psychological trends.

Sociology as a whole is less inclined than the Maslows or the Murphys to speak of creativity as a basic personality characteristic. One critic, for instance, reviewing Murphy's last book, applauds its "high moral purpose" but is critical of its tendency to indulge "in exhortation rather than in scientific method." [13] There is general agreement on the fusion of the biological-psychological-social. Sociology goes further in breaking down the lines between person and society; some, but not all, members of the discipline go so far as to argue for a *cultural determinism* or an almost total absence of judgment, choice, or personal influence. The concept of social role has become a sociological tool to indicate how a part of the total identity of the person "is brought into action at a given time by a special set of group phenomena."

According to the late Znaniecki,[14] a group is a creative synthesis of personal roles. Thus one person may belong to several groups and perform in various ways as he moves back and forth between such roles as father, worker, friend, lodge member, and church worshipper. The social circle has its unique norms for its participants; it establishes expectations or functions for its members; it allocates respective positions of esteem or status; it contributes to perceptions of itself as a collective "self" and to pictures that each member has of himself.

An illustration of the use of the social role concept is a study of leisure and "life-style" by Havighurst and Feigenbaum,[15] who sought to relate the leisure activity of 234 persons (aged 40–70) in Kansas City to their roles as parent, spouse, homemaker, worker, citizen, friend, and club or association member. Life-style was defined as the characteristic way in which these roles are combined. A rating scale was devised to measure the person's competence in fulfilling each of his roles and another to represent general expectations of these roles, including one for the role of "user of leisure time." The "significance" of his favorite activities was evaluated on the basis of many factors: autonomy, creativity, enjoyment, instrumentation or expressiveness, ego integration or role diffusion, vitality or apathy, expansion or constriction of interests, development of talent, relation of leisure to work, service or pleasure, status and prestige, new experience or repetition, relaxation, and gregariousness or solitude. Presence of the first seven was treated as signifying a higher role performance.

Life-styles were isolated by these combined factors, and the resultant patterns or styles were grouped into four:

1. "Community centered" (high performance in all roles).
2. "Home centered high" (fall below group 1 in roles of friend, citizen, and club member).
3. "Home centered medium" (family centered but lower than 2).
4. "Low level" (low scores on complexity, with more important family and work role performance).

As we may have anticipated, the community-centered style of leisure was generally carried on away from home—in theaters, concerts, clubs, etc.—by more autonomous persons, seeking novelty and looking for a goal beyond the activity itself. They fell into the upper middle class.

The others engaged in family activities, whether around the home or in family-centered church outings, fishing trips, or sociability with neighbors; there was more division by sex groups.

The authors conclude that in the selection of activities "the personality, more than the situation, determines the life style." The evidence for this is derived by taking a number of community and home-centered people, equating them for age and socioeconomic status, and discovering that location in the suburbs was not a determining factor. The authors do note the importance of children in the home.

It would appear, however, that the presence of children is more a matter of situation than of personality; further, some questions may be raised on the relative merits or significance of the 14 items used as criteria; the situation has also been defined too narrowly on the single criterion of location within the Kansas City metropolitan area. On the last point, a large number of situational factors have been listed in this volume; they range from the location of work and hours (Chapter 3), possession of equipment in the home and general family life

(Chapter 5), birth into subcultural groups (Chapter 7), facilities of the community (Chapter 8), nature of the political system (Chapter 9), and allegiance to religious or secular ideology (Chapters 10 and 11). These items, alone or in combination, do not explain choices in leisure, but they set the objective conditions. If, after all such considerations are disposed of, we ask, "Why did Mr. X engage in O rather than in S activity," and no further explanations are in sight, this residue may very well be called "personality."

This is not to undervalue the concept personality but rather to render it ultimately undefinable, for it is not a thing, or an entity, but a configuration, a "field," a process in which the person constantly interacts within situations. As the social group is a synthesis of roles, so the personality is a synthesis of actions in which elements of individual and group life can hardly be distinguished.

The composition of play or leisure roles depends on the type of activity; the essential distinction of the leisure role from others is in the purpose or direction of leisure—purposes we have suggested in Chapter 2. These purposes or elements, perception of freedom from commitment, from economic functions, etc., can take place in areas near or relatively far from home; it is thus reasonable to construct categories of the kind used by Havighurst and Feigenbaum with the full awareness that we have arbitrarily selected some issue or assumption of something important.

Thus, if instead of ecological concerns leisure-styles are to be directed to distinctions in reference to the use of bodily skills, expenditures of money, or hours of activity, several other kinds could readily be drawn. The elimination of location does not eliminate a host of other conditional factors.

The most important influence upon the individual is the general norm of accepted behavior in the circles or segments of life within which he moves. There can be little doubt that many books are read, many movies are seen, many places are visited, and some symphony concerts are attended because these are the things to do; in other circles, taverns may be frequented, women patronized, bets laid, or strangers "rolled," for these, too, may be the things to do. Conformity by the suburbanite has been much in the minds of recent scholars, as seen in this comment by Reuel Denney: [16]

Suburb man's purposeful use of his leisure to identify with the community bears out Thorstein Veblen's observation that people are torn between using their leisure for the fun of it, and using it to maintain status. In fact, for many a suburb man, leisure can be work. Many a salesman or junior executive feels it obligatory to belong to that country club, or to attend this dinner party where the big shots will be found. Instead of going to the ball games, he is impelled, by the social pressures surrounding him, to play a round of golf, to buy a boat, or to purchase a home movie camera similar to that which the Smiths have. The suburbs impose other exactions on leisure hours. Parents must attend PTA meetings, participate in motor pools, and join in community activities, if they ever want to get the kids into the tennis club.

It is quite impossible to uncover the point at which this kind of pressure becomes not an imposition but a natural part of one's life, so that the pressured one now applies similar pressures on others; in short, the personality and the milieu blend, and the social controls, as we indicated in Chapter 18, are "what's in the air." It is possible to overemphasize this element of "what's in the air" with a philosophy of *Zeitgeist, Weltanschauung,* or similar expressions that have dominated many neo-Platonic historians and metaphysicians; yet it is also possible to exaggerate will, motive, purpose, teleology, choice, or other symbolic references to the triumph of the individual over his culture.

Teleological or purposive activity

In the conceptualization of leisure (Chapter 2) we spoke of one of its elements as pleasant expectation and recollection, of another as the whole range of moral evaluation, and of a third as a perception of freedom. These present goals *beyond* the activity; they are ends such as pleasurable anticipation, identification with the "good," and being "free." Yet the problem of motives has long bedeviled thinkers of all eras. We have no intention of paraphrasing the classic arguments and positions with which the serious student of leisure—or any type of human behavior—has already wrestled. Yet a few observations pertinent to the present topic are in order.

Somehow there has arisen in many contemporary circles the notion that double motivations are unhealthy, that, for instance, leisure that smacks of conformity cannot at the same time be pleasurable and emotionally or mentally satisfying; that those who conform are acting involuntarily, caught, overwhelmed, defeated. This notion oversimplifies. One may, indeed, be a voluntary, conscious, and entirely happy conformist, as may be the case even of the critic of conformity. Similarly, the urge to be or the insistence on being free, creative, or independent can be quite imposed and result in great unhappiness. The arts, for example, are notable for persons who were pushed into creativity by someone or other and in a sense commanded to be free.

The critic of the "mass mind"—a term invariably intended to suggest a uniquely new and American phenomenon—is prone to overlook the thousand years preceding European industrialization, when a mass mind and mass culture (and a low state of culture it was for the masses) were based upon the Church. Then, as now, forces of society, in a very natural and predictable way, weighed heavily on each man and woman, so that the *inner-directed* person of our time corresponds to the *other-directed* of Church and feudal society. The conditions of freedom change and cannot be defined in social vacua. Nor are "happiness," "needs," "desires," and "goals" isolated terms. We have no way of telling whether our nation is happier now or less happy than it was a century ago, and the decision cannot be made by editorial writers. Until one sets forth his assumptions and methods, he cannot tell us whether our society is more creative or less creative than it was in prior generations, and this book has already laid its case for the former judgment in reference to art in America. For these opinions there are no objective formulas.[17]

However, we have incontrovertible evidence that the person of our time has access to a wider variety of things, kinds of people, ways of thought, and styles of life than his father had. He can move faster, be heard farther, and is more likely to be literate and formally educated. His likelihood of being ignorant of such leisure possibilities as adult schools and books is much less.

If man indeed has free will, then today he has a wider palette on which to paint his fantasies. If he is, on the other hand, by and large the reflection and articulation of the "arc of culture" around him, then he is embarrassed by a diversity of physical and mental riches. It is an old song that tells of the many going to Hell, for they are not in the singer's key; the song—and the cacophony—were heard long before the age of television.

Character, purpose, will, personality—these are familiar coins in contemporary explanations of human action. On the other side of the coin we read such terms as structure, pattern, mode, fashion, and organization. Three specific aspects of the *structure* of leisure now concern us as supplements to the explanations of this chapter.

The structure of leisure   20

Our present purpose is to select three aspects of leisure structure for some detailed study: isolated and patterned experience, time, and group composition.

Isolated and patterned experience

An isolated experience, as we use the term, is relatively unrelated to previous habits of the person. It is strange to him and not expected of him by others. It is novel to him but not necessarily an odd or novel experience to others. Examples can be anything: the art exhibit attended by Mr. Jones on Monday, the burlesque show by Mr. Brown on Tuesday, the concert by Mrs. Black on Wednesday, the bridge party by her new daughter-in-law on Thursday. If each of these persons were to be interviewed by a Gallup poll worker on the following Saturday and asked about his leisure activities of the week, four items would be tabulated. In each case the item might be an unrelated, disparate bit, either entirely new or seldom followed by these persons. Of course, the identity of a new experience for Mr. Jones at the art exhibit—by inference—tells us something about him, but it is a deductive conclusion. A more accurate identification of leisure or life patterns is achieved by seeing the person over a period of time.

Patterns of leisure behavior are of two types: X, Y, Z or X_1, X_2, X_3. The first indicates that there is some relationship between qualitatively *different* experiences, such as taking a walk, seeing a TV show, or playing poker. The second indicates a simple repetition of a similar experience, such as watching TV several times a week.

In either case—X, Y, Z or X_1, X_2, X_3—there are at least three ways in which the items of experience are integrated or interrelated.

261

COMMON EXTERNAL FACTOR. The evening walk, the evening TV show, and the evening poker game are related to a common factor, hours of work. Any other variable can be extracted from discussions in Chapters 3 through 11. For example:

Related Experiences		Common External Factors
X	Play with baby	
Y	Drive family for the ride	Be a father
Z	Attend PTA meeting	
X	Watch Yankees play	
Y	Visit Statue of Liberty	Live in New York City
Z	Hear Chinese music	
X	Travel to Europe	
Y	Ride to hounds	Be economically well off
Z	Collect stamps	

FUNCTIONAL DEPENDENCE. In such a case, the items are related substantively through something inherent rather than external: one travels to Italy and therefore prepares by studying the language; or one joins a community theater, having been stimulated by meeting an amateur actor at a party; or one is a member of an athletic club and later finds oneself taking long hikes.

LOGICAL-MEANINGFUL.[1] The activities are consciously related by the participant, so that an idea or connecting thread runs through the experiences. Painting abstractions, reading the *Partisan Review*, and drinking espresso in the right (basement) coffeehouse is avant-garde, and whatever else I do I want to be avant-garde. Joining the right country club, reading *Fortune*, and gambling in Monte Carlo is clear evidence of being a *somebody*, and that is my ambition—to be a *somebody*. Volunteering my free hours to the Grey Ladies, to becoming a Cub Mother, and serving on a committee of the League of Women Voters is part of being useful, a good citizen; this is one of my needs and wants—to be and to be known as a good and useful person.

We have, then, a range from least to most integration between leisure experiences:

1. Isolated items of leisure.
2. Patterned experiences, integrated by (a) a common external factor, (b) functional-dependence, and (c) logical-meaningful dependence.

Our next problem is to note a number of relationships that ____ exist between isolated and patterned leisure experiences. It should be clear that these terms are relative and are perceived as new or old by the participant.

AN ISOLATED EXPERIENCE CAN SERVE AS A CREATIVE EXPLORATION IN ESTABLISHING A PATTERN. The newly married couple, just moved into Chicago, draws up a list of places to visit: Brookfield Zoo, Museum of Science and Industry, etc.; in the course of time they may decide to repeat the museum visit many times. As these places are explored, unexpected experiences and unscheduled places may turn up.[2]

AN ISOLATED EXPERIENCE CAN SERVE AS A CREATIVE ELEMENT TO INTERRUPT A SLAVISH INNER CONFORMITY TO ESTABLISHED BEHAVIOR PATTERNS. This may occur accidentally or deliberately. Small examples occur when the family decides to eat out or to take a camping trip for the first time next summer rather than to return to grandfather's farm. More serious examples occur when a new experience, such as betting on a horse, violates one's previous norms of conduct. One of the writer's students uncovered a family that had moved to Boston from Atlanta. Although their leisure patterns in Georgia had been based on close family and neighborhood interests, the parents were consciously attempting to have the children acquaint themselves with the larger community.

A MEANINGFUL PATTERN MAY SERVE TO PROVIDE A FEELING OF ROOTEDNESS AND IDENTITY. The repetition of activity in bridge club or family provides a person with a social role for which he may be well prepared. He has a feeling for these groups in which he is an accepted part; he knows what will be expected of him, what he may expect in return, and how he is considered by the others.

A MEANINGFUL PATTERN MAY SERVE TO ELIMINATE DISCOVERY IN LEISURE BY BECOMING A PERSONAL RITUAL AND TRADITION. Such, in fact, was the intent of those who imposed restrictions on the free-time behavior of the early American pioneers: one's free time, they implied, should not ever be really free, for free time or a free idea is always a potential threat to the order and can arise even innocently from apparently inconsequential moments and actions.

MEANINGFUL LEISURE PATTERNS ARE CAPABLE OF CREATIVE GROWTH AND MATURATION. The familiar and the new can be balanced. The issue of balance can be seen in an analogy between the person and the society. In a chapter called "The problem of society—how we become selves," George Mead had this to say: [3]

> This is the problem of society, is it not? How can you present order and structure in society and yet bring about the changes that need to take place. . . . How can you bring those changes about in orderly fashion and yet preserve order? To bring about change is seemingly to destroy the given order . . . the problem, to incorporate the methods of change into the order of society itself.

In a chapter on modifications of leisure we face this issue, the place of the new.

Significance and limitations of the dichotomy

There is a danger in social analysis of becoming a prisoner of one's own categories. There is no point in carrying the isolated-patterned dichotomy too far. Its limitation is the difficulty in determining accuracy. For example, how many times does an act have to be performed before it becomes part of a pattern? Does a weekly cycle mean the same thing as a yearly cycle? A second difficulty might lie in an interpretation of patterned as necessarily noncreative. This is by no means true: one may attend art classes month after month and find them highly refreshing and creative, whereas new experiences can be dull, flat, and unchallenging. On the other hand, to draw the distinction of new-old, independent-ritualistic, exploratory-habituated, or fresh-familiar contributes toward a theoretical sophistication in dealing with such practical issues as whether the new time of retired persons should be given to an enlargement of past activities or to the encouragement of new ones.

Time

"Patterning" has already indirectly raised the matter of time. Let us view this concept more closely. Three broad divisions suggest themselves: objective or astronomical, subjective or psychological, and cultural or patterned time: (a) the chronological sequence of 1-2-3 o'clock, (b) the attitudes or meanings about time held by the person, or his perception of the sequential relations of events, and (c) institutionalized segments, such as "holidays," hours "for work," hours "for sleep," etc., as passed on through the generations.

The chronological aspect of time makes possible a coordination of behavior between strangers; as in the parallel case of money,[4] a mechanistic measuring stick assists in the ordered living of complex societies. All conscious men know, or should know, that wit/ span of 12 hours, the fifth is "after" the fourth or that "we w.. at 4 P.M." is an understanding that assumes that both parties are aware of time and read the clock. Yet, immediately, even at this level, the three divisions (objective, subjective, and cultural) fade into one symbolic unity in which our language becomes both master and tool of our thought. No one has written more brilliantly on this aspect of language than Benjamin Lee Whorf. His central position is that "concepts of 'time' and 'matter' are not given in substantively the same form by experience to all men but depend upon the nature of the language or languages through the use of which they have been developed." [5]

Whorf's classic elaboration of this point indicates that even so-called astronomical or objective measures of time are far from objective. Anthropologists and historians have provided many illustrations that underlie linguistic references. The historian E. R. Leach notes that "different societies have found different kinds of dimensions convenient, partly because their social and religious organization called for different types of technological thinking." [6] The need to allocate water for irrigation in ancient Egypt led to a division of days into hours. Other methods and referrents have been movements of the earth, sun, and moon; the recognition of seasons; the ripeness of wild food plants; the first appearance of migratory birds; and the devices of the calendar-shaman in Borneo.

A team of scholars working with Margaret Mead has this to say of "time" in the Greek way of life: [7]

Greeks "pass" the time; they do not save or accumulate or use it. . . . The clock is not master of the Greek: it does not tell him to get up, to go to the field. . . . At church the people are not impatient while waiting for Mass to begin; and the church fills only gradually. They know when to go to church; yet when a foreign visitor inquires as to the time of a certain Mass, the subject creates a discussion; and eventually the answer will be something like: "Between 2 and 3." And when Greeks who follow their traditional ways invite, they say, not: "Come at 7 o'clock," but: "Come and see us." To arrive to dinner on time is an insult, as if you came just for the food. You come to visit, and the dinner eventually appears. . . . For the Greek traditionally, to work against time, to hurry, is to forfeit freedom. His term for hurry means, originally, to coerce oneself: and a visitor arriving out of breath may say, "I have hurried," but the form in which the word is more often used is "Don't hurry." . . . In spite of the prevalence of timepieces, the church bell and the school bell, and even a cannon blast continue to have active functions in calling adults or children to pre-arranged gatherings or communal village work. Even in the cities, people are called "Englishmen" when they turn up on the dot at meetings or appointments. People often arrive an hour late to an appointment to find that the other person is also just arriving, or if they find him gone, they usually accept the fact with neither apology nor frustration.

Within each social system, the person assumes his attitude toward time as entirely natural. The American attitude includes a considerable enslavement to and reverence for time and clocks. As George Soule says of our views,[8]

> "Time is money." We "save" time, "spend" time, and "waste" time, just as we save, spend and waste money or material goods. When zest flags, "time lies heavy on our hands," we "kill time."

To this list we can add other familiar concepts: time "flies," "goes," "runs out," "drags," "disappears," "passes by," "escapes," "vanishes," or "creeps up." There is some truth in George Woodcock's comment that the clock was the most important instrument of the Industrial Revolution.[9]

It would seem that a combination of disciplines would long ago have made significant contributions to unraveling the intermeshing of astronomical, cultural, and personal conceptualizations of time. Such is not the case. This may come about in time through the attempt of social psychiatrists to relate time to consciousness as an awareness or continuity of past, present, and future. A. E. Fessard speaks of the "unified configuration" or "temporal *Gestalt*."[10] K. S. Lashley writes of "serial order" in behavior.[11]

We submit the position that a serious study of leisure may contribute insights into time and, conversely, that further considerations of time are basic to depth understanding of leisure.[12] The following notes are no more than suggestions toward some directions in this research area.

CONCEPTS AND ATTITUDES ABOUT TIME ARE CENTRAL ISSUES FOR AN UNDERSTANDING OF THE "AGING" PROCESS. The elementary truth in Franz Werfel's poem, *The Calendar of Sleep*, is apparent: [13]

The nursling sleeps the night and day right through,
Time is to him as meadow-grass it were.
Youth's sleep tips up the scales by adding to
The waking hours which endlessly recur.
The man, who futile problems must pursue,
Consumes eight hours in sleep, though he demur.
The aged rise betimes, refreshed anew,
By curtailed slumber rendered livelier.
The westward slope of life has this relief:
God lengthens time, as time becomes more brief.

Time is lengthened or made brief by the age we are, the nature of the present task, or the presence of futile problems. It may well be that time scales can be developed to reveal its length or brevity in one's consciousness and thereby provide an index of interest, attention, concentration, and over-all aging.

What must be clearly recognized in the use of statistical indices of time is that we are dealing with perceptions and contents. No one has stated this with more felicity than Sebastian de Grazia:

> Thus, by using a strictly quantitative assembly-line conception of time—time as a moving-belt of equal units—one ignores the significance of much activity. A moment of awe in religion or ecstasy in love or orgasm in intercourse, a decisive blow to an enemy, relief in a sneeze, or death in a fall is treated as equal to a moment of riding on a bus or shoveling coal or eating beans.[14]

A NEW CONCEPTION OF LEISURE AS ABSENCE OF COMMITMENT MIGHT BE RELATED TO ONE'S RELATIVE FREEDOM FROM THE CLOCK. It has long been observed that the simple rural folk society is both spontaneous in many of its celebrations and unsophisticated in its "temporal *Gestalt*." For instance, among Spanish Americans,[15]

> There is little place for planning. . . . Gatherings, celebrations, are usually spontaneous. Children are sent from house to house announcing the dance or the *fiesta* or the "spread," borrowing implements or crockery, asking for help.

Many persons, when asked about moments or times when they felt freest, have spoken to the writer about "forgetting the time." It is a common observation that work or social visits are pleasantest when time is ideally forgotten. Here, then, is a dimension of freedom that awaits exploration in a variety of settings, with hypotheses that cut across them: classroom, prison, military service, factory, European meal, automat experience in New York, time on a date, and so on.

In a recent series of researches at McGill University, it was found that college students experience hallucinations when they are kept in bed for many hours. Yet is not leisure capable of hallucinations that might have equally pregnant insights into the mind or into the subtleties of social relationships?

THE ASTOUNDING FACET OF CONTEMPORARY AND EMERGING LEISURE IS OUR POSSESSION OF BULKS OF TIME. It is one thing to have a total of 14 days vacation each year if they are distributed throughout the year; it is quite another matter if this becomes one continuous period. We can illustrate the difference between "bulk" and "distributed" time by some examples in a compilation by Judith Chase. Writing of "the average woman," Miss Chase notes [16] that in the course of her lifetime this mythical creature

> spends 13 weeks at the hairdresser, and 9½ in the kitchen;
> cooks 47,000 meals;
> talks over eight years;
> listens to 44,270 radio serials [this was written in 1943];
> sleeps 22½ years;
> grows 11 yards of hair; and
> argues 258 times with her husband.

These are distributed activities. She actually sleeps only several hours at one time, cooks one meal, etc. Now, if to the foregoing list we add that she has 31,200 hours of free time, a reader would perhaps take this figure in stride as distributed time. The truth is quite to the contrary. The working man or woman who retires at the age of 60 has some chance of living to 75. Multiply 15 years by 52 weeks by 5 days by 8 hours and the result is 31,200 hours of free, bulk, consecutive hours of leisure time, which—before retirement—would have been filled with work commitments.

Luckily, perhaps, our average woman or man about to retire does not carry out this simple multiplication. The fear of retirement might increase.

An equally simple observation is that bulk time lends itself to bulk, continuous, or patterned activity. A month's continuous vacation lends itself to a motor trip across much of the United States; four weekly vacations do not. An interesting fact emerges: of the two basic leisure patterns we have already indicated (travel and television), the first depends on bulk time, the second on segmented or chopped-up time. Units of the first are often days, if not weeks; of the second, half-hour units or programs. If travel leads peculiarly to the forgetting of time, the mass media keep their viewers highly conscious of minutes and nationally synchronized clocks.[17]

Group structure

Much of our leisure time is spent with other people, whether informally at a party, more formally at a club or as an athletic team, audience, touring group, or artistic enterprise. We have brought in the social role theory at several points before this, and we draw on it again to introduce a theory of group analysis uniquely pertinent to our purpose.

Role is a description of one's social circle, function, status, and "self." Thus we speak of one's role as minister, doctor, professor, plumber, or housewife. All ministers, all doctors, etc., have in common certain elements pertaining to the quartet of elements, even though, as persons who fulfill these roles, there are wide divergences. Thus all of us speak easily of the clerk who served the customer, as we do of the patient-doctor, policeman-criminal, and teacher-student.

A quick review of the kind of leisure activity described in this book suggests these elementary examples of role interrelationship:

Sociability: typical roles—host, guest, friend, lover, child.
    1. Circles: family, club members, party companions
    2. Functions: to be at ease, help others to relax
    3. Status-rewards: popularity, recognition, friendship, love
    4. "Self": shy, open, "life of party," reserved, loved

Association: typical roles—member, officer, organizer.
    1. Circles: lodge brothers, political party members
    2. Functions: elect, debate, introduce motions, converse
    3. Status-rewards: office, honor, right to attend or vote
    4. "Self": patriotic, punctual, needed, level-headed

Game: typical roles—shortstop, South hand, partner.
    1. Circles: team, fellow students, playmates
    2. Functions: catch the ball, bid, win, cooperate
    3. Status-rewards: victory, prestige, awards
    4. "Self": hero, good sport, victor, clever one

Art: typical roles—creator, performer, promoter, audience.
    1. Circles: orchestra group, chorus, salon group
    2. Functions: listen, play a part, sell tickets
    3. Status-rewards: aesthetic experience, applause
    4. "Self": sensitive person, good performer, composer

Movement: typical roles—tourist, student, guide, agent.
    1. Circles: tourist party, trailer camp community
    2. Functions: receive impressions, ask questions, buy gifts
    3. Status-rewards: prestige, fulfillment of curiosity
    4. "Self": member of upper class, successful

Immobility: typical roles—listener, watcher, reader, student.
    1. Circles: family, theater, audience
    2. Functions: respond to materials on TV, in books, etc.
    3. Status-rewards: entertainment, information, news
    4. "Self": one who seeks improvement, rest, relaxation

A detailed analysis could be made of each of these groups, with methods and categories familiar to all social scientists: how members are selected, indoctrinated, expelled; the social controls that operate; how members communicate; the carry-over of values into the group from other experiences; and so on. One practical aspect or application of such research has already been suggested at the close of Chapter 4 in a discussion of baseball games at mental hospitals. Yet the issue of how play groups function suggests a unique aspect, one that offers insights for group theory in general. The remainder of the chapter is devoted to this uniqueness.

The teleopractic group as play group [18]

Every student of social groups is aware of categories that call attention to such group characteristics as composition, permanence, functions, interests, structures, cohesiveness, and sanctions. These categories, and in essence many of the analyses related to them, stress the static nature of group life inherent in the familiar term structure. Yet a group is more than structure. As a dynamic "synthesis of social roles," interrelationships within the group may change so sharply that a substantially new group will emerge. This dynamic process of transformation goes on in a family as children and parents grow older, as someone leaves the home, as father loses his job. Yet in both cases, family and congregation, a new direction or goal is not sought; change is inevitable, but it is not consciously embodied as a desirable aspect in respect to more or less specific ends.

There is another kind of group whose function is not just to survive but whose entire activity is consciously geared to a future event, experience, or even crisis. A military unit drills for anticipated battle; an athletic team looks ahead to its "meet"; a workers' union directs its energies toward negotiation or strike; and a group of actors rehearses for its public performance. The matter goes further than the general preparation. Often, the "enemy," the "public," and the "opponent" are known in detail, and plans are shaped accordingly. Indeed, the very day and hour of the "crisis," "meeting," or "show" is often known, if not arbitrarily selected. These facts color such aspects of group life as the selection and training of members and the presence of objective criteria for evaluating success.

It is immediately obvious that many play and leisure groups fall into the second or teleopractic category. Our now-familiar types of leisure activity may be so divided:

Teleopractic Groups	Nonteleopractic Groups
Association	Sociability
Game	Movement
Art	Immobility

A club often performs; it is on display as it fights for a social change or as it parades down the street. The athletic team and artistic group exist primarily to be viewed or heard by others who are not themselves participating. On the other hand, a party, a travel group, or an audience are simply living; their essential character as groups is not affected by the process of having existed.

It is evident that a fast distinction between these groups is difficult, yet it is clear enough so that research can be focused on the differences. Two hypotheses are examined in relation to the goal-minded group:

1. *As this type of group approaches its goal, a significant change takes place in the social roles of its members.*

2. *A significant change takes place in technical relations of members.*

The group selected for observation was a symphony orchestra during four rehearsals, just after one concert had been played and another was to be given. We will recall from Chapter 1 that there are more than 1000 community orchestras, which in their yearly average of about six concerts each reach a total of many millions of listeners. A similar analysis of groups is also applicable to several thousand theater groups, more than 700 community opera groups, and untold thousands of athletic associations across the country.

In the present case the writer-participant kept a record of time spent in playing and in talking, thus developing a content-analysis of rehearsals. The details will be omitted. It became clear that persons perform in an orchestra on a dual level. As *social* persons they are recognized as Mr. Jones, John, Mary, etc. As *technical* persons they are completely identified with the instruments they play. For example, the first and second clarinet parts are played in a relationship of pitch, time, nuance, etc., which is prescribed by the composer and conveyed by symbols in a musical score. No consideration is given, ideally, to the fact that the performers reading them are bankers, coal miners, or clerks. When Jim and Sue exchange comments on the weather, it is as social persons; when they discuss a musical phrasing, it is as technical colleagues.

For social and technical we shall employ E. T. Hiller's concepts, extrinsic and intrinsic.[19] What is evident is that *intrinsic roles assume dominant importance as the concert approaches.* Members tend more and more to business. In the first rehearsal we noted a very noisy group over which no control was attempted by the conductor. By the fourth rehearsal this had changed to little noise and some control.

The change was to be expected. An approaching crisis becomes a closer reality in dimensions of time and awareness. In the process, discipline may be more rigid from the top but also more self-imposed. For instance, approach of battle brings tensions that combine repressed fear, mental numbness, "jitters," and the like. The leader approaches the crisis as a climax to a time-growth during which he has attempted a dual task.

1. He learns to know his members both in their intrinsic and extrinsic roles and to effect a reconciliation between the two. For instance, we noted that the orchestra conductor opened his first rehearsal by promising the woodwinds and brasses that later he would include selections that would demand more of their music. Here he is speaking to persons *qua* persons who want to play as much as possible and not to clarinets et al. who have no right to question either his intentions or the orchestrations of composers.

2. As time goes on, the conductor deliberately minimizes his concern with extrinsic aspects and concentrates more upon intrinsic or technical elements. This reaches a point where if some person made a nuisance of himself as a *person* and thus interfered with the musical results, the conductor might replace him with a substitute.

A second general observation relates to changes in the types of communication and integration between persons in their roles as musicians.

Three vehicles of communication exist in the orchestra: speech, gestures, and the music itself. Speech consists of three kinds: (*a*) ordinary conversation, such as, "Let us play the X symphony"; (*b*) metaphorical or poetic expression to describe a desirable conception, such as, "It portrays a sick man, fighting for life with Death, and in delirium recalling his childhood, youth and manhood" (Strauss, *Death and Transfiguration*); (*c*) terms to define more exactly such interpretative concepts or technical procedures as retard, senza sordino, and vibrato.

It was evident that as the concert drew near more time was taken in talking by the conductor. Although in the fourth rehearsal there were frequent stops and corrections, fully 70 per cent of the first rehearsal was spent in playing. Further, the nature of speech employed by the conductor was at first largely technical, but when the orchestra had overcome details it was increasingly imaginative. These patterns vary from one group or conductor to another.

Beyond word-of-mouth communication, the conductor used motions of his body or face and, more directly, of his arms and hands in a pattern of movements generally uniform among conductors. Here the integration of players is purely by sight.

Last, music itself is the most important communication between members of the orchestral group. The written integration exists in symbols—notes, dynamic markings, etc.—all of which appear on the stands placed before the musicians, who have been trained in (*a*) an understanding of these printed symbols, (*b*) a conception of how these symbols are performed on instruments, and (*c*) a conception of how one instrumental sound is blended with another. Little deviation is permitted from these aesthetic norms. There is no room for free expression of Tiger Rag while others are in the thick of Beethoven. Max Weber's comments on the inherent antipathy between charisma and discipline holds true here and should be familiar to the student of groups.[20]

Speech, one of the three systems, gives way entirely at the concert. Integration of the musical activity becomes increasingly a matter of meaningful gestures and of reliance on fitting one's part into an aural pattern. In summary, *as the goal of performance approaches, relationships between communicative systems and norms change.*

Among the theoretical problems suggested by the foregoing method, the most important is that of relating group functions to internal synthesis of roles. Other applications can be made to concepts for the study of morale, to the impact upon personality of long-continued association with such goal-oriented groups, or to the transformation of a group from one type to another.

Yet other and more immediate interpretations can be drawn for the teleopractic as a leisure group. Recall that the performing group is involved in activities whose success is more easily measurable and whose membership is replaceable by others more capable. It depends on a recipient, audience, or outsider. Successful participation makes more demands upon the person. The striking feature, also, of these activities is that there is a more continuous commitment in time, energy, and training. Yet, as in all leisure, the voluntariness is a primary quality. Why, then, do so many people seek out an activity in which they gladly commit themselves to lodge rules, game regulations, or artistic standards and exacting skills?

Our answer takes us back to Chapter 2. Reference was made there to Huizinga's analysis of play as *order:* "Since order has a tendency to be a thing of beauty in and of itself, we have the affinity of play to aesthetics. Order within play contains all the elements of beauty such as tension, poise, balance, and contrast." [21]

For many persons, the order of discipline of their community orchestra or of the lodge proceedings is precisely the control or focus of security through discipline and restriction that they need and get in no other way. Such persons do not want or seek freedom in leisure, unless we mean freedom through identity and fusion with a collective undertaking. Again we return to one of the central themes of our approach to leisure: its fulfillment may include man's "entire range of significance and weightiness"; it may bear a "close relation to cultural values." [22] Leisure may, indeed, prove to be a source of human identity and personal values which in former days were obtained from work and religion. In this sense, its essential ingredient is commitment, self-effacement, ritual, belonging. Such is man's strange choice: that as he continues to work in a permissive atmosphere he is denied freedom in at least some of the activities he freely chooses!

The second observation is that in this same devotion to mastery of details and to controls set up by the nature of the aesthetic enterprise a person can achieve a self-expression of deep meaning to him. A pertinent question, therefore, is this: how does the teleopractic experience affect the person as he goes through the process of creating or performing? The full answer assuredly cannot be expected here, for we stand only at the threshold of a field of investigation that must await the closer cooperation of many disciplines. A few directions are suggested by hypotheses, which draw upon the three elements of leisure structure discussed in the present chapter.

1. *The creative or teleopractic experience permits the possibility of patterning that is more than repetition, for the content and meaning grows as performance or "crisis" comes into view.*

2. *Since the subjective perception of time is in the sequence or gestalt of meaningful events, time spent in creative or teleopractic leisure experience invites a special anticipation and recollection, different from other kinds of experiences.*

3. *Since the inherent nature of the teleopractic group is to lead toward increasing functionalism in technical rather than social roles, such groups provide much possibility for bringing together persons who share a common leisure interest, although they may come from various backgrounds.*

Structure—whether of leisure patterns, time, or groups—suggests a static situation. Yet a constant value in many studies of leisure is dynamic: how can we change, modify, and hopefully improve others? This concern brings us directly into the applications of leisure theory to front-line policy and practice.

The modification of leisure experience 2 I

I n his *Christian Missions and Oriental Civilizations*, Maurice Price
tells this story: [1]

> Several years ago a missionary in China was preaching in a country chapel
> to a large crowd mostly made up of "raw heathen." Few of the crowd
> showed any interest. But one man at the back of the assembly showed
> from the beginning of the talk an extreme interest in the speaker. He
> moved from his seat at the back to one nearer the front. The missionary
> noticed him and began to center his remarks upon this man. The man
> moved again, when a vacancy occurred, to the very front of the crowd,
> all the time appearing to drink in literally every word as it fell from the
> preacher's mouth. At the end of the sermon the missionary invited in-
> quirers to remain. This man remained and the missionary went to him
> first. . . . "Yes, I want to ask you a question," answered the Chinese, to
> a request for some expression from him, "I have been watching all through
> the service that gold tooth in your mouth, and I would like to know if
> it grew there, or how you got it, and whether it is real gold."

Here, in a nutshell—or a gold tooth—we have the essence of our
present issue: the values and methods of those who seek to change
others, the motivations and destiny of those who are exposed to such
values and methods.

Why should anyone be concerned with what is done in free time
by others? We may recall Dr. Kenneth Benne's comment on the 1956
conference on leisure. The conference in Boston "came back again and
again to this question. How central is the importance of free and rational decision and choice for the individual within this whole process
of spending leisure time? Most of us affirmed the general value of rational choice." [2] Free choice, he added, implies criteria of values; and
the danger exists that we will impose a fixed eternal value rather than
allow the person to be active in developing his own value system.

This matter of values or assumptions is—or "should be"—of immediate concern to a small army of professional "change agents"; psychiatrists, teachers, ministers, social workers, recreationists, judges, mental hygienists, and others. Their daily business is based on assessing the condition of a client—a congregant, patient, student, prisoner, or player—and prescribing how the patient *should* act, speak, or live, even though the prescription is by indirection. And there are all the rest of us, laymen who provide amateur advice in ordinary conversation. We sometimes see in the other person what we want to see in a way that one sociologist calls the self-fulfilling prophecy.[3] That is, we assume that the watching of TV is *bad,* we find considerable evidence of *bad* there, and proceed to lecture on the ills of mass media.

The motives of the "change agent"[4] are many, as are the motives of those who are the subjects of change. Somewhere in the situation there is a dissatisfaction, a feeling that what is being done is not what "could be." I may, for some reason, develop the desire to go beyond my weekly card party; perhaps my new wife has convinced me, or I wish to move up in the social scheme of things; in a new suburban environment I want to be like my neighbors, or I have just returned from military service and rubbed elbows with brighter men than I. Some good Samaritans are determined to improve me and others like me: that fellow, they imply, is wasting his potential; he should be doing something more creative; he certainly cannot be happy just playing cards, or, if he is, he is deceiving himself; he should be more concerned with current world affairs; he should be going to concerts; he should read a book; he "should be . . ." he *should be.* . . .

The sources of these *should be's* are many: the nature of our own education, our family background, our church teachings, our temperament, the papers we read, the friends we keep, the climate of opinion around us.

There are several kinds of questions implicit in all this concern:

1. What right or ethical justification have I to lead others in new directions?

2. What is the model of personal well-being that I use as a criterion for myself or others?

3. What is the model of the "good life" in general that I hold?

4. What knowledge have I of the consequences that may arise if I succeed in changing someone's behavior, including my own?

5. Do I proceed to change the ways of my friends (or congregation, child, wife, patient, etc.) by hunch, intuition, persuasion, intimidation, common sense, trial and error, or has social science other methods to suggest?

6. How do I tell when a change has been made in respect to its permanence, depth, success?

7. Is it possible to change the meaning or character of a particular activity so that it will take on new significance, or does a modification of leisure imply only new activities?

Differential modification

We will recall the position taken in Chapter 18 that personality types may be identified by their reaction to or acceptance of various kinds of social control. Expressive or creative persons respond most immediately to knowledge; object-oriented persons, to symbols of status; and people-oriented, to controls that stem from conformity.[5]

The suggestion can hardly be avoided that the directions of modification in leisure, which will be most acceptable to the subject or client, are thereby indicated. What this further implies is that not all activities are equally acceptable or desirable for all persons, that the goals of the change agents cannot be universal, and that, in fact, the social scientist is raising the wrong question when he seeks professional consensus on personality goals. For example, in a volume on social change the authors write,[6]

> What . . . is a good measure of mental health? Is it how well the individual feels? How others feel about him? What his therapist thinks about him? Can mental health be measured by verbal instruments, calibrating, so to speak, the words which the individual uses about himself and his world? Or by projective tests which submit his perceptions and interpretations? Or by various techniques of role playing? Or by direct observation of his behavior? Do we need information about his conscious processes, his unconscious processes, or both, or neither?

To carry the implications of this approach further, the multigroup nature of American society and the multitype personality of which Riesman and others speak point toward the futility of goal consensus. The lead to such research conclusions was best illustrated by *The Authoritarian Personality*,[7] in which it was shown that there is a personality profile, a consistency, in which one may hate other people because this fulfills a need, it projects a normal side of the person's nature. On the commercial side, the hidden persuader of radio and television has now concluded that he must level his advertising to a certain type of person for a certain product for a certain price, and a whole group of young social scientists have now put their categories and formulas up to the highest-paying persuader.

It stands to reason that within any society there will be differences in the way people act, think, see, perceive, react, challenge, accept, feel, or perform similar tasks. The classifications into which they are put, or the items for observation, are themselves a manifestation of the culture; the writer recently entertained several persons from the Soviet Union who were traveling with a dance company, and the difference that intrigued them was that he wrote with the left hand. The problem for science is to decide on a question for study and then to work with as many classifications as it wants: someone may want to measure skin color by two grades, another by twenty-two; we can divide mental abilities, height, muscular ability, strength, or taste for vegetables, etc., into a few or many.

However, it becomes another matter when these categories are taken too literally by the scientist as a basis for reforming or making over man. Man is a many-sided creature. It is fair to say that there are elements of creativity and that they may be found in some persons more than in others; or that there are characteristics we can associate with liking people or being oriented to them; equally, that there is something we can observe about how man reacts to objects about him. The question is, shall we conclude that because a particular man emphasizes one set of elements in his behavior he *is* that kind of man, or shall we say he emphasizes these items because of a combination of circumstances? His choice has been limited, his world is finite, his exposures selective. To provide the client with leisure according to a recipe of what he *now appears to be* is to assume an inflexibility, a lack of growth potential, and a surrender to the past.

If, however, social science seeks to go beyond the measurement and the classification of men *as they are* and beyond the issue of classifying activities to meet the assumed needs *as they are*, then it will find itself on a dimension new to its positivistic tradition. The issue has already arisen among social gerontologists. Shall the worker with older persons find out what they want or need (in accordance with their profiles or descriptions of the personality "configuration") or shall a new world of possibilities be set up on a basis of values of the good life? This is perhaps what Ralph Linton meant when he said,[8]

> This is a vital problem for a changing world. If education can reach the deeper levels of personality, the personality norms of society can be changed consciously and purposefully. If these levels cannot be reached after early childhood, the outlook is much less promising, in fact well-nigh hopeless. . . .

Similarly, Gardner Murphy does not speak of different types of men as he discusses the possibility of encouraging man's "third human nature" or creativeness. He discusses, rather, the nature of the creative process and the conditions under which it finds expression. He identifies five principles for permitting the discovery of human potentialities: [9]

1. Avoid the assumption that we can simply give the individual "all he needs," for many of the needs "just disappear when gratified, and nothing more can be done."

2. Avoid overemphasizing the competitive, not that it is always bad, but "it frustrates and benumbs most of those who fail, and, for those who succeed, it can at best give only the ever iterated satisfaction of winning again."

3. Study and develop the satisfactions of man "that are capable of *progressive development*."

4. Emphasize *active effort at self-fulfillment* rather than passive exposure to culture.

5. Work on the final principle that those satisfactions are best that make *one sensitive to new experience.*

> The heart of the human potential lies in that sensitive, flexible creative, self-fulfilling deployment of perception, feeling, and impulse in which no single drive controls the architectural pattern; in which no single task of selection, discrimination or action rivets the mind to any self-sufficient goal; but in which each activity, satisfying in itself, is an aspect of a larger activity—a phase of a plan, a phase of a life, a phase of the nexus of the lives of many. . . . The philosophical, religious, political, and other value-fulfilling phases of human life express the humaneness of movement in the direction of integration—fluid, sensitive, ever changing integration as a step toward further integration.

Modification of external common factors

The position that Murphy represents in the foregoing statements is, as he notes, of the stamp that William James called "soft determinism," or choice that springs from character. Distinct from this is "hard determinism," or fatalism, which sees the elements of control outside of man. It is the present writer's position that the dichotomy is too black and white, that the internal and the external forces that shape man's life are not so simply distinguished, and that man's objective world is in part always beyond control and prediction, in part increasingly within his control.

Several items of the external world were referred to in Chapter 20 as common external factors and were spelled out in all of Part 2: work conditions, family, community, and others. This is not the place nor can it be our purpose even to list, much less to detail, the changes that are possible in this level. These changes range from the construction of recreation centers, the development of adult-education curricula and agencies, the creation of programs for retired persons, to the organization of leisure-time activities by schools, unions, and voluntary organizations. Public, commercial, and personal equipment and facilities are involved, and the automobile and television are only two of countless types of equipment that can effect the behavior of significant groups and that lead us to a vital point: *the values, the kinds of "self-fulfillment" that man seeks and finds may be closely affected by external means. However, industrialism is more than a technical achievement; it is a source of values.* The reordering of the community or the society may proceed on the unified dimension of the "soft" and the "hard" determinism of which William James speaks. One example is provided by youth gangs and their control.

The last decades have witnessed an approach to gangs of young people that begins with a close understanding based on careful descriptive studies. Thrasher was a pioneer with his Chicago studies.[10] Whyte's *Street Corner Society* has become a popular work.[11] Clifford Shaw went beyond his writings to establish a working organization by which a worker would be placed immediately within a criminal hangout.[12] Danville, Illinois, was one such area. The worker made friends with the gang by proving himself, but neither as gang member nor as an arm of the law. By winning their confidence, he was able to establish neighborhood committees who would obtain jobs for boys leaving the penitentiary, counsel the boys in the delinquent district on vocational or personal matters, and in other ways provide constructive assistance. These committees consisted of persons, perhaps the grocer, the barber, or the tailor, who carry weight with the boys.

Arthur Miller, the playwright, describes how he brings this concept to life in a new script.[13] Jerry Bone works with the South Bay Rangers, who are led by Paul Martense. Jerry can keep up his part of the conversation. "I'm down for that, man. . . . You cats are really steamin', man. . . ." But Miller has terms such as "escape" and "maturing" falling from his lips. Jerry will win their confidence as he treads the thin line between knowing everything the boys do and demonstrating responsible citizenship. In the end, Paul the gangster takes Jerry's place as the Youth Board worker.

> There will be Jerry's attempt to transform the gang into a social club devoted to constructive ends like holding dances. We will see that these boys do not know how to dance . . . their first lesson in democratic debating procedure . . . making a swimming pool out of the water tank on the roof of the housing project, and the lesson in physics that resulted.

Herbert A. Bloch and Frank T. Flynn discuss the problem of juvenile delinquency and its relation to play.[14] "That so much delinquency oc-

curs in unsupervised free time has led many observers to believe that
the misuse of leisure time is the principal cause of delinquency." However, Bloch and Flynn are more cautious in their interpretation: not all
children who have habitually misused time have turned to crime;
others who have been exposed to well-organized recreational activity
have turned into criminals. For example, the Burgess-Shanas study of
over 15,000 boys and almost 8000 girls in Chicago revealed that delin-
quents had spent *more* time in recreational projects than others.[15]
There was a difference in type of participation:

> Active delinquents and predelinquents *shunned* supervised activities, pre-
> ferring competitive sports and motion pictures. Moreover, their mobility
> from recreation center to center was considerably higher than that for
> nondelinquents. Since those who begin as nondelinquents in "delinquency
> areas" are not immune from the deviation pressures that create delin-
> quency, it is interesting to note that the rate of later delinquency was
> three times as high for those who did not attend the original recreation
> centers as for those who did.

Yet, again, the authors urge caution in simple cause-and-effect interpretation. The presence of a recreation agency by itself does not tell
the whole story. Evidence appears to show that "the most successful
recreation programs were those that were organized as phases of a
wider program for community development."

The nature of family life has often been noted to explain the strong
control over young Chinese, even within our own country. A further
example of this is provided in a report from Italy, which has one of
the lowest juvenile delinquency rates in the world. A wave of hooli-
ganism was reported in the summer of 1959 in the prosperous northern
areas, such as in Milan.[16] According to newspaper accounts, youngsters
seem best behaved in the cities of the poor south. There, family bonds
are still tight, "and crime is still a serious thing that is committed for
the sake of honor, vendetta, passion or money—not for play."

The report on the Italian scene may misinterpret the serious turn
that play can take, but again the mention of family suggests a basic
principle in the modification of human activity: *a need for the co-
ordinated effort of many types of agencies and institutions, and, in
the case of the juvenile delinquent, the need for close community planning among public and private welfare agencies.*

Other principles are noted in the next section, and are placed separately so that we may again consider leisure modification on a more
general plane.

Some principles of change as control over leisure

1. Leaders in change are urged to think above and beyond the specific activity level in terms of larger processes, end, and goals. According to the Lippitt group, some persons oppose change from a fear of failure or awkwardness.[17] It is the leader's strategy in such cases to move a step at a time but to have his general direction in mind.

2. Suggestions for leisure changes should be made on a positive rather than on a critical note. As Allport notes, "It is an axiom that people cannot be taught who feel that they are at the same time being attacked." [18] The hortatory approach usually accomplishes little, as we noted earlier in this chapter. Bales writes,

> A whole series of studies show that if one wishes to change attitudes and subsequent behavior of a group, discussion and decision where all members participate as directly as possible tend to be more effective than "enlightenment" or "persuasion" by the lecture method, or by an unqualified order from above.[19]

3. The most important persons affecting our actions are not necessarily persons of fame or institutional position in the society but those closest to us. With the child as with the adult, modifications of behavior are most likely to come from peers. Furthermore, word of mouth is more effective than statements in writing.

4. Consumers of leisure entertainment in the "public arts" [20] of the mass media are more powerful than they usually believe in effecting the practices of sponsors or producers. Those who would modify leisure can be effective in convincing the public of its power in this regard.

5. A change in activity may imply a change in social status. On this point we quote from Professor Richard T. La Pierre.[21]

> It is because the adoption of anything new demands some learning and the abandonment of some familiar device, or at least established attitudes and values, that only those individuals who are already discontented with what exists will be tempted by the new. For them to adopt the new usually means, however, that they run counter to the norms of some, if not all, of their status groups. Moreover, if they persist in so violating the norms, they may be excluded from those groups. The would-be cultural conqueror cannot at the outset provide these marginal individuals with a new status alternative. He says, in effect, "I can heal your wound, assure you a place in heaven, protect your feet from sharp stones, or teach you how to live a longer and more fruitful life." But he cannot offer them what they, like every other individual, want most—status among their own kind.

He summarizes. No effort at cultural conquest can succeed unless the conqueror is able to gain status value for what he represents. The point is most appropriate to leisure activities, since this is frequently the lever by which the American seeks to pull himself up to other social levels. The best prospects for Christian missions among the Chinese, notes La Pierre, were those whose positions among their own were already weak, who were viewed by their neighbors as failures. Conversion deepened their marginality. The parallel does not hold entirely true for leisure; leisure conversion has less significant consequences for the most part, yet the major lesson remains. By moving into new leisure patterns one runs the risk—or seeks the gain—of mingling in new social circles. Such may be the intent. That such exploitation may be conscious and premeditated is not to gainsay the possibility of genuine gain from the new activity. Such is the dilemma often met by the critic of the American art scene, for that area is useful to the social climber. But does the climber never experience a genuine consequence? Are the by-products of behavior sometimes not so significant as the clear objectives? Is the "change agent" justified in seeking the concealed end by fostering more palatable beginnings?

A case study

Of principles and general observations there are many more. How do these principles work in a concrete situation? What other issues arise in their application?

During the period 1952–1957 the present writer found himself in a favorable position to observe and participate in a community venture; in the first two years, he was president of Community Arts in Champaign-Urbana, Illinois. A community orchestra was organized in the first year. By the second year—and all under a common name and administrative organization—a contemporary dance group, a theater, a chorus, and a painting group were created. As many as 450 persons a week were sometimes engaged in all of these groups.[22]

On the surface the Community Arts project is easy to describe. Each group had its officers and was represented on the central board. A monthly bulletin provided internal communication. During the year there were many performances of one group or another for combined audiences totaling in the thousands. The quality of performance was mixed, sometimes reaching high levels; the organization as a whole was by this time well known and received in the community and the local press. It had no official tie with the state university located in the community or with any other agency.

If we now look below the surface, several items are immediately apparent. Here was a leisure enterprise that operated on several dimensions. Although limited to the performing arts, there was broad scope and choice, so that various artistic interests or proclivities could be served within the same circle of friends. These activities obtained public response and acquired group reputation or status, which was shared by the participants. As to be expected, there is a wide range of abilities in each of the arts; there was a range in the ages, educational experiences, occupations, income, ethnic and racial origins, religious beliefs, and personal needs. The variety of needs that was satisfied, or was at least apparent to the observer, covered the gamut from a genuine self-expression on high levels of achievement to personal therapy, status-searching, exhibitionism, skill improvement, domestic escape, keeping busy, and accommodating friends. Finally, performance activities called upon persons to fill such diverse roles as creators, performers, critics, audiences, stage crews, sellers of tickets, publicity persons, and the like.

In short, personal, group, and aesthetic possibilities were present in the situation. How was this large project created? How did its development modify the leisure patterns of its participants?

Something has been said of the motivations of change agents. As the participant-observer in this case, the writer can attest to several motives, avoiding self-analysis on deeper psychological levels.

1. He had long spoken and written on the meaning of community artistic efforts and had been instrumental in promoting such programs before; thus the present situation had been tested by him in other forms.

2. He had for some time felt that the community or voluntary association was a natural stage for a close rapport between amateur and professional art.

3. He was convinced that many persons in Champaign-Urbana were living under the illusion that they were active in the arts because they were present at first-rate productions of the university.

4. He was conscious of the introduction of television to the community and believed that its rate of absorption depended in part on creative patterns previously established.

5. When the project was underway, the final motivation set in: the challenge, fun, and satisfaction of seeing an idea take form and substance and the mastery over the myriad problems that inevitably arise in a voluntary and democratic adult activity.

A series of preliminary meetings was held with a few persons after the rough idea of forming a symphony orchestra had been discussed with a local conductor with wide experience, the willingness to experiment, and a philosophy of art and life. A high school orchestra room was obtained without charge for weekly rehearsals; 35 persons appeared the first evening in response to telephone calls and a newspaper invitation. The first psychological step had been achieved: no one could now say, there is no need for this; for 35 men and women there apparently was some need. About six weeks later, a concert was played for an audience of 500 persons. By then about 650 hours of time had been affected or modified for the participants. By 1959 a total of at least 3000 hours had been collectively spent in rehearsal and performance by these members (the group had grown in size), not to speak of additional hours of practice by individual members who might otherwise have neglected their instruments, the many hours spent by other persons in promoting the activity, or the collective time of the combined audiences. The repertoire included such compositions as the Schumann Fourth Symphony, the Goldmark Rustic Wedding Symphony, the Brahms Academic Festival Overture, and a number of concerti, often reaching a very respectable quality of performance.

By the second year, 1953, Community Arts had created additional units. The dance group quickly grew from six to 60, 50 persons attended the first theater meeting, a chorus of about 20 persons was organized, and several dozen painters began to work together. The community soon became accustomed to a stream of art exhibitions, plays, and concerts; those who desired to develop their skills had a home. It would be difficult to estimate the total hours—perhaps 100,000 or more "man-hours"—spent in direct creative activity by some or in organizing and promoting these activities by others.

What would these people have been doing otherwise? What were their many motives? How deeply rooted were their artistic experiences and how significant the by-products—the personal friendships, the excitement, the frustrations, the arguments, the opportunities for leadership? Were personalities reached on the deeper levels that Linton called for, or does all this add up to superficialities, mere recreation, fun, relaxation, sociability, and nothing more? And if this local activity is to provide only one example of similar development in the thousand communities which now possess community orchestras, in the many hundreds which have opera companies, or in the numerous painting and writing and theater groups across the country, again the question becomes insistent: is there not, among all this effort, some real degree of aesthetic seeking, artistic growth, meaningful new interrelation of persons? The writer's conclusions about his own activities and those of the many thousands of others now engaged in some form of building constructive leisure are based upon the analysis of the potential of the American scene—already analyzed in this book—and on concrete experience on the community level. The fundamental conclusion reached is that *leisure patterns are in part a projection of past traditions and actions, in part a consequence of technological or other forces outside the community's immediate control, and in part the result of the strength of leadership directing itself to goals and dedicated to a philosophy*. We may now view the enterprise further in reference to the kinds of issues raised throughout our theory of leisure:

WORK. Since this was a self-created leisure activity—not an offering of an established institution such as a school—we could establish hours to fit the conditions of our jobs. In our own quarters we could also function during holidays, week ends, and other odd times.

We discovered that participants came from a wide variety of occupations and that the university-town dichotomy was easily bridged. The role of singer in the chorus or actor in the theater was sufficiently general to minimize educational backgrounds, and the sociability that grew naturally out of joint creative activity developed friendships with little regard to academic degrees; marked differences in wealth remained a more resistant distinction but was more evident as a factor in the kind of activity chosen.

PERSONALITY. The painting and theater activities seemed to be more conducive to self-discovery. Several cases were uncovered in which persons from those groups became aware of themselves in a new light and in which self-discovery was accomplished with the direct aid of one other person in the group. Since the roles in musical activity were more "institutionalized" and demanded more prior training, the participant stood to gain experience and a chance to "keep his fingers alive," but less of a creative emergence was noticed. On the other hand, the leisure-time orchestra provided an opportunity for several talented young people to be given a boost in their professional aspirations by presenting them as soloists.

Havighurst's familiar thesis was proved again and again: that the same activity meant many things to different members and that the motivations or effects of these artistic activities ranged from sincere desire to engage in the artistic process to romantic interest in another member, therapy in the midst of emotional ills, excitement of performance, the exercise of power, and so on.

As to relationships of leaders and members, the largest single clue to the success or failure of such a project seemed clearly to rest on the matter of the presence of leaders, however such persons are conceptualized. The philosophy or the soundness of the project was insufficient to carry along by itself: constantly the leadership had to reformulate the value of the project to the community or to untangle personal conflicts (usually over the element of power or social visibility) or to arrange small details that would otherwise be left undone. A primary element in the process of leadership, it was found, is a feeling for the emerging *phases* (timing, life cycle) of a large project, particularly in the passage from the first to the second generation of leadership in the various units.

FAMILY. One unique feature of the aesthetic enterprise, which we saw clearly, was the possibility of serving family units, either with the entire family participating at one time (as in the orchestra) or with various members of the family involved in related aspects of the artistic enterprise, such as performer, ticket seller, stage crew, and audience.

SOCIAL CLASS. We have noted the bridge that grew from these activities across the town-gown axis. The theater seemed to attract more of the country-club set than the other activities, and in conversation with a newspaper editor on the dynamics of this community we were told early in our history to seek out such persons in order to attract the interest, and potential contributions, of the older residents. One incident was noteworthy on class: the Oddfellows volunteered at one time to become the fund-raising agency. Eventually their president came to the conclusion that his group had not been successful because it did not occupy a position of status, especially when it came to the arts, and that his members felt uncomfortable when they approached "upper-class" persons.

SUBCULTURES. The arts as a common concern made it easy to bridge differences of ethnic origin and even (in a community that is on the borderline between the South and the North) of racial groups. The theater offered some resistance early in its history, but music was an easy device for bringing together persons of different religions and colors. In an early stage of the whole project the initiator's motives were questioned in an anonymous quarter, and it was not done by facing him with the direct question but by pointing to his minority background.

COMMUNITY. One of the convictions of the initiator at the beginning of the enterprise was that the community was living under an illusion that it was a creative center. True, a great university is the heart of the community, but the community only watches and participates as an audience in the multiple creative activities on the campus. Thus the leadership felt that it could best begin, not by arguing the need for aesthetic creativity on a general level, but by developing specific activities in which a real group of persons found their own needs realized. Perhaps one practical lesson from this is that we do not have to begin with surveys to find out whether there is a need for a given leisure enterprise. We can create the need, not by responding to requests for the organization of such activity, but by setting up the channel through which man can explore and manipulate and exercise his curiosity.

POLITICAL UNITS. The Community Arts project made no special plea for older persons or for any other segment of the population as it approached a municipal agency for the use of school facilities. It did find a considerable interest among local officials for adult leisure activity in general. In practice, we found that it was entirely possible, in all activities except the contemporary dance, to mix persons of all ages. The orchestra ranged from 11 or 12 to over 87 in age distribution. We also found that our original concept of structure was sound: we were freer by having been generated from within ourselves—freer to function closely with the university as well as the local government, churches, unions, businessmen, and so on. This democratic base was not lost upon the members.

VALUES. The whole problem of the unique values which the arts offer as a leisure experience brings us finally to the nature of creativity itself. It is a question larger than the arts, of course, and raises the point of alternative values to be gained from the various kinds of leisure activities suggested in Chapter 22.

In a recent statement on the nature of the "creative arts" within the framework of adult education, we started with three assumptions: [23]

> (1) There is no clear conception of the resultant form or end of the experience, for these take shape in the course of the experience; (2) the participant contributes to the shaping of the material or medium so that its final result includes an effect upon *him;* and (3) participation may take place on the many dimensions of skills, standards, tastes, or traditions, each of which may provide a degree of creative fulfillment which is to be judged in the context of the situation rather than by professional standards.

More generalized, by the first assumption we mean that *man's life cannot be wholly in the past, the present, or the future; a creative life takes its roots from all three;* for example, as we turn our analysis to the older person, it is with the intent of drawing upon the past less than he might be tempted and to help envision for him a future more than he had hoped. The creative life therefore draws upon many ways and contents, but it looks with favor upon complex rather than simple activity, for in complexity is the challenge that takes effort and moves along on a wave of emotional and intellectual anticipation.

The second assumption makes of the man more than a bystander, or even more than *homo faber;* for now man does not weave the basket or play the tune or build the table: the basket is now part of him, he is the tune, the table has not been made but *he has been made* (reborn, says Erich Fromm) in the act of creating the table. *Thus leisure becomes more than time spent. It becomes at its best a way of progressive rebirth, regrowth, reacquaintance with oneself, renewing and refulfilling.* Its essence is on several dimensions—doing, seeing, conceiving, planning, evaluating, contemplating—and by drawing upon one's mature experiences with life these can go on simultaneously or move back and forth with ease from one to the other.

The final assumption is that the concern that we can bring to the leisure activity—the arts as well as the others—exists on several levels. *It is necessary that the degree of creativity or the level of performance be estimated in reference to the function and meaning of the experince to the person* and, thereby, that we had better unlearn the professional's judgment of effort by the criteria of excellence that stems from a long tradition.

For ultimately a theory of leisure can be little less than a theory of man and a theory of the emerging culture. Such macrocosmic theory rests on the unity of all ages in man and on the unity of concerns that treat of man's continuity. The sciences and the humanities join, for as Albert Einstein noted in a foreword to Galileo's Dialogue,[24]

> There is no empirical method without speculative concepts and systems; and there is no speculative thinking whose concepts do not reveal, on closer investigation, the empirical material from which they stem.

Thus we turn, finally, to the central issue of all creative values in leisure.

Evaluation and Implication
of Leisure

Creative values
and prospects in the new leisure 22

The major conclusion that underlies all else is that leisure, however it is defined and analyzed, is not a peripheral phenomenon, extracurricular to life and its value systems: its social and psychological roots arise from the culture; the criteria of its judgment are imbedded in the culture; indeed, what people do in time free of commitment to work is a valuable clue to the directions of the culture itself.

But the desirable relationship of leisure to cultural values is a debatable matter.

Thus we will recall that Louis Kronenberger, conscious of current tendencies toward conformity and social status, argues for a leisure that is an end in itself, its own justification.[1]

Quite another set of values was set out by conferees called together in 1956 by the Jewish Theological Seminary. Having asserted that "To waste time is to waste ourselves," the conference concluded that the least adequate leisure is *mass entertainment;* more preferable is *play, sporting* and *gaming;* most preferable is *recreation,* which consists of three groups: artistic creation and appreciation, study and discourse, and prayer and worship. Worship is placed above the rest, for, in addition to the element of freedom, worship seeks "the aid of the transcendent." [2]

We will recall that Joseph Pieper speaks of the ultimate leisure as a *divine* time—a mental and spiritual attitude of inward calm and silence, a capacity for steeping oneself in the whole of creation, and climaxed in the act of celebrating creation on holy days and feast days. Drawing on St. Thomas Aquinas and Aristotle to develop a pre-Calvinist conception of effort and suffering, Pieper notes that man must be more than worker if he is to lead a full human existence.[3]

These discussions arise in a consciousness that there is something unique about the leisure of today and tomorrow. Before returning to the problem of values and criteria, it is well to re-examine this uniqueness.

The new leisure—social and psychological

The social and psychological nature of our new leisure springs from the overwhelming fact that American society evolved without going through a feudal phase. As de Tocqueville noted, the American was born free without having to become so. In spite of the range of very rich to very poor, a truly corporate society was impossible when a large and ill-defined middle class became the predominant economic and psychological stratum. For there is here neither a genuine reactionary or conservative tradition nor a radical or revolutionary strand or school. The businessman in our culture has no security beyond his ability to make money—hardly the basis for a philosophical position! The worker, who might conceivably have pondered a mass revolt in the 1930's, found his Bismarckian ally in F.D.R. and the New Deal, thus together—and almost in spite of the business segment—preserving the capitalistic order.

The American businessman is certainly no aristocratic counterpart of his European feudal blood or bank brother, for he has not learned the elementary rules of aristocratic manners—how to be an expert at play and an amateur at work. The American worker, for his part, is no brother in spirit or consuming standards to his feudal neighbor, for his necessities as a middle-class Common Man call for food, clothing, heat, transportation, entertainment, medication, and community services which exceed those available to the wealthiest feudal czars, princes, merchant kings, and their Pompadours! As to our middle class—and, according to a Gallup Poll, 87 per cent of us claim membership in that democratic haven—it has defied and confused our social scientists (except for a few of the more empirically obsessed) by playing golf, taking showers before dinner, wearing sports clothes, buying symphony tickets, going to Miami, and seeing the world in eighty payments.

The new leisure—technological

The technological basis of the new leisure is manifest in all directions. In 1850, we have previously noted, the average work week for farmer and laborer was about 72 hours; the 72 became 60 by 1900 and 44 by 1940; now it rapidly approaches 35. But more than time is at stake, for bulk time differs from scattered and sporadic time. Forty million workers now have contracts for several weeks vacation with pay. This is bulk time; it permits a long trip or paints a large room. Further, the average middle-class home in America has in it enough vacuum cleaners, waffle irons, air cleaners, dishwashers, clothes scrubbers, and other gadgets to equal the energy of 90 male servants. This supplements time, providing a style of life, a form. And this family, in almost no American home a myth or mere statistical construct, has other gadgets, such as TV, radio, and phonograph, which fill up the time freed by their kilowatt cousins, providing a content for the time just released. In addition to these benefits, we have at our disposal better lights, frozen foods, telephones in all colors, unpaid-for cars with fins, paper-covered books, and countless other paraphernalia that enrich time, helping us to "save" it, "pass" it, "spend" it, "kill" it, or "use" it for a variety of purposes.

Nor is this the end. The technological base of our leisure will inevitably expand. We are geniuses at inventing needs as well as machines, but the position of classical economics that labor will ultimately be kept making machines to make machines has about it an eerie quality of self-deception at a time when George Soule reports that sooner or later we will control the sun's energy in ocean water, and one acre so controlled will give the world enough power to run its wheels for 300 centuries.[4]

The new leisure and the total milieu

Yet, in larger terms, this new technological and social orientation is only part of a total culture in which fundamental values and social controls are reoriented, reordered, or redirected. Work, religion, family, education—all are altered in meaning and influence.

It is a new leisure, on the one hand, that de Tocqueville had told us would come with the mass, democratic society: a time of ease, low taste, vulgarization. But it is a leisure, on the other hand, that foretells a heaven on earth, that supplants the Christian concept of the Devil and the Flesh with the Judaic concept of the good, earthly life of optimistic outlook and a unity of Spirit and Flesh. It is a leisure permitting of the best and the worst in man. It is a leisure in which all men may find their wants met—the loafer and the doer, the scholar and the sportsman, the Las Vegas gambler and the suburban gardener, the numismatist and the Saturday night astronomer, the hot-rod fanatic and the Lucy Ball fan, and the Presley, Proust, and Puccini audiences.

It is a leisure—and a culture—in which some of our best-read social-science sermons persist, by grandiose psychoanalysis, in telling us that

we are rootless, alienated, other-directed, suffering from malaise, hyp-
notized by status, overwhelmed by conformity, and weakened by
anomy. However, as we look at some of the concrete manifestations of
this leisure, it becomes apparent that our exegesis incorporates Paradiso
as well as Inferno.

True, 40 million dollars was invested in drive-in theaters in 1953, but
in 1952 836 million dollars was spent for flowers, seeds, and potted
plants and another 200 million dollars for garden tools. True, there are
10 million readers of *Confidential*-type magazines every month, but a
century ago their counterparts were illiterate as well as lost. Our pulpit
oratory could thunder about the noncreative millions who watch TV
for an average of 16 hours each week, and we could ask about the 16
or more hours spent by their whittling forefathers who engaged in
meaningless conversation even below Paar into the morning hours. On
the side of Light we could speak of the 1000 community orchestras
or the 5000 community theaters; yet Darkness swells in our tears for
the large audience to spectator sports. So, depending on our likes and
dislikes, our assumptions and our ethnocentric temper, we could pull
out all manner of figures—like organ stops—to produce the effect we
desire or to pad the sermon we prefer. Finally, with due apology to
the ladies of the congregation, we could bow our heads and pay our
respects to Mark Twain's profane trinity: liars, damn liars, and statis-
ticians!

Certainly our thinking must go below the facts, for contrary to our
imperialistic empiricists, facts do not speak for themselves; nor, as
Mannheim warned us in his *Ideology and Utopia*, should we assume
that only those things that can be measured are important. The quality
of creativity, broadly conceived, remains the paramount issue.

The nature of creativity and its evaluation

If we would judge which of the leisure activities measure up to creative values, we must be directly concerned with the model of the Good
Life. This is precisely a model we no longer have. The church model
of the selfless, cooperative man? The rural-American model of Li'l-
Abnerian honesty and naïveté? The medieval model of Man on Horse-
back? The Adam Smith–Herbert Hoover model of the faithful little
capitalist, saving for a rainy day? If these are dated and scarcely pertinent to the hydrogen-bomb age, we hardly have a new model. Not
even a mold for one comes out of Detroit. *The fact is that this very diversity of values, the destruction of the monolithic, authoritarian dog-*

mas should be a cause for rejoicing, a fruition of liberal humanistic struggle of the last thousand years. Uprootedness is freedom giving, and freedom brings with it the task of finding new values, new relationships of man to man or man to God; and assuming that aesthetic values, like all others, are a part of the culture stream, even a new aesthetic philosophy must be sought.

Our conception of creative values must encompass a wider range than the arts, for many of our attitudes about the arts are class-bound, fascist in their implications, snobbish, dogmatic, and unconcerned with man. A basic position of this volume has been that the new leisure, because it is more than a recuperation from work, can become a potential source of the deepest values and can provide a variety of activity for creative expression.

Social scientists assume that the quality of being *creative*—not unlike the quality of being *good, beautiful, talented, just,* or *sacred*—is not inherent, universal, self-evident, divine, objectively definable, or supracultural. This lack of precision need not make us unhappy, for one of the sources of strength in creative activity, art for example, is that, being indefinable, its functions and relationships within the culture are flexible and always relevant. Besides, there is some internal ugliness about a static conception of something as dynamic as creativity. On the other hand, we cannot naïvely ignore the established traditions within the context of a given culture that condition us to distinguish the creative from the imitative or fake.

Finally, creativity can function on a personal dimension, as in self-expression or realization; on a dimension of social process, such as production, distribution, or consumption of art work; or on the ultimate dimension of consummation in a musical, pictorial, dramatic, literary, or architectural product, which, says the philosopher D. W. Gotshalk, exhibits an "internal perception." [5]

Is everyone capable of some degree of creative activity? Gardner Murphy's recent volume, *Human Potentialities*, speaks of creativity in every man as his "third nature." [6] Whether or not we care to place it side by side with the biological and cultural natures is not at issue here, for by eliminating the universal objective criteria from creative effort it becomes possible to agree that every person, in all ages, from all backgrounds, can set himself a challenge, a possibility of growth, by direct participation in creative values or as consumer and distributor of such values.

It was Maholy-Nagy, a great figure of the Bauhaus in Munich, who wrote: [7]

Everyone is equipped by nature to receive and assimilate sensory experiences. Everyone is sensitive to tones and colours, has sure touch and space reactions, etc. This means that by nature everyone is able to participate in all the pleasures of sensory experiences, that any healthy man can also become a musician, painter, sculptor, architect, just as when he speaks he is a "speaker."

Whether or not everyone can deal directly with such forms of constructive, perceptive, and symbolic expression, he can come to grips with it in its other dimensions of personality exploration or in the social process essential to creativity. This can be demonstrated if we review briefly several functional classifications of leisure employed in previous chapters.

Types of leisure and creative values

First, creative values may be found in which the person is directly related with another person in his leisure. In its pure form this relationship has "no objective purpose," as Georg Simmel wrote, "no content, no extrinsic results, it entirely depends on the personalities among whom it occurs." Models are found in family relationship and among friends. Here the normal or key role of banker, baker, or Baptist is suspended as one becomes, momentarily, a bartender, bon vivant, conversationalist, confidante, or flirt. The creativity here can be at a minimum, as, freed of all responsibility except tact, people flit about from one sandwich to another in a noisy room. Yet conversation at its best can be intense, exciting, exploring of other lives, clarifying of one's own. The intrinsic valuation of persons takes time and effort; it involves exposure, for to know others well is to become well known.

Of course, the very lack of content defines the limitation of sociability as leisure. It may develop expertness in relating to others in form, in manners, in pleasantry, or in depth, but its success has no consequence unless the depth focuses on interests larger than a liking for persons.

We come, then, to a second type of leisure, association with other people, not because we like each other, but because both of us share a wider concern, liking, interest, cause, or theme for action in which our joining is only a means. Now we have an end, a common objective— a society to champion women's rights, contemporary music, antivivisectionism.

Now it is more than process; the creativity in associating with others lies in the growth or groping toward purpose publicly stated and defended. A result of internal movement or struggle is the emergence of leaders and followers as well as group solidarity or weakness. Although the goal itself may range from simple and unimportant to complex and significant, a content of another sort arises from knowing that one is wanted, needed, missed, excused for being absent, hooted for being noisy, elected to office for being vocal, ejected for being rambunctious, sainted for being pure, commemorated for one's virtues, or honored for one's dedication. Here, therefore, is creativity through meaningful relationship with others in a collective possession of interest.

A third and a fourth type of leisure differ in the direction of our approach to the world. In our leisure devoted to movement we go physically to meet the world; in the leisure of immobility we remain in our community or living room as the mass media and mass literacy bring the world to us.

In travel we go to the world. An enormous amount of this takes place. Well over a million of us visited Europe in 1960; in 1956, within our own country, all of us together drove over 3 *trillion* miles. Our motivations ranged from genuine curiosity, to visiting someone, restlessness, purchasing of tourist loot, taking photographs, a romantic quest, or the need to be a somebody who has been atop the Eiffel Tower, inside the Kremlin, or at a table of Antoine's in New Orleans.

It need hardly be said that not all persons are emotionally prepared to travel as a creative experience, that is, to become active travelers rather than consumers of scenery and guide patter. For example, research for the Council for Student Travel in New York has sought to recognize kinds of students who should *not* be encouraged to go abroad. Yet the creative possibilities in this new-found leisure for the many are enormous for personal growth as well as for world commonality. Represented at their best are relationships to new folkways, values, and institutions, as well as to physical surroundings. However, these experiences, too, are limited, for we cannot reshape the world we come to see; we can only look at it, aim the 35 millimeter camera, and recollect and relive it with scrapbooks and trays of slides.

Our next form of leisure develops when we remain in home or community, and the world comes to us through the printed page, the television screen, the picture, the phonograph record, or the motion picture. In placing all of these into one category, our explicit assumption is to deny the outmoded dichotomy of active-passive. We intimate that none of the media by which the world's wisdom and its foibles are brought to us is generically better or worse, creative, or parasitic; each provides a possible continuum from complete boredom, disinterest, and insensibility to complete and exciting creativity, inner struggle, and participation in the world.

The last two categories of leisure are games and art. The game, of course, provides a microcosm of the world: freedom through order and discipline, a morality of *sportsmanship, gamesmanship,* and *co-operation,* which is freely transposed to the world outside the playground, an "interlude" in life, as Johan Huizinga calls it. The creative value is in the mastery of the opponent, but, more important, it is in the mastery of oneself in the face of organized opposition. Its strength and discipline also set its creative limits.

In art we come to our final leisure form. Its uniqueness as a ground for creative value is that it encompasses all of those we have now reviewed. In leisure-centered art we may find sociability with people, a common interest that brings us together with those of diverse backgrounds, with a grasp of the world through its symbolic testaments of past and present, or with the requisite victory over techniques and pure forms as in a game. Art can do these, and go further, for quite like science it comes to grips directly with creativity and its accompanying values and attitudes.

Possibilities for creative leisure

We may return now to our larger theme, to leisure as a whole, and ask two final questions:

1. How may we assess the possibility for the fullest development of creative values in the new leisure?

2. If so developed, what contribution can a creative leisure make to the total value-structure of the emerging society?

As to the actual potential of a creative leisure, several conclusions are submitted.

First, what happens to American life, including its leisure directions, follows from three types of conditions: the projection of present trends, the emergence of unexpected or unpredictable calamities, wars, or scientific breakthroughs, and the directions given to human events in accord with assumed goals and historical traditions. *The burden of our analysis has been that the tendencies, values, and interpretations of American life are so diverse and multidirectional that the last consideration—goals taken by our leadership—must consciously and strategically isolate the assets about us and build upon them with a realistic faith.*

Second, we submit that the direction of American life as a whole has been increasingly humanistic: industry's managerial revolution, with its view of the worker as whole man; science, most dramatically in the position of physics, that morality, as well as molecules, is its concern; religion, more earth-bound than in earlier days; education, concerned as much now with people as with subject content; government, conscious of human welfare as much as with control. Creative or aesthetic philosophy can hardly remain divorced from this trend.

Some say that the destructive elements of our life already are deeply rooted and will be hard to eradicate. The evidence of conformity and status searching in the writings of such men as C. Wright Mills and now Vance Packard cannot be lightly dismissed. Yet the writer, for one, is not overwhelmed with the hopelessness of the tendencies they describe. With Joyce Cary, Peter Drucker, and some pages of David Riesman, we agree that the mass mind has been overdrawn. Looking back to the past, all societies have been status conscious. But to ignore the differences in taste or style of life as depicted most clearly by Russell Lynes would be to close our eyes to such social symbols as cars and houses and hi-fi and boxed cigarettes. *Yet there is considerable evidence that aesthetic interests have never been pursued more genuinely in the history of this country or with greater variety and independence.*

Of this there is neither positive proof nor disproof. In the past, as now, forces of society weighed heavily on each man and woman, so that the "inner-directed" person of our time corresponds to the "other-directed" of Church and feudal society. The conditions of freedom change and cannot be defined in social vacua. Nor are happiness, human needs, desires, and goals isolated terms. We have no way of telling whether our nation is happier now than it was a century ago, and the decision cannot be made by editorials. Until we set forth our assumptions and methods, we cannot tell whether our society is more or less creative than in prior generations, and for these assumptions there is no objective validity.

However, we have incontrovertible evidence that the people of our time have access to a wider variety of things, kinds of persons, ways of thought, and styles of life. They can move faster, be heard farther, and are more likely to be literate and healthy. The likelihood of their being ignorant of such leisure possibilities as adult schools is much less.

If man has Free Will, then today he has a wider palette on which to paint his chosen fantasies; if he is, by and large, the reflection and articulation of his arc of culture, then he is embarrassed by the diversity of riches about him. That he may seek to escape his freedom is, indeed, a fact. But this escape does not necessarily sing of man going to Hell because all men do not sing on one key; the song and the cacophony have been heard many times in ages past, even before the jingles of TV.

These speculations have to be far-reaching or we may be caught short. What happens, for instance, when the worker is given an option of working four hours per day or six months of full days, leaving six months to fish, loaf, or meditate? What happens as jet travel modifies our habits of time and space use?

What people will do with their leisure at the turn of the twenty-first century, or how much time they will have, is not merely a matter of taste or personality or current values. January 1, 2000, is close at hand—those who will be retiring from work then are college students now.

The population of the world, according to the United Nations, may increase by four billion over the present and will by then increase each year at the rate of 126 million.[8] Harrison Brown glumly suggests that 100 billion persons could be supported on earth if "we were willing to be crowded together enough, to eat foods which would bear little resemblance to the foods we eat today . . . if we . . . construct floating islands where people might live and where algae farms could function. . . ." [9] George Soule, assessing our potential energy supply, asserts that if only 10 per cent efficiency were to be achieved in releasing usable energy by fission "one cubic mile of sea water would supply enough energy to do the world's work for three hundred centuries—at the 1950 rate of consumption." [10]

Our total population and our energy potential are in turn related to the destinies of our present underdeveloped, preindustrial countries. And whether such areas as India, China, and Africa are industrialized by economic help from the current democratic or totalitarian powers will contribute to our own political and social complexion in the United States. If the current cold war maneuverings for the support of these many millions result in atomic or hydrogen wars, there need be little concern for the quality of work and nonwork life four decades from now. If total war can be prevented or our competition can be channeled into other avenues, the process of industrialization and urbanization will inevitably continue.

Vast markets for our goods may open in other parts of the world, although at this moment there is considerable evidence that Russia will expand in world trade in larger proportion than we. Or, as seems certain in the short-range view, the trends of the past decades will continue, and our economy will expand even as we work the less. It is conceivable, if Russian economic competition meets the predictions of their own leaders, that an attitude of guilt will develop among Americans who talk, much less demand, shorter hours, an attitude that could become common if the press and molders of opinion took this line.

Larger issues

Yet life and work are more than a matter of hours—free or committed. The same forces that reduce hours are interwoven with political, social, economic, and philosophical strands. Although projections of single elements, such as population or energy production, can be somewhat feasible, it is the compounding and the interweaving of influences that result in subtle and elusive by-products of attitudes and behavior. It is not possible to go back a half century and say that man was essentially what he is now in spite of TV or missiles whizzing by in planetary orbits; for these developments are very new, indeed, and have not yet become childhood experiences of contemporary mature persons. It is reasonable to assume that our children and theirs will be absorbed daily (as men have always been) with small details of family, friendship, and personal drama. But the style of life, the larger patterns, the milieu, the flow of information, the fears and roots, the controls, these will not be the same a half century hence.

In 1955, Morris L. Ernst looked forward to 1976: [11]

> . . . close to one half of our people will, all through their adult lives, take courses by correspondence, or otherwise and effectively explore those aspects of life and the unknown which excite their curiosities. The new exciting leisure will establish prestige values of unorthodoxy; . . . millions of us will go abroad. . . . Our own people will learn at least three languages in childhood, as the Swiss do; . . . the cravings for narcotics and excessive alcohol will decline as people need fewer spurs for courage, and less forgetfulness; . . . our spiritual road map will carry the direction pointers: 1976—This Way—Energy, Leisure, Full Rich Life.

And, in part, the optimism of Ernst, if caught by strategic leaders, is a part of what *will* happen in 1976 or 1996 or 2026. For what we want and expect in the years ahead will play a part in the directions that their leadership will take, in the zeal that they will display in carrying out new social tasks or, indeed, the gloom that they will assume and the potential leadership they will consequently abdicate. The future hinges in part, on our goals, desires, values, and purposeful application of available knowledge. These goals, in turn, can be defined only as each of us individually, and all of us collectively, sets out a position of values or assumptions.

Several such assumptions found their way into Utopia. Thomas More, for instance, foresaw a society in which man worked six hours a day and in which free time was used to cultivate the mind, to tend gardens, play games, travel, and converse with friends. H. G. Wells's residents of The Modern State would live in a world without toil, but leisure for itself would be feared. Edward Bellamy's Julian West went to sleep in 1887 and awoke in the world of 2000—where people retire at 45.

> Of course not all, nor the majority, have those scientific, artistic, literary, or scholarly interests which make leisure the one thing valuable to their possessors. Many look upon the last half of life chiefly as a period for enjoyment of other sorts; for travel, for social relaxation in the company of their life-time friends; a time for the cultivation of all manner of personal idiosyncrasies and special tastes, and the pursuit of every imaginable form of recreation; in a word a time for the leisurely and unperturbed appreciation of the good things of the world which they have helped to create. But whatever the differences between our individual tastes as to the use we shall put our leisure to, we all agree in looking forward to the date of our discharge as the time when we shall first enter upon the full enjoyment of our birthright, the period when we shall first really attain our majority and become enfranchised from discipline and control, with the fee of our lives vested in ourselves. . . . [12]

Assumptions for our own time must look ahead in view of our rapid technology and the corresponding leisure-aristocracy of the middle classes. They must be assumptions based on a leisure with dignity.

As we noted in the early pages of this book, this search for a new way of leisure touches upon the concerns and professions of many—"the city planner, recreationist, gerontologist, family counselor, clergyman, educator, businessman, hospital administrator, government official, physician and psychiatrist, philosopher, criminologist, publisher, advertiser, disc jockey, union leader, and industrialist. . . ." The social scientist can hardly deny either the importance of the issue or the opportunity for contributing to its solution by his own insights into a search that is in some major part a social inquiry.

That inquiry will be incomplete, however, until it is taken over by those who are less abashed and more experienced in forging and enunciating values than the social scientists. For leisure in America is not, *ipso facto*, a problem or a blessing; it is a phenomenon of abundance and material wealth. There is a tendency in some quarters to point the finger at leisure, to associate it with insignificance and decadence. But this is to think in past terms. Out of that leisure may arise humanitarian values to help move us into the Hydrogen Age. Leisure, a by-product of technology, may become a potent condition in which thoughtful, responsible, and well-fed men will seek to assess themselves and to grow again. This prospect invites us all to ponder this new source and this new result of wealth—leisure—and to encourage a broader social inquiry.

Notes

1. Arthur Schlesinger, Jr., Our New-Found Leisure Won't Bore Us If Some of It Is Employed in Reading, editorial, *Saturday Evening Post*, April 18, 1959.

2. *St. Louis Post Dispatch*, July 30, 1956.

3. *Business Week*, September 12, 1955.

4. H. D. Meyer and C. K. Brightbill, *Community Recreation*, Heath, 1948.

5. United Nations Department of Public Information, *The New Industrial Revolutions*, January 1956, p. 4.

6. For further estimates of expenditures, see *America's Needs and Resources*, Twentieth Century Fund, 1955, p. 366, based on U. S. Department of Commerce figures. Yet the same Department report notes that the *total* expenditure for "strictly recreational goods and services" was only 10.5 million dollars in 1952. This illustrates how estimates in this field must be taken cautiously.

7. Robert Coughlan, *Life*, December 28, 1959, Vol. 47, No. 26, 69.

8. W. S. and E. S. Woytinsky, *World Population and Production: Trend and Outlook*, Twentieth Century Fund, 1953; extracted from Table 142, pp. 280–281.

9. Henry Cantril, *Public Opinion, 1935–1946*, Princeton University Press, 1951.

10. Associated Press, February 21, 1959.

11. At this point and at many others this book deals with questions of methods of studying leisure. Indeed, whenever it is employed as a textbook, students are urged to be conscious of methodology as well as of substance. The student is referred to M. H. and E. S. Neumeyer's *Leisure and Recreation* (3rd ed.), Ronald, 1958. Each chapter is followed by projects that suggest many excellent assignments. Chapter 15 of the Neumeyer book is on "recreation research." See also Florence G. Robbins, *The Sociology of Play, Recreation, and Leisure*, Brown, Dubuque, Iowa, 1955, which is especially useful for students entering the recreation field. In reference to issues that relate to leisure to older persons, see *Aging and Leisure*, Oxford University Press, 1960, a project of

the Research Subcommittee of the Section on Psychology and the Social Sciences, The Gerontological Society, Inc., Robert W. Kleemeier, editor and Chairman.

12. Testimony by Helen Thompson, American Symphony Orchestra League, at *Hearings before a Special Subcommittee of the Committee on Education and Labor,* House of Representatives, 83rd Congress, Washington, D. C., June 8 and 9, 1954, on "Federal Grants for Fine Arts Programs and Projects," p. 227.

13. Testimony of Ralph E. Becker, Washington Counsel, League of New York Theatres and the National Association of Legitimate Theatres, Inc., before committee noted in footnote 12; hearings of July 5, 6, 1956, and January 20, 26, 27, 1956, on bills "Distinguished Civilian Awards and Cultural Interchange and Development," p. 110.

14. *Life, op. cit.,* special issue, "The Good Life," all devoted to leisure.

15. Max Kaplan, *Gerontological Geiger-Counters and the Study of Free Time,* for the Twelfth Annual Conference on Aging, "Designs for Retirement," University of Michigan, June 23, 1959.

16. David Dubinsky, Union Education for Leisure, *Education,* Vol. 71, No. 2, October 1950.

CHAPTER 2

1. There is scarcely need here to qualify this statement. The issue of the differences and functions of various fields of knowledge escapes any facile, one-sentence formulation. One of philosophy's functions is just this, an investigation of the kinds of knowledge and comparative methods. A whole branch of interest, the "sociology of knowledge" has been evolving in recent decades. The reader will find fruitful discussion in such books as Karl Mannheim, *Ideology and Utopia,* Harvest Books; Thomas Merton, The Sociology of Knowledge in *Twentieth Century Sociology,* 1945, edited by Moore and Gurvitch; and Florian Znaniecki, *Cultural Sciences,* University of Illinois Press, 1952, especially Chapter 6, Natural Order Among Data.

2. See Ernest Nagel, *An Introduction to Logic and Scientific Method,* Harcourt, Brace, 1934.

3. Joyce O. Hertzler, *Society in Action: A Study of Basic Social Processes,* Dryden, 1954, p. 76.

4. A. L. Kroeber, *Anthropology,* Harcourt, Brace, 1948, p. 253.

5. Clark Wissler, *Man and Culture,* 1923, p. 74, quoted in M. Herskovits, *Man and His Works,* Knopf, 1948, p. 230. See also Herskovits' chapter, A Theory of Culture, pp. 625–641.

6. M. Herskovits, *Man and His Works,* Knopf, 1948, Chapter 37, pp. 625–641.

7. Margaret Mead (editor), *Cultural Patterns and Technical Change,* UNESCO report, Mentor, 1955, pp. 174–175.

8. A. I. Richards, *Land, Labour and Diet in Northern Rhodesia,* London, 1939, pp. 392–394, quoted in Herskovits, *op. cit.,* p. 272.

9. George Soloveytchik, *Switzerland in Perspective,* Oxford University Press, 1954.

10. Leisure, *Encyclopedia of Social Sciences,* 1937, Vol. 9.

11. Murray, *A New English Dictionary on Historical Principles.*

12. *Webster's New International Dictionary* (2nd ed.).

13. For example, see Brian Sutton-Smith and Paul V. Gump, Games and Status Experience, *Recreation,* Vol. 48, April 1955, 172–174; same authors, The "It" Role in Children's Games, *The Group,* February 1955.

14. Johan Huizinga, *Homo Ludens: A Study of the Play Element in Culture,* Beacon, 1950, Chapter I.

15. The following definition illustrates this view: Leisure "is the time we are free from the more obvious and formal duties which a paid job or other obligatory occupation imposes upon us. In accepting this definition, we are not over-looking the interdependence of work and leisure. Such terms are mere pragmatic ways of designating aspects rather than separate parts of life. It remains a fact, however, that nearly all people can and do classify nearly all their activities according to these two categories in a way that is deeply meaningful to themselves. As such, the categories are . . . useful for our purpose." George A. Lundberg, Mirra Komarovsky, and Mary A. McIllnery, *Leisure: A Suburban Study,* Columbia University Press, 1934, pp. 2–3. For another discussion, see Neumeyer and Neumeyer, *Leisure and Recreation* (3rd ed.), Ronald, 1958, pp. 14–26.

16. In his *Essays from Max Weber.* See also Weber's famous discussion of authority—the rational-legal, traditional, and charismatic "ideal types."

17. Talcott Parsons, *The Structure of Social Action,* Free Press, 1949, p. 606.

18. Later there will be occasion to bring in David Riesman's writing, i.e., that work-play is less distinguishable. We will finally look upon this as an over-simple statement but one that deals with a fundamental issue.

19. See Chapters 4, 19, 20.

20. Florian Znaniecki, *The Method of Sociology, op. cit.,* p. 32, "If the humanistic coefficient were withdrawn and the scientist attempted to study the cultural system as he studies a natural system, i.e., as if it existed independently of human experience and activity, the system would disappear and in its stead he would find a disjointed mass of natural things and processes, without any similarity to the reality he started to investigate."

21. Not all sociologists agree on the approach to society by a study of its values. Yet the literature of social science is necessarily replete with discussions of value. See the important discussion in W. I. Thomas and Florian Znaniecki, *The Polish Peasant in Europe and America,* Note on Methodology (reprinted edition) Knopf, 1927. Here the concept of value is paired with attitude. Znaniecki, in his several important books on theory in the last quarter century, has moved beyond this position. See his reinterpretation in *Cultural Sciences,* p. 238 ff., and in *The Method of Sociology,* Farrar and Rinehart, 1934, pp. 39–43.
There is the large question whether social science should go beyond

treating the values of those it studies as *data* and commit *itself* to positions and judgments. If the reader has done any substantive work in the social sciences he has already come across the many arguments. If not, his reading has not begun. He might start with the introductory chapters of such textbooks as Kingsley Davis, *Human Society*, Macmillan, 1949; Arnold W. Green, *Sociology*, McGraw-Hill, 1956; Lundberg, Schrag and Larsen, *Sociology*, Harpers, 1954; and along the way, he should read Max Weber's essay, Science as a Vocation, as well as David Riesman's Some Observations on Social Science Research. The last essay is in *Individualism Reconsidered*, Free Press, 1954.

22. George A. Lundberg, Mirra Komarovsky, and Mary A. McIllnery, *Leisure: A Suburban Study*, Columbia University Press, 1934, p. 19.

CHAPTER 3

1. Bernard Karsh, The Meaning of Work in an Age of Automation, *Current Economic Comment*, University of Illinois, Vol. 19, August 1957, **3**, 3–13. See also T. Caplow, *The Sociology of Work*, University of Minnesota Press, 1954. For a more limited study, N. C. Morse and R. S. Weiss, The Function and Meaning of Work and the Job, *American Sociological Review*, April 1955. The broadest statements on work and the economy in relation to other institutions can be found in anthropology texts and monographs.

2. Adriano Tilgher, *Work: What It Has Meant to Men Through the Ages*, Harcourt, Brace, 1930, exerpt in *An Introduction to Social Science*, edited by D. Calhoun, A. Naftalin, B. Nelson, A. Papandreou, and M. Sibley, Lippincott, 1957, Part II, p. 105.

3. C. Wright Mills, *White Collar: The American Middle Classes*, Oxford University Press, 1956.

4. See Chapter 8, Leisure and Community.

5. Brief summaries of the famous studies by Elton Mayo and others will be found in *Fatigue of Workers*, National Research Council, Committee on Work in Industry, Section IV, The Western Electric Researches, Reinhold, 1941.

6. J. A. C. Brown, *The Social Psychology of Industry*, 1954, Chapter 7, Work, Its Nature, Conditions and Motivation.

7. H. D. Meyer and C. K. Brightbill, *Community Recreation*, Heath, 1948, Chapter 14; also, Max Kaplan, Recreation and Music in Industry, *Current Economic Comment*, University of Illinois, November 1953.

8. *America's Needs and Resources*, Twentieth Century Fund, 1955, p. 730.

9. *Ibid.*, p. 39.

10. Robert Coughlan, *Life*, December 28, 1952, p. 69.

11. Twentieth Century Fund, pp. 43–45. The Director of the Fund, Dr. August Heckscher, amplified these points in his annual report for 1956: "The prevalence of free time in a society is not necessarily a limiting factor upon output.

In the enjoyment of leisure men and women create demands which stimulate the economic system, fostering trades and industries and developing new geographic regions. The pressure for shorter working hours (without cutting pay) acts at the same time as a spur to make management seek constantly more efficient methods of production. Men are replaced by machines; machines are replaced by new machines of greater subtlety and effectiveness. Thus it is that throughout the industrialized West the drive for shorter hours has in the past hundred years been one of the factors bringing about an astonishing increase in productivity."

12. John Weeks, *Among the Primitive Bakonga*, Seeley, Service, London, 1914, p. 128.

13. *America's Needs and Resources, op. cit.*, Chapter 20.

14. See Chapters 6 and 7.

15. Among the many references on automation are some good introductory readings: Robert Bendiner, The Age of the Thinking Robot, and What It Will Mean to Us, *The Reporter*, April 7, 1955; send to the Education Department, UAWCIO, 8000 E. Jefferson Ave., Detroit, for material from labor's point of view, especially on its demands for the guaranteed annual wage; *Business Topics*, April 13, 1955, Automation—From Four Viewpoints; *America's Needs and Resources, op. cit.*, pp. 869–872. An illustration of these machines from the last source, p. 871: "Multiplying, 6,834,872 by 1,488,639 takes a man five minutes or more using pencil and paper, but an electric computer completed at the University of Toronto in 1952 could multiply 500 pairs of such numbers in two seconds. This seems like fast work, but only a year later the Argonne Laboratory of the Atomic Energy Commission completed a new model, the Oracle, able to multiply 683,487,234,834 by 438,342,784,386 about 2000 times in one second. A mathematical problem which would take two mathematicians working with ordinary electric calculating machines five or six years to complete can be done by this new machine in half an hour or less."

16. This report from London provides one illustration (*St. Louis Post Dispatch*, January 22, 1957): London, Jan. 21 (INS)—A 33-year old Briton has quit his soft job in an automation-run plant and applied for what he calls a "man's job." George Mee of Derby complained that his job in the plant, which produces ground mica for use in paint, was "too monotonous." He said he had little else to do but read newspapers and fill in football pool coupons. His salary was $40 a week—which goes substantially further in Britain than it does in the United States. He starts work tomorrow as a moulder in a foundry at Kerby. The work there, he said, "will be hard and hot, but it's a real man's job." As for his former work in the push-button plant, George said, "Automation—anyone can have it. I did less than half an hour's actual work in each 12-hour shift."

See Everett C. Hughes, Work and Self, in J. H. Rohrer and M. Sherif, *Social Psychology at the Crossroads*, Harper, 1951.

CHAPTER 4

1. Howard S. Becker, Becoming a Marihuana User, in *Mental Health and Mental Disorder*, edited by Arnold Rose, W. W. Norton, 1955, pp. 420-433.

2. *Ibid.*, p. 421.

3. *Ibid.*, p. 425.

4. *Ibid.*, pp. 427-428.

5. David Riesman, *The Lonely Crowd*, Yale University Press, 1950.

6. David Riesman, Some Observations on the Study of American Character, *Psychiatry*, Vol. 15, No. 3, August 1952, 333-334.

7. *Ibid.*, p. 334.

8. *The Lonely Crowd, op. cit.*, Chapter XV.

9. Thorstein Veblen, *Theory of the Leisure Class*, Macmillan, 1912.

10. *The Lonely Crowd, op. cit.*, p. 124.

11. *Ibid.*, p. 160.

12. For a critique of Riesman, see Dennis H. Wrong, Riesman and the Age of Sociology, *Commentary*, April 1956, 331-338.

13. Erich Fromm, *The Sane Society*, Rinehart, 1955.

14. *Ibid.*, p. 66.

15. *Ibid.*, p. 91.

16. *Ibid.*, p. 95.

17. *Ibid.*, p. 110.

18. *Ibid.*, p. 124. See also H. Jelden, Erholung—Ein Lebensproblem der Gegenwart (Recreation—A Vital Problem of our Time), *Soz. Welt.*, 1955, 6, 2/3, 110-116.

19. Leo Lowenthal and N. Guterman, The Agitator Utilizes Social Malaise, *Readings in Sociology*, Barnes and Noble, 1951, pp. 270-275, reprinted from *Prophets of Deceit*, Harper, 1949, pp. 14-19.

20. *The Sane Society, op. cit.*, pp. 136-137.

21. W. I. Thomas and Florian Znaniecki, *The Polish Peasant in Europe and America*, Knopf, 1927.

22. Robert MacIver, *The Web of Government*, Macmillan, 1947.

23. Pitirim Sorokin, *Society, Culture, and Personality*, Harper, 1947, p. 348.

24. Florian Znaniecki, *Social Role of the Man of Knowledge*, Columbia University Press, 1940; Social Groups as Products of Cooperating Individuals, *American Journal of Sociology*, May 1939.

25. Johan Huizinga, *Homo Ludens: Study of the Play Element in Culture*, Beacon, 1950, Chapter 1.

26. For a study of the hospital as a social institution, see Alfred H. Stanton and

Morris Schwartz, *The Mental Hospital: A Study of Institutional Participation in Psychiatric Illness and Treatment*, Basic Books, 1954; see the long bibliography following the paper by H. E. Freeman and L. G. Reeder, Medical Sociology: A Review of the Literature, *American Sociological Review*, Vol. 22, No. 1, February 1957, 78–81.

27. Chapter 19.

CHAPTER 5

1. Examples of good introductory discussions of these family trends: Robin M. Williams, Jr., *American Society, A Sociological Interpretation*, Knopf, 1952, Chapter 4; Willard Waller-Reuben Hill, *The Family: A Dynamic Interpretation*, Dryden, 1951.

2. Alexis de Tocqueville, *Democracy in America*, Vintage, 1954, Vol. II, pp. 117–118. (A. A. Knopf, 1945.)

3. William Albig, *Modern Public Opinion*, McGraw-Hill, 1956, p. 280.

4. *Recreation*, December 1946, 472.

5. *Life*, December 24, 1956, 65.

6. *Consumer Behavior, Vol. II, The Life Cycle and Consumer Behavior*, New York University Press, 1955.

7. *Ibid.*, Careers and Consumer Behavior, pp. 1–18.

8. L. Schneider and S. Lysgaard, The Deferred Gratification Pattern: A Preliminary Study, *American Sociological Review*, 18, 1952, 142–149.

9. David Riesman and Howard Roseborough, Careers and Consumer Behavior, *Consumer Behavior*, New York University Press, pp. 6–10.

10. A. S. Bennett Associates, *National Survey of Public Interest in Music*, conducted for American Music Conference, 1948.

11. *Ibid.*, Table XXIX.

12. Report from conversation with Professor Dallas Smythe, University of Illinois Institute of Communications, 1957.

13. See Chapter 15 for empirical evidence of the view here expressed.

14. Nelson N. Foote, Sex as Play, *Social Problems*, Vol. 1, No. 4, April 1954, p. 161.

15. Robert Coughlan, Changing Roles in Modern Marriage, *Life*, December 24, 1956.

16. Margaret Mead, *Male and Female*, Mentor, 1955, p. 13.

17. E. T. Hiller, *Social Relations and Structures*, Harper, 1947, p. 402.

18. B. Malinowski, *A Scientific Theory of Culture and Other Essays*, University of North Carolina Press, Chapel Hill, 1944.

19. A. S. Bennett Associates, *National Study of Public Interest in Music*, mimeographed, American Music Conference, 332 S. Michigan Blvd., Chicago, 1948.

20. A. S. Bennett Associates, *National Study of Public Interest in Music,* Summary of Findings, Part I (d), mimeographed, American Music Conference, 332 S. Michigan Blvd., Chicago, 1948.

21. David L. Cohn, *The Good Old Days,* Simon and Schuster, 1940, p. 308, quoted in Twentieth Century Fund, *America's Needs and Resources,* 1955, p. 179.

22. George Nelson, Down with Housekeeping, *Holiday,* March 1956, Vol. 19, No. 3.

23. The second table drawn from the Wharton Study is found in Chapter 7.

24. Twentieth Century Fund, *America's Needs and Resources,* 1955, p. 98.

CHAPTER 6

1. Milton Gordon, Social Class in American Sociology, *American Journal of Sociology,* LV, No. 3, November 1949, 265.

2. L. Warner and P. S. Lunt, *The Social Life of a Modern Community,* 1941, and *The Status System of a Modern Community,* Yale University Press, 1942; Kingsley Davis, *Human Society,* Macmillan, 1949, Chapter 14.

   A. B. Hollingshead, *Elmtown's Youth,* Wiley, 1949, and Selected Characteristics in a Middle Western Community, *American Sociological Review,* XII, August 1947.

   F. S. Chapin, *Contemporary American Institutions,* Harper, 1935.

   Louis Guttman, A Review of Chapin's Social Status Scale, *American Sociological Review,* VIII, No. 3, June 1943.

   R. and H. Lynd, *Middletown,* 1929, and *Middletown in Transition,* Harcourt, Brace, 1937.

3. M. Gordon, *op. cit., passim.*

   Paul K. Hatt, Occupation and Social Stratification, *American Journal of Sociology,* LV, No. 6, May 1950.

   L. Gross, The Use of Class Concepts in Sociological Research, *American Journal of Sociology,* LIV, No. 5, March 1949.

   O. C. Cox, *Caste, Class, and Race,* Doubleday, 1948.

   C. R. Page, *Class and American Sociology: From Ward to Ross,* Dial, 1940.

   H. W. Pfautz and O. D. Duncan, Critique of Warner's Work in Stratification, *American Sociological Review,* Vol. 15, No. 2, April 1950.

   There are many discussions of social class by popular writers who have contributed to the subject, such as C. Hartley Grattan's The Middle Class, Alas, *Harper's,* October 1948, No. 118.

4. *Ibid.,* 214–215.

5. R. MacIver, and C. H. Page, *Society,* Rinehart, 1949, p. 350.

6. E. T. Hiller, *Principles of Sociology,* Harper, 1933, pp. 36–37.

7. Wilbert E. Moore, *Industrial Relations and the Social Order,* Macmillan, 1946, p. 483.

8. *Ibid.,* pp. 483–484.

9. C. L. Lastrucci, The Status of Occupational Research, *American Sociological Review*, XI, No. 1, February 1946.

10. David Hume, *Essays*, 1907, Vol. 1, p. 245, quoted in D. Martindale and E. D. Monachesi, *Elements of Sociology*, 1951, pp. 359–360.

11. Joseph A. Kahl, *The American Class Structure*, Rinehart, 1957, pp. 184–220. For a clever division into four classes of the consumers of leisure themselves, see Russel Lynes, *Life*, December 28, 1959, 86–89.

12. W. J. Cash, in his brilliant *Mind of the South*, has stripped American history of much of its false conception about the nature of the southern "aristocracy." Doubleday Anchor, 1954.

13. Edmund Wilson, *To the Finland Station*, Doubleday Anchor, 1953, p. 304.

14. Thorstein Veblen, *Theory of the Leisure Class*, Macmillan, 1912.

15. Chapter 4.

16. Veblen, *op. cit.*, p. 48.

17. David Riesman, Veblen and the Business Culture, in *Individualism Reconsidered*, Free Press, 1954, pp. 271–304. See also Riesman's *Thorstein Veblen*, Scribner's, 1953.

18. Max Kaplan, *Art in a Changing America*, Music Educators National Conference, Washington, D. C., 1958, p. 26.

19. R. Clyde White, Social Class Differences in the Use of Leisure, *American Journal of Sociology*, September 1955, Vol. LXI, No. 2.

20. Alfred C. Clarke, The Use of Leisure and its Relation to Levels of Occupational Prestige, *American Sociological Review*, Vol. 21, No. 3, June 1956.

21. R. Clyde White, *op. cit.*

22. Leonard Reissman, Class, Leisure and Social Participation, *American Sociological Review*, Vol. 19, No. 1, February 1954.

23. Karl Mannheim, *Ideology and Utopia* (translated by Louis Wirth and Edward Shils), Harcourt, Brace, 1936, pp. 43, 52–53.

CHAPTER 7

1. Robert Bierstedt, The Sociology of Majorities, *American Sociological Review*, Vol. 13, December 1945, 700–710.

2. *Webster's New International Dictionary*, 1935.

3. See Chapter 6.

4. Frank Tannenbaum, *Darker Phases of the South*, 1924, pp. 139–140, quoted in G. Myrdal, *An American Dilemma*, Harper, 1944, Vol. 11, p. 1435.

5. *Ibid.*, p. 1435.

6. Gunnar Myrdal, *op. cit.*, Vol. 11, p. 986.

7. Ahad Ha'am, Flesh and Spirit in *Selected Essays*, Jewish Publication Society of America, 1912.

8. A. J. Heschel, *Man Is Not Alone: A Philosophy of Religion,* Jewish Publication Society, 1951, p. 264.

9. For further examples on the Judaic balance, see A. Cohen, *Everyman's Talmud,* Dutton, 1949, pp. 230–235.

10. Salo W. Baron, *A Social and Religious History of the Jews,* Columbia University Press, 1937, Vol. 2, p. 110.

11. Israel Abrahams, *Jewish Life in the Middle Ages,* Meridian Books, 1958, p. 373.

12. *Ibid.,* p. 398.

13. Israel Abrahams, *The Jew in the Medieval World: A Source Book,* 315–1791, Union of American Hebrew Congregations, 1938, pp. 418–421. Leon's famous dialogue on gambling was written at the age of 14. Cards obsessed this very learned man to his old age.

14. *Ibid.,* pp. 408–409.

15. *Ibid.,* p. 331.

16. Of course, individual beggars persisted, often with the attitude that they were providing an opportunity to the giver for a religious deed.

17. Eli E. Cohen, Editor, *American Jewish Yearbook,* Jewish Publication Society, 1950, p. 55.

18. Nathan Glazer, Why Jews Stay Sober, *Commentary,* February 1952, Vol. 13, No. 2, 181–186; for rates of alcoholic psychoses among Jews, see Table 7, pp. 110–111, Arnold Rose, editor, *Mental Health and Mental Disorder,* Norton, 1955.

19. See Chapter 21, Minorities and Art, pp. 614–644, *Racial and Cultural Minorities,* by G. E. Simpson and J. M. Yinger, Harper, 1953; Alain Locke, *The Negro in Art: A Pictorial Record of the Negro Artist and the Negro Theme in Art,* Associates in Negro Folk Education, 1940.

20. Oscar Handlin, What Will U. S. Jewry Be Like in 2000? *The National Jewish Monthly,* May 1957.

21. Oscar Handlin, *op. cit.,* p. 5.

22. Franklin Frazier, *Black Bourgeoisie,* Free Press, 1957.

CHAPTER 8

1. C. Kluckhohn and H. A. Murray, *Personality in Nature, Society, and Culture,* Harvard University Press, 1948, p. 35.

2. Ferdinand Tonnies, *Fundamental Concepts of Sociology: Gemeinschaft und Gesellschaft* (translated by C. P. Loomis), New York, 1940.

3. Howard Becker is one who has cautioned against the free use of such terms as secular and segmented, as synonymous. His own distinction of sacred-secular is well known: see Chapter 5 in *Through Values to Social Interpretation,* Duke University Press, 1950. See also Robert Redfield's famous characterization in The Folk Society, *American Journal of Sociology,* Vol. LII, pp.

293–308. A critique of this concept may be found in Oscar Lewis, *Life in a Mexican Village: Tepoztlan Restudied*, University of Illinois Press, 1951.

4. See Notes 16 and 17 of Chapter 2.

5. G. Lundberg, M. Komarovsky, and M. A. McIllnery, *Leisure, A Suburban Study*, Columbia University Press, 1934.

6. *Ibid.*, p. 2.

7. *Ibid.*, Chapter II, pp. 24–57.

8. *Ibid.*, p. 85.

9. *Ibid.*, Chapter IV, pp. 87–125.

10. *Ibid.*, pp. 130–131.

11. *Ibid.*, Chapter VI, pp. 170–189.

12. *Ibid.*, p. 217.

13. See Chapter 10.

14. Lundberg, Komarovsky and McIllnery, *Leisure: A Suburban Study*, Chapter VIII, pp. 218–252.

15. *Ibid.*, Chapter 10, pp. 307–344.

16. For instance, their description of club life as "Commodities to be purchased rather than . . . experiences to be lived," p. 85.

17. R. S. and H. M. Lynd, *Middletown, A Study in American Culture*, Harcourt, Brace, 1929, and *Middletown in Transition*, 1937.

18. *Middletown*, p. 226.

19. *Ibid.*, p. 253.

20. *Ibid.*, p. 250.

21. *Middletown in Transition*, p. 290.

22. *Ibid.*, p. 260.

23. *Ibid.*, pp. 274–277.

24. *Ibid.*, p. 283.

25. *Middletown*, p. 244.

26. *Ibid.*, p. 245.

27. *Middletown in Transition*, p. 293.

28. Ernest Greenwood, *Experimental Sociology, A Study in Method*, King's Crown Press, 1945.

29. B. S. Rowntree and G. R. Lavers, *English Life and Leisure*, Longmans Green, 1951, Chapter 14, pp. 375–414.

30. *The Chicago Recreation Survey*, Chicago Recreation Commission, 5 vols., 1937–1940.

31. *Ibid.*, Vol. II, p. 1.

32. *Ibid.*, Vol. II, p. 1.

33. *The Chicago Recreation Survey*, Chicago Recreation Commission, Vol. II, p. 5.

34. *Ibid.*, Vol. II, p. 10.

35. *Ibid.*, Vol. II, p. 162.

36. Philip M. Hauser, *Chicago 1965, Bulletin of the Housing and Redevelopment Coordinator*, City of Chicago, University of Chicago, June 1956, p. 1.

37. See "Megalopolis," a Research Project in Progress, 1957, Annual Report of the Twentieth Century Fund, pp. 36–37.

38. About one in every five Americans moves every year. Among these, 10 millions move to other states; at least 10 per cent of the states have received their populations from other states. In seven western states and Florida more than half the population are immigrants. In part this is due to the transfer of industrial workers and to military orders, but many other reasons enter.

39. A recent study of leisure in Vienna based on 4000 questionnaires also illustrates the point; "Comparing the data with the time between World War I and World War II it appears that the visiting of coffeehouses, restaurants and sports events has decreased, and traveling and the use of autos and motorcycles have increased." Summary by F. Goldsmith in *Sociological Abstracts*, Vol. 7, No. 2, April 1959, No. 5834. Source, L. Rosenmayr, Die Freizeit in der modernen Gesellschaft (Leisure-time in Modern Society), *Soz. Welt.*, 1955, 6, 4, 297–310.

40. Jessie Bernard, *American Community Behavior*, Dryden, 1949.

CHAPTER 9

1. See the studies on this in *The American Soldier: Adjustments During Army Life*, Samuel Stouffer et al., Princeton University Press, 1949.

2. See Howard Becker, *German Youth: Bond or Free*, Routledge Kegan Paul, London, 1946.

3. An interesting monograph called *Czechoslovak Youth*, which describes the political and sports activities of the 1,116,000 members in 20,000 units of the Union of Youth, came out of Prague in 1956. "It aims at inculcating in its members loyalty and devotion to their country, organizes their efforts in the building of socialism, encourages in them a love and respect for work, makes them familiar with their own and world culture, and instructs them in the fundamentals of scientific socialism." P. 26.

4. *America's Needs and Resources*, Twentieth Century Fund, 1955, pp. 348–350.

5. H. D. Meyer and C. K. Brightbill, *Community Recreation*, Heath, 1948, Chapter 1.

6. Report submitted to the writer by Cyril M. Whittom, Chief, Community Service Projects, Federal Works Agency, Denver, Colorado, November 19, 1940.

7. Grace Overmeyer, *Government and the Arts*, Norton; also, Hearings before a Special Subcommittee, Committee on Education and Labor, 83rd Congress, on Bills for Federal Grants for Fine Arts Programs and Projects, June 8 and 9, 1954; same title, 84th Congress, 1955.

8. Meyer and Brightbill, *op. cit.*, Chapter 3, The Federal Government and Recreation, pp. 59–71.

9. Robert Moses, in *The New York Times Magazine*, January 8, 1956.

10. Malcolm Knowles, *Time*, November 15, 1954, 54.

11. *The New York Times*, July 4, 1958.

12. For example: (The following numbers appear on the cover system behind the numbering; no month or year is given.)

No. 1 (16) Winter Holiday, p. 16; Social Center in a Siberian Steel City, p. 52.

No. 3—TV for Children, p. 14; Baltic Theatre Festival, p. 26.

No. 5—A Tajik Village Club, p. 10; Saturday Night Dance, p. 28; Under the Big Top, p. 40.

No. 5 (20): Eighty-man Amateur Symphony Orchestra, p. 16.

No. 6—Moscow Schedules July Sports Festival, p. 61.

No. 6 (21) Vacation Time, p. 32.

No. 14—No Scrap Heap for Aging Workers.

13. Ivan Kozlov, Vacation Time, *U. S. S. R.*, No. 6 (20) 32.

14. Randall was chairman of the Commission of Foreign Economic Policy in 1954. He was asked to submit a report on international travel, as directed by the Mutual Security Act of 1957.

CHAPTER 10

1. Gus Dyer, 1939, syndicated newspaper article, quoted in H. E. Barnes, *Social Institutions*, Prentice-Hall, 1942, p. 85.

2. A. J. Heschel, *Man Is Not Alone: A Philosophy of Religion*, Jewish Publication Society, 1951, pp. 28–29.

3. A. L. Kroeber, *Anthropology*, Harcourt, Brace, 1948, pp. 458–550.

E. R. Leach, Primitive Time-Reckoning, in C. Sinter, E. J. Holnyard, and A. R. Hall, eds., *A History of Technology*, Oxford University Press, 1954, pp. 110–127.

4. The last four paragraphs are based upon F. R. Dulles, *America Learns to Play: A History of Popular Recreation*, Appleton-Century-Crofts, 1940, pp. 5–6. See also Clarence E. Rainwater, *The Play Movement in the United States*, University of Chicago Press, 1922. For an interesting contemporary commentary on these issues, see the Commonwealth of Massachusetts report, *Legal Holidays and Their Observance*, Legislative Research Council, February 24, 1960.

5. Johan Huizinga, *Homo Ludens: A Study of the Play Element in Culture*, Beacon, 1950, pp. 18–27.

6. Plato, *Laws*, VII, p. 796.

7. Josef Pieper, *Leisure, the Basis of Culture* (translated by A. Dru), Pantheon, 1952.

8. *Ibid.*, p. 26.

9. Josef Pieper, *Leisure, the Basis of Culture* (translated by A. Dru), Pantheon, 1952, p. 40.

10. *Ibid.*, p. 44.

11. *Ibid.*, p. 47.

12. *Ibid.*, p. 55.

13. *Ibid.*, p. 73.

14. Full title of the conference: *Problems and Challenges of the New Leisure: an Examination of a Contemporary Moral Dilemma.*

15. David Allen, Why Man Gambles—And Should He? *The New York Times*, August 14, 1955. See also D. Allen, *The Nature of Gambling*, Coward-McCann, 1952; Clyde B. Davis, *Something for Nothing*, Lippincott, 1956; discussions on gambling in England, B. S. Rowntree and G. R. Lavers, *English Life and Leisure*, Longmans, Green, 1951.

16. See Chapter 14.

17. Kenneth D. Underwood, *Protestant and Catholic: Religious and Social Interaction in an Industrial Community*, Beacon, 1957.

18. *Ibid.*, p. 222.

19. *Ibid.*, p. 232.

20. *Ibid.*, p. 236.

21. *Ibid.*, pp. 238–239.

CHAPTER II

1. Since this question of values is fundamental to an understanding of the sociological position, a range of views is illustrated in the list of writings recommended below:

Chester Alexander, Is Sociology an Exact Science?, *American Sociological Review*, February 1946, Vol. 11, No. 1.

Read Bain, Sociology As a Natural Science, *American Journal of Sociology*, July 1947, Vol. LIII, No. 1.

Jesse Bernard, The Art of Science: A Reply to Redfield, *American Journal of Sociology*, July 1949.

Beatrice Boran, Sociology in Retrospect, *American Journal of Sociology*, January 1947.

Morris R. Cohen and Ernest Nagel, *An Introduction to Logic and Scientific Method*, Harcourt, Brace, 1934, Chapter 18, Logic and Critical Evaluations, pp. 352–375; Section 3, The Logic of Critical Judgments on Art, pp. 357–361.

John Dewey, Liberating the Social Scientist, *Commentary*, October 1947.

Robert Endleman, The New Anthropology and its Ambitions, *Commentary*, September 1949.

Nathan Glazer, What is Sociology's Job?, *Commentary*, February 1947.

Sidney Hook, Scientific Method on the Defensive, *Commentary*, June 1946.

William L. Kolb, The Changing Prominence of Values in Modern Sociological

Theory, pp. 78–92 in *Modern Sociological Theory*, Dryden, 1957, edited by Howard Becker and Alvin Boskoff.

W. Z. Laqueur and George Lichteim, *The Soviet Cultural Scene, 1956–57*, Atlantic Books, 1958, Chapter 21, The Soviet Attitude to Sociology, pp. 185–201.

George Lundberg, Semantics and the Value Problem, *Social Forces*, October 1948.

George Lundberg, The Senate Ponders Social Science, *Scientific Monthly*, May 1947.

Gunnar Myrdal, *An American Dilemna*, Vol. 11, pp. 1041–1064.

Robert Redfield, The Art of Social Science, *American Journal of Sociology*, November 1948.

Svend Riemer, Values and Standards in Research, *American Journal of Sociology*, September 1949.

Albert Salomon, Prophets, Priests, and Social Scientists. *Commentary*, June 1949.

Max Weber, *From Max Weber: Essays in Sociology*, Oxford University Press, 1946, Politics as a Vocation and Science as a Vocation.

A. B. Wolfe, *Conservatism, Radicalism, and Scientific Method*, Macmillan, 1923, Chapter IX, pp. 200–251.

F. Znaniecki, *The Method of Sociology*, Farrar and Rinehart, 1934, pp. 36–43, and *Cultural Sciences*, University of Illinois Press, 1952, pp. 172–177.

2. Robert Bierstedt, *The Social Order*, McGraw-Hill, 1957, p. 20.

3. Norman Birnbaum, Science, Ideology, and Dialogue, *Commentary*, December 1956, Vol. 22, No. 6 (Summary and Analysis of the World Congress of Sociology–Amsterdam, August 1956).

4. Jessie Bernard, *American Community Behavior*, Dryden, 1949, p. 10.

5. See also the debate between Reuben Maury and Bishop I. Bromley Oxnam in *PB, The Pocketbook Magazine*, December 1954.

6. Louis Kronenberger, Leisure, Our Most Personal Possession, *House and Garden*, April 1956. For a similar position, see Frederick D. Wilhelmsen, The Attack on Leisure, *National Review*, November 23, 1957, 474. By "attack," the author means any effort to assist persons to use leisure for any purpose aside from letting man "not simply to be doing but to be." Note this interesting and presumptuous judgment: "Adult education classes; folk dancing by people who are not a folk; Great Books seminars; guided tours through museums filled with things made by other men in other times—all of them along with 'Do It Yourself' tend to absorb man's increasing leisure into a kind of desperate conformism and groupism that fears instinctively to let humanity alone so that it might simply be." The question may be raised how far Mr. Wilhelmsen would go in defining the nature of the "attack": would it include all attempts to create facilities in the community? An opposite view is this, by Charles Brightbill, Professor of Recreation at the University of Illinois, in a paper, Public Recreation—Its Great Omissions and Misconceptions: "Starting with the playgrounds and small parks in New England at the turn of the century there has always been a need for public recreation. If anything, the need

is far more pronounced than ever before. So long as democracy aims primarily at affording the chance for its people to pursue happiness, so long as government bears the first responsibility for the health, safety and welfare of the people and alone enjoys the privilege of exercising the powers of eminent domain, so long as large financial resources are needed to acquire and maintain adequate land and property resources and so long as these things must be done on a continuing basis, that long there will be need for recreation supported by tax funds."

CHAPTER 12

1. An amusing illustration of a quick transition from one type of content to another is found in a study of El Cerrito, New Mexico, by Olen Leonard and C. P. Loomis, *Culture of a Contemporary Rural Community*, U. S. Department of Agriculture Rural Life Studies, November 1, 1941, p. 49. Describing the community dances in this Spanish community, they write: "For the older members of the group these dances serve still another purpose. They serve as a medium for airing any political view or conducting any business that concerns the group. It is generally recognized and never questioned that such a person has a right to stop the dance when he wishes and talk as long as he likes. If the wine is adequate and the audience at all appreciative he may stop the dance several times during the course of the evening for such speeches."

2. E. T. Hiller, *Social Relations and Structures*, Harper, 1948.

3. *Ibid.*, pp. 192–193.

4. Georg Simmel, Sociability, an Example of Pure, of Formal Sociology, in *The Sociology of Georg Simmel* (translated by K. Wolff), Free Press, 1950, pp. 40–57.

5. *Ibid.*, p. 45.

6. Kurt Lewin, *Resolving Social Conflicts*, Harper, 1945.

7. Leo Bogart, Adult Talk About Newspaper Comics, *American Journal of Sociology*, July 1955, **61**, 26–30.

8. *Fortune*, A Dramatic New Office Building, September 1957.

9. William Whyte, The Transients, in *Prize Articles of 1954*, New York, 1955, originally in *Fortune*, 1954.

10. Gunnar Myrdal, *An American Dilemma*, Harper, 1944, Chapter 1, American Ideals and the American.

CHAPTER 13

1. Donald Bell, The Theory of Mass Society, *Commentary*, Vol. 22, No. 1, July 1956, 80.

2. Arnold Rose, Professional and Voluntary Organizations and Aging, preliminary title and chapter in manuscript for inclusion in *A Handbook of Social Gerontology*, University of Chicago Press, 1960, Clark Tibbitts, editor.

3. Busy Brotherly World of Freemasonry, *Life*, October 8, 1956, 104.

4. F. A. Bushee, Social Organizations in a Small City, *American Journal of Sociology*, November 1945.

5. Stuart Queen, Social Participation in Relation to Social Disorganization, *American Sociological Review*, April 1949, **14**, 2.

6. Floyd Dotson, Patterns of Voluntary Associations Among Working Class Families, *American Sociological Review*, **16**, 1951, 687–693.

7. Mirra Komarovsky, The Voluntary Associations of Urban Dwellers, reprinted in *Sociological Analysis*, editors, Wilson and Kolb, Harcourt, Brace, 1949, pp. 378–392.

8. Pitirim Sorokin, *Altruistic Love: A Study of American Good Neighbors and Christian Saints*, Beacon Press, 1950.

9. Pitirim Sorokin, *Fads and Foibles in Modern Sociology and Related Sciences*, Regnery, 1956.

CHAPTER 14

1. Jerome Fried, Games, in *Standard Dictionary of Folklore, Mythology and Legend*, Funk and Wagnall, Vol. 1, pp. 431–439.

2. Ralph Linton, *The Study of Man*, Appleton-Century-Crofts, 1936.

3. Florian Znaniecki, Social Groups as Products of Participating Individuals, *American Journal of Sociology*, Vol. 44, 1939, 799–811.

4. Fried, *op. cit.*, 433.

5. Jean Piaget, *Language and Thought of the Child*, Harcourt, Brace, 1926.

6. Johan Huizinga, *Homo Ludens: A Study of the Play Element in Culture*, Beacon, 1950, pp. 19–27.

7. Gregory Stone, *Some Meanings of American Sport*, College Physical Education Association, 60th Annual Meeting, Columbus, Ohio, October 1957.

8. *Ibid.*

9. *Ibid.* For a humorous but biting comment, which relates to this theme, the reader will enjoy Lorraine L. Hopkins' The Little Leagues, *Atlantic Monthly*, Vol. 202, No. 3, September 1958, 85–88.

10. *Ibid.*

11. This material on games and sports in Europe is reproduced with the kind permission of Dr. Seward Staley. The report has been printed in full under the title, The European Sport Scene, *American Academy of Physical Education; Professional Contributions*, American Association for Health, Physical Education and Recreation, No. 6, 1958, pp. 12–24.

12. Fried, *op. cit.*, p. 439. See also David Riesman (with Reuel Denney), Football in America: a Study in Culture Diffusion, *Individualism Reconsidered*, Free Press, 1954, pp. 242–257.

13. *America's Needs and Resources*, Twentieth Century Fund, 1955, p. 361.

14. Stone, *op. cit.*

15. Stone, *op. cit.*

16. Howard S. Becker, The Professional Dance Musician and His Audience, *American Journal of Sociology*, LVII, September 2, 1951, pp. 136–144.

17. For a parallel to professionalism and amateurism in the arts, see Chapter 15.

18. Chapter 5, page 59.

19. R. S. and H. M. Lynd, *Middletown in Transition*, Harcourt, Brace, 1937, pp. 269–271.

20. Playing Cards—A National Survey, *Hobbies*, December 1942, quoted in Irving Crespi, The Social Significance of Card Playing as a Leisure Time Activity, *American Sociological Review*, Vol. 21, No. 6, December 1956.

21. Lynd, *op. cit.*, pp. 270–271.

22. Crespi, *op. cit.* Material on Korean and Japanese games adopted from student paper by Miss Alice Moy, University of Illinois, 1957.

23. Mr. Sam Davison, sportswriter for the *Chicago Daily News*, commented on August 21, 1957, on these developments in the baseball world: "Changing habits of the consumers, including the family car and the new cult of togetherness, play a big part. Participation sports, such as boating, bring increased money to many industries, but less attendance for spectator sports."

CHAPTER 15

1. Portions of this section are adapted from Max Kaplan's The Social Role of the Amateur, *Music Educator's Journal*, February–March 1954, 26–28.

2. A. M. Carr-Saunders and P. A. Wilson, Professions, in *Encyclopedia of the Social Sciences*.

3. E. T. Hiller, Social Relations and Structures, Harper, 1948, p. 544.

4. R. MacIver and C. H. Page, *Society, An Introductory Analysis*, Rinehart, 1949, pp. 478–483.

5. Chapter 3, p. 31.

6. Based on theories of Florian Znaniecki, *Social Role of the Man of Knowledge*, Columbia University Press, 1940; Social Groups as Products of Cooperating Individuals, *American Journal of Sociology*, May 1939. For a lengthy restatement and application, see Max Kaplan, *The Musician in America: Analysis of his Social Roles*, unpublished Ph.D. dissertation, University of Illinois, 1951.

7. Talcott Parsons, *Essays in Sociological Theory*, Free Press, 1949, The Professions and Social Structure.

8. See John H. Mueller, *The American Symphony Orchestra: A Social History of Musical Taste*, Indiana University Press, 1951.

9. Max Kaplan, *The Musician in America, op. cit.* See also *The National Crisis for Live Music and Musicians*, Research Company of America, Conducted for the American Federation of Musicians about 1956.

10. Howard Hanson, quoted in *The New York Times,* December 31, 1950, by Harold C. Schonberg.

11. Broadcast Music, Inc., leaflet, *Concert Music, U.S.A.,* 1958.

12. Alexis de Tocqueville, *Democracy in America,* Vintage, 1945, Vol. 2, pp. 53–54. This chapter is also included in B. Rosenberg and D. M. White (editors), *Mass Culture,* Free Press, 1957. Other writings that should be seen are Gilbert Seldes, *The Public Arts,* Simon and Schuster, 1956; American Round Table Series, *An Inquiry into Cultural Trends,* Yale University and The Advertising Council, 1957; D. W. Brogan, The Problem of High Culture and Mass Culture, *Diogenes,* 1954, No. 5; Reuel Denney, *The Astonished Muse,* University of Chicago Press, 1958.

13. Unpublished study by Los Angeles Bureau of Music, J. Arthur Lewis, Director, 1958, Special Survey of U. S. Cities—over 25,000 Population—Expenditures for Music.

14. Max Kaplan, Music in Adult Life, *Adult Leadership,* Vol. 5, January 7, 1957.

15. John W. McConnell, Chapter 13, *Aging and Society,* Clark Tibbitts, Editor, to be published in 1960 by University of Chicago as a project of the Inter-University Training Institute in Social Gerontology, tentative p. 16.

CHAPTER 16

1. James L. Bossemeyer, Executive Vice President of the National Association of Travel Organizations, says that our total expenditures for domestic tourist travel is 18 billion dollars! See his full statement in Travel: American Mobility, *The Annals of the American Academy of Political and Social Science,* Vol. 313, September 1957, pp. 113–116. For a comparable study of Great Britain, see *Holidays in 1951, Results of the British Travel and Holidays Association.*

2. *The Travel Market: A National Study,* Curtis Publishing Company, Research Department, 1955.

3. Twentieth Century Fund, 1955, p. 263.

4. James Bossemeyer, Travel: American Mobility, *op. cit.,* p. 114.

5. *Ibid.,* pp. 114–115.

6. *Christian Science Monitor,* June 23, 1958.

7. *Travel USA Newsletter,* National Association of Travel Organizations, Washington, Vol. VIII, No. 4, June 1958.

8. Rose Macaulay, Pleasures of Travel, *The Listener,* Vol. LVII, No. 1451, January 17, 1957, p. 113.

9. C. Wright Mills, *White Collar,* Oxford University Press, 1951, Chapter 11, pp. 239–258.

10. An example of over-analysis is illustrated by an elaborate study of prostitutes which showed that these girls had come from broken homes, had low intelligence, and odd notions about life, etc. Subsequently another investigator discovered that this group of women needed the money; they left the First Profession almost to a man as soon as they were given jobs with better income!

11. Walter Lippman, *Public Opinion,* Penguin, 1946, p. 61.

12. P. G. Anson, In *Landscape, Magazine of Human Geography*, Rudal Press, Santa Fe, Vol. 6, No. 1, Autumn, 1956, p. 40.

13. George Horne, *The New York Times*, February 2, 1958.

14. *The New York Times*, November 3, 1957.

CHAPTER 17

1. David Riesman, *Individualism Reconsidered*, Free Press, 1954, p. 206.

2. As an example of such a study, see Television within the Social Matrix. Robert V. Hamilton and Richard H. Lawless, *Public Opinion Quarterly*, 1956, **20**, 2, Sum, 393–403; and Social Norms in Television-Watching, Kent Geiger and Robert Sokol, *American Journal of Sociology*, LXV, 2, September 1959, 174–181.

3. Marjorie Donald and Robert J. Havighurst, The Meaning of Leisure, *Social Forces*, Vol. 37, No. 4, May 1959, 355–360.

4. John Houseman, Battle Over Television, *Harper's*, No. 1200, May 1950.

5. *Christian Science Monitor*, November 22, 1957.

6. This summary is by Vashti McCollum, in a paper for the author, dated May 1957. Her information is based on TV Should Go East With Homicide, *Saturday Evening Post*, 224:10, July 7, 1951; Dallas Smythe, Three Years of New York Television, 1951–1953, NAEB, Urbana, Illinois, July 1953, pp. 4–5; Parents, Children, and Television, The First Television Generation, Information Service, National Council of Churches of Christ, Vol. 23, No. 17; and *Interim Report* of the Kefauver Sub-Committee to Investigate Juvenile Delinquency, 1955.

7. The Witty study was reported by Godfrey Sperling in *The Christian Science Monitor*, December 29, 1958.

8. *The Pleasures of Publishing*, Columbia University Press, Vol. 25, No. 2, February 1958.

9. Kurt Enoch, The Mass Media: Challenge/Chimera? *Essential Books*, June 1956, p. 13.

10. Arnold Hauser, *The Social History of Art*, Knopf, 1952, Vol. 2, p. 949.

11. Morris Cohen, *Preface to Logic*, New York, 1949, pp. 74–75.

12. George Lundberg et al., *Leisure: A Suburban Study*, Columbia University Press, 1934, quoted in *Mass Leisure*, edited by E. Larrabee and R. Meyersohn, Free Press, 1958, p. 195.

13. Russell Lynes, The Pressures of Leisure, *What's New*, 1958, No. 208.

14. See the de Tocqueville and Whitman selections in *Mass Leisure, op. cit.*

CHAPTER 18

1. E. T. Hiller, *Social Relations and Structures*, Harper, 1947, p. 21.

2. James Feibelman, *The Theory of Human Culture*, Duell, Sloan, and Pierce, 1946, p. 6.

3. Kingsley Davis, *Human Society*, Macmillan, 1948, p. 510, "The very non-rationality of religious behavior is the thing that gives religion its vitality in human life."

4. A. Hollingshead, *Elmtown's Youth, The Impact of Social Classes on Adolescents*, Wiley, 1949, pp. 398–399.

5. Fred C. Kelly, The Great Bicycle Craze, *American Heritage*, Vol. VIII, No. 1, December 1956, pp. 68–73.

6. J. H. Barnett, The Easter Festival: A Study in Social Change, *American Sociological Review*, 14, 62–70.

7. W. G. Sumner, *Folkways*, Ginn, 1906.

8. Simmel, The Stranger, in *The Sociology of Georg Simmel*, Free Press, 1950, pp. 402–408; for the Philistine, Bohemian, and creative types, see W. I. Thomas and F. Znaniecki, *The Polish Peasant in Europe and America*, Knopf, 1927.

9. The best contemporary discussion we know is by E. T. Hiller, Social Relations and Structures, Harper, 1948, Part 6, pp. 331–650.

10. Jerome Dowd, *Control in Human Societies*, Appleton-Century, 1936.

11. T. W. Adorno, A Social Critique of Radio Music, *Kenyon Review*, Vol. 7, 1944.

12. Kurt Lewin, *Resolving Social Conflicts*, Harper, 1948.

13. Charles F. Marden, Secret Societies, in *Social Control*, edited by J. S. Roucek, Von Nostrand, 1947; and Georg Simmel, *op. cit.*, The Secret Society, pp. 345–378.

14. Thorstein Veblen, *The Theory of the Leisure Class*, Mentor, 1953, Chapters 3 and 4.

15. A chapter was written in the history of "gentlemen's agreements" among tennis and athletic clubs in the summer of 1958, when Ralph Bunche's son was denied membership in the West Side Tennis Club. There was an immediate reaction in the press, suggestive of either an unlikely naïveté or a previously well-hushed fact. The club quickly straightened out the matter when its president resigned and Bunche was officially invited to join. (He did not join.)

16. Morris Rosenberg, *Occupations and Values*, Free Press, 1957, Chapter 11.

17. August Heckscher and Sebastian de Grazia, Executive Leisure, *Harvard Business Review*, July–August 1959.

18. Morris Ernst, *Utopia, 1976*, Rinehart, 1955.

CHAPTER 19

1. Robert J. Havighurst, The Leisure Activities of the Middle-Aged, *American Journal of Sociology*, LXII, 2, September 1957, 152–162.

2. Committee on Social Issues of the Group for the Advancement of Psychiatry, *The Social Responsibility of Psychiatry: A Statement of Orientation*, Report 13, July 1950, Topeka, Kansas.

3. Robert S. Lynd, *Knowledge for What? The Place of Social Science in American Culture*, Princeton University Press, 1939, Chapter 2.

4. Ralph Linton, The Personality of Peoples, *Scientific American*, August 1949, 14.

5. Robert S. Woodworth, *Dynamics of Behavior*, Holt, 1957, p. 62.

6. William McDougall, *An Introduction to Social Psychology*, W. Luce, Boston, 1926, Chapter 2.

7. W. I. Thomas, *The Unadjusted Girl*, Little, Brown, 1923.

8. *Ibid.*, pp. 124–133.

9. *Ibid.*, p. 133.

10. Abraham Maslow, *Motivation and Personality*, Harper, 1954.

11. Gardner Murphy, *Human Potentialities*, Basic Books, 1958, Chapter 5.

12. *Ibid.*, Chapter 2.

13. Robert Bierstedt, *Saturday Review*, December 13, 1958.

14. Florian Znaniecki, Social Groups as Products of Cooperative Individuals, *American Journal of Sociology*, May 1939, and his Social Organization and Institutions, in *Twentieth Century Sociology*, editors, Gurvitch and Moore, Philosophical Library, 1945.

15. Robert J. Havighurst and K. Feigenbaum, Leisure and Life-Style, *American Journal of Sociology*, LXIV, 4, January, 1959, 396–404.

16. Reuel Denney, Individuality and the New Leisure, *Esquire*, October 1958, Vol. L, No. 4.

17. See Joyce Cary, The Mass Mind: Our Favorite Folly, *Harper's*, 1222, March 1952.

CHAPTER 20

1. We make use here of Pitirim Sorokin's terms, albeit in a different context. See his *Social and Cultural Dynamics*, American, 1937, Vol. 1, Chapter 1.

2. The term "serendipity" is used in social science to note unexpected scientific insights; why not apply this term to modes of social experience?

3. George H. Mead, *Movements of Thought in the Nineteenth Century*, University of Chicago Press, 1936, pp. 361–362.

4. Georg Simmel, The Metropolis and Mental Life, in *The Sociology of Georg Simmel*, Free Press, pp. 409–424.

5. B. L. Whorf, *The Relation of Habitual Thought and Behavior to Language*, Four Articles on Metalinguistics, Foreign Service Institute, U. S. Department of State, 1950, p. 44.

6. E. R. Leach, Primitive Time-Reckoning, *A History of Technology*, Vol. 1, Oxford University Press, 1954, pp. 110–127.

7. Margaret Mead, editor, *Cultural Patterns and Technical Change*, Mentor, 1955, pp. 70–72.

8. George Soule, *Time for Living*, Viking, 1955, p. 90.

9. George Woodcock, The Tyranny of the Clock, *Politics Magazine*, October 1944, in *An Introduction to Social Science*, edited by Arthur Naftalin et al., Lippincott, 1953, Part 1, pp. 209-212.

10. A. E. Fessard, Mechanisms of Nervous Integration and Conscious Experience, p. 233, *Brain Mechanisms and Consciousness*, UNESCO Conference, Oxford, 1954.

11. K. S. Lashley, The Problem of Serial Order in Behavior, quoted in Fessard, *ibid.*, p. 233.

12. For a detailed examination of time, see Hans Reichenbach, *The Directions of Time*, University of California Press, 1956, and his *Philosophy of Space and Time*, Dover, 1958.

13. Werfel, *Poems*, Princeton University Press, 1945.

14. Sebastian de Grazia, How People Spend Their Time, *Aging and Leisure*, Robert W. Kleemeier, editor, Oxford University Press, 1960.

15. Mead, *op. cit.*, p. 163.

16. Judith Chase, The Average Woman, *Collier's*, February 27, 1943.

17. See Chapter 17, p. 227.

18. This section is based on part of the author's M. A. thesis, *The Symphony Orchestra as a Social Group*, University of Illinois, 1948.

19. E. T. Hiller, Social Relations and Structure, Harper, 1948, Chapters 13 and 14.

20. Max Weber, *Essays in Sociology*, Oxford University Press, 1946, pp. 253-266.

21. Chapter 2, p. 21.

22. Chapter 2, p. 24.

CHAPTER 21

1. Maurice Price, *Christian Missions and Oriental Civilizations*, Private Printing, Shanghai, 1924, p. 4.

2. Chapter 10, p. 156.

3. Robert Merton calls this the "self-fulfilling prophecy." See his *Social Theory and Social Structure*, Free Press, 1949.

4. This term is used in Ronald Lippitt, Jeanne Watson, and Bruce Westley, *The Dynamics of Planned Change, a Comparative Study of Principles and Techniques*, Harcourt, Brace, 1958.

5. Chapter 18, p. 242.

6. Lippitt, *op. cit.*

7. T. W. Adorno et al., *The Authoritarian Personality*, Harper, New York, 1950.

8. Ralph Linton, The Personality of Peoples, *Scientific American*, August 1949, 15.

9. Gardner Murphy, *Human Potentialities*, Basic Books, 1958, Chapter 5.

10. Frederick Thrasher, *The Gang*, University of Chicago Press, 1927.

11. William S. Whyte, *Street Corner Society*, University of Chicago Press, 1943.

12. Clifford Shaw and others, *Juvenile Delinquency and Urban Areas*, University of Chicago Press, 1942.

13. Arthur Miller, Bridge to a Savage World, *Esquire*, Vol. I, No. 4, October 1958.

14. Herbert A. Bloch and Frank T. Flynn, *Delinquency, The Juvenile Offender in America Today*, Random House, 1956, pp. 202–205.

15. *Ibid.*

16. Paul Hoffman, *The New York Times*, July 12, 1959.

17. Lippitt, *op. cit.*, p. 180.

18. Gordon Allport, quoted in Robin Williams, Jr., Propositions on Inter-Group Hostility and Conflict, in *Sociological Analysis*, edited by L. Wilson and W. L. Kolb, Harcourt, Brace, 1947, p. 752.

19. Robert Bales, A. Paul Hare, and Edward F. Borgatta, Structure and Dynamics of Small Groups: a Review of Four Variables, in J. B. Gittler (ed.) *Review of Sociology*, Wiley, 1957, p. 407.

20. Gilbert Seldes, *The Public Arts*, Simon and Schuster, 1956.

21. Richard La Pierre, *A Theory of Social Control*, McGraw-Hill, 1954, p. 498.

22. Another discussion of the Community Arts project may be found in the writer's *Art in a Changing America*, Music Educators National Conference, Washington, 1958.

23. Max Kaplan and Carol Pierson, Creative Arts in Adult Education, *Handbook of Adult Education—1960,* Malcolm Knowles, editor, Adult Education Association of the U.S.A., 1960.

24. Albert Einstein, Foreword to *Galileo Galilei*, trans. Stillman Drake, University of California Press, 1953, xvii.

CHAPTER 22

1. See Chapter 11, pp. 165–166.

2. See Chapter 10, p. 155.

3. See Chapter 10, p. 153.

4. George Soule, *The Shape of Tomorrow*, Signet, 1958.

5. D. W. Gotshalk, University of Chicago Press, 1947.

6. Gardner Murphy, *Human Potentialities*, Basic Books, 1958, Chapter 5.

7. Maholy-Nagy, *The New Vision*, New York, 1939, p. 15, quoted by Sir Herbert Read, Adult Education and the Arts, *Arts in Society*, University of Wisconsin, January 1958, p. 19.

8. Kingsley Davis, The Other Scare: Too Many People, *The New York Times Magazine*, March 15, 1959.

9. Harrison Brown, *The Challenge of Man's Future*, Viking, 1954, pp. 220–221.

10. George Soule, *op. cit.*, p. 99.

11. Morris Ernst, *Utopia, 1976*, Rinehart, 1955, *passim.*

12. Edward Bellamy, *Looking Backward, 2000–1887*, Houghton-Mifflin, 1931, pp. 196–197.

Name index

331

Subject index

336